The Cuba Interviews

T. K. Hernández

The Cuba Interviews

Conversations on Foreign Investment and Economic Development

Foreword by Dr. John M. Kirk

With Contributions by
Mark A. Entwistle
Dr. Juan Triana Cordoví
Élise C. Hartill

palgrave
macmillan

T. K. Hernández
ON, Canada

ISBN 978-3-031-30202-2 ISBN 978-3-031-30203-9 (eBook)
https://doi.org/10.1007/978-3-031-30203-9

This Palgrave Macmillan imprint is published by the registered company Springer Nature Switzerland AG
The registered company address is: Gewerbestrasse 11, 6330 Cham, Switzerland

To my mother for her tireless strength, support, and belief in this work.

Acknowledgments

There were many people involved in creating this book and without their belief in this work and my intentions, it would never have existed.

First, I must extend thanks to those who gave me the opportunity and privilege to interview (in alphabetical order): Hermenegildo Altozano, Sebastiaan Berger, Gerard Byrne, Dr. José Ramón Cabañas Rodríguez, Felix Chevalier, Dr. Yamila de Armas Águila, Dr. Dmitry Chelovskiy, Marta Deus, Ambassador Berris Ekinci, Mark A. Entwistle, Ambassador Julio Garmendía Peña, Ambassador Andrei Anatolyevich Guskov, Dr. Osvaldo Héctor Ardisana, Ana Teresa Igarza Martinez, Paul Johnson, Xiangzhong Kong, Judy Kruger, Minister Rodrigo Malmierca Díaz, Dr. Mayda Mauri Pérez, Ambassador Marcelino Medina González, Dr. Emily Morris, Huong Nguyen, Tom Popper, Andrew G. Purcell, Gail Reed, Vice Minister Déborah Rivas, Peter Stickland, Dr. Antony Stokes, LVO, OBE, Desmond Taljaard, Dr. Juan Triana Cordoví, Dr. Mitchell Valdés-Sosa, Vice Minister Josefina Vidal Ferreiro, Fred Wade, Dan Whittle, James Williams, Minister-President Marta Wilson González, and Daniel R. Zim. Their time and collaboration were crucial for the work and most appreciated. Without their perspectives, thoughts, and ideas on investment in Cuba, this book would surely never come into being.

My deep gratitude goes to three experts on Cuba who contributed to this volume. I am very honored. Dr. John Kirk, Professor Emeritus of Latin American Studies at Dalhousie University for writing the Foreword, for his guidance and immense support in the preparation of the proposal, his wisdom in answers to many questions I had while preparing the manuscript. Second, Dr. Juan Triana Cordoví, economist from the University of Havana for his chapter, "Foreign Direct Investment, What Can We Expect?", and his extensive work on the updating of the chapter, and his earlier interview with me. Third, Mark Entwistle, former Canadian Ambassador to Cuba and Partner at Acasta Cuba Capital, for the chapter "The Cuban Black Box: Understanding Why Cuba Does What It Does." Earlier, he granted an interview and subsequently updated it with an intensive analysis of the Biden presidency.

My thanks to Élise C. Hartill, an ocean scientist, more qualified than I to discuss the protection of oceans and fisheries, who conducted the interview with Dan Whittle, attorney and senior director at the Environmental Defense Fund.

This book would never have been possible without the support and efforts of two of Cuba's ambassadors to Canada. I must extend gratitude to their Excellencies, Josefina Vidal Ferreiro, and Héctor Igarza Cabrera, for their belief and support of the work from the first inception to final days before manuscript submission. There were moments in which I thought this book would never get written and for that reason, I am grateful for their kindness during that time.

Special "gracias" to others: Tom Popper, who gave me the best advice I ever received. "Make it happen," he said when it looked like things would never happen. And author Keith Bolender, who assisted with a major edit during the rewriting of the introduction to this book and provided me guidance and support throughout the entire process. And Sebastiaan Berger for answering the nagging question in the back of my mind (why an investor would invest in a country perceived as high-risk).

Special gracias also to Vice Minister Rivas for her confidence in my work and personal help to me, just a foreign journalist and writer in her country.

I also express my thanks to the staff at the Cuban Embassy in Ottawa, the Consulate of Cuba in Toronto, and the Centro de Prensa Internacional in Havana, including Areadna Quintana Castañeda, Mariem Martinez, Tania López Larroque, and Aileén Carmenaty Sánchez for arranging interviews and many press visas. I have to particularly thank Aileén at the Press Office and Lessner Gómez Molina, Director of the Office of Tourism in Toronto for their help on a Sunday in obtaining a report I needed quickly during the final proofing stage. Special gratitude to Hector Amed Velázquez Méndez, coordination specialist at the CPI for his "legwork" in the final days of manuscript preparation.

Additionally, a thank you to others who helped in small and large ways: Sue Ashdown, Vitaliy K., Aaron Kelly, Natalya Otcheskaya, and Helen Yaffe.

I am grateful to Palgrave Macmillan, which accepted the proposal of the work for publishing in the uncertain times of the 2021–2022 and to the editing team Meera Seth, Bronwyn Geyer, Susan Westendorf, Wyndham Hacket Pain, Abarna Antonyraj, and Nandakini Lahiri. I thank also Matthew Savin, Jill Balzano, and Lauren Dooley for their 'behind the scenes' work as members of the production management team.

Finally, I cannot forget the patience of my family for their assistance as readers and critics and bearing the perceived burden of my never-ending discussions on Cuba. They gave me the necessary motivation and solitude for an author to produce a work.

Contents

1 **Foreword by Dr. John M. Kirk** 1
John M. Kirk

2 **Introduction** 7
Motivations 7
The Coming of Trump 12
The Backbone: The Havana Syndrome 14
Winding Down: The Payout 15
The COVID Pandemic 17
The Final Interviews 20
Conclusion 21
Outline 23
References 29

3 **Foreign Direct Investment, What Can We Expect? By Dr. Juan Triana Cordoví** 35
Juan Triana Cordoví
The Economy 2015–2020 36
FDI: A Synthesis of Its Evolution in Cuba 38
Is Cuba an Attractive Market for Investment? 39
FDI and Ordenamiento Monetario 41
FDI in Post-pandemic and Post Ordination Times 44
Conclusions 47

Annex 47
References 49

4 The Cuban Black Box: Understanding Why Cuba Does What It Does by Mark A. Entwistle 51
Mark A. Entwistle
Reference 58

Part I Government

5 Currency Reform, Wages, and the New Entrepreneurs: Ambassador Julio Garmendía Peña 61
References 71

6 "Business Is Great"—Dr Antony Stokes, LVO OBE, Ambassador to Cuba of the United Kingdom 73
References 77

7 Interview with Josefina Vidal, Ambassador of Cuba in Canada 79
References 90

8 Interview with Foreign Investment Minister Rodrigo Malmierca Díaz 91
Follow-up to the Interview: July 2022 95
References 99

9 "One Door Closes, Another Opens," Interview with Ambassador José Ramón Cabañas Rodríguez 101
References 106

10 Expanding Political Dialogue and Links Between Cuba–Canada, First Deputy Minister Marcelino Medina González 107

11 Interview with Her Excellency, Berris Ekinci, Ambassador of Turkey in Cuba 111
References 119

12 Interview with Andrei Guskov, Russian Ambassador to Cuba 121
References 126

Part II The Economy and Foreign Investment

13 Interview with Economist Juan Triana 129
Reference 134

14 Day Zero to the Future–Economist Dr. Emily Morris Discusses the Cuban Economy 135
Follow-up to the Interview: June 2022 141
Reference 144

Part III The Industrial Zones

15 ZED Mariel: Interview with General Director Ana Teresa Igarza 147
References 155

16 Interview with Huong Nguyen, Business Manager, ViMariel 157

Part IV Banking

17 Interview with Minister-President Marta Sabina Wilson González 169
Annex 1A 177
Annex 1B 177
Annex 2 178
References 179

Part V The Lawyers and the Law

18 The What's-next Scenario for Helms–Burton Claimants—Daniel R. Zim, Attorney 183
References 189

19 Interview with Hermenegildo Altozano, Partner, Bird & Bird, Spain 191
Annex 197
References 200

20 Protecting Foreign Investors–Interview with Déborah Rivas, Vice Minister, MINCEX 201
Follow-up to the Interview: May 2022 206

Annex 207
References 216

Part VI Business

21 Felix Chevalier on the Houston Trade Mission to Havana 219

22 The Quiet Optimism in the American Business Community 223
References 226

23 "Facts and Knowledge Are the Antidote to Threat" Mark Entwistle, Former Ambassador to Cuba 227
Follow-up to the Interview: April 2022 234
Annex 236
References 260

24 "Cuba's Day in the Sun Will Come"—Fred Wade, President, Fireworks FX 261
References 266

Part VII Oil and Energy

25 Is Energy Self-Sufficiency in the Cards for Cuba? Peter Stickland, CEO, Melbana Energy 269
References 272

26 Interview with the Chief Representative of Greatwall Drilling, China 273
Reference 276

27 Melbana CEO Announces New Partnership with Sherritt: "The Best Opportunity We Have for Delivering the Best Outcome" 277

Part VIII Healthcare, Biotechnology and Medical Tourism

28 Cuba's Medical Tourism Business—Its Past, Present, and Future, Dr. Osvaldo Héctor, Servicios Médicos Cubanos 285
Reference 289

29 The Future Direction of CSMC, Dr. Yamila De Armas Águila, President, Comercializadora De Servicios Médicos Cubanos 291
Follow-up to the Interview: May 2022 293

30 A US Journalist Reports on Health from Havana, Gail Reed, MEDICC 301
References 309

31 VP of BioCubaFarma Discuss Partnerships, COVID-19, and the Future of the Company—Dr. Mayda Mauri Pérez 311
References 319

32 Wrong Conclusions from Incomplete Science: Dr. Mitchell Valdés-Sosa Discusses the NASEM Report on the "Havana Syndrome" 321
References 328

33 NEYROS CEO Discusses Joint Research with Cuba on New Parkinson's Medication 331
Update to This Interview 333
References 334

Part IX Tourism

34 "No One Remembers the Silver Medalist," Interview with Desmond Taljaard, London & Regional Properties Ltd. 337
Follow-up to the Interview: April 2022 340
References 341

35 Travel to Cuba—A New Era Dawns, Tom Popper, President, InsightCuba 343
Follow-up to the Interview: April 2022 347
References 352

36 "Start as You Intend to Go on," says CEIBA Investments Portfolio Manager, Sebastiaan Berger 353
Description of CEIBA Investments Limited and Meliá Hotels International Construction Projects 355

Follow-up to the Interview: January 2022 360
References 361

37 Archipelago's Hotel Investment and Expansion in the Time of Pandemic: Interview with Managing Director, Gerard Byrne 363
References 369

Part X Agriculture

38 USACC Chair Talks Agricultural Trade with Cuba 373
Follow-up to the Interview: April 14, 2022 381
References 382

Part XI The Non-state Sector: Micro, Small, and Medium Enterprises (MSMEs)

39 The Cuban Entrepreneurs: "Running Up That Hill," Interview: Marta Deus 387
References 393

Part XII The Nonprofit Organizations

40 Interview with James Williams, President of Engage Cuba 397
References 402

41 Environmental Defense Fund and Cuba's Long-Term Mutually Beneficial Relationship, Dan Whittle 403
Élise C. Hartill
Reference 415

Index 417

Notes on Contributors

Dr. John M. Kirk is professor emeritus of Latin American Studies, Dalhousie University, Canada, and the author/co-editor of 17 books on Cuba. Some of his recent works include *Healthcare Without Borders: Understanding Cuban Medical Internationalism*, *Cuba at the Crossroads*, *Cuban Medical Internationalism: Origins, Evolution, and Goals*, and *Jose Marti: Mentor of the Cuban Nation*. He is currently working on a book analyzing Canada–Cuba relations.

Dr. Juan Triana Cordoví is a senior professor at the Center for the Study of the Cuban Economy, University of Havana. He holds a Bachelor's in Economics, a Master's in Cuban and Latin American Studies, and a Ph.D. in Economy. From 1995 to 2004, Dr. Triana was Director at the Center for the Study of the Cuban Economy, University of Havana. In 1997, Dr. Triana was awarded for his work in Economics by the Ministry of Science, Technology and the Environment (CITMA). He is also a four times winner as coauthor for *Best Book in Economy* from the National Social Sciences Prize from CITMA. He is an internationally published author of more than 25 books as a coauthor and numerous articles on strategies for economic change, opportunities, challenges, perspectives, reflections on economic matters pertaining to Cuba.

Mark A. Entwistle was the former Canadian ambassador to Cuba from 1993 to 1997. He is also co-founder and co-managing director of Acasta Cuba Capital Inc. an advisory and specialist business development firm in

Toronto Canada enabling clients to understand the market in Cuba and pursue commercial opportunities.

Élise C. Hartill holds an M.Sc. in Marine Biology from the School of Marine Science at the University of Maine. During her undergraduate career, Ms. Hartill studied tropical coral ecosystems in Bonaire and the Dominican Republic with Dr. Robert Steneck and cold-water coral with Dr. Rhian Waller. Her undergraduate thesis describes the reproductive biology of an Antarctic deep-sea coral, and her master's thesis describes the ecology of cold-water corals in Alaskan fjords. She is a National Geographic Explorer, having received an "Early Career Grant" in 2019 to develop and expand place-based science programming for students in rural Alaska. Her research was published in the journals *PLoS One* and *Frontiers in Marine Science*. She is now the Communications Coordinator with Maine Youth for Climate Justice, a coalition of over 400 youth across the state of Maine who organize for climate justice, she is also co-chair of the Climate Education working group with the Nature-Based Education Consortium.

T. K. Hernández, with many years of experience in Cuba prior to its official opening to international tourism, is co-founder and editor at Cuba Business Report. As a journalist, her work has been published in various online news media publications. She has supported fundraising for Cuba's last two hurricane disaster relief campaigns and is a member of the Canadian Network on Cuba (CNC-CCFA). She graduated from Western University with a bachelor's degree in European Literature and holds a certificate in Economic Development from Oxford University. She is also a member of the Society of Professional Journalists, and ACES International Alliance of Editors. Ms. Hernández is the author of two published books.

Abbreviations

ANEC	Asociación Nacional de Economistas y Contadores de Cuba
BCC	Banco Central de Cuba (Central Bank of Cuba)
CECMED	Cuban Regulatory Authority
CEOG	Cuba Energy Oil and Gas (conference)
CIDEM	Center for Pharmaceutical Research and Development
CIGB	Center for Genetic Engineering and Biotechnology
CIM	Center of Molecular Immunology
CIPI	Center for International Policy Research
CITMA	Ministry of Science, Technology and Environment
CNEURO	Center for Neuroscience
CSMC	Comercializadora de Servicios Médicos Cubanos (CSMC S.A)
CUPET	Unión Cuba-Petróleo
ECLAC	Economic Commission for Latin America and the Caribbean
EDF	Environmental Defense Fund
ELAM	Latin American School of Medicine
FDA	U.S. Food and Drug Administration
FDI	Foreign Direct Investment
FEMA	Foreign Extraterritorial Measures Act (Canada)
FIHAV	Feria Internacional de la Habana/Havana International Trade Fair
INDER	National Institute of Sports, Physical Education and Recreation
MEP	Ministry of the Economy and Planning
MICONS	Ministry of Construction
MINAG	Ministry of Agriculture
MINCEX	Ministry of Foreign Trade and Foreign Investment
MINEM	Ministry of Energy and Mines
MINJUS	Ministry of Justice

MINREX	Ministry of Foreign Affairs
MINSAP	Ministry of Public Health of the Republic of Cuba
MLCs	*Moneda Libremente Convertible:* Freely Convertible Money (Foreign Currency)
MOU	Memorandum of Understanding
MSMEs	Micro, Small, or Medium Enterprises
NDA(s)	Non-Disclosure Agreement (s)
OCPI	Cuban Industrial Property Office
OFAC	Office of Foreign Assets Control
ONRM	National Office of Mineral Resources
PAHC	Pan American Health Organization
PCC	Communist Party of Cuba
PSC	Production Sharing Contract
SMC	La Comercializadora de Servicios Médicos Cubanos (CSMC S.A.)
SMEs	Small, Medium-Sized Enterprises
TSRA	Trade Sanctions and Export Enhancement Act of 2000
UN	United Nations
UNDP	United Nations Development Program
USACC	United States Agriculture Coalition for Cuba
USDA	United States Department of Agriculture
WB	World Bank
WHO	World Health Organization
WTTC	World Travel & Tourism Council

List of Figures

Fig. 5.1	His Excellency, Julio Garmendía Peña (Photo courtesy of the Embassy of Cuba in Canada)	62
Fig. 6.1	At the official residence of his excellency, Ambassador Dr. Antony Stokes, LVO, Ambassador to Cuba of the United Kingdom	74
Fig. 7.1	Her Excellency, Josefina Vidal, during her term as Ambassador at the Embassy of Cuba in Canada. The Ambassador is now Vice Minister of Foreign Affairs (Photo by the editor)	80
Fig. 8.1	Rodrigo Malmierca Díaz, Minister of Foreign Investment and Trade (MINCEX) (Photo courtesy of MINCEX)	92
Fig. 9.1	Dr. José Ramón Cabañas Rodríguez, formerly the Ambassador of Cuba in Washington, D.C. He is now the Director of the Center for International Policy Research (Photo courtesy of Dr. Cabañas)	102
Fig. 10.1	His Excellency, Marcelino Medina González, is now the Ambassador of Cuba in Spain (Photo by the editor)	108
Fig. 11.1	Her Excellency, Berris Ekinci, Ambassador of Turkey in Cuba (Photo by the editor)	112
Fig. 12.1	His Excellency, Andrei Anatolyevich Guskov (Photo courtesy of the Embassy of the Russian Federation in Cuba)	122
Fig. 13.1	Dr. Juan Triana Cordoví (Photo from the personal collection of Dr. Triana)	130
Fig. 14.1	Dr. Emily Morris (Photo by Michael Lachmann)	136

Fig. 15.1 Ana Teresa Igarza, General Director at the Mariel Special Development Zone (Photo by the editor) 148

Fig. 16.1 Huong Nguyen, Business Manager at ViMariel (From the personal collection of Nguyen) 158

Fig. 17.1 Minister-President, Marta Wilson González, of the Central Bank of Cuba (Photo by the editor) 170

Fig. 18.1 U.S. attorney Daniel R. Zim (From the personal collection of Mr. Zim) 184

Fig. 19.1 Spanish attorney, Hermenegildo Altozano, CUPET Conference, 2019 (Photo by the editor) 192

Fig. 20.1 Déborah Rivas Saavedra, Vice Minister from the Ministry of Foreign Trade and Foreign Investment (MINCEX) (Photo by the editor) 202

Fig. 21.1 U.S. attorney, Felix Chevalier and Jeffrey DeLaurentis, Chargé d'affaires ad interim of the Embassy of the United States, Havana, 2017 (Photo from the personal collection of Mr. Chevalier) 220

Fig. 23.1 Mark A. Entwistle, former Canadian Ambassador of Canada to Cuba, co-founder of Acasta Cuba (Photo by Juanita Montalvo) 228

Fig. 24.1 Fred Wade, president of Fireworks FX, at the top of the lantern dome of the Capitolio, 300 feet above the streets of Havana (From the collection of Mr. Wade) 262

Fig. 25.1 Peter Stickland, Non-Executive Director at Australia's Melbana Energy Limited (Photo courtesy of Mr. Stickland) 270

Fig. 26.1 At the Greatwall Drilling site near Matanzas with Kong Xiangzhong (From the personal collection of the editor) 274

Fig. 27.1 Melbana Energy's CEO, Andrew G. Purcell (Photo courtesy of Mr. Purcell) 278

Fig. 28.1 Dr. Osvaldo Héctor from SMC in Montreal with Services Santé International President, Alain Leclerc 286

Fig. 29.1 Dr. Yamila de Armas, President of the CSMC at our interview (Photo by the editor) 292

Fig. 30.1 Gail Reed, Executive Editor at MEDICC Review, at home in Havana (Photo by the editor) 302

Fig. 31.1 Dr. Mauri in her office at BioCubaFarma (From the personal collection of Dr. Mauri) 312

Fig. 32.1 Dr. Mitchell Valdes-Sosa (From the personal collection of Dr. Valdes-Sosa) 322
Fig. 35.1 Tom Popper, now CEO, 82° West Consultants at the Special Development Zone of Mariel in 2022 (Photo from the personal collection of Mr. Popper) 344
Fig. 36.1 Sebastiaan Berger from CEIBA investments in London (Photo by Charles Sturge) 354
Fig. 37.1 Archipelago International Overseas' Managing Director, Gerard Byrne (From the personal collection Mr. Byrne) 364
Fig. 38.1 Paul Johnson of the USACC (From the personnel collection of Mr. Johnson) 374
Fig. 39.1 Entrepreneur, Marta Deus at her office in Vedado (Photo by the editor) 388
Fig. 41.1 Dan Whittle, Senior Director, and Attorney at EDF.org at the Encuentro de Pesca Sostenible en Cuba event, 2018 (From Mr. Whittle's personal collection) 404

List of Tables

Table 2.1	U.S. tourists to Cuba: 2011–June 7, 2023	10
Table 2.2	Foreign investment: 2017–2021 (Estimated)	18
Table 2.3	International tourist arrivals: 2009 to June 7, 2023	22
Table 3.1	Cuba: main macroeconomic indicators	36
Table 3.2	Foreign investment in Cuba	44
Table 13.1	Year-over-year change in quarterly GDP (2020/2019) (%)	131

CHAPTER 1

Foreword by Dr. John M. Kirk

John M. Kirk

Having taught about Cuba for over four decades at the university level in the United States and Canada, I am fully aware of the lack of positive information about the island published in North America—other than travel coverage about the wonderful beaches, salsa music, and mojitos. Misinformation is sadly a common feature of the (limited) coverage of life in Cuba today, with an extraordinary mixture of lies and half-truths being commonplace. In addition, there are many areas of the Cuban development model that are simply ignored.

So little is said, for instance, about the healthcare system (with results rivaling those found in many countries of the Global North, at a fraction of the cost), or the achievements in education (Cuba has a higher literacy rate than Canada or the United States). Likewise, little attention was paid to Cuba's approach to COVID-19. Few people know that, in addition to a remarkably low level of COVID-related deaths (when adjusted for population, 1/50 the rate found in the United States), Cuba

J. M. Kirk (✉)
Halifax, Canada
e-mail: John.Kirk@dal.ca

Dalhousie University, Halifax, Canada

T. K. Hernández, *The Cuba Interviews*,
https://doi.org/10.1007/978-3-031-30203-9_1

also sent almost 5,000 medical specialists to 40 countries to participate in campaigns against the virus.

Moreover, next to nothing is said about the economy of Cuba (other than criticizing its inefficiencies), much less the potential of investing in Cuba. Indeed, many people are unaware that it is even possible for foreigners to invest in the island, despite the fact that there are over 200 foreign companies established with offices there. That is why this collection of insightful interviews, gathered with great care by T. K. Hernández over the past six years, is so important—since it breaks some of the more common myths about these topics. The bottom line found in these interviews is very clear: Cuba is in the process of introducing significant economic reform, and medium-and long-term investments are definitely worth considering.

This book is a veritable treasure trove of pertinent information on the economic system, and investment scenario, in contemporary Cuba. Anybody interested in wanting to find out how the Cuban economy works, and what the experience of foreign investment in Cuba has been, will find it extremely informative and helpful. This is particularly relevant in light of the election of the Biden administration in the United States (and indications that U.S. policy will revert to the lines adopted by the Obama administration), as well as significant economic changes in Cuba.

There are many questions that need to be considered when reflecting on investing in Cuba today. What is the current economic situation there? How attractive is the investment scenario? What are the principal investment opportunities and challenges? What is the experience of companies that have invested there? How significant are the recent economic reforms in Cuba? How will the election of Joe Biden affect U.S.-Cuban relations, and the potential to invest there? This book seeks to provide insights into these, and other crucially important matters related to the economy and investment experience.

Cuba is at a significant crossroads in its history. For four years the Trump administration had introduced scores of measures in an attempt to destroy the socialist system and bring about regime change there. Laws limiting the amount of remittance money from members of the diaspora had been passed, causing severe difficulties for many Cuban families that depended upon that support. Cruise traffic—bringing annually hundreds of thousands of American vacationers—had been outlawed, resulting in the cancellation of 800,000 bookings on cruise liners.

Washington also prohibited flights to all cities in Cuba apart from Havana, again creating major obstacles for Cuban Americans seeking to visit families on the island. Bills were passed limiting the potential for companies (anywhere in the world) to trade with Cuba, and any who dared to trade with Cuba using U.S. dollars faced legal charges and hefty fines. Despite the clear limitations of international law, Americans and Cuban Americans were encouraged to use the Helms–Burton legislation, enacted in 1996, and sue any foreign investors who were "trafficking" in property on the island allegedly owned by the complainants.

Fortunately, the Trump era has passed. The election of Joe Biden has made it clear that his government will be reverting to some of the key initiatives of the Obama administration in its Cuba policy. It is important to remember the significance of this. The Obama years had shown clear possibilities in improving U.S.-Cuban relations and had resulted in meaningful economic reforms on the island. Small businesses sprang up, hundreds of private restaurants and bed-and-breakfast operations (many listed on Airbnb) opened, tourism soared with hundreds of thousands of Americans visiting the island annually, and the administration by American hotel chains of several Cuban hotels (for the first time in sixty years) started. At the same time the Cuban government initiated a series of modernizing reforms, supporting these changes. With the election of Joe Biden, Obama's vice president, it now looks as if a return to some of the Obama initiatives will result.

Meanwhile, significant changes have been occurring on the island, despite the ravages of COVID-19. For instance, after fully a decade of debating the need to bring about monetary unification (uniting the two monetary systems, the Cuban peso—mainly used by Cubans—and the Convertible peso, or CUC used by foreigners), this reform actually took place in early 2021. This is an enormous benefit for foreign investors, making planning and administration cost transparent after decades of two very different monetary systems. Investment has immediately become more cost-effective and attractive.

The Cuban government has also brought about a significant reform in labor law. Until 2021 self-employment was reduced to just 127 types of businesses or occupations that Cuban citizens could seek. This has now changed drastically, and while the government has provided a list of 124 activities which will continue to be controlled by the state, everything else (over 2,000 different employment opportunities, trades, and business areas) is now open to individuals and businesses. The self-employed sector

(600,000 strong, or 13% of the workforce) continues to grow, and cooperatives and small and medium-sized businesses now have the potential to develop. In addition, subsidies to state companies have been reduced, as the government seeks to develop a more robust economy. Private businesses have also been granted access to wholesale suppliers and markets, and are now allowed to import and export products (although only through government agencies). These changes have all been introduced in the early months of 2021, and illustrate the government's intention of supporting self-employment and the small business sector. In the past these had been shunned; now they are seen as an essential part of the economy.

In terms of an opening to foreign investment, in March 2021 the Cuban government announced its intention to continue offering investment opportunities to the international community, listing over 500 specific project possibilities. Another significant change is that, for the first time since 1959, the government has now stated that Cubans living abroad were also welcome to invest in the island. In addition, as a means of reducing bureaucratic hurdles and red tape, a "single window" has been introduced by the government to facilitate foreign trade and investment. As can be seen, following decades of tight, central government control, important innovations and initiatives have been introduced. There is a clear opening to the private sector, both on the island and abroad, and foreign investment is both sought and needed. Given these circumstances it is important to have updated, pertinent information on the realities of the Cuban economy, and investment opportunities.

The collection of interviews found in this book goes a long way to inform readers about the impact of these changes, particularly in terms of investment experience in several key areas. In this book we see the opinions of ambassadors, ministers, economists, lawyers, academics, scientists, journalists, and ecologists, in all an international "Who's Who" of international (and Cuban) insights into the economy and investment practices. The actual interviews—which are the main core of the book—are preceded by an insightful introductory chapter by one of Cuba's leading economists, Juan Triana, setting the scene and explaining the nature of economic realities in Cuba today.

The interviews, concise and focused, are divided into 12 sections: government, economy and foreign investment, industrial zones, banking, business, law, oil and energy, health and biotechnology, tourism, agriculture, the non-state sector, and NGOs, with an array of specialists providing information on both possibilities and specific investment experiences. These are the key sectors of the Cuban economy, the areas of greatest potential. There are two central thrusts to the collection of interviews—information on the economic reality of the island (with excellent contributions from British academic Emily Morris and her Cuban colleague, Triana) and information on the sectors with the greatest investment potential. The actual experiences presented by individuals involved in these areas are particularly helpful.

There are many different perspectives, ranging from various Cuban government representatives to participants in U.S. trade missions, from investors in key sectors to managers of investment projects. Particularly helpful are the views of Mark Entwistle, the former Canadian ambassador to the island and in recent years a consultant on trade with, and investment in, Cuba. In addition, given the long-standing U.S. opposition to Cuba (and in particular, the Helms–Burton legislation introduced during the Clinton administration) the legal analysis provided in the two interviews is instructive and helpful.

There is a nucleus of niche investment areas in Cuba, and information on all is provided in this collection. These areas of greatest potential are energy, tourism/hospitality, and health/biotechnology, and specific direct experiences from each sector are provided here. The oil and gas section contains an interview with the CEO of an Australian oil exploration company and also with a representative of a Chinese company. Cuba produces about one-half of the oil and gas it needs and is keen to increase this potential (as well as to develop "green energy"), and therefore be less dependent upon foreign sources.

The tourism/hospitality industry, the best-known internationally, has been shown to have enormous potential in Cuba, with the number of tourists rising from 745,000 in 1995 to 4.7 million in 2018. After the COVID-19 pandemic is finally over, it is expected that this will again prove to be one of the key drivers of the Cuban economy, as vacationers flood to the pristine Cuban beaches. Insights and advice are presented by several international investors in this area, including the managing director of a global investment firm, the president of a U.S. company that had offered people-to-people travel opportunities, the portfolio manager of an investment company with several hotels in Cuba, and the managing Director of a South Asian company managing several hotels on the island.

The wealth of their experience is impressive, and their advice, extremely helpful.

Insight into the health sector is provided in six interviews. It is not well known that the major source of hard currency income for the Cuban government comes from the exportation of medical services, in large part because the country has a surplus of medical personnel (on a per capita basis three times the number of physicians found in either Canada or the United States). At present there are over 30,000 medical personnel from Cuba working overseas. On the island, the company Servicios Médicos Cubanos provides a wide variety of medical services for foreigners (from cancer and hip surgery to diabetes treatment and cosmetic surgery), and two of the interviews speak to this service. Medical tourism is an area yet to be fully developed in Cuba and offers enormous potential, given the low costs and high quality of medical care. Cuba has also produced a variety of internationally recognized pharmaceutical products (including CIMAvax, a lung cancer vaccine in trials at Roswell Park Cancer Center in New York, as well as four COVID-19 vaccines), and Gail Reed provides insights into the potential in this sector.

It is often said that Cuba (population 11.2 million) is a small country with a large international footprint. But little is mentioned, or indeed known, about the investment opportunities in Cuba. This book seeks to fill that gap. Following years of sanctions and a variety of pressures from the Trump administration, and as it emerges from COVID-19, Cuba has brought about a series of significant economic reforms. Little is known about these changes in economic policy and the opening to foreign investment, and there is a great deal of misinformation about the significance of these developments.

A new investment climate, combined with changes in national economic policies, make this an opportune time to explore the investment potential on the island—particularly in the post-Trump era. No finer source of updated information on this topic exists than this collection of interviews, replete with advice, and the experience of specialists in various investment areas in Cuba. The book, painstakingly edited by Ms. Hernández, represents obligatory reading for all traveling along this road. Despite widespread media ignorance and misinformation, the economic reality on the island is changing dramatically. Cuba is indeed open for business, as this book shows clearly.

CHAPTER 2

Introduction

I never initially intended to gather these interviews into book format. The value of these conversations from a historical perspective, and as a story of economic development, inspired me to do so. I realized they presented an "open window" into a nation perceived by the Americans as "shuttered" to the outside world (Jones, 2012).

These interviews occurred between 2016 and 2022 in London, Washington, DC, Toronto, Ottawa, and Havana.

Motivations

I admit, the excitement of the Obama years captured me. This was my initial motivation in conducting the interviews collected here. My approach was structured by the contextual history and politics of the Barack Obama and Raúl Castro announcement in December 2014, when for the first time in nearly sixty years, Cuba and the United States opened a path toward normalized relations. It came to be equally influenced by the bleak days of the Trump presidency and the emergence of the so-called Havana Syndrome, a series of health incidents reported by more than a dozen American and several Canadian embassy staff starting in late 2016. Finally, the project was shaped by the onset of the global pandemic, the election of Biden in 2020 and his "unmet promises" regarding Cuba,

T. K. Hernández, *The Cuba Interviews*,
https://doi.org/10.1007/978-3-031-30203-9_2

along with the winding down of the syndrome through to the economic recovery of the island under the post-pandemic new normal.

My second motivation was the desire to address the difficulty in obtaining interviews and information in Cuba that hinders attempts to present a clear picture of foreign direct investment (Feinberg, 2012). This work aspires to fill some of those gaps and supplement future analysis.

I have attempted to present a "balanced perspective" throughout the book—this can only be arrived at by assuming an international viewpoint. The interviews contain the thoughts and opinions of stakeholders who work and invest within and beyond Cuba's borders. One of this book's main objectives is to supplement FDI analysis through participants' direct experiences—which demonstrate both a continued global interest and participation despite the limitations imposed by the government of the United States of America.

These interviews paint a more complete picture of Cuba. They provide an open window through which to examine its economic changes and investment potential, an understanding of which is vital for anyone who wishes for a deeper insight into Cuba. This "open view" will be useful to those who want and need to know more about the island, ninety miles south of the United States.

Having an international perspective is important because few journalists or authors can write without a lifetime of political socialization shaping their construct of the world. As an outsider to the United States, I, like many others, view the American press as engaged in a sort of media war against Cuba best analyzed by author Keith Bolender in his book, *Manufacturing the Enemy: The Media War Against Cuba*. Of course, there are those who write objectively about Cuba, but the norm is a daily barrage of criticism, "*contra-Cuba*," most especially from the corporate media.

This compilation of interviews, conducted for the publication *Cuba Business Report* took place with government representatives and international businesspeople from a variety of industry sectors. These individuals discuss their experiences, bilateral relations, trade and investment, economic development, collaboration, and legal issues. They talk candidly of goals, achievements, and challenges in Cuba. We hear the voices of reason and progress. The ones who lead and invest, who create opportunities for themselves and others, initiate change, trigger sustainable development, build infrastructure, improve lives, strengthen the economy, lessen suffering, and create hope. They stimulate forward progress. They are the visionaries with plans for both the nation and humanity, seeking to realize the full potential of Cuba, driving a new era of sustainable development and growth. These voices come from Australia, Canada, China, Cuba, England, The Netherlands, Indonesia, Italy, Ireland, Russia, Spain, Turkey, Vietnam, and the United States.

This work could not exist without a constant reference to the United States. I have interviewed Americans; I have friends who are American. I have traveled extensively throughout the country. As with everything, what happens in the United States has enormous repercussions around the world. American policy has directly affected revolutionary Cuba's economic and social development for the past 60 years. American politics permeate the story of Cuba, sadly to the serious detriment of the Cubans and American business interests.

Therefore, what I present is a diverse collection of views. These will be helpful for those interested in foreign investment, the society in which they propose to invest, the laws and reforms that will play out on those investments, and the business climate of Cuba.

These interviews began in what I would call "the optimism of the hype years," when Cuba and the United States attempted to construct a new relationship. The announcement by presidents Castro and Obama on December 17, 2014, took the world by surprise. In July 2015, the opening of embassies in each other's capital cities generated an optimism not witnessed for decades.

American business executives poured into Cuba, all eager to sign agreements, launch cruises, book flights, manage hotels, rent bed-and-breakfasts, and export coffee, cigars, and rum.

The "hype years" took off with a bang. France's president welcomed Raúl Castro on his first visit to Paris, Cuban flags fluttered in the breeze along the famous Champs-Élysées (Horobin, 2016). As if by magic, an abundance of specialists appeared on the scene. Consultancy firms sprang up; high-priced "need-to-be-there" conferences were launched by a new breed of experts. International business, already with a foot in the door, sensed the real possibility of encroaching American competition and it became a mad race for dominance in the Cuban market.

Obama and his wife made it all official with their visit in 2016. There was a rapid rise in government trade commissions (U.S. Embassy in Cuba, 2019), corporate executives from Airbnb, Google, General Electric, JetBlue, Marriott, MasterCard, PayPal, Pfizer, Starwood, Xerox, (Burnett, 2014), and politicians (Correspondent, 2018) all touched down in Havana. Ironically, even Trump Organization executives[1] paid multiple visits over the years to explore business opportunities. (Drucker & Wicary, 2016). A sudden deluge of U.S. tourists, curious about Cuba—the "forbidden fruit"—jumped at the chance to visit (see Table 2.1). Beyoncé, Rihanna, and the Rolling Stones landed in Havana. Chanel models strutted their stuff on the perfect del Prado runway. Hollywood touched down and filming began in Havana. Even Jill Biden, wife of then-Vice President Joe Biden, paid a visit in October 2016 (The White House, Office of the Press Secretary, 2016).

The business community was eager to move forward with relationships with Cuba in those glory days; it was a time of hope and excitement.

In 2015, a bipartisan advocacy group formed under the name "Engage Cuba" delivering to America the simple and direct messaging: *engage with Cuba*.

Table 2.1 U.S. tourists to Cuba: 2011–June 7, 2023

Year	*Number of visitors*
2011	73,566
2012	99,052
2013	93,420
2014	92,325
2015	162,972
2016	284,552
2017	618,346
2018	638,365
2019	498,538
2020	58,147
2021	1,872
2022	100,494
2023	70,694

Source: Oficina Nacional de Estadistica e Información (ONEI). (2022). Información de la Dirección de Identificación, Inmigración y Extranjería cierre de diciembre 2022. Arribo de viajeros. Visitantes internacionales. Cierre diciembre 2022.

[1] Bloomberg's article "Did Donald Trump's Executives Violate the Cuban Embargo?" points to a series of trips to Cuba over the years by executives of the Trump organization. Drucker, J., & Wicary, S. (2016, July 28). *Did Donald Trump's executives violate the Cuban embargo?* Bloomberg. https://www.bloomberg.com/features/2016-donald-trump-golf-cuba/.

From 1992 to 2018, U.S. tourism to the Island rose steadily (Table 2.1). In 2011, Obama restored the "people-to-people" travel license, whereby each year an average of approximately 95,000 Americans visited until 2014. The Obama "'feel good effect' and the marketing headlines urged, 'go now… before it changes,' kicked in." Under licenses and agreements, the cruise ships began sailing in May 2016 to dock at ports in Cuba, *legally*. U.S. airlines launched commercial flights to all destinations on the island. The number of American tourists soared, reaching a peak of 638,365 visitors by the end of 2018 (ONEI, 2021).

But in 2019, the numbers fell to 498,538 visitors, no doubt a result of the Havana Syndrome story, John Bolton's Troika of Tyranny campaign, the proliferation of lawsuits resulting from Trump's unprecedented implementation of Title III of Helms–Burton, and the creation of a blacklist of Cuban hotels, which threatened prosecution of any American who stayed in one. Senator Marco Rubio and others feared the consequences of increased tourism to and from Cuba. They feared losing their grip on the "Cuba issue." Americans couldn't be told what was happening there because of the "eye-opening" experience of travel.

By the close of 2018, politics would change with the arrival of national security adviser John Bolton. Rubio urged more "practical steps." Bolton designated Cuba, Venezuela, and Nicaragua as a Troika of Tyranny.[2] The American government complained of Cuban support for Venezuelan President Nicolás Maduro. They accused Cuba of stationing troops in the country when, in fact, there were only doctors, a deal between the two nations, an exchange of Venezuelan oil for Cuban medical services.

Indeed, the Havana Syndrome came to play an outsized role in the destruction of the blossoming bilateral relations under Obama, but the Troika of Tyranny became an essential ingredient to the mix. Today, it is interesting to observe that both machinations have reached their conclusions and vanished into the ether.

My first interviews during the Obama era reflected the optimism of those years. I continued interviewing government officials and executives following the 2016 election of Donald Trump. That moment in history

[2] Rogin, J. (2018, November 2). *Opinion | Bolton promises to confront Latin America's "troika of tyranny"*. *The Washington Post*. https://www.washingtonpost.com/opinions/global-opinions/bolton-promises-to-confront-latin-americas-troika-of-tyranny/2018/11/01/df57d3d2-ddf5-11e8-85df-7a6b4d25cfbb_story.html.

established the onslaught of what I call the "bleak years." American executives, still hoping to move forward with Cuba, sensed the impending disaster. My interview, "*The Quiet Optimism in the American Business Community*," reflected this mood. Privately, several people expressed a sense of dread at the prospects of a Trump presidency. Looking back with the crystal clarity of hindsight, the foreboding was entirely accurate.

As Obama left office in January 2017, his last act was the cessation of the "wet foot, dry foot" policy, thus ending the ability of Cubans to claim special immigration status once they set foot on American soil (Cuban Adjustment Act, 1966). For the time-being, this put an end to precarious journeys undertaken by Cuban emigres who wished to reach a country that existed mainly in their imaginations, a perceived paradise where the streets are paved with gold, where the wildest dreams could come true.

The Coming of Trump

The effects of both Trump's hostile policies against Cuba combined with the COVID pandemic were devastating to Cuba's economy when measured by its GDP, which plummeted 11%.[3] Globally, the pandemic wreaked economic havoc, throwing countries into crisis mode with the border closures, the loss of tourism, stalled manufacturing, and disrupted supply chains. These also affected Cuba, but more dramatically. Crippling sanctions in a time of pandemic, a lack of access to markets in the first place and international financial aid, the loss of foreign currency earnings from the collapse of tourism and foreign trade in goods, and lockdowns, compounded the crisis.[4] Trump's activation of the Helms–Burton Title III Act (waived by all previous U.S. presidents since Clinton) intensified the problem by permitting U.S. interests to sue Cuba over claims of "confiscated" properties. In total disregard for the pandemic, Trump increased sanctions by a further 243 measures.

[3] In his address to parliament in December 2020, Economic Minister Alejandro Gil reported the decline in GDP and predicted a 6–7% growth in 2021. Reuters Staff. (2020, December 17). *Cuban economy shrank 11% in 2020, government says*. Reuters. https://www.reuters.com/article/cuba-economy-idUSL1N2IX1V9.

[4] For further reading of the trends and causes of the economic crisis in Cuba during the pandemic, see the United Nations Economic Commission for Latin America and the Caribbean document Economic Survey of Latin America and the Caribbean · 2020, available at: https://repositorio.cepal.org/bitstream/handle/11362/46071/19/ES2020_Cuba_en.pdf.

These were the "bleak years," indeed. Despite this, foreign investment led by the Russians and Chinese never ceased, filling the gap exposed by the American absence. Mainstream media responded with an almost surprising naïveté that the Russians and Chinese were in Cuba involved in major infrastructure, technology, and biopharma projects. It is almost as if those reporters were oblivious to the rules of the school playground, when there's a bully in the playground one finds new friends. But the Chinese and Russian friendships were not, by any means, new. These are long-term, uninterrupted, mutually beneficial relationships.

The world's interest in Cuba continues to this day. This is a nation that, against all odds, has survived over six decades of what amounts to, and is aptly named, an economic and financial blockade imposed by its superpower neighbor to the north. But my task here is not to explain Cuba's history—other experts on these matters can better establish Cuba's survival into the twenty-first century.[5]

It would be a failure to ignore the repercussions of 60 years of blockade when analyzing the Cuban economy. Embargoes and blockades penalize the targeted economy. In 2018, the Economic Commission for Latin America and the Caribbean (ECLAC) said the organization estimates damages at $130 billion (Bárcenas, 2018).[6] In 2021, Cuba reported $144.4 billion[7] of losses over the last six decades (Prensa Latina, 2021). On a daily basis, this developing economy loses $12 million (Morejón, 2022).[8] These measures affect not only each and every citizen, but also the health and biopharmaceutical industries, foreign investment, energy supply, food security, factory production, education, transportation, and access to banking institutions.

[5] For further reading on Cuba's economic survival, read Helen Yaffe's book, *We are Cuba: How a Revolutionary People Have Survived in a Post-Soviet World* (2020).

[6] In her speech on opening day of the Economic Commission for Latin America and the Caribbean (ECLAC), May 2018, in Havana, Alicia Bárcena, Executive Secretary of the organization stated the cost of the blockade of Cuba was $130 billion. "We evaluate it every year, as an Economic Commission, and we know that this blockade has cost the Cuban people more than 130 billion dollars, at current prices, and that it has left an indelible mark on its economic structure."

[7] Cuba's Foreign Minister Bruno Rodríguez Parrilla reported $144.4 billion in 2021. View at: https://www.plenglish.com/news/2021/05/22/rodriguez-denounces-us-blockade-costs-cuba-millions-of-dollars-a-day/.

[8] Cuba's Ministry of Foreign Affairs reported $12 million, in daily losses.

The Backbone: The Havana Syndrome

The Havana Syndrome, launched quietly in late 2016, served as the backbone for Trump's anti-Cuba propaganda that supported the hostile measures to come.

What the U.S. government now calls Anomalous Health Incidents (AHI) (U.S. Department of State, 2021) first emerged in a CIA officer in Havana in December 2016 (Entous & Anderson, 2018). Journalists and others, without any scientific investigation as to cause, were quick to call it a sonic weapon attack by Cuba or a foreign adversary. In total, 1,100 U.S. and Canadian embassy staff (Isikoff, 2022), and CIA agents reported injuries. Its symptoms included concussions, vertigo, tinnitus, extreme fatigue, hearing and vision loss, nausea, and headaches. Scientific investigation found other causes, including pesticides, cicadas, and mass psychogenic illness. The CIA and FBI investigations eventually concluded that no foreign actors played a role, and it "could be attributed to alternative environmental and medical factors" (Isikoff, 2022). The claims of attacks gravitated to a breakdown in US–Cuba relations, the closure of the embassy in Havana, and more sanctions. As a result, in the glaring absence of fact-checking, the last five years of sensationalist reportage amounts to nothing less than a conspiracy theory.

Trump first announced his plans to limit travel and trade at the Manuel Artime Theater in Little Havana on June 16, 2017; however, at no point in his speech (U.S. Embassy in Uruguay (2021) did he refer to the upcoming controversial event soon to rear its ugly head: the Havana Syndrome. Had he known, there is no doubt in my mind he would have included it in his rabble-rousing diatribe. This is interesting because, at the time of the speech, the State Department had been following it for at least six months. It begs the question, why did he not know? It would have fit, more than perfectly, into the theme and tone of his speech. Framing Trump's anti-Cuba agenda, the Havana Syndrome would become key to the escalated sanctions against Cuba, one monstrous news event predicting another.

The Trump administration, heavily swayed by the anti-Cuba community and the vote in Miami, tore down every advance made by Obama and the Cuban government. Not that this was unusual. If one thing characterizes U.S. policy toward Cuba, it is the bipolar political dance of one step forward and two steps back *modus operandi*.

The curtailing of Americans' limited right to travel to Cuba was on the horizon. By August 22, two CIA agents reported bizarre and unconfirmable audio sensations in their rooms at the Hotel Nacional and the Hotel Capri in Havana. Washington responded with a security message banning U.S. citizens from those hotels. As early as September 15, Senator Rubio, without evidence or investigation, had already determined these were "acoustic" attacks (Rubio, 2017), and urged the expulsion of Cuban diplomats and the closure of the U.S. Embassy in Havana. "They did some bad things in Cuba," Trump said on September 29, 2017 (Holland, 2017).

Fifteen Cuban diplomats were expelled in October. Two days later, Secretary of State Rex W. Tillerson said on the television program *Face the Nation* that he was, "considering closing the recently reopened United States Embassy in Havana" (Harris, 2017). By October 25, Trump had restricted U.S. travel even further by banning flights to all destinations in Cuba except the José Martí International airport in Havana. In November, the State Department published its first list of blacklisted hotels.

Trump's administration, continuing with the goal of crushing the Cuban economy, then attacked remittances (an income estimated to be in the range of $1.53 to $3.72 billion) sent by Cuban Americans to their families in Cuba (Runde, 2022). A month and a half later, Trump effectively terminated almost all remittances by making it illegal for Western Union to operate on the island.

Winding Down: The Payout

From acoustic, sonic, and microwave weapons, to cicadas, pesticides exposure, unexplained health incidents, and mass psychogenic illness (the most likely evaluation), the "syndrome" spread to cities around the world, including Guangzhou, Vienna, Berlin, Colombia, Kyrgyzstan, Uzbekistan, Vietnam, and Washington, DC. Its only victims were American embassy staff (but not their bosses), CIA agents, and Canadian diplomats. A report released by the U.S. Academy of Science in December 2020[9] claimed the cause was microwave weapons. A secret report by the

[9] National Academies of Sciences, Engineering, and Medicine. (2020). *An Assessment of Illness in U.S. Government Employees and Their Families at Overseas Embassies*. The National Academies Press. https://doi.org/10.17226/25889.

JASON advisory group in 2018, obtained by Buzz Feed News in 2021,[10] dismissed that theory. Final reports by the CIA and FBI concluded there was no evidence of an attack by a foreign player. The entire scheme wound down when Joe Biden signed the HAVANA Act in October 2021[11] to compensate the government personnel who experienced the traumatic brain injuries and other symptoms.

As a further closure to these "health incidents," in an interview conducted by NBC's Andrea Mitchell, CIA Director William J. Burns also concluded:

> You could find reasonable alternative explanations, whether it was other environmental factors or preexisting medical conditions or other kind of medical explanations. (NBC News, 2022, 40:39/48:05)

The "Havana Syndrome" combined with Trump's 243 new sanctions, the fallout from the pandemic, as well as Bolton's Troika of Tyranny, together represent another four years of failed U.S.–Cuba policy. As a closing act of the Trump regime, Cuba was added back onto the list of state sponsors of terrorism by then-Secretary of State Mike Pompeo, who falsely accused Cuba of "repeatedly providing support for acts of international terrorism in granting safe harbor to terrorists" (U.S. Embassy Havana, 2021). In reality though, it was a move to hogtie any future administration.

In a final assessment, the Trump administration's actions against Cuba were a series of unfortunate events, resulting in "a rollercoaster of cruelty"[12] for the Cuban people. These actions created a humanitarian crisis in Cuba, levied colossal fines against international businesses and banks, destroyed American businesses, and curtailed American citizens' right to travel to the island.

[10] https://www.buzzfeednews.com/article/danvergano/havana-syndrome-jason-crickets.

[11] Statement of President Joe Biden on Signing HAVANA Act into Law. (2021, October 8). The White House. Retrieved from Statement of President Joe Biden on Signing HAVANA Act into Law. https://www.whitehouse.gov/briefing-room/statements-releases/2021/10/08/statement-of-president-joe-biden-on-signing-havana-act-into-law/.

[12] The words of Johana Tablada de la Torre, Deputy Director General for the United States of the Ministry of Foreign Affairs of Cuba, July 2022.

Carlos Fernandez de Cossio, General Director at Cuba's Foreign Ministry stated on the Cubavision TV program:

> Perhaps we will never know what truly happened with the so-called health syndrome or health symptoms of U.S. diplomats in Havana. The U.S. government showed no willingness to cooperate, to find the answers. Clearly, it's not their aim. This whole situation has served the purpose. It has served as an excuse to diminish the bilateral relationship (Cubavisión Internacional, 2020).

The COVID Pandemic

The COVID-19 pandemic was an unexpected bonus for the Trump administration and its attempts to wear down the economy of Cuba. The intensification of sanctions during the pandemic was without regard for basic human rights. Trump enforced these despite the World Health Organization's declaration of a global pandemic on March 12, 2020, and further calls from UN Secretary-General António Guterres and UN Special Rapporteurs to end sanctions during the pandemic. Even the Secretary-General's "appeal for the waiving of sanctions that can undermine countries' capacity to respond to the pandemic" was ignored (Guterres, 2020). It amounts to nothing more than a complete lack of concern for human rights (Rodríguez, 2020) coming from a nation that supposedly prides itself on its care of duty.

Cuba took precautions to control the virus and closed its borders to tourism. At the same time, the country was sending its doctors overseas to support more than forty countries in their battles against the pandemic (Reuters, 2020). Its biotechnology sector developed five COVID vaccines, immunized its population, and achieved the highest vaccination rate in the world (Mathieu et al., 2020).[13] *The Lancet*, a peer-reviewed medical journal praised the nation's management of the pandemic, declaring it a "successful Covid-19 pandemic response" (Burki, 2021). All these accomplishments occurred while the U.S. administration blocked food, fuel, medicines, and medical supplies and canceled remittances to Cuban families.

[13] In comparison to the rest of the world, Cuba's vaccination rate is the highest, published online at: https://ourworldindata.org/coronavirus [Online Resource].

Meanwhile on the Island, its borders closed to international tourism and its citizens under stringent mask mandates, Cuba was planning for the future. Foreign investment in the Mariel Special Development Zone increased, and Vietnam's ViMariel, a 100% foreign capital partnership completed the infrastructure of its industrial park within the Zone. Today, the ZED Mariel has taken on the appearance of a developed industrial city since its opening over eight years ago. As at the date of writing, May 2022, committed investments stand at $3 billion with 62 businesses in operation or under construction. In Havana, high-rise hotels under construction, including the towering *Lo Más Grande*, dot the skyline. Cuba continued to build relations with other nations while promoting its investment opportunities at virtual business events. Its new entrepreneurial sector, another path to economic development, expanded rapidly. Foreign investment was publicly identified as vital to economic development, as was the recognition of the necessity of its promotion. The island began a program of reforms starting with a unification of its dual currency on January 1, 2021, known as "Day Zero," in efforts to revitalize the economy under the "new normal."

Much of the FDI data shown in Table 2.2 comes directly from public speeches or interviews with the Minister of Foreign Trade and Investment, Rodrigo Malmierca Díaz. In Chapter 8, Minister Malmierca confirmed that in 2020 over 30 businesses received approval for more

Table 2.2 Foreign investment: 2017–2021 (Estimated)

Year	*Annual flow*	*Cumulative*
2017	$2 billion[a]	$2 billion
2018	$1.5 billion[a]	$3.5 billion
2019	$1.7 billion[a]	$5.2 billion
2020	$1.9 billion[a]	$7.1 billion
2021	$708 million[b]	$7.808 billion

Sources

[a]The Economist Intelligence Unit. (2021, January 11). Government reports boost in foreign investment. https://country.eiu.com/article.aspx?articleid=1280582711&Country=Cuba&topic=Economy&subtopic=Forecast&subsubtopic=External+sector

[b]Rodríguez, J.L. (2022). Evolution of the world economy in 2021 and its impact on Cuba. Outlook for 2022. https://content.csbs.utah.edu/~al/EcReportCuba/CubaJLR22_05Eng.pdf

than $2 billion of committed capital. However, foreign investment did not fare so well in 2021 at the height of the pandemic, falling to $708 million (Rodríguez, 2022). During the first six months of 2022, Cuba approved nine businesses with foreign capital (one in the ZED Mariel); over 50 others are in negotiations (Ruiz Miyares, 2022).

At the same time as recovery, the economy reeled in the fallout from the pandemic, in the adjustment to economic reforms, increasing sanctions, and the loss of earnings from tourism. The shortages of basic goods and medicines, the loss of remittances, and skyrocketing inflation compounded the problems creating excessive hardship for Cuban families. But this is not the first time the nation faced a crisis of such magnitude. In the 1990s, Cuba experienced extremely difficult economic circumstances during the Special Period in Time of Peace following the collapse of the USSR. The nation survived.

Cuba also faced other challenges.

At the height of the resurgence of the pandemic in Cuba, protests arose across cities throughout the island on July 11, 2021, resulting from a combination of electricity blackouts, food, fuel, and medicine shortages, but stoked by social media manipulation. These hardships stemmed in large part from the escalation of sanctions and US-funded regime change programs (Yaffe, 2021). While the Cubans have genuine justification to complain about the shortages caused by 60 years of the blockade and an unexpected pandemic, the protests would not have happened without the funding of the anti-Cuba dissidents. As William LeoGrande so aptly put it, Biden's support of the US-funded dissidents signifies the president's "embrace of regime change strategy" and the "resurrection of the Washington 'pipe dream' of the Cuban government's collapse" (LeoGrande, 2021).

Washington's regime change strategy, considered a cruel absurdity by the rest of the world, is still in force. The Cuban government has survived four years of the Trump agenda, a global pandemic, and Biden's passivity which, by any evaluation, are not small feats. It can also be concluded that the American-funded protests in July did not bring about the "pipe dream."

What's left for the American regime change strategy? There's nothing. The Havana Syndrome is wrapped up. The Troika of Tyranny is worn out. There is no doubt the blockade creates massive suffering for the Cubans and wreaks tremendous economic damage on their nation. In a final assessment, the only real achievement of the blockade was its original intention, made clear by the now-infamous memorandum by Lester Mallory in 1960 under the Kennedy administration:

> If the above are accepted or cannot be successfully countered, it follows that every possible means should be undertaken promptly to weaken the economic life of Cuba. If such a policy is adopted, it should be the result of a positive decision which would call forth a line of action which, while as adroit and inconspicuous as possible, makes the greatest inroads in denying money and supplies to Cuba, to decrease monetary and real wages, to bring about hunger, desperation and overthrow of government. (Mallory, 1960)

The Final Interviews

The final interviews for this book took place in Havana in May 2022 when I had the chance to speak with a group of remarkable women. It was an honor and a privilege. These women are at the pinnacle of their careers, highly successful and in leadership roles—positions they have attained through education, professionalism, wisdom, and a passion for their work. These women, highly driven super-achievers, are the Minister-President of the Central Bank of Cuba, the General Director of Mariel Special Development Zone, the president of the *Comercializadora de Servicios Médicos Cubanos* (CSMC), the Deputy Minister of MINCEX, the business manager of Vietnam's ViMariel, and one of the strongest female representatives of the emerging non-state sector. It was not planned for the interviewees to be predominantly female, but it does confirm what Josefina Vidal, Vice Minister of Foreign Relations, told me in our 2019 interview. She spoke of how women were involved in the Revolution and of their changing role in Cuban society. She told me the status of women today is closer to that of men than in many other places. As evidence, she pointed to the high percentage of women in government, second only to Rwanda.[14]

I originally intended to have thirty interviews for this book; however, I realized the full picture was not complete. With the pandemic, currency unification, economic reforms, and the growth of the private sector, this book was forced to expand.

[14] See Chapter 7, interview with Josefina Vidal.

It is important for readers to understand that these interviews were not censored. That said, I was later obliged because of an ongoing Helms-Burton court case, to remove two interviews and the name of a company. In all the other interviews, I asked the questions I wanted, what I thought most people wished to know. Of these conversations, I eliminated the "filler words" included in our everyday oral conversations and edited the grammar, both my own and that of the speakers whose first language is not always English. These interviews were conducted in person, by telephone, by Zoom, and by email.

Conclusion

It is undeniable that the blockade by the United States of America has only two purposes—to create suffering for the Cuban people and bring about regime change. By its very essence, it inhibits economic development. It complicates FDI, the activities of international business investors and banks, the ability of Cuba's entrepreneurial sector to scale, and clamps down on the rights of Americans to travel where they choose.

If this book opens a window to Cuba, then it fulfills its ambitions. It is my deep conviction that we cannot view Cuba solely from the eyes of the United States; we must observe "through Cuban eyes." Just as our seas and climates do not respect arbitrarily drawn borders, we too must blend views from Cuba with those of the rest of the world. However, we cannot deny the existence of international boundaries. Cuba, as a sovereign and independent nation, will determine its own path.

Economists of the future who analyze this island's economy are obliged to provide continual reference to the U.S. embargo and the effects of the pandemic. COVID took the world by surprise; few nations were prepared. We cannot compare this economy to any other that does not also face the same aggressive program of sanctions—it is impossible and renders a comparison invalid. Post-COVID economies, especially in Latin America and other developing nations, have experienced the fallout of the pandemic, the problem of vaccine accessibility, sharp decreases in tourism, international supply chain issues, and a plunge of 45.4% of foreign investment inflow, estimated at \$87.6 billion in 2020 (World Investment Report, 2021). Subsequently, the first six months of 2022 show investment inflows to the region are 15% below pre-pandemic levels (UNCTAD, 2022).

On a more positive note, forecasts predicted the recovery of Cuba's tourism industry by the end of 2022, but the numbers have not yet reached pre-pandemic levels. By December 31, 2022, Cuba recorded 1,614,087 international visitors, an increase of 452.8% from the same month last year (ONEI, 2022). Cuba's peak tourism months are November, December, and January, when winter braces the nations of its most frequent guests, the Canadians. It is safe to wager, those numbers will continue to grow (see Table 2.3).

As a final note, the people I interviewed surprised some. They asked, "How did you get those interviews?" My simple answer is, and will remain, "I asked."

One of my last private conversations on the streets in Havana was with a young entrepreneur. We both agreed that if the United States dropped its blockade, Havana would become something like the "Paris of the

Table 2.3
International tourist arrivals: 2009 to June 7, 2023

Year	*Number of arrivals*
2004	2,048,572
2005	2,319,334
2006	2,220,567
2007	2,152,221
2008	2,348,340
2009	2,429,809
2010	2,531,745
2011	2,717,215
2012	2,840,000
2013	2,850,000
2014	3,000,000
2015	3,152,400
2016	3,585,200
2017	4,143,400
2018	4,111,600
2019	4,275,558
2020	1,085,920
2021	356,470
2022	1,614,087
2023	1,177,513

Source Oficina Nacional de Estadistica e Información (ONEI). (2021, December 2). 15.6 Visitantes por países.xls. and Arribo de viajeros. Visitantes internacionales. Cierre diciembre 2022

Caribbean." Then, we stopped in silence for a moment, one of those pauses between two people who become lost in thought, contemplating a vision's magnificence.

This is how you do it. We are all in this together.

Outline

The book begins with two chapters by Dr. Juan Triana Cordoví, Cuba's leading economist from the University of Havana, and Mark A. Entwistle, former Canadian ambassador to Cuba. They "set the scene" in two ways. Dr. Triana addresses the economy and foreign direct investment (FDI). Mr. Entwistle proposes the concept of a black box as a way for outsiders to decode the mystery of Cuba.

The book is divided into parts. These sections are government, economy, foreign investment, industrial zones, banking, law, and business. Following those parts are interviews with executives from the sectors of Oil and Energy, Healthcare, Biotechnology & Pharmaceuticals, Tourism, Agriculture, the Entrepreneurial Sector, and Non-Profits.

Part I examines the perspectives of government officials of Cuba, the United Kingdom, Turkey, and Russia—nations involved in investment and trade with the island. The topics covered in these interviews are the economy, currency unification, foreign investment, joint ventures, entrepreneurs, society, bilateral relations, and Trump, among other subjects.

Part II comprises analyses of the economy from different perspectives: one from within and one from beyond the borders of Cuba. In Chapter 13, Dr. Triana presents the Cuban perspective. Chapter 14 contains the view from abroad, from Dr. Emily Morris, a research associate at the UCL Institute of the Americas and formerly associated with the Economist Intelligence Unit. As a facilitator of international research collaboration, she is involved in a sustainable development project in Cuba.

Part III examines the importance of industrial zones in developing countries. Industrial zones have long been identified as a beneficial component of economic development. They generate employment, enable technology transfer, increase connectivity, and, importantly, build infrastructure. In Chapter 15, I interviewed the General Director of the

Mariel Special Development Zone. In Chapter 16 , I spoke with the Business Manager of ViMariel S.A., an industrial park within the ZED Mariel built by a Vietnamese corporation.

Two of my questions to the interviewees were to counteract a BBC Mundo article, "*Puerto de Mariel: La Vitrina capitalista Cubana Que Aún no funciona,*" published in 2015, portraying the ZED Mariel as a failure in benefitting the surrounding people and communities, less than two years after the signing of the original agreement (Redacción BBC Mundo, 2015). The article was published one year and 11 months after the signing of the legislation to establish the Zone. What the journalist failed to investigate or fact-check for his or her article was the time required for investment promotion, land surveys, construction of roads and railways, waste management systems, factories, communications infrastructure, and any other type of development *and* the time needed for the trickle-down effect to reach surrounding communities. It is yet another example of anti-Cuba journalism. A few of my questions to the interviewees addressed these matters specifically. Today Cuba's ZED Mariel resembles an industrial zone like anywhere else in the world. Residential neighborhoods have been built for employees. Many of its investors have reinvested in the Zone. In Chapter 15, I interviewed Ana Teresa Igarza Martínez, General Director of the Mariel Special Development Zone. In the following chapter, I spoke with Huong Nguyen, Business Manager of the ViMariel economic zone within the ZED Mariel.

Part IV, Banking, covers the role the sector plays in development. Chapter 17 is an interview with the then-Minister-President, Marta Wilson of the Central Bank of Cuba. The interview addressed the challenges and successes and looked at private sector services and recent legal reforms. There is an acknowledged need to modernize the banking system. However, under U.S. sanctions, challenges remain because of the difficulties of technology acquisition under those restrictions.

Part V, "The Lawyers and the Law," examines legal issues of investment in Cuba. Two of these interviews are with lawyers from different sides of the Atlantic. A third interview takes place with the Vice Minister at the Ministry of Foreign Investment and Trade (MINCEX) in Chapter 20. My interview in Chapter 18 began as a conversation with Cuban American attorney Daniel R. Zim. We discussed the "what's-next scenario" for Helms–Burton Title III claimants following activation of the legislation. In Chapter 19, I spoke with Spanish attorney Hermenegildo Altozano, a longtime expert on foreign investment in Cuba. We discussed Helms–Burton, recent reforms, and investing in Cuba. The final interview with the Vice Minister of MINREX in Part V, explains legislative protections for foreign investors. The interview was updated in May 2022.

Part VI examines the theme of business in Cuba. Chapters 21–24 give a sense of what it was like to attempt to do business in Cuba and what it is currently. I interviewed several Americans and Canadians who pursue these opportunities. I began these interviews during the Obama administration and continued throughout Trump's. In Chapter 21, I spoke to an American attorney from Houston who was active in U.S.–Cuba business while Obama was president. Our conversation covered market entry, trade missions, and business trips to Cuba. Chapter 22 reflected the cautious optimism of the American business community on the eve of the Trump presidency. Chapter 23 is an interview with Mark Entwistle, the former ambassador to Cuba. The interview "Facts and Knowledge are the Antidote to Threat" is a discussion on the U.S. embargo. In 2022, Mr. Entwistle and I spoke again, a conversation in which he shared his analysis of the Biden presidency in terms of U.S.–Cuba relations.

In Chapter 24, I interviewed a Canadian company president of Fireworks FX that provided the firework celebrations for Havana's 500th anniversary. He spoke of his company's business entrance and activities in Cuba, the importance of relationships, and why he thinks the American embargo presents opportunities for foreign businesses.

Parts VII through to Part X focus on Cuba's key industry sectors. I interviewed executives of the oil and energy, healthcare, biotechnology and pharmaceuticals, tourism, and agriculture sectors.

Chapters 25–27 include oil and energy sector interviews, which occurred between 2016 and 2021. I held two separate two interviews with members of the board of the Australian oil exploration company, Melbana Energy Limited. Melbana has been involved in oil exploration in Block 9 on Cuba's north shore since 2015. By 2021, the company began a drilling program in a proven hydrocarbon system.

Chapter 26 comprises an interview with the Chief Representative of China's Greatwall Drilling. The company provides services at the oil well sites.

Part VIII examines the sectors: healthcare, medical tourism, biotechnology, and pharmaceuticals—of primary interest to investors. I held six interviews with Cuban doctors, executives, and an American who lives on the island and works for the non-profit organization publication,

MEDICC Review. The topics cover the achievements of the healthcare system, the numerous opportunities for research collaboration and investment, its innovative pharmaceutical products, its coronavirus protocols, vaccine innovation, joint ventures, and medical tourism.

Chapter 28 contains an interview with Dr. Osvaldo Héctor Ardisana from Comercializadora Servicios Médicos Cubanos (CSMC S.A.) in 2017. He is responsible for the North American and English/French-speaking Caribbean markets. Our conversation explored the history and present state of Cuba's medical tourism industry and its services.

Chapter 29 includes two interviews I had with Dr. Yamila de Armas Águila, the president of the CSMC. The first one occurred in 2018, followed by a second in 2022. These interviews illustrate the evolution of Cuban perspectives on its medical tourism industry, from recognition of its assets to the necessity of promotion in a globally competitive industry.

Chapter 30, an interview with Gail Reed, presents the views of an American who has lived and worked in Cuba for many years. Ms. Reed is now the executive editor of MEDICC Review, a peer-reviewed journal focusing on US–Cuba health collaboration.

Chapter 31 presents an interview with the Vice President of BioCubaFarma. BioCubaFarma oversees 32 companies involved in research and development, pharmaceuticals, and medical devices. The interview examines BioCubaFarma's international collaboration with the Roswell Park Cancer Center, China, and Russia. Dr. Mauri discussed the future direction of BioCubaFarma, its product portfolio, challenges and successes during the pandemic, and COVID-19 drug trials.

Part VIII, Chapter 32, includes an interview with Dr. Mitchell Valdés-Sosa, a respected neurologist and the Director at the Center for Neuroscience (CNEURO). The interview occurred following the publication of the National Academies of Sciences, Engineering, and Medicine (NASEM) report in the United States. The NASEM report determined that radio frequency wave exposure (microwave weapons) was the explanation for symptoms experienced by embassy staff in Havana. Cuban scientists rated the report as an "unlikely hypothesis," and "not established science," a conclusion eventually reached by the FBI, CIA, and the JASON advisory group Reports.

Chapter 33 is an interview with a Russian company involved in a joint venture with Cuba's CNEURO. The interview is an example of collaboration in research and development of new pharmaceutical drugs that can benefit millions of people.

Part IX features four interviews with investors in Cuba's tourism sector, one of its largest income-generating industries. International border closures, combined with the addition of U.S. sanctions, affected the sector. The effects of lockdowns were catastrophic to the entire travel industry. For Cuba, reliant on a steady inflow of tourists and managing a pandemic at the same time, this was devastating to its economy. It was also challenging for hotel developers forced to put projects on hold.

Three interviews were with hotel real estate developers from companies of Southeast Asia, the United Kingdom, and an investment company that partners with Spain's Meliá Hotels International.

Chapter 34 was the first interview I did with a foreign investor of Cuba. In 2016, I spoke with the director of an international property development firm based in the United Kingdom. In 2015, the company received master plan approval. The following year, the construction of a luxury golf resort, apartments, and villas began. It would have been the first time since the Revolution that foreigners could have purchased property on the island. Both parties were very excited about the project. It was a "bold scheme" during the time of Obama-influenced optimism. In April 2022, I spoke again to the director for an update on the property. It has been put on hold. Two factors are the direct cause of the suspension of construction: the pandemic and the extraterritoriality of the U.S. government's broadening restrictions on trade and investment.

Chapter 35 looks at American travel to Cuba following the Trump announcement of a ban on cruises and people-to-people travel in June 2019. I interviewed Tom Popper, formerly the president of an American travel company. The company was the first to provide people-to-people travel services in the United States. In 2022, we updated the interview. We discussed the latest American travel restrictions and his continued involvement with Cuba, but this time, in a new role.

Chapter 36 is an interview with one of the most successful long-term investors on the Island. This conversation was with Sebastiaan Berger, the Portfolio Manager of CEIBA Investments. His company partnered with Meliá Hotels on three projects in Cuba. These projects faced setbacks because of the pandemic and the collapse of tourism. We later updated this interview in January 2022. The question asked, "Why would a successful investor invest in what we perceive as a high-risk environment?" Mr. Berger's answer is interesting.

In 2021, I interviewed Archipelago International's Managing Director, Gerard Byrne. Archipelago International is Southeast Asia's largest privately owned hotel group. The company manages five hotels and resorts across the Island. Chapter 37 explores the company's history in Cuba from 2015 to today. The interview focused on hotel investment and expansion during the pandemic. Nevertheless, despite the delays, Archipelago opened its new five-star hotel, the Grand Aston La Habana on the Malecón, in March 2022.

Chapter 38 examines the activities of the United States Agriculture Coalition for Cuba (USACC). The USACC represents American farm groups that want increased trade with Cuba. At present, normal two-way trade does not exist; a boat will send products to Cuba and leaves Cuban ports empty. In addition, American farmers are not permitted to offer credit terms to Cuba because of U.S. restrictions. The interview examines the multiple benefits of a closer trade partnership between the United States and Cuba. It was updated in April 2022 after the USACC held its first conference in Havana after COVID lockdowns, consequently becoming the first American organization to host such an event in Havana since then. The USACC event was well attended by American farm groups and high-level Cuban government officials.

Part XI, The Non-state Sector: Micro, Small, and Medium Enterprises (MSMEs) features an interview that illuminates the challenges and successes faced by the sector. The interview is with one of Cuba's most well-known entrepreneurs, Marta Deus. She is the founder of three successful business ventures and a strong representative of the sector. Ms. Deus is the founder of three companies, a magazine, a consulting services firm for entrepreneurs, and Mandao, a food delivery service.

Part XII looks at the roles of NGOs and non-profits in economic development. The first interview is a conversation of 2016 with James Williams, the then-president of Engage Cuba in Washington, DC. It was a lobby group representing businesses and individuals who wanted to end the trade and travel embargo against Cuba.

Chapter 41, the final interview of the book is a conversation with EDF's senior advisor and attorney, Dan Whittle. The interview demonstrates the benefits of the 20-year relationship between Cuba and the EDF in protecting marine ecosystems, oceans, and fisheries. Ultimately, relationships of cooperation and dialogue between nations will bring positive outcomes to global issues that affect us all.

References

Bárcenas, A. (2018, May 21). *The 2030 agenda outlines a path to launch a new style of development*. Speech by Alicia Bárcenas. Granma. Retrieved July 20, 2022, from https://en.granma.cu/cuba/2018-05-21/the-2030-agenda-outlines-a-path-to-launch-a-new-style-of-development

Bolender, K. (2019). *Manufacturing the enemy: The media war against Cuba*. Pluto Press.

Burki, T. (2021, April 1). *Behind Cuba's successful pandemic response*. The Lancet Infectious Diseases. Retrieved June 17, 2022, from https://www.thelancet.com/journals/laninf/article/PIIS1473-3099(21)00159-6/fulltext

Burnett, S. (2014, June 30). *Google executives visit Cuba*. Time. Retrieved June 9, 2022, from https://time.com/2938843/google-visit-cuba/

CEPAL. (2020). *Economic survey of Latin America and the Caribbean · 2020 CUBA 1. General trends*. CEPAL. Retrieved July 14, 2022, from https://repositorio.cepal.org/bitstream/handle/11362/46071/19/ES2020_Cuba_en.pdf

Correspondent, S. (2018, June 5). *Cuba president welcomes US senator, Google CEO*. Prothomalo. Retrieved August 8, 2022, from https://en.prothomalo.com/international/Cuba-president-welcomes-US-senator-Google-CEO

Cuban Adjustment Act, Pub. L. No. 89-732, 80 Stat. 1161. (1966). https://www.govinfo.gov/content/pkg/STATUTE-80/pdf/STATUTE-80-Pg1161.pdf

Cubavisión Internacional. (2020, October 21). Chapter 5 Archivo.Cu [Video]. YouTube. https://www.youtube.com/watch?v=kgunmy68mBY

Dirección Comercial del Mintur. (2023, June 8). INFORME COMERCIAL. COMPORTAMIENTO DEL ARRIBO DE VISITANTES A CUBA. Havana; Cuba.

Drucker, J., & Wicary, S. (2016, July 28). *Did Donald Trump's executives violate the Cuban embargo?* Bloomberg. Retrieved July 19, 2022, from https://www.bloomberg.com/features/2016-donald-trump-golf-cuba/

Entous, A., & Anderson, J. L. (2018, November 9). *The mystery of the Havana Syndrome*. The New Yorker. Retrieved June 10, 2022, from https://www.newyorker.com/magazine/2018/11/19/the-mystery-of-the-havana-syndrome

Feinberg, R. E. (2012). *The new Cuban economy: What roles for foreign investment?* Latin America Initiative at Brookings, 16–18. https://www.brookings.edu/wp-content/uploads/2016/06/cuba-economy-feinberg-9.pdf.

Guterres, A. (2020, March 26). *Secretary-General urges G20 countries to suppress COVID-19 transmission, keep households Afloat, amid pandemic's 'human crisis.'* United Nations. Retrieved June 11, 2022, from https://press.un.org/en/2020/sgsm20024.doc.htm

Harris, G. (2017, September 17). *Tillerson says U.S. may close Cuba embassy over mystery ailments*. The New York Times. Retrieved June 11, 2022, from https://www.nytimes.com/2017/09/17/us/politics/tillerson-cuba-embassy.html

Holland, S. (2017, September 29). *Trump says Cuba 'did some bad things' aimed at U.S. diplomats*. Reuters. Retrieved July 15, 2022, from https://www.reuters.com/article/us-usa-trump-cuba-idUSKCN1C42W4

Horobin, W. (2016, February 1). *France seeks closer ties with Cuba during Castro visit*. The Wall Street Journal. Retrieved July 15, 2022, from https://www.wsj.com/articles/france-hosts-state-dinner-for-cuban-president-1454331794

Isikoff, M. (2022, September 14). *Top U.S. officials cast fresh doubt on sensational 'Havana Syndrome' claims*. Yahoo! News. Retrieved September 14, 2022, from https://news.yahoo.com/top-us-officials-cast-fresh-doubt-on-sensational-havana-syndrome-claims-090025560.html

Jones, O. (2012, October 30). *Cuba is opening its doors, to allow Cubans to leave*. Big Think. Retrieved March 22, 2022, from https://bigthink.com/politics-current-affairs/cuba-is-opening-its-doors-to-allow-cubans-to-leave/

LeoGrande, W. (2021, October 27). *Taking page from Regime Change Playbook, it's back to confrontation with Cuba*. Responsible Statecraft. Retrieved June 9, 2022, from https://responsiblestatecraft.org/2021/10/27/taking-page-from-regime-change-playbook-its-back-to-confrontation-with-cuba/

Mallory, Lester D. (1960, April 6). *Memorandum from the Deputy Assistant Secretary of State for Inter-American Affairs (Mallory) to the Assistant Secretary of State for Inter-American Affairs*. U.S. Department of State. Retrieved July 9, 2022, from https://history.state.gov/historicaldocuments/frus1958-60v06/d499

Mathieu, E., Ritchie, H., Ortiz-Ospina, E., et al. (2020, March 5). *Coronavirus (COVID-19) vaccinations*. Our World in Data. Retrieved July 19, 2022, from https://ourworldindata.org/covid-vaccinations

Morejón, R. (2022, April 29). *Twelve million dollars a day is only one of the costs of Washington's blockade*. CUBADIPLOMATICA. Retrieved July 14, 2022, from https://misiones.cubaminrex.cu/en/articulo/twelve-million-dollars-day-only-one-costs-washingtons-blockade

National Academies of Sciences, Engineering, and Medicine. (2020). *An assessment of illness in U.S. government employees and their families at overseas embassies*. The National Academies Press. https://doi.org/10.17226/25889

NBC News. (2022, July 20). *LIVE: Andrea Mitchell interviews CIA Director William Burns* (Video). YouTube. https://www.youtube.com/watch?v=p6M4W-OB6Ak

Roca, Abisais. (2021, December 21). 15.6 Visitantes por países.xls. Oficina Nacional de Estadistica e Información (ONEI). http://www.onei.gob.cu/

ONEI. (2022, December). *Arribo de viajeros. Visitantes internacionales. Cierre diciembre 2022*. Retrieved January 27, 2023, from http://www.onei.gob.cu/node/18036

Prensa Latina. (2021, May 22). *Rodriguez denounces US blockade costs Cuba millions of dollars a day*. Prensa Latina. Retrieved August 20, 2022, from https://www.plenglish.com/news/2021/05/22/rodriguez-denounces-us-blockade-costs-cuba-millions-of-dollars-a-day/

Redacción BBC Mundo. (2015, October 13). *Puerto de Mariel: La Vitrina capitalista Cubana Que Aún no funciona*. BBC News Mundo. Retrieved April 19, 2022, from https://www.bbc.com/mundo/noticias/2015/10/151013_economia_demoras_puerto_mariel_lf

Reuters Staff. (2020, December 17). *Cuban economy shrank 11% in 2020, government says*. Reuters. Retrieved July 6, 2022, from https://www.reuters.com/article/cuba-economy-idUSL1N2IX1V9

Ritchie, H., et al. (2020, March 5). *Coronavirus pandemic (COVID-19)*. Our World in Data. Retrieved August 17, 2022, from https://ourworldindata.org/coronavirus

Rodríguez, J. L. (2022). *Evolution of the world economy in 2021 and its impact on cuba. Outlook for 2022*. Retrieved September 18, 2022, from https://content.csbs.utah.edu/~al/EcReportCuba/CubaJLR22_05Eng.pdf

Rodríguez, R. (2020, December 18). *U.S. economic sanctions on Cuba in the context of the pandemic COVID-19*. Ethics & International Affairs. Retrieved July 17, 2022, from https://www.ethicsandinternationalaffairs.org/2020/u-s-economic-sanctions-on-cuba-in-the-context-of-the-pandemic-covid-19/

Rogin, J. (2018, November 2). Opinion | *Bolton promises to confront Latin America's 'troika of tyranny'*. The Washington Post. Retrieved August 30, 2022, from https://www.washingtonpost.com/opinions/global-opinions/bolton-promises-to-confront-latin-americas-troika-of-tyranny/2018/11/01/df57d3d2-ddf5-11e8-85df-7a6b4d25cfbb_story.html

Rubio, M. (2017, September 15). *Rubio, colleagues ask Tillerson to expel Cubans, close embassy after attacks on U.S. diplomats*. U.S. Senator for Florida, Marco Rubio. Retrieved August 10, 2022, from https://www.rubio.senate.gov/public/index.cfm/2017/9/rubio-colleagues-ask-tillerson-to-expel-cubans-close-embassy-over-attacks-on-u-s-diplomats

Ruiz Miyares, J. (2022, July 22). *Minister briefs deputies on the status of foreign investment on the Island*. Retrieved August 22, 2022, from https://www.radiohc.cu/eo/noticias/nacionales/294086-minister-briefs-deputies-on-the-status-of-foreign-investment-on-the-island

Runde, D. F. (2022, August 15). *U.S. policy on remittances to Cuba: What are some viable options?* U.S. Policy on Remittances to Cuba: What Are Some Viable Options? | Center for Strategic and International Studies. Retrieved

June 10, 2022, from https://www.csis.org/analysis/us-policy-remittances-cuba-what-are-some-viable-options

The Economist Intelligence Unit. (2021, January 11). *Government reports boost in foreign investment*. Retrieved June 20, 2022, from https://country.eiu.com/article.aspx?articleid=1280582711&Country=Cuba&topic=Economy&subtopic=Forecast&subsubtopic=External%2Bsector

The United States Government. (2021, October 8). *Statement of President Joe Biden on signing Havana Act into law*. The White House. Retrieved August 17, 2022, from https://www.whitehouse.gov/briefing-room/statements-releases/2021/10/08/statement-of-president-joe-biden-on-signing-havana-act-into-law/

The White House, Office of the Vice President. (2016, October 6). *Dr. Jill Biden travels to Cuba* (Press release). https://obamawhitehouse.archives.gov/the-press-office/2016/10/06/dr-jill-biden-travels-cuba

UNCTAD. (2021, June 21). *World Investment Report*. Retrieved April 20, 2022, from https://unctad.org/webflyer/world-investment-report-2021

UNCTAD. (2022, June 9). *World Investment Report 2022*. UNCTAD. Retrieved August 15, 2022, from https://unctad.org/webflyer/world-investment-report-2022

U.S. Department of State. (2021, November 5). *Anomalous health incidents and the health incident response task force*. U.S. Department of State. Retrieved July 15, 2022, from https://www.state.gov/anomalous-health-incidents-and-the-health-incident-response-task-force/

U.S. Embassy in Cuba. (2019, July 15). *Brief diplomatic history*. U.S. Embassy in Cuba. Retrieved June 9, 2022, from https://cu.usembassy.gov/our-relationship/policy-history/

U.S. Embassy in Cuba. (2021, December 8). *U.S. announces designation of Cuba as a state sponsor of terrorism*. U.S. Embassy in Cuba. Retrieved June 18, 2022, from https://cu.usembassy.gov/u-s-announces-designation-of-cuba-as-a-state-sponsor-of-terrorism/

U.S. Embassy in Uruguay. (2021, January 21). *Remarks by President Trump on the policy of the United States towards Cuba*. Retrieved June 18, 2022, from https://uy.usembassy.gov/remarks-president-trump-policy-united-states-towards-cuba/

Vergano, D. (2021, September 30). *A secret state department report says Microwaves didn't cause "Havana Syndrome"*. BuzzFeed News. Retrieved August 15, 2022, from https://www.buzzfeednews.com/article/danvergano/havana-syndrome-jason-crickets

Weissenstein, M. (2016, November 1). *Cuba falling short of foreign investment goals*. AP NEWS. Retrieved July 17, 2022, from https://apnews.com/article/c375a1ff434c444ebaabf418828426c5

Yaffe, H. (2020). *We are Cuba! How a revolutionary people have survived in a post-Soviet world*. Yale University Press.

Yaffe, H. (2021). *Cuba after the July 11 protests—Yaffe*. American University. Retrieved June 9, 2022, from https://www.american.edu/centers/latin-american-latino-studies/cuba-after-the-july-11-protests-yaffe.cfm#_edn1

CHAPTER 3

Foreign Direct Investment, What Can We Expect? By Dr. Juan Triana Cordoví

Juan Triana Cordoví

Foreign direct investment (FDI) is one of the country's main sources of financial resources, along with income from service exports and remittances.

The goal/need for FDI in Cuba was set at $2.5 billion per year more than five years ago. Since then, the country's growth needs have increased at the same time as its external financing requirements, due to the deterioration of its external accounts (both exports of goods and services), repeated defaults on debt payment commitments and non-payment of dividends to investment companies based in the country for several decades.

At the same time, the U.S. blockade of Cuba, codified in the Helms–Burton law and increased quantitatively and qualitatively by President Donald Trump (there are more than 242 concrete actions of the Trump administration) has had a strong impact on the global performance of the economy and especially on the attraction of FDI flows, both because of

J. T. Cordoví (✉)
Havana, Cuba
e-mail: jtriana@ceec.uh.cu

T. K. Hernández, *The Cuba Interviews*,
https://doi.org/10.1007/978-3-031-30203-9_3

the activation of Title III of that law and because of the uncertainty that it generated and still generates on possible businesses in Cuba.

This paper attempts to synthesize some of the features that have distinguished the process of assimilation of foreign direct investment (FDI) in our country. It will be approached in this order: necessity, historical aspects, institutional adaptation, behavior, and challenges.

The Economy 2015–2020

Although it is debatable today to argue that the necessary growth rate should be between 5.5% and 6.5%, it could be that a higher GDP growth rate is needed, due to the weak behavior of the GDP in the last five years (see Table 3.1), it seems highly unlikely that at least in the next two years the dynamics of the Cuban economy will reach those goals.

After several attempts to transform the national economy since almost the beginning of the 1990s, there are still deep flaws that show that the objectives of those different attempts have only been partially achieved,

Table 3.1 Cuba: main macroeconomic indicators

Main macroeconomic indicators						
	2015	*2016*	*2017*	*2018*	*2019*	*2020*
GDP* (growth rate) %	4.4	0.5	1.8	2.2	−0.2	−11
GFC* (GFC/GDP) %	14.6	15.6	15.4	15.8	15.9	n.d
(Investment/GDP)**	6.78	7.12	8.32	9.30	9.50	n.d
Balance of Goods and Services	10,510	10,219	10,297	10,275	8,832	n.d
Goods	3,350	2,317	2,402	2,373	2,062	n.d
Services	11,702	10,270	10,172	11,484	9,901	n.d
Deficit	−8,352.0	−7,953.00	−7,770.00	−9,111.00	−7,839.00	n.d

Note *Constant prices; **Current prices

Source ONEI. (2020). *Anuario Estadístico de Cuba (AEC) 2019*, chaps. 5 and 8

while at the same time, some of the most significant structural flaws, far from diminishing, have been consolidated:

- Low capacity of the "leading sectors" to generate ecosystems[1] that allow them to take full advantage of their potential and generate spillovers to other sectors.
- High technological obsolescence of a substantial part of the productive system (agricultural and industrial).
- Inadequate incentives for innovation, productivity growth, and technological change.
- Insufficient gross capital formation (GCF),[2] low rate of investment, and problems in its sectoral allocation.
- Persistence of a vicious circle between the dependence of GDP dynamics on imports, weak export performance, and reduced import capacity.
- Tendency of all economic actors (families, companies, government) to use income for consumption rather than savings.
- Weak flow of external financing (credits and foreign direct investment).
- Business fabric with low competitiveness and low internal integration

At the same time, it is good to signify that there have been changes in the structure of GDP, reinforcing the role of services in it, (the services sector generated 69.3% of GDP in 2019), but favoring trade and gastronomy (25 percentage points corresponded to trade and hospitality, while 24.4 corresponded to public health and education (ONEI, 2020).

The need for a more aggressive policy toward FDI is evident in the participation of Gross Capital Formation (GCF) in the same which fails to exceed 20% and the low participation of the investment rate in GDP calculated at constant prices, one of the main reasons for the low growth capacity of the national economy.[3]

[1] Neither the expansion of the tourism sector, nor the emergence and consolidation of the biotechnology sector, nor the export of medical services have been able to do so. This is particularly notable at the territorial level, as it has not been possible to replace the role played by the sugar cane industry prior to 1989.

[2] Gross capital formation has not exceeded 15% of GDP in the last ten years.

[3] The possibility of deficient data capture on investment should also be considered, given that part of it, that corresponding to private investment, is not included as such

FDI: A Synthesis of Its Evolution in Cuba

The evolution of the perception of FDI has been very special and is associated with its history and the adoption, since 1961, of a political regime diametrically opposed to capitalism and also to the confrontation with U.S. policy toward the country. Cuba was an investment zone practically without restrictions for U.S. capital during the first half of the twentieth century. Then, from the beginning of the 1960s until practically the beginning of the 1980s, FDI was identified as a sworn enemy of development aspirations, an instrument of neo-colonialism and U.S. imperialism (something that was by no means untrue).[4] Access to FDI became virtually impossible, first because it was neither politically nor ideologically desired, and because the US blockade imposed too high a price on foreign investors. The low financing that the country received from the Union of Soviet Socialist Republics also made it possible to avoid the need for it.

In the 1980s, Decree Law 50 was passed, but nothing proactive was done to really attract FDI until the collapse of the socialist camp became a concrete reality. Saving socialism also meant opening the national and socialist economy, practically 100% nationalized, to FDI—what a paradox!

Thus, Foreign Direct Investment was assumed as a "necessary evil," which then with the first law for FDI approved in 1995 became a "dangerous complement," to later about 2010–2011 converted into a complement and in 2014, when the second law was approved, transformed into a "strategic necessity for our development," a criterion endorsed in the documents of the Communist Party of Cuba (PCC, 2016).

This contradiction between the necessary and the undesirable also promoted a "way of acting" toward FDI and foreign investors, where political and ideological prejudice was predominant. If one reviews the Cuban legislation in detail and the way it is done, it is possible to verify that the preference for the "control" of foreign investment and foreign investors has prevailed over the promotion and facilitation of investment.

in the national accounts. Unconfirmed estimates put this private investment at between $450 million and $600 million.

[4] The influence of Dependency Theory on the perception of the role of FDI as an instrument of exploitation of developed capitalist countries over underdeveloped countries cannot be underestimated either.

It has been, however, an asynchronous and asymmetric process. That is, it has not been well-connected in time with the country's needs for external savings flows and, at the same time, it has been more the effort made from the political discourse than the institutional arrangements to capture those flows and facilitate the realization of business.

The norm that today governs the policy toward foreign investment is Law 118 and its regulations which have been systematically "modernized" at various times.[5] All this regulatory effort has allowed barely less than half of the FDI inflows declared necessary more than a decade ago to be achieved, with an estimated total amount (including business in the Mariel Special Development Zone (ZEDM) of $8 billion committed between 2019 and 2020 (Rodríguez, 2020). This means about $1.3 billion per year of committed capital, far from the target.

Is Cuba an Attractive Market for Investment?

Promoting a country or territory as a destination for FDI is, above all, to highlight the competitive advantages of the country in relation to other destinations. In the case of Cuba, its competition is the Caribbean region. Until 2017, Cuba was the Caribbean country that received the least investment flows, with the exception of Haiti (Monreal, 2017).

The advantages of Cuba in relation to other countries are very clear and are recognized by foreign investors: security of the country, qualification of the workforce, low levels of corruption compared to other countries, political stability, geographical location, high standards of health and education of the population.

The disadvantages are also clear: economic blockade and financial persecution by the United States which exerts extraterritorial pressures on potential partners, high degree of centralization of economic decisions and very little autonomy of state enterprises to "do business," highly centralized planning expanded to all levels of the economy, weak national banking system with little or no autonomy, absence of international banks operating in the country, state monopoly on exports and imports, impossibility of investing outside the sphere of state enterprises or without their mediation in the process, macroeconomic distortions, the greatest

[5] Decree 325 that explained the procedures was replaced by Decree No. 347 with the purpose of facilitating the procedures to establish an FDI in Cuba.

of which is the existence of multiple exchange rates, overvalued exchange rates, distorted relative price systems, etc., etc., etc.

But promotion is not enough. Doing business is also a great challenge. FDI facilitation is another of the great challenges in our region (ECLAC, 2018). *Investment facilitation*[6] refers to creating the conditions for investors to easily materialize their projects. In general, there are international standards with which we are compared.[7] Although it is true that there is no study on the investment climate, nor on the business environment in Cuba,[8] some of the elements that could improve the perceptions of foreign investors are known. Some of them are listed below:

1. Improve transparency in such sensitive issues as the valuation of the assets that appear as a contribution from the Cuban side.
2. Allow direct contracting of the labor force at prices appropriate to the region or voluntary use of the services of labor contracting companies.
3. Ensure the return on your investments.
4. Facilitate import and export issues.
5. Grant facilities to settle in Cuba: immigration procedures, purchase of houses and cars, personal bank accounts, etc.
6. Keep in mind that some services have the highest rates in the entire Caribbean region: mobile phone and internet services, electricity, legal services.
7. De-bureaucratize the negotiation chain.
8. Guarantee more professionalism and decision-making capacity of the negotiating groups.

[6] To date, national and international investment policies pay relatively little attention to investment facilitation. Of the 173 new investment promotion and facilitation policies introduced worldwide between 2010 and 2015, only a minority include investment facilitation measures (UNCTAD, 2018).

[7] This includes issues related to immigration and customs regulations, settling in the country where the investment is to be made, facilities to establish residence, the existence of high levels of bureaucracy to establish business, facilities to contact potential counterparts, the existence of professional consulting services at adequate rates, agile and modern banking and financial services, infrastructure services also modern and at rates comparable to the average for the region, and so on.

[8] In 2019 Moody's rated Cuba at Caa2 (https://datosmacro.expansion.com/ratings/cuba).

In the annual balance sheet of the Ministry of Foreign Trade and Foreign Investment, it was reported that 34 new businesses were created during 2019; however, no estimate was given as to the amount of capital committed (Del Sol, 2020).

FDI and Ordenamiento Monetario

2020 has been perhaps the most difficult year faced by the Cuban economy. On the one hand, an international environment characterized by a world economy[9] in recession estimated at a fall of close to 6% (WB, 2020), with great uncertainty. On the other hand, the worsening of the attacks by the U.S. administration and, finally, the COVID-19 pandemic, have introduced new variables to consider in the present and future of the national economy. To this must be added old unresolved structural flaws, debt payment crisis with creditors (Paris Club, Russia), debts with suppliers accumulated for years and unpaid dividends for years to foreign companies with investments in the country.

There have been some changes in the institutional design that can be interpreted as a response of the Cuban authorities to the need to attract new capital flows. Among them:

- The creation of the single window for foreign investment (Cubadebate, 2019) is undoubtedly relevant, as it would shorten the time associated with procedures.
- The opening of some space for foreign investment in the Territorial Development Strategy, which gives some capacity to territorial governments to establish projects using these resources.
- The constitution of Technology Parks in the Universities, which also allow the establishment of business with foreign companies.
- The possibility for the non-state sector to do "business" with foreign companies based in the country.
- New incentives for state-owned companies to do business with companies located in the ZED Mariel.
- The elimination of the negative list of self-employment which should lead to a better business environment.

[9] ECLAC estimates the fall for Latin America at 9.1% (in ECLAC-UN, 2020).

- Allow also local governments to promote and manage FDI projects up to a certain $ amount.

However, given the recomposition of trade and investment flows caused by COVID-19 and its recessionary effect on a global scale,[10] the high uncertainty in the future in terms of the economy, on the one hand, and the worsening of measures against Cuba by the Trump administration, on the other, it does not seem real to expect increases in investment flows to Cuba. This again forces a deeper look at the possibilities of reducing as much as possible the weaknesses of the national economy, in order to increase its competitiveness and resolve the shortcomings in the institutional design, to make it even easier for new business with foreign capital.

The so-called "*Ordenamiento Monetario*" initiated in January, which in essence is nothing more than a profound reform and structural adjustment of the economy, logically has an impact on foreign direct investment and has a significant impact on the current and future behavior of FDI, both for the profound changes it introduces in general macroeconomic aspects, as well as for those others that specifically regulate foreign direct investment.

The unification of exchange rates and currency should allow businesses, whether Cuban or foreign, to work in a more transparent monetary environment, while significantly reducing "currency arbitrage."

The devaluation of the official exchange rate from 1 CUP equals one dollar to 24 CUP equals one dollar should, at least theoretically, mean an incentive for companies operating under the Foreign Direct Investment regime, especially for those that export. However, it should also be considered that this same devaluation has an impact on the prices of imported inputs, making them dramatically more expensive, in the same way, the prices of domestic inputs—by virtue of the transfer of costs to prices—should also be modified upward, impacting the operating costs of these companies.

[10] "The COVID-19 crisis will lead to a dramatic fall in FDI. By 2020, global FDI flows are projected to decline by as much as 40% from their 2019 value of $1.54 trillion. This would bring FDI below $1 trillion for the first time since 2005. FDI is projected to decline by a further 5% to 10% in 2021 and to begin its recovery in 2022. A rebound in 2022 is possible, with FDI returning to the pre-pandemic trend, but this is only the highest expectation" (UNCTAD, 2020).

To what extent this process results in more benefits than costs for foreign companies, given the characteristics of the Cuban economy, which is highly discretionary in its management, will depend on the specific situations of each company.

It should be noted that in order to avoid excessive price increases, the Cuban government has intervened in the price mechanism, setting "monetary converters" different and lower than the official exchange rate for setting new prices and at the same time has set maximum limits for the prices of some retail products, which has put a strain on the balance sheets of some of these joint ventures that mainly depend on the domestic market and sell their products in CUP.

On the other hand, the decision to convert the balances in convertible pesos equivalent to dollars of the bank accounts that these companies held in Cuban banks at a rate of 1 dollar equal to 1 CUP (BCC, 2020) basically operates as a disincentive (see Annex, Resolution 181).

Regarding the payment of salaries to its employees, it follows from the approved rules that:

1. As of January 1, 2021, all the different rates or converters that were applied are replaced by a single rate that is adopted for the entire economy $1 USD to 24 CUP, whether in the ZEDM or in a mixed enterprise in the national economy.
2. The magnitude of the salary to be paid by foreign companies in all cases must be negotiated between the Cuban employer and the foreign company.[11]
3. In no case can the Cuban worker be paid less than what is stipulated in the new scale for his or her position.
4. The so-called bonuses can be maintained; they are negotiated between the worker and the employer and will be paid to the worker in Cuban pesos.
5. The commission that was previously charged by the employers and which was 20% is now subject to negotiation between the employer and the foreign employer and in no case will it reach that 20%.
6. Workers under this modality will pay their taxes (including bonuses) as established by Cuban law.

[11] The resolution .... Article 12.1. "The salary is fixed by agreement between the employing entity and the company with foreign capital, taking into account the complexity, working conditions and additional requirements of the positions" (MTSS, 2020).

FDI in Post-pandemic and Post Ordination Times

A combination of external and internal factors that make the recovery of the Cuban economy more difficult have confirmed the strategic role of FDI in the future dynamics of the economy. Thus, in the report on the National Economic Plan 2022, one of the main directions is identified as "Redoubling efforts to attract foreign direct investment" (MEP, p. 40).

The first official and public report on foreign investment produced by the National Office of Statistics and Information (see Table 3.2) shows that in 2020, foreign investment in its different modalities experienced a modest growth in terms of the number of existing companies compared to 2019.

The share of FDI in gross capital formation was 7.2% in 2019 and decreased to 5.4% in 2020.[12] Its contribution to gross formation by sector highlights that the agriculture and fisheries sectors have benefited the least, something that is contradictory to the country's own needs.

While the Ministry of Foreign Trade and Investment confirmed that in 2021 there were 302 businesses with foreign investment in the country: 104 joint ventures, 54 companies with totally foreign capital, and 144 international economic association contracts (Figueredo et al., 2021). Between 2020 and 2021 only 47 new projects have been approved, of which only 25 are under implementation.

Table 3.2 Foreign investment in Cuba

Number of businesses by FDI type		
	2019	*2020*
Number of businesses with foreign investment	281	318
Businesses with foreign investment in the ZED Mariel	42	45
Joint ventures	98	103
Joint ventures in the ZED Mariel	11	13
100% foreign companies	46	50
100% foreign companies in the ZED Mariel	29	30
International Economic Associations	137	165
International Economic Associations in the ZED Mariel	2	2

Source ONEI, *Inversión Extranjera en Cuba*. Table 1.1, p. 5

[12] Author's calculations based on Foreign Investment in Cuba, Selected Indicators, table 1,3 p. 7.

A group of constraints facing foreign investment have been identified and officially made public (Figueredo et al., 2021).

1. **Cuba's qualification as a high-risk country.**
    a. Relations with the United States, marked by the persistence and intensification of the blockade, whose legal basis includes provisions of an extraterritorial nature.
    b. High levels of indebtedness of the country (negatively influencing the country risk rating, business performance, access to external credit, and the ability of foreign partners to regularly expatriate their dividends).
2. **In the Cuban economy, there are characteristics that discourage foreign investment and affect the functioning of businesses, including their ability to link up with the rest of the economy.**
    a. Problems of convertibility of the Cuban peso.
    b. Costs of goods and services in the country that are not competitive.
    c. Constructive capacity deficit and problems in the execution of investment processes.
    d. The Cuban financial system is underdeveloped and there is no domestic financial market to which foreign investment can easily have access.
    e. Cuba is lagging behind in process automation and connectivity.
3. **The policy toward foreign capital contains principles that are not in line with the interests put forward by foreign investors.**
    a. Inability to hire staff directly and problems in the operation of the employers.
    b. Non-transfer of ownership of certain assets to foreign investment modalities.
    c. Restrictions on the use of external guarantees that compromise the retention of flows in banks abroad.
    d. Restriction of foreign investment to participate in the retail market.
    e. Inability of foreign personnel working as managers or technicians in foreign investment modalities to acquire certain goods.

f. Definition of terms of validity of the business, as opposed to the claim of foreign entrepreneurs to create companies that do not disappear, unless they go bankrupt or other imponderables happen.
g. Limiting foreign direct investment to activities that have the capacity to generate income in MLC to ensure the financial sustainability of the project in foreign currency. This excludes the construction or repair of roads, highways and associated infrastructure, public transport, and housing construction, among others.

4. **Errors and deficiencies in the work of agencies, entities, and companies linked to foreign investment.**
   a. Insufficient preparation of the personnel in charge of the activity and of the negotiating groups at the level of companies and business groups.
   b. Lengthy negotiation processes with foreign investors.
   c. Complex and extensive approval process for businesses with foreign capital.
   d. Delays in the completion of economic studies due to lack of information and errors. Difficulties and errors in the documents in the files (legal and land registry clearances and legal documents).
   e. Incorrect conception of projects with foreign investment.
   f. Little space has been given to the territories to attract foreign investment, which has been reversed in the last year, but it is still insufficient.
   g. Promotion is not sufficiently proactive or intentional.
   h. Little attention has been paid to promotional work aimed particularly at foreign investors established in the country in order to achieve greater amounts of reinvestment (Figueredo et al., 2021).

Similarly, there is a delay in approving new procedures that would allow foreign investors' interests in Cuba's small and medium-sized private enterprises to become new businesses.[13]

[13] Nine months after the opening to SMEs, which as legal entities are legally entitled to participate in projects of this type, the procedural problems to facilitate the access of this type of companies have not been solved.

From the macroeconomic perspective, the new exchange rate and monetary distortions that have arisen as a result of the regulation, especially the exchange rate distortion and the inconvertibility of the official currency together with the increase in unpaid payment obligations, as well as the delay in the payment of dividends to these companies also generate uncertainty and at the same time have a negative impact on interest in the Cuban market.

Conclusions

Cuba is not a highly demanded investment place, on the contrary. This makes it necessary to achieve better levels of competitiveness and better standards of investment facilitation.

The change of administration in the United States, which could have been a stimulating factor for FDI, as occurred with the Obama Administration, has had the opposite effect and far from contributing to reduce uncertainty in the Cuban market, it has increased it. In that sense, Title III of the Helms–Burton Act is a factor that discourages foreign investors, and it will be unrealistic to expect a substantial change in the perception of foreign investors.

The opportunity to turn the new Micro, Small and Medium Enterprise sector and Local Development Projects into an attractive destination for foreign capital will depend to a large extent on the internal political balance and on the adoption of adequate procedures and the necessary incentives, which today are still far from international standards.

However, the challenge will remain to make the best possible use of these external investment resources, which is closely linked to the absorptive capacity of the national economy, and to ensure that the multiplier effect on the domestic economy is greater than the import effect generated. All this will depend essentially on medium- and long-term factors linked essentially to the productive transformation of the economy.

Annex

Gaceta Oficial de la Republica de Cuba—2020-860-EX73

RESOLUCIÓN No. 181/2020

POR CUANTO: Por el Decreto-Ley 17 "De la Implementación del Proceso de Ordenamiento Monetario," del 24 de noviembre de 2020, se dispone la unificación monetaria y cambiaria, así como el retiro de circulación del peso convertible en el plazo de ciento ochenta (180) días, contados a partir de su entrada en vigor; por lo que resulta necesario regular el tratamiento a las cuentas bancarias de las modalidades de inversión extranjera y de los usuarios y concesionarios de la Zona Especial de Desarrollo Mariel.

POR TANTO: En el ejercicio de las facultades y atribuciones conferidas en el Artículo 25, inciso d), del Decreto-Ley 361 "Del Banco Central de Cuba," del 14 de septiembre de 2018.

RESUELVO

PRIMERO: A partir de la unificación monetaria y cambiaria las empresas mixtas, los contratos de asociación económica internacional y las empresas de capital totalmente extranjero establecidas en Cuba al amparo de la Ley 118 "Ley de Inversión Extranjera," del 29 de marzo de 2014, operan cuentas bancarias en pesos cubanos y moneda extranjera. El concepto de moneda extranjera se refiere a las divisas que acepta el Banco Central de Cuba.

SEGUNDO: Los bancos convierten a pesos cubanos de forma automática, el saldo de las cuentas bancarias en pesos convertibles de las empresas mixtas, los contratos de asociación económica internacional o las empresas de capital totalmente extranjero establecidas en Cuba, a la tasa de cambio de un peso cubano por un peso convertible.

TERCERO: Las cuentas bancarias en moneda extranjera de las empresas mixtas, los contratos de asociación económica internacional y las empresas de capital totalmente extranjero, se mantienen operando hasta que se agote el saldo; a partir de decretada la unificación monetaria y cambiaria estas cuentas bancarias solo aceptan débitos.

CUARTO: A partir de la entrada en vigor de esta Resolución, las empresas mixtas, los contratos de asociación económica internacional y las empresas de capital totalmente extranjero, abren nuevas cuentas bancarias en moneda extranjera donde se acreditan las aportaciones dinerarias del inversionista extranjero y los financiamientos externos.

QUINTO: Los recursos financieros de las cuentas en moneda extranjera mencionadas en los apartados Tercero y Cuarto, pueden ser utilizados en operaciones de comercio exterior e inversiones, para pagar deudas o comprar pesos cubanos a la tasa de cambio que se establezca.

SEXTO: Los ingresos por exportaciones se convierten a pesos cubanos a la tasa de cambio que se establezca y se acreditan a la cuenta en pesos cubanos.

SÉPTIMO: Los usuarios y concesionarios de la Zona Especial de Desarrollo Mariel.

continúan realizando sus operaciones monetarias mercantiles en moneda extranjera y a ese efecto operan cuentas bancarias denominadas en esa moneda. Además, pueden abrir cuentas bancarias de gastos en pesos cubanos, las que se nutren mediante transferencias bancarias desde su cuenta en moneda extranjera a la tasa de cambio vigente.

La cuenta en pesos cubanos se limitará solo a las actividades de los usuarios y concesionarios con el resto de la economía.

DISPOSICIONES FINALES

PRIMERA: Las cuentas bancarias en pesos convertibles con respaldo de liquidez se convierten a dólares estadounidenses a la tasa de cambio del día previo a la unificación monetaria y cambiaria.

SEGUNDA: La presente disposición jurídica entra vigor el 1ro. de enero de 2021.

PUBLÍQUESE en la Gaceta Oficial de la República de Cuba.

ARCHÍVESE el original en la Secretaría del Banco Central de Cuba.

DADA en La Habana, a los veintiséis días del mes de noviembre de dos mil veinte.

Marta Sabina Wilson González
Ministra Presidente
Banco Central de Cuba

References

Central Bank of Cuba (BCC). *Resolution 181*, in Official Gazette of the Republic of Cuba, Official Gazette No. 73 Extraordinary of December 10, 2020.

Cubadebate. (2019, December 19). *One-stop foreign investment window in Cuba will begin in January 2020*. Cubadebate. http://www.cubadebate.cu/noticias/2019/12/19/ventanilla-unica-de-inversion-extranjera-en-cuba-iniciara-en-enero-de-2020/

Del Sol, Y. (2020, February 29). *Annual balance of MINCEX: "Making foreign investment projects sustainable"*. Cubadebate. http://www.cubadebate.cu/noticias/2020/02/29/balance-anual-del-mincex-hacer-sostenibles-los-proyectos-de-inversion-extranjera/

ECLAC. (2018, September). *Foreign Direct Investment in Latin America and the Caribbean 2018*. ECLAT. https://www.cepal.org/en/publications/43690-foreign-direct-investmentlatin-america-and-caribbean-2018

ECLAC-UN. (2020). *Health and economy: A necessary convergence to face COVID-19 and resume the path towards sustainable development in Latin America and the Caribbean*. https://repositorio.cepal.org/bitstream/handle/11362/45840/S2000462_es.pdf?sequence=4

Figueredo, O., Montero, A. A., Ferrer, L. I., Blanco, A. J., & Pérez, I. (2021, December 21). *Inversión Extranjera: "Pese a las acciones desarrolladas, no Se Han logrado Los resultados deseados"*. Cubadebate. Retrieved May 20, 2022, from http://www.cubadebate.cu/noticias/2021/12/20/inversion-extranjera-pese-a-las-acciones-desarrolladas-no-se-han-logrado-los-resultados-deseados/

Ministry of Economy and Planning (MEP). *Main aspects of the National Economic Plan 2022*. https://www.granma.cu/file/pdf/especiales/Plan%20de%20la%20Econom%C3%ADa%202021.pdf

Ministry of Labor and Social Security (MTSS). *Resolution 33 in the Official Gazette of the Republic of Cuba, No. 69*, Extraordinary of December 10, 2020.

Monreal, P. (2017). *Foreign investment: How much should we aspire to?* Blog El Estado como tal. https://elestadocomotal.com/2017/05/27/inversion-extranjera-a-cuanto-debemos-aspirar/

ONEI. (2020). *Anuario Estadístico de Cuba. Año 2020a Enero-Diciembre 2020. Cuentas Nacional*. Retrieved June 30, 2022, from http://www.onei.gob.cu/sites/default/files/anuario_estadistico_de_cuba_2020_.pdf

PCC. (2016). *National plan for economic and social development until 2030*. Havana.

Rodríguez, J. L. (2020, February 18). *Cuba and its economy in 2019: A year of progress amid difficulties (II)*. Cubadebate. http://www.cubadebate.cu/opinion/2020/02/18/cuba-y-su-economia-en-2019-un-ano-de-avances-en-medio-de-dificultades-ii/

Rodríguez, J. L., & Pichs Madruga, R. (2022, February). *Resumen Sobre La Evolución De La Economía Mundial En 2021*. Centro De Investigaciones De La Economía Mundial (CIEM).

UNCTAD. (2018). *World Investment Report 2018*. https://unctad.org/es/system/files/official-document/wir2018_overview_es.pdf

UNCTAD. (2020). *World Investment Report 2020*. https://unctad.org/en/PublicationsLibrary/wir2020_en.pdf

World Bank. (2020, June 8). *COVID 19 (coronavirus) plunges global economy into worst recession since World War II*. https://www.bancomundial.org/es/news/press-release/2020/06/08/covid-19-to-plunge-global-economy-into-worst-recession-since-world-war-ii

CHAPTER 4

The Cuban Black Box: Understanding Why Cuba Does What It Does by Mark A. Entwistle

Mark A. Entwistle

Even though Cuba dwarfs its neighbors in the Caribbean region, it is a comparatively small country both in terms of population and landmass. It is the 83rd most populous country in the world and Cubans make up about 0.15% of the global population. It is the 106th largest country in the world, contributing about 1% of the world's landmass. When ranked by annual GDP, it is more or less the 196th largest economy in the world.

Yet Cuba has taken up a much larger footprint than these figures might suggest in people's imagination, in its past and present contribution to world arts and culture—music, dance, visual arts, and more—and in the political bandwidth assigned to it in the foreign policies of the world's powers. Despite its current economic and social challenges, Cuba exudes a sense of potential.

M. A. Entwistle (✉)
Toronto, Canada
e-mail: mae@acastacapital.com

T. K. Hernández, *The Cuba Interviews*,
https://doi.org/10.1007/978-3-031-30203-9_4

Cuba sits 90 miles from the United States, a twist of geographic fate that has meant that the history of Cuba has been interwoven with that of the United States in different ways for at least a hundred and fifty years, including at least three serious discussions in the United States about annexation in the nineteenth century. This American attention has not always been salutary.

Culturally, Cuba is a richly woven fusion society of Spanish and African origin, via colonization and the slave trade, respectively, overlaid subsequently by French, Chinese, Jewish, Italian, Russian, and other influences over the years. Indigenous Siboney, Taino, and Guanahatabey populations and their cultures were effectively annihilated following European contact in the sixteenth century.

All countries have national myths. The modern Cuban identity, forged in the wars of independence against Spain in the second half of the nineteenth century, created the image of the "mulatto society," blended, mixed, all citizens equally Cuban. The nation "with all and for all" of José Martí, the founding father of Cuban nationalism. That narrative of Cuban national identity persists to this day in the broad refusal to confront issues of race in Cuba. There can be no race issue because that matter was resolved many generations ago when Creole patriots and ex-African slaves joined in a national project to rid the island of the Spaniards. This unwillingness to acknowledge a national race question, or in our current parlance, systemic racism, existed well before the Cuban Revolution of 1959 and has persisted throughout the Revolutionary Period.

Politically, contemporary Cuba is a product of a revolutionary experience that has created institutions and political norms that differ from those prevalent in the liberal democratic world. Historically, in the period of the Republic from 1902 to the coup d'état led by Fulgencio Batista in 1952, the fledgling democratic institutions were weak, and political corruption marred almost all elections. Ironically, probably the only national election held before the Cuban Revolution in 1959 that could be considered free and fair from a distance was that of 1940, won by the same Mr. Batista. Even as the revolutionary Cuban government is criticized for failing to protect individual political rights, to freedom of speech and assembly, for instance, there is no glorious democratic pre-revolutionary past to hold up as an example. The Cuban people have had virtually no civic experience with clean and healthy functioning representative democracy throughout their history.

Cuba is many things, but it is not an autocracy. Those who portray Cuba as such, or as an unfettered dictatorship, miss the much more nuanced dynamics of how decisions are made in Cuba. Even under the more mercurial leadership style of Fidel Castro, while he unquestionably exercised expansive personal authority, the daily operations of the State were more structured, process-driven, consultative, and systematic than one might have imagined from the outside. Different authority centers act as a Cuban version of checks and balances. The Cubans have a strong governance capacity.

Nor is it precisely a "Communist" state. The short-form label derives from the existence of the Communist Party of Cuba, but that name infers as much from the early years of the Revolution when Fidel Castro engineered a hostile reverse takeover of the old Moscow-allied Communist Party to acquire its organizational capabilities as any ideological predilection. In fact, there were Communist Cabinet Ministers in Batista's wartime government from 1940 to 1944 because they were a political presence in Republican Cuba from the mid-1920s. Contemporary Cuban socialism is an adaptable animal.

Cuba is a perfect case for which to deploy a black box model. The analytical approach, as applied to political science, tries to conceptualize political decision-making in an environment where the process itself is unknown, hidden from public view, and not transparent. A set of inputs, whether they be construed as factors, considerations, or pressures, go in and a more or less rational outcome emerges from the other end. The black box idea applies to all systems of government, including representative democracies like Canada, the United States, or the United Kingdom because there is a veil of secrecy surrounding the making of public policy. In many cases, that secrecy is acceptable to a reasonable degree according to the Westminster rule of Cabinet secrecy and collective responsibility.

Cuba is no different in the general opaqueness and lack of public transparency surrounding its public policy and political decision-making processes. The difference is in degree because of a lack of data transparency and public accountability mechanisms, like freedom-to-information acts or institutions like public ombudspersons. But the Cuban black box has to be customized somewhat to allow for recognition that there is a "national security" filter that is applied over all Cuban decision-making that can distort or skew the theoretically rational outcomes.

This national security override is the political product of the U.S. trade and investment embargo and its underlying objective of regime change in Cuba. The core aim of American policy vis-à-vis Cuba remains unchanged to this day, even if dressed differently, such as during the historic opening in U.S.–Cuba relations led by former Presidents Barack Obama and Raúl Castro from December 2014 until January 2017.

From a Cuban perspective, the U.S. embargo and regime change policy is perceived as an aggressive and existential threat to not only the survival of the leadership group but to the Cuban State itself. In response, the Cuban leadership has adopted a distrustful wartime psychology that looks little different from the wartime worldview of any nation that feels itself under hostile assault or siege. This can have the effect of taking some policy options off the table that could have been outcomes in a different scenario, up to allowing a justification for the curtailment of rights in the name of national security.

The Cubans are not overly ideological in their approach to problem-solving. They are more accurately political pragmatists. The black box model presupposes rational decision-making in producing political and policy outcomes, and, by and large, that would apply to Cuba. But the national security override or filter described above can sometimes introduce a measure of seeming irrationality, especially regarding economic policymaking.

To best understand the twists of the Cuban Rubik's Cube, it may be helpful to consider the factors that are the inputs to the Cuban black box. These factors are in dynamic interplay with each other, sometimes to be balanced in one way and sometimes in another. Some are policy considerations, and many can be seen as competing political pressures.

There are three principal baskets of such political inputs: history, domestic, and external considerations. Within each basket, there are several sub-categories of factors. A review of this menu of inputs to the Cuban black box, and the full landscape of considerations and pressures, helps explain why the Cubans do what they do.

Regarding the history basket, every country has a story that creates the precursor conditions that lead to the present. But, in Cuba, the shadow of history is a more potent force than usual. Part of this dynamic is related to historical memory. Michael Bustamente, Assistant Professor of Latin American History at Florida International University, has written recently an important book entitled *Cuban Memory Wars: Retrospective Politics in*

Revolution and Exile,[1] which finally examines the complex way in which Cubans interpret, sculpt, and mold the past to fit images of their Cuba (Bustamente, 2021).

For Cubans, the lessons of history are not merely academic observations but rather building blocks of identities. One reason there can be such a misunderstanding between the Cuban and American governments is that the posture of the former can be almost paralyzed by a sense of history while that of the latter is almost completely ahistorical, except for grievance over the expropriation of properties owned by U.S. nationals in the first years of the Revolution.

In a Cuban context, such history-derived considerations involve an almost obsessive concern about sovereignty, a sense of the fragility of Cuban independence, a hyper-sensitivity to the idea of a return to U.S. hegemony over Cuba, and as a by-product, fierce self-reliance. One could plausibly argue that, despite the foundation of the Republic in 1902, Cuba has only been independent for three decades since the collapse of the former Soviet Union in 1991. Almost four hundred years as a Spanish colony, followed by six decades of American hegemony from 1898 to 1959 and then another roughly three decades in the orbit of the former USSR. Wrapped in the flag of patriotic Cuban nationalism, deservedly or not, the Cuban political leadership can be hyper-sensitive about never returning to hegemonic relationships with any foreign powers, including in the ownership of national assets and resources deemed strategic. The international economic policy imperative of Cuba could be described as diversification of reliance.

Related to perceptions of the past, Cubans have a sense of their own exceptionalism. This informs Cuba's relations with other Latin American neighbors in the hemisphere but is also another reason that explains the difficulties between Cuba and the United States. American exceptionalism is perhaps a defining characteristic of their ethos. Despite the obvious asymmetrical power relationship, economically, politically, and militarily, between Cuba and the United States, there is, however, a clash of exceptionalism. As a result, the Cuban expectation is that they are treated with respect.

Regarding the basket of domestic inputs into the Cuban black box, these involve pressures such as a fraying social contract, a deep fatigue

[1] Bustamente, M. (2021). *Cuban memory wars: Retrospective politics in revolution and exile*. University of North Carolina Press.

in the Cuban people, demography, and alienation of younger generations from the narrative and symbols of a revolutionary past, including a demand for greater respect of the individual.

In the absence of multi-party democratic elections in which ideas compete, for example, political legitimacy in Cuba flows from an unwritten and implicit social contract between the State and the Cuban people. It is a kind of glue that holds the sociopolitical arrangement together. In effect, the people provide time and space to the political leadership in return for a list of expectations being met, as much quality and freely accessible health care and education as possible, adequate food and transportation, reliable power and electricity supply, especially in the urban centers.

More recently, the younger urban professional class has added another item to the social contract—affordable and open access to the Internet. In the current macroeconomic challenges facing Cuba, themselves the product of a trifecta of conditions including Cuban economic policy decisions, the chilling effect in global capital markets of four years of torqued aggressiveness from the former Trump administration and the almost catastrophic impact of the COVID-19 global pandemic, the social contract is under duress.

Cuba has politics. They are not partisan party politics as is understood in liberal democracies, but to think the Cuban political system is only a set of directives and edicts delivered from on high by a distant and disconnected elite underestimates the Cuban version of retail politics, especially in the provinces. There is plenty of feedback on the pulse and mood of the Cuban people from the barrios, municipalities, and provinces through institutions of local government and personal relationships on the street. The political leadership is increasingly sensitive to emerging public opinion and, over the past few years, has changed course on several decisions in the face of negative public reaction. To the degree that the core elements of the social contract—health care, education, food supply, transportation, electricity, and Internet access—cannot be delivered, this creates a political challenge for the leadership. Those factors must be protected.

Other social and demographic pressures have political implications. At one end of the demographic profile, aging senior citizens increasingly need old age security and pension support from the State. While younger Cubans do not generally have the same connectivity to the historical anchors of the past as do their parents and are less receptive to the political messaging of continuity. The migration impulse remains strong, which steadily eats away at the morale of the society.

Regarding the basket of external inputs, these constitute another category of pressures and involve the weight of foreign debt, the general wariness in the global capital markets of Cuba as a destination for investment, and, of course, the direct and extraterritorial effects of the U.S. trade embargo.

Cuba's foreign debt exposure can be complicated, carried as both sovereign and commercial debt. Soon after taking over the presidency from his ailing brother Fidel in 2008, former President Raúl Castro made it a priority to adopt a more systematic and focused approach to the challenge of putting its foreign debt house in order. This was important to signal the international financial community that it took its obligations seriously and would be a reliable partner for the global capital markets.

From 2011 to 2016, Cuba secured billions of dollars of bilateral debt relief through forgiveness or new debt swap facilities with China, Mexico, Russia, France, Spain, Japan, and other countries. Most importantly, it reached an agreement with the multilateral Paris Club of creditor nations in December 2015 to forgive $8.5 billion of total debt of $11.1 billion, on which Cuba had defaulted in 1986, with repayment of the outstanding balance in annual payments through to 2033. However, in October 2019, Cuba could not make the entire scheduled payment and could not pay anything in 2020; arguing the ongoing and serious damage to the economy caused by the COVID-19 pandemic, the Cuban government asked for a payment moratorium until 2022. The Paris Club appeared to agree with the conditions.

Cuba's economic future will depend to a large extent on increased flows of direct foreign investment. The modest domestic State capital pools are simply insufficient and there is no real private capital accumulation. Continued debt restructuring, as well as recent monetary reform related to currency unification to create a single national peso currency, should over time help encourage new investment and improve the fiscal environment once a recovery from the COVID-19 pandemic can begin.

We can imagine the dynamic inside the Cuban black box, where constant policy trade-offs are made. The permutations of political equations are endless.

For example, to make an important foreign debt repayment, scarce financial resources would need to be withdrawn from an investment to strengthen the electrical grid or purchase agricultural inputs with which to increase food production and enhance food security, risks weakening the social contract and creating additional political pressure. Or, to stimulate economic development through foreign investment, changes have already been made to legal frameworks to allow 100% foreign-owned companies to operate more widely in the Cuban marketplace and foreign investors to own the majority stake in joint ventures registered in Cuba. However, such effective semi-privatization challenges the idea of sovereign and independent control of the national economy that has animated much of the Cuban leadership since 1959. Or, what to do about allowing accumulation and deployment of capital by individual Cuban citizens in the economy, and how will that affect the perception of the social contract?

These constant and daily political equations make up the algebra of Cuba.

Reference

Bustamente, M. J. (2021). *Cuban memory wars: Retrospective politics in revolution and exile*. The University of North Carolina Press.

PART I

Government

CHAPTER 5

Currency Reform, Wages, and the New Entrepreneurs: Ambassador Julio Garmendía Peña

In March 2017, I met with His Excellency, Julio Garmendía Peña, Ambassador of Cuba to Canada, at the Embassy of the Republic of Cuba for an in-depth discussion (Fig. 5.1).

Ambassador Garmendía and I discussed a wide variety of topics ranging from currency unification, wages, Canada and Cuba, Québec in Cuba, the economy, foreign investment, the entrepreneurs, and the subject on everybody's mind at the time, a Trump question.

Ambassador Garmendía was born in 1952. He holds degrees in Russian Language, Literature and Translation from the Soviet Union (1975) and a degree in Political Science from the University of Havana (1980).

The Ambassador is a career diplomat having served as Deputy Economic Counselor (1982–1985), and Economic Counselor (1986–1989) at the Embassy of Cuba in the Soviet Union. From 1994 to 1999, he was Minister Counselor, Deputy Chief of Mission at the Embassy of Cuba in Russia. From 2004 to 2008, he served as the Ambassador to the Ukraine.

Today, Ambassador Garmendía serves as Cuba's Ambassador to Russia in Moscow.

He is fluent in Russian and English.

Hernandez: Thank you for granting this time with me. I have some general questions about Cuba of interest to many people. The

T. K. Hernández, *The Cuba Interviews*,
https://doi.org/10.1007/978-3-031-30203-9_5

Fig. 5.1 His Excellency, Julio Garmendía Peña (Photo courtesy of the Embassy of Cuba in Canada)

first thing I'd like to discuss is currency unification. Are there any updates on the monetary system you could share? Are we looking at change this year?

His Excellency, Julio Garmendía Peña, Ambassador of Cuba to Canada: First of all, I'm sure you know the reason why we have two currencies in Cuba. There was a time when we began to develop tourism and the only currency was the Cuban peso but lots of tourists were coming, bringing dollars or other currencies which began to circulate underground because it was not legal. This created a disbalance in society and certain problems so we decided as a way of solving the issue was to create the CUC (the convertible peso). I would say that it solved the problem at that time because a lot of people that had dollars or other currencies, no longer had to commit a crime.

Dollars became legal exchange at that time.

Ambassador Garmendía: Yes. And many, many people that worked in tourism that had (foreign) currency were able to exchange it legally, but with time it led to a distortion of the economy. And, of course, with other consequences for society, differences in society. When we began to update our economic model five years ago, one of the goals we set in our guidelines to achieve that update was to put an end to the double currency and have one Cuban peso. But it came to be more difficult than we thought because of the 1–24 the exchange rate.

The sudden change from one night to the next day can create certain chaos in the society. We have been working on that for some years now, and we expected to complete the unification process last year, but evidently it was not possible taking into consideration other factors. We hope it will happen this year, but the Central Bank of Cuba and the competent authorities are the ones in charge of that decision.

People are expecting it to happen in April.

Ambassador Garmendía: Whenever it comes, but most of the people realize it is a need because the two currencies—from the macroeconomic point of view—make a distortion to the economic indices or the numbers. An example, energy is priced in one currency and people pay in Cuban pesos so you never know the exact figures to create the GDP.

There's something else I'm curious about. The average wage in Cuba. I know there is free health care, education, and the government supplies basic food items to all Cubans through the ration card system (the *libreta*). Are there plans to increase the average wage of 20–25 CUCs a month? If one looks at the cost of living in Cuba, luxuries such as hotels are expensive for Cubans earning only 20 to 25 CUCs.

Ambassador Garmendía: Well, you are right in some aspects of your questions but in other Latin American countries not every citizen can go to hotels, only those people that have a good salary can afford that. You cannot compare Cuba with Canada, or Brussels, or Europe.

We have to be compared with our environment, with our region, Central and South America and the Caribbean. We are a country that doesn't have enough natural resources and Cuba has been under a blockade for almost 60 years. But the Cuban government has worked to improve the salaries of the people, especially in some sectors or branches of the economy.

For example, in healthcare. Doctors and nurses and other healthcare personnel receive more salary than average Cubans, but it's still not enough, of course. People that work in some industries that are prioritized, for example, nickel, oil, receive much more money than a Cuban that works for the government.

Farmers receive a lot of money because they produce and sell their production. People that work in the cigar or tobacco industry also earn more than the rest of the workers in other branches of the economy.

Now we have the emerging sector of the economy, the new entrepreneurs, the people that work for themselves, *paladars*, taxi drivers, hair salons. There are more than 200 different activities allowed to carry out self-employment. And those people receive a lot of money compared to those that work for the government.

If you go to a hotel, especially in the summer, you can find lots of Cubans. Now there is a difference, the State has been working to improve the wage, but if today you double the income of everybody, tomorrow there will not be products in the stores. The inflation rate will rise very high. It depends on productivity and production as well. You cannot increase salary without a material response from industry. That's one way to see this.

Another way to view this is that Cubans receive 20 to 25 CUCs, but you cannot consider that figure alone because your children can go to school and do not pay one cent. This includes university education, and a doctorate if you are able to—it's all free. You receive free healthcare. If you need a heart operation, you pay nothing. You receive housing. Most Cubans are homeowners and do not pay taxes for housing.

You receive different social benefits from society which, if you add in the international values of those services, you can reach a salary close to what a Canadian with low income receives. That's my opinion. I don't want to convince you of that, but that's my point of view.

Let's move onto the subject of Canadian business. We hear little in the press on Canadian business in Cuba. I think this is because Canadians go quietly about their business. Is this a correct assumption? Has there been an increase in the Canadian investment in Cuba?

Ambassador Garmendía: I would say there has been little time to see an increase, but we have seen an increase in different countries willing to come to Cuba. In fact, we have worked during these two years with lots of companies who are interested in exploring in Cuba. That doesn't mean that everybody signs a contract or is already investing. Usually ten people apply and one decides to invest. But at the end of the day, there is renewed interest from Canadian companies.

Of course, I should add that in any case, the presence of the blockade bothers many in this case. Because many Canadian companies that have interests or links to the United States are afraid of being charged or fined by the U.S. institutions. They are very cautious about involvement with Cuba. And that's a reality, and they have to count on that.

Yes, I think that's true, there's a lot of fear of the American blockade for international business.

Let's discuss Québec business in Cuba. Philippe Couillard, the Premiere, led a trade delegation to Havana last September. At that time, I believe there was the intention of setting up an office. Is this in the works? When is the expected opening date?

Ambassador Garmendía: It's not a trade office, it's an office they call an "antenna." They have one in Mexico. It is for the development of the complexity of relations with the country where they are present. Trade, yes, but also cultural links, state relations, etc. They are planning to open an office, within the framework of the Embassy of Canada in Havana, beginning from there.

It appears that Québec has a large business presence in Cuba. The fact is the Québécois people love Cuba. Would you agree that the province has the greatest business presence on the Island?

Ambassador Garmendía: Québec has, for a long time, been a very important province for Cuba–Canada relations. I think this is the province which sends the most tourists to Cuba. The Québécois are maybe 55 or 60% of the total number of tourists from Canada. I can't say the exact figure, but they do send lots of tourists to Cuba.

Secondly, there has been an initiative of the government of Québec to reinforce the relationship with Cuba in different fields including trade, investments, and other activities of mutual interest. For example, they have a very outstanding development in clean energy production, and this is a sector Cuba is interested in.

We think Québec is a good example of a province that can help Cuba change our pattern of energy production, which now is based mainly on fossil fuels (oil and gas). We have a lot of potential in clean energy sources that we could take advantage of such as wind, for instance.

Québec is also known for the successful development of cooperatives in numerous sectors of its economy. This is one of the directions Cuba is updating its economic model, creating cooperatives not only in the field of the production of food but also in other activities. Québec is in the avant-garde of cooperatives in different services and activities, so we think we can take from them many experiences.

Québec has outstanding universities, and they proposed (during the visit last September) to have an exchange in the framework of higher education. They offered ten scholarships for Cubans. Québec is willing to work harder in the different branches of the economy, and I think it's a good example of how Canadian provinces can work with Cuba.

We've been reading in the press there are an increasing number of memorandums of understanding (MOU) and agreements with other nations. Is there a growth in this activity since things changed in December 2014?

Ambassador Garmendía: For sure. A lot of companies from Europe, even from Asian countries, have come to Cuba. In this period, it coincides with the new bill of Foreign Investment[1] in Cuba and the decision of the government to create the Special Development Zone of Mariel, which has special conditions for foreign investors and different tax policies. It's convenient for investors, so lots of people from all over the world have been coming to Cuba.

I wouldn't say that the results are those that we expected, we still think there are many more opportunities, and we have to be more, say, aggressive in the work with foreign investors. You have to understand that Cuba is an organized country, and we have our priorities in foreign investment. That means we have identified projects, and we have created a portfolio[2] of projects for foreign investment that has been approved by the National Assembly.

It's a difference with other countries of the region and of the world where any investor can come and decide to create a chain of McDonald's, or Starbucks, or Tim Hortons. We are not going that way. We have identified clearly where we want to invest, which is mainly in Marxist terms, in the first sector of the economy. That means the sectors of the economy that produce goods, factories, enterprises, services.

[1] Law No. 118, Foreign Investment Law replaced Law No. 77 in 2014, Gaceta Oficial de la Republic de Cuba.

[2] Cuba's Portfolio of Foreign Investment Opportunities can now be found online at https://inviertaencuba.minces.gob.cu/en/; Cartera de Oportunidades 2021-2022. MINCEX. (2020). https://inviertaencuba.mincex.gob.cu/en/

Is there a race to get to Cuba for these foreign companies, to establish themselves before the Americans arrive?

Ambassador Garmendía: It has been said, but I would have a different approach. Business is business, people see opportunities, and now there are opportunities for business in Cuba. And international business can feel that, and they are coming with or without the Americans.

Of course, maybe in the consciousness of investors, there is something that says "Go Now" because it's a good moment. They know that if tomorrow the embargo/blockade is lifted, many American companies will come as would any other investor in the world. But at the end of the day, those foreign companies from Europe, Asia, the Middle East realize there are opportunities with the new Foreign Investment law and the Special Development Zone of Mariel. It's a good time to come to Cuba and find those opportunities.

The Americans will come, but they will have to participate in equal conditions that anybody else must. They will have to compete. If there is a better technology from Europe, we will choose the company that responds to our needs. That's the reality.

Which country has the greatest presence in Cuba in terms of investments? I would say Spain because I see Spanish brands most frequently.

Ambassador Garmendía: Not only do they have lots of investments, you are correct, there are two or three hotel chains: Sol Meliá, Iberostar, and Barceló that have been present in Cuba for more than 25 years. They have been working with Cuban counterparts and they are happy. There are also Spanish companies in other spheres such as food production, wine, good Spanish wines, and supplying spare parts for transportation, etcetera.

What about the Chinese in Cuba?

Ambassador Garmendía: China is also an important part of Cuban trade. I wouldn't say they are higher than the Spanish, I would say they are participating well in the economy. We do have some interesting projects with China.

For example, in the sphere of biotechnology we have a joint venture with China, but they are also an important trade partner. They supply locomotives for trains, they participate in other development of our railroads. Of course, they take part with high tech in different ways. They are important partners for Cuba, but they are important partners in the world today for many countries.

At last year's FIHAV (Havana International Trade Fair, 2016) and at other times, both President Raúl Castro and other Ministers have emphasized the necessity of speeding up the process of foreign investment? What's the status on this considering the need for investment and increasing GDP?

Ambassador Garmendía: I told you that for a period of time, Cuba saw foreign investment as a complement to the economy. Two years ago, Cuba decided that foreign investment should be an important part for the development of the economy. That's why one of the measures we took was to change the legislation which comprised the 118 bill, and other instruments that facilitate and provide easier mechanisms for investors to come and work with Cuban partners.

We still are not satisfied with the speed that foreign investment is taking part in Cuba's economy. We should work harder, I think. Even Raúl said this in the National Assembly last December. That is why our Minister of Foreign Investment and Trade (Rodrigo Malmierca Díaz) is going abroad and presenting those opportunities. The Embassies also have the task to participate in different events and to explain to investors the opportunities that Cuba offers.

I'm sure it'll speed up once the embargo is lifted.

Ambassador Garmendía: That's one main obstacle. It's a very important obstacle. If there wasn't an embargo, the blockade as we call it, I'm sure that many companies, for example, Canadian companies that have an important part of their business related to the United States will come to Cuba and work.

For example, Sherritt International, came, and they began to work in a factory that belonged to a U.S. company before 1959. Of course, they were immediately sanctioned. The executives of Sherritt and their families cannot visit the United States.

I think if you work in new investments, and this a message for Canadian companies, there is no reason legally for any American company or its justice system to apply any fine or measure for working with Cuba.

Ambassador Garmendía: The bad news is that, still, it is not legal to make transfers in American dollars. So you have to find a way. We've had good experiences working with Canadian banks to make the transfers in Canadian currency. We have to find a mechanism, I won't open them here, but those who want to work with Cuba have mechanisms created by Canadian banks that operate very efficiently.

You are an example of how the blockade functions. Some people think this is a theory that has been invented by Cubans. It is not. It is there, it works, it damages the Cuban people and others. And it damages the American people, too.

We want you to have a vision of Cuba as a country that is not perfect. We have lots of problems to solve. We have made mistakes. We have corrected them. We are always willing to do better than we do. The project that the Revolution has developed is mainly directed to the well-being of the people. Sometimes we haven't achieved that because we haven't had a lot of resources because of the U.S. blockade or our own mistakes.

But the reason of our project is the people. We work for the benefit of the people.

In recent years, the Cuban Government has been working to improve basic services such as water supply to the population. We have been doing important investments in some provinces. We have had drought, like Las Tunas or Ciego de Avila. Last year it was almost everywhere. It's not a drought, there is not enough underground water. You see everything green, but there is not enough water for human use. Sometimes we have had the effect of the climate change.

We have been creating channels from province to province to carry water from one place to another. Huge investments have led to an improvement in the water supply to the population. We also had an old system of water distribution, especially in Havana, and we have had to renew all that. It's a complicated process in a city like Old Havana.

On the electricity supply, Cuba guarantees this service to the housing sector in 98% of its territory. I think you won't find that in any other country of Latin America.

You know that one of the main incomes of Cuba today is not tourism or nickel. It is medical services. We have three ways of Cuban participation in world healthcare. One of these ways is where we send our doctors and medical personnel to countries, and we don't receive any money. The second case is where the receiving country pays part of those services, those that are middle income, on different continents.

The third case is where countries pay because they can afford it. Our doctors go to those places where local doctors do not want to go. That's the case of Brazil and South Africa[3] for example. In Brazil we have today, as I'm sure you know, more than 5,000 doctors working in areas where Brazilian doctors do not go, in remote areas of Brazil in different states, mostly in the Amazon which is risky. But our doctors are ready for that.[4]

I would like to finish this interview with a "Trump question". I have to ask this. It's on everybody's mind these days. If President Trump reverses Obama's progress, will "business as usual" continue between Cuba and Canada?

Ambassador Garmendía: I think history has proven that Canadian–Cuban relations have endured any conjuncture. There was no break, and we will work together in one way or another. We appreciate very much most Canadian companies that work with Cuba do that seriously, openly, and respectfully. We have the experience, as I said, of Sherritt which has been working with Cuba for more than 20 years.

They began trade in 1991, and then they created the joint venture. But in any case, it's a good example, and now Sherritt is drilling for oil. Sherritt is now processing the accompanying gas with a very interesting project in two places, near Havana and in Varadero. It is converting gas into propane gas for cooking.

We have these examples which are good and speak clearly about the relations that can be created if there is a decision to work together.

We think that we are going to continue working with Canadian companies because we appreciate very much their will to work seriously with Cuba. Even if tomorrow the blockade is lifted, we will continue working with these companies.

We cannot put all eggs in the same basket in any case. That happened once, and we had a very bad experience with the United States. In 1959, everything was American in Cuba. We have to diversify our economy and that's why we work with China, with Spain, with Russia, and with Canada.

[3] See Dr. John M. Kirk's book, *Healthcare Without Borders: Understanding Cuban Medical Internationalism: Cuban Medical Internationalism from the 1970s: The African Experience*. University Press of Florida.

[4] According to PAHO (2018), 18,655 Cuban doctors (Alves, 2018) were working under the Mais Médicos (More Doctors) program serving 8,000,000 families in remote areas of the country. It was predicted that the withdrawal would have disastrous results for Brazil. In November 2018, Cuba withdrew its doctors after "contentious remarks" by the right-wing president Jair Bolsonaro and the attempt to alter the contract shared with Cuba, Brazil, and the WHO. For more information: *The Lancet*. https://doi.org/10.1016/S0140-6736(18)32975-1.

Of course, in the region we have good connections with countries such as Mexico, Venezuela, Brazil, and others.

I would like to say that we hope that common sense will prevail and our bilateral relations with the United States continue based on mutual respect, respect to sovereignty, and without interference in internal affairs. We hope that.

Ambassador Garmendía, thank you.

References

Alves, L. (2018). Cuban doctors' withdrawal from Brazil could impact health. *The Lancet*. Retrieved March 11, 2022, from https://doi.org/10.1016/S0140-6736(18)32975-1

Kirk, J. M. (2015). *Healthcare without borders* (1st ed.). University Press of Florida.

Pan American Health Organization. (2018). Introduction: Social cultural interactions of Cuban doctors in Brazil. In *Sociocultural interactions of Cuban doctors participating in the more doctors program in Brazil* (pp. 10–11). PAHO.

CHAPTER 6

"Business Is Great"—Dr Antony Stokes, LVO OBE, Ambassador to Cuba of the United Kingdom

Dr. Antony Stokes, Her Majesty's Ambassador to the Republic of Cuba, was kind enough to grant an interview in October 2017 in Havana. It took place at the British Ambassador's residence on the final day of the CUPET Cuba Energy Oil and Gas Conference (CEOG). Ambassador Stokes had delivered a keynote address on the opening day of the conference (Fig. 6.1).

Ambassador Stokes has served as the British Ambassador in Havana since October 2016. He has held previous postings as Ambassador-at-Large for Climate, and from 2010 to 2014 as Ambassador to the Socialist Republic of Vietnam. His former assignments include missions in Latvia, South Asia, and South Korea.

The Ambassador studied at Queen's College, Cambridge and University College London and holds a Ph.D. in Fibre Optics. Prior to the Foreign Service, he held management positions in the private sector.

In the following interview, the Ambassador discusses the opportunities that exist for British business in Cuba, first steps into the Cuban market, and Britain's vision of the UK–Cuba relationship.

Hernández: Do you think the CEOG conference was a success?

Ambassador Dr. Antony Stokes: I believe it was a great success, although the real test of that is feedback from the participants. I am answering yes because of what they have told me fresh from two days of doing business here. Many are going off on a trip tomorrow to the

T. K. Hernández, *The Cuba Interviews*,
https://doi.org/10.1007/978-3-031-30203-9_6

Fig. 6.1 At the official residence of his excellency, Ambassador Dr. Antony Stokes, LVO, Ambassador to Cuba of the United Kingdom

Greatwall Drilling Company oil field Matanzas, so it's not quite finished yet.

But from what I've heard of the business relationships being built, it was highly focused both from CUPET, the Cuban side, the hosts whom I know were very keen to make this happen—and from potential partners, British and wider international businesses.

As far as British business is concerned, the volume, the level of business is less than it should be. I think the potential is there, but we need to work hard to realize that potential.

This market is not for everybody, because it takes patience. And it takes perseverance and presence here in the country. I think these are key ingredients for success, but if you can do that, there are real opportunities.

Tell me more about UK–Cuba bilateral relations. How long has this relationship been "going strong"?

Ambassador Stokes: I have been lucky in arriving here in Havana after many years of improving relations between the two countries. They really stepped-up in May 2016 when then-Foreign Secretary Philip Hammond visited and signed bilateral agreements covering debt repayment, education, financial services, energy, and culture. Since then, we have seen a lot of activity. But we have a lot more to do if Britain is to realize its potential here. We can succeed partly by building partnerships in areas where the United Kingdom has particular strengths, like those mentioned above.

We can make this relationship quite unique: both island nations have enormous creativity and soft power, greater than you might expect from their size. We talk about partnership between "*dos islas creativas y dinamicas,*" two creative and dynamic island nations: that's our vision.

How many British companies are currently doing business in Cuba and in what sectors are they invested?

Ambassador Stokes: Not as many as we would like in the future. Over 40 companies have been doing business here, but not all have a presence in Cuba. We want to see more, and there is no doubt that there is great interest in Cuba from British business; we have had to employ an additional member of staff in Havana to handle all the inquiries.

Oil and gas, tourism, food, drink, pharmaceuticals, professional services, and more. Another good example is renewable energy: construction on Cuba's first biomass plant has just begun,[1] led by a British company using British technology (Pérez Sanchez, 2020).

Let's say I'm a British company and I want to "open up shop" in Cuba. How will the British Embassy in Havana help me?

Ambassador Stokes: Great to hear from you! We are here to support you. The office of our Department for International Trade, within the British Embassy, helps UK business export to and invest in Cuba. They are well-connected with a wide Cuban government and business network, and they will offer further assistance once you have established yourself here, as well as market information and introductions. The British business group, the Cuba Initiative,[2] meets here regularly and is a useful source of help and information (The Caribbean Council, 2017). This

[1] The stone laying ceremony took place April 2017 and was attended by the ambassadors of the United Kingdom and China. Construction began in March 2018. The first biomass-fired 60-MW power plant at Ciro Redondo located in Ciego de Ávila was synchronized to the national grid on March 16, 2020. Cuba's First Biomass-Fired Power Plant Inaugurated. https://www.powermag.com/cubas-first-biomass-fired-power-plant-inaugurated/, July 1, 2020.

[2] The Cuba Initiative is membership organization of the Caribbean Council, founded in 1995, co-chaired by Rodrigo Malmierca, Minister of MINCEX and Lord David Triesman, British Parliamentarian.

is not a market which is right for every business, but there are real opportunities for British business to grow a much bigger profile.

What's the UK perspective on the proposed rollbacks by President Trump of Obama's opening of the Cuba–US relationship? From the Canadian point of view, Prime Minister Trudeau said it would be "business as usual for Canadian business." The Chinese, the Spanish, and the Russians appear to have the same attitude. Will it be business as usual for British investment in Cuba?

Ambassador Stokes: I hope it is more than business as usual. We have our own bilateral relationship with Cuba, and we've been developing that, very much focused on where we see an advantage for Cuba and Britain to work together. That will be our focus. The European Union, with Britain still a member of the EU, recently reached an agreement called the Political Dialogue Cooperation Agreement[3]—which will come into provisional force on the first of November (European Union Publications, 2020). That new agreement is a more positive and ambitious environment for EU member states to work with Cuba politically, economically, and commercially than previously, so we think we're in a positive place when we look at the future. We will build further on this after we leave the EU. We're in a better place, a stronger place with more opportunity to do business and engage more with Cuba.

What are the future prospects for UK business in Cuba?

Ambassador Stokes: We believe the UK spirit is to become even more global, and that means not only working in the largest markets in the world but also smaller markets such as Cuba.

You need to be careful. Success here takes patience and time in the country, as well as the right product or offering. But there are particular opportunities here in energy including renewables, biotech and pharmaceuticals, agriculture, and tourism including infrastructure and construction. Britain has strong business leadership in each of these sectors. We also have a wealth of commercial expertise in fin-tech and banking, which will become more important if Cuba is to realize its

[3] Political Dialogue Cooperation Agreement (PDCA) between the European Union and its Member States, of the one part, and the Republic of Cuba, of the other. Signed in Brussels on December 12, 2016, with provisional application as of November 1, 2017. http://publications.europa.eu/resource/cellar/a9979e32-7274-11ea-a07e-01aa75ed71a1.0001.02/DOC_1, February 26, 2020.

economic potential. Right now, we are working on opportunities to establish a strong British presence in finance here, which could be great news for both countries.

This is a good time to strengthen our bilateral trade and collaboration with Cuba because of the way Britain is championing global trade and investment as it establishes a global agenda in leaving the EU. The United Kingdom is a beacon for open trade, and we will continue to be an outward-looking, globally minded, big-thinking country: a champion for free trade.

Are you proud of British advances in Cuba?

Ambassador Stokes: I am proud to be in a position to support more British business success in the future. I have a wonderful job and it is a privilege to represent Britain here at a time when both countries are at important moments in their histories. For the United Kingdom, leaving the EU is an invigorating challenge and for Cuba, unlocking the potential of the economy and the innovative brilliance of the people here will need foresight and skill. If we can seize the opportunities that now present themselves, the future will be exciting.

Thank you, Ambassador Stokes, for taking the time to answer my questions on British business in Cuba. It was a wonderful opportunity to speak with you.

References

Caribbean Council. (2017). *The Cuba initiative*. Retrieved November 24, 2021, from https://caribbean-council.org/membership/cuba-initiative/

European Union Publications. (2020). *Political dialogue and cooperation agreement with Cuba*. Retrieved November 24, 2021, from http://publications.europa.eu/resource/cellar/a9979e32-7274-11ea-a07e-01aa75ed71a1.0001.02/DOC_1, February 26, 2020.

Pérez Sanchez, A. (2020). Cuba's first biomass-fired power plant inaugurated. *Power Magazine*. Retrieved August 31, 2021, from https://www.powermag.com/cubas-first-biomass-fired-power-plant-inaugurated/

CHAPTER 7

Interview with Josefina Vidal, Ambassador of Cuba in Canada

In this interview, Her Excellency, Josefina de la Caridad Vidal Ferreiro, the Ambassador of Cuba in Canada, speaks about the role of Cuban women in government and shares some interesting perspectives on the lives of women in her country. We also touched on the subject of economic development, politics—in terms of Helms–Burton Title III, foreign investment, and shared a little about her personal life and career. Our interview took place in late January 2019 at the Embassy of Cuba in Ottawa (Fig. 7.1).

Ambassador Josefina Vidal was born in 1961. She holds a Bachelor's Degree in International Relations from the Moscow State Institute of International Relations, (MGIMO) (1984).

After several years working as an Assistant Researcher at the University of Havana Center for the Study of the United States (1984–1990), she joined Cuban Foreign Service where she has enjoyed a long diplomatic career. She served as an Analyst at the Cuban Embassy in France (1990–1997) and as First Secretary at the Cuban Interests Section in Washington (1999–2003).

Following her roles abroad, Ms. Vidal spent 15 years at the Cuban Foreign Ministry, first as Deputy Director (2004–2006) and then Director (2006–2012) of the North America Division.

In 2012, she became Director General of the newly created United States General Directorate until 2018. In this capacity, she led the Cuban

T. K. Hernández, *The Cuba Interviews*,
https://doi.org/10.1007/978-3-031-30203-9_7

Fig. 7.1 Her Excellency, Josefina Vidal, during her term as Ambassador at the Embassy of Cuba in Canada. The Ambassador is now Vice Minister of Foreign Affairs (Photo by the editor)

delegation that negotiated the reestablishment of diplomatic relations with the United States in 2015.

In January 2018, she was awarded the rank of Ambassador of the Republic of Cuba, and in March, she became the Ambassador to Canada.

She is fluent in English and French and has a knowledge of Russian. Ambassador Vidal is married.

This interview was published originally on Cuba Business Report, used as part of a presentation for the MEDICC conference "Women, Leadership and Health Equity in Cuba." It later appeared in the British magazine, Cuba Si.

Hernández: Good morning, Ambassador. Thank you for taking the time to meet with me. I have a few questions to ask you about women in government in Cuba. The Island is in second place in the

world for the number of women in lower parliament. Of the 605 seats, women hold 322 of those seats. This is a statistic from May 2018. Are these numbers correct?

Ambassador Josefina Vidal: Yes, they are correct. Of the 605 seats, 322 are held by women which represents 53.2% of the total seats of the parliament. That proves the Cuban parliament is second place in the world with the largest presence of women in government after Rwanda. There are three important positions in the parliament, the President, the Vice President, and the Secretary of the Cuban National Assembly. The Vice President and the Secretary are women. There are 10 permanent committees and four of them are chaired by women, so you see, we have seen over time the role of Cuban women growing and their presence in the Cuban Parliament representing different municipalities of the country.

Also, you have to take into consideration there are the provincial governments and in 10 of the 15 Cuban provinces (14 provinces and 1 special municipality), the heads of the provincial governments are women.

Is the age of this group younger now?

Ambassador Vidal: It is younger. I didn't bring that number, but I think the average age of the Cuban parliament now is 49 years old. It's a very young parliament.

The Berkley Center reported in 2015 that the Cuban Communist Party comprises seven percent of women (Wadley, 2015). **Has this number changed?**

Ambassador Vidal: I don't have the statistics for the Communist party as a whole all over the country to know how many women are members affiliated with the Communist party, and I cannot validate this data because I don't know if the source is accurate. But I have the number for the members of the Central Committee of the Cuban Communist Party. There are 148 members in total in the Central Committee, 67 of the 148 are women, which represents 45.47%.

What are the challenges women in politics face today?

Ambassador Vidal: There was a revolution in Cuba 60 years ago, and there was also a revolution for the role of women in society that changed overnight in a very significant way. But for many years we didn't have the same presence of women in politics that you were seeing in other sectors of the society, scientists, doctors, nurses, teachers, in culture, artists. You didn't see that number growing as fast in the political sphere. But in the last few years that number has been growing. You see now more women involved in politics in Cuba.

Do you think the problem during the time after the Revolution was because women didn't possess the correct educational requirements or connections to the right people?

Ambassador Vidal: I think it's more of a traditional, cultural nature, not a problem but a reality. Although we have given women from the very beginning of the Revolution the same rights as men to have access to different positions in society, there is still the weight of the domestic work at home in the lives of women. There is a conflict between public and domestic life, because most of the work at home still is on the shoulders of women. No matter how much we have done, no matter how much progress Cuban men have made, still women are very much responsible in the house for looking after the children, the family.

We have a growing problem in Cuba with the aging population. Now you find more and more women have to take care of their older parents. And that is growing because the Cuban population is aging rapidly. You find some indicators in Cuba which normally are not present in developing countries and are more indicators of developed countries. But in Cuba we have this contradiction, because of the access to education, to health, to social security, the aging population is growing quickly and the younger population is not growing as fast. Now you have women not only looking over the children, the education of children, but also aging parents. A lot still has to be done from, let's say, in the educational, cultural work so there is a more balanced share of responsibilities at home between all members of the family.

I won't say only between men and women, all members of the family, so women are released from this conflict they have between the amount of work they have to do at home and political responsibility. I think we have to do more from the social point of view to recognize more, the women who are in politics because sometimes you know, it's not done intentionally. If you have a lot of responsibility in politics or in any kind of administrative position, be it research, university, or hospital, whatever, it will add more work to you and that puts a lot of pressure on women. Maybe we have to recognize that what they do is important, that what they do is viewed well by the society. To compensate for the idea that this is too much for women, you know, it's more of a cultural and, let's say, cultural and educational issue.

It's not just a matter of the government approving policies that help in that regard. For example, we have a new maternity law. The maternity law permits not only women but also men to receive part of their salaries if they take care of the child if it's more important economically for the family that the woman works because it brings more to the family. You find a few more men doing that now.

But we need more, we need to show there are policies, legislation, oriented to help change the balance of the whole situation, but we need to do more from the cultural and educational standpoint.

Out of curiosity, how long is the maternity leave for women in Cuba?

Ambassador Vidal: One year and you receive 65% of the salary so you can be at home with your child and receive a big part of your salary. Now we give that possibility for men to take care of their children, which is good. This is quite new.

But you still don't find many men doing this, but there are some. And now, even if the woman and the man are important for the whole family that they work, we are paying grandparents to take care of the small children. This is quite new too.

To help the entire family, if the woman and the man need to work and there is a retired grandmother or grandfather, they can take care of the children. The grandparents are being paid for the work of taking care of the children. This is very good. The government continues looking for solutions, for creating the right conditions so that women can work and have more responsibility in society, a work-life balance.

Are there programs in Cuba to advance the status of women in government and society? You've explained some of the maternity benefits. For example, does the Federation of Cuban Women still play a prominent role in Cuban Society?

Ambassador Vidal: The Federation of Cuban Women has always been very important, although it has been changing over time, adapting to the realities of the country. At the beginning and even now, the Federation was key and was very important for approving non-discriminatory legislation in Cuba and to design and implement government policies and programs that could help to achieve equality between the sexes. Many laws, such as the maternity law I explained, have been enacted in Cuba, mainly at the initiative of the Cuban Federation of Women. The maternity law is one of them, but there is the Family Code. This is very important. This is a law in Cuba to establish the rights and duties of the family. It will be reviewed after the Constitution is approved to look at the concept of family, at the concept of marriage, to expand that possibility in Cuba.

The Family Code and the labour laws are very advanced, among the most advanced in Latin America, because of the many rights for women.

The Federation of Cuban Women has played an important role in international organizations such as the United Nations and its agencies that promote the improvement of the status of women. Cuba was the first country to sign and the second to ratify the Convention on the Elimination of all Forms of Discrimination Against Women.[1] That gives you an idea of the importance we attribute in Cuba to gender equality and the role of women in society.

In the most recent period, the Federation of Cuban Women is more focused on other social issues that are important not only for women but for society in general. For example, they still look about how to fight against the remnants of, you say, machismo. That's important because that still exists; it has not been eliminated in Cuba, although we have made a lot of progress.

At the same time, the Cuban Federation of Women is paying a lot of attention to gender violence. I cannot say that this is a major social problem in Cuba, even when you compare Cuba with other countries, it is not, let's say, as present. The manifestations are different. According to a study I read, in Cuba gender violence is more of a kind of a psychological violence. It is less physical, less economic; it is more emotional, psychological. Economic, no, not too much because women, many of them are independent, they work, they sustain themselves, they do not depend on men, the majority of them. Yes, there is some physical violence as anywhere else, but it's not so present as you see in other countries because there is a lot of focus and attention. For example, in Cuba, the Federation of Cuban Women established *Casas de Orientación* for women and the family all over the country. Those institutions are present in every municipality to give support to females, heads of families, single mothers, anyone who needs some assistance, guidance, help, even for orienting those who are victims of violence.

Recently, last year, the Federation of Cuban Women signed a collaboration agreement with the Attorney General's office for the use of a telephone line to report acts of violence against women. They're looking

[1] Convention on the Elimination of all Forms of Discrimination Against Women was opened for signature at the United Nations Headquarters on March 1, 1980. Cuba signed on March 6, 1980. Ratification, Accession, Succession: July 17, 1980. https://treaties.un.org/pages/ViewDetails.aspx?src=TREATY&mtdsg_no=IV-8&chapter=4&clang=_en.

a lot after this specific issue. Also, the Federation of Cuban Women is paying a lot of attention to social cases of, for example, dysfunctional families. They do some kind of social work too in the fight against addiction, mainly among young people. They're looking at how to assist, how to help where they detect there are young who are addicted to drugs. This is not a big problem in Cuba, because our drug policy is very tough, but it exists. The Federation of Women is doing a superb job in that regard.

You see now it's not so much as at the beginning of the Cuban Revolution to encourage women to go to work, to go to study, to become independent economically though they still do that because not all Cuban women work.

According to our statistics, when you look at the civil State sector of the economy, women who work at State institutions are 49% of the entire workforce, so it's almost half of the workforce in the State sector of the economy. Not all women work, so still the Federation of Cuban Women promotes that and does this kind of work to encourage women to work, to study, but they don't have to put much emphasis as they did many years ago. Now they still do that but at the same time, they also have as a role to help society, to help families and I think it's very important.

What in your view on gender equality in Cuba? Is there a glass ceiling for women, as there is everywhere else in the world?

Ambassador Vidal: We spoke a little about this already. Throughout history, you find women who played a very significant leading role in the struggle for the independence of Cuba from Spain, in the subsequent revolutionary struggle in the '30s, '40s, '50s. But it wasn't after 1959 when conditions were created in Cuba that women could develop their potential. Actually, when you look at the statistics in the fifties, only 10% of the workforce of the country was women. There is a complete change now looking at the number of women working in the civil sector of the State economy, which is 49%. There has been an enormous change, as I mentioned. A revolution occurred in the status of women; women started working massively in Cuba, participating in the country's social life, reaching economic independence, autonomy, freedom from the previous dependence on men.

I think we have made a lot of progress when you compare Cuba with other countries with the same level of development. I think we did it because from the very beginning, the government set as a goal for the Revolution to increase the role of women in the society.

It came from the top down.

Ambassador Vidal: Yes, yes, it's not a coincidence that Vilma Espin, who was the wife of Raúl Castro and who was involved in the Revolution, was the person who created the Cuban Federation of Women. From the very beginning she had the support of the government to do that. Many Cuban women from all over the country were brought to big cities to study, to work, to be trained. There were many illiterate women. There was a program in Cuba to overcome this problem. That was solved at the very beginning.

Fidel, at that time said women were a revolution within the revolution, and that without women the Revolution would have been impossible. That gives you an idea about how, from the very beginning, women were seen as an important factor in Cuban society for all the changes we wanted to do in our country. Now we can say there is no sector in Cuba, political, economic, social, cultural, scientific, sports, and even defense in which women are not present. They are present everywhere.

Was there, in the beginning, resistance among men?

Ambassador Vidal: I'm sure, I was young, but I am sure there was resistance for many years, as you are suddenly trying to change a society. Actually, there were many films done in the 1960s and '70s and their main topic was the struggle for women to get freedom from the dependence on man.

I have some numbers for you about the role that women play now in our country:

- 67.2% of technicians and professionals in Cuba are women,
- 48% of political and administrative leaders,
- 81.9% of teachers, professors, and scientists,
- 80% of prosecutors, presidents of provincial courts, professional judges.

It has never been a problem for Cuban women from the very beginning of the Revolution to receive the same salary as a man for the same work. It was a surprise for me to see that the Canadian Parliament just passed that legislation.

Sexual reproductive rights are guaranteed. You know this is a problem in many countries. But we cannot think that everything is done, so we have to continue doing our educational work, it's a permanent activity that we have to do.

My next question is about a quote by Fidel. He said, "We must have a party of men and women, a leadership of men and women, a state of men and women." We discussed this in part, but how else have women achieved equality in Cuba?

Ambassador Vidal: In Cuba there are no quotas. But, the State, the party, are looking to giving the same opportunities to everyone, regardless of being black, white, women, men, homosexual. In our Ministry, 44% of our ambassadors are women and it was not like that many years ago. It was rare in the first years after the creation of our Ministry 60 years ago. So you have to give the same opportunities to all, and that has helped to increase the presence and the role of women.

What do you see personally as Cuba's challenges over the next five years?

Ambassador Vidal: I think our main challenge is how to make our economy more efficient and how we accelerate the development of the economy so that we can deliver more and respond to the increasing needs of the society and the population, and improve the standard of living. I think this is needed. We have wonderful people, well-trained, a strong culture, and in the State and the government we are very well aware of that. This is one of the key goals of the process of huge economic transformation we are going through in the country.

The goal is to accelerate our development, to be more efficient, to produce more so that we can improve the life of our people. And you know, we have made our own mistakes in the economic field, and that is why we have been reviewing many policies in the last eight years.

But it's not all our mistakes. There are the mistakes we have made because making a revolution is not easy. No one had a model how to do that, we have had to learn in the process over the years, to rectify many things that we were doing after we realized that wasn't the right way to do it and that we had to make changes.

But you cannot forget all the pressures, the permanent and constant external pressures of the U.S. blockade that is still in place, and still makes our life very hard, very difficult. That's why we say that, despite the mistakes we might have made, the blockade is the major obstacle for the development of the Cuban economy in all its potential, because it's not just a matter of what we want to do; we want to do many things and many times we find in our operations abroad, in our financial, trade operations, lots of obstacles because of the U.S. policy. So that fact has to be taken into account, as it costs a lot of money to the Cuban economy and affects the life of the people directly. It's a reality, it's not propaganda. We have many examples every year of how the blockade affects our people, affects the economy, because with the idea and the goal of affecting the government, the Americans have been hurting the people.

Those are our challenges, how to continue improving our economy, how to make it more efficient so that we can improve the life of the people and satisfy their needs. At the same time, how we do that in an international environment in which the United States seems to be moving to a policy of confrontation with Cuba, once again, unfortunately.

A lot of companies want to do business with Cuba. I've talked to many investors with good projects for Cuba, and they complain about the length of time it takes and some investors end up walking away.

Ambassador Vidal: We are working on that. This is a problem we have already identified, and we have been changing the procedures for foreign investors to do all the paperwork in Cuba, in a more expedited way. We will create a "one-stop shop" for foreign investment which will facilitate the entire process. And the government is paying a special attention to foreign investment, with our President himself looking closely at the issue.

What is your perspective of the latest backtracking by the Trump administration—the most serious tightening of the U.S. trade embargo/blockade against Cuba in over two decades—Helms–Burton Act Title III—giving Americans the right to sue companies profiting from nationalized properties?

Ambassador Vidal: The current U.S. government adopted several measures a year ago, to crack down on travel to Cuba, business with Cuba. It issued a list of hundreds of Cuban companies and entities with which the Americans cannot have any transaction. Now they're considering other actions against Cuba… like implementing Title III of the Helms–Burton Act, which would be a gross violation of international law, the rules of international trade and the sovereignty of states. It will affect foreign investors, traders, everyone.

The head of the European Union, Federica Mogherini,[2] High Representative of the Union for Foreign Affairs and Security Policy/

[2] Federica Mogherini served as High Representative of the Union for Foreign Affairs and Security Policy and Vice President of the European Commission from November 2014 to November 2019. https://www.un.org/internal-displacement-panel/content/ms-federica-mogherini.

Vice President of the Commission, said that the United States would not dictate EU policy (France 24, 2019). A Britain politician expressed the same position recently.

Ambassador Vidal: She said that a year ago when she was in Havana. I saw that.

It is important that people know the United States is reinforcing the blockade and is permanently looking for other ways to tighten it, and to go further in its confrontation with Cuba. They are talking again about putting Cuba back in the so-called terrorist list to which we have never belonged.

There is a group of hardline people which represent a minority in the United States, in Florida mainly, who don't want to see any rapprochement between Cuba and the United States. They're working fast, now that they occupy important foreign policy positions, looking for ways to revert everything that was done under the Obama administration.

There is not enough about Cuba in the mainstream/corporate media. There's a lot in the Cuban press, but how many people read that outside of Cuba? I mean, a lot of what you've told me here today is published nowhere in the mass media.

Ambassador Vidal: You are right. At the end of last year, I attended a reception for the whole diplomatic corps here, where I had the opportunity to talk to the Canadian Minister of Womens Issues. When I said to her that more than half of the Cuban Parliament are women and that over 65% of the professional and technical working force is women, and we have always received the same salary as men and our reproductive sexual rights are totally guaranteed, she asked me, how did you do that? I said, we had a Revolution 60 years ago, and that completely changed the lives of women in Cuba.

In the American press, we always hear about racism and the lack of religious freedom in Cuba.

Ambassador Vidal: Pure propaganda.

A personal question for you. How did you enter the field of politics? Was it your goal to be an ambassador?

Ambassador Vidal: No. As a child I used to tell my mother that I would like to study something that permitted me to learn foreign languages, to know other cultures, other countries, other places. My mother, she passed away, spoke English very well. So when I was in the last high school year, 12th grade, and I was thinking about what I wanted to study at the university, I said to myself, why not study international relations?

So this is what I decided to do. After graduating from the University, I worked for several years at the University of Havana, and then I decided to join the Foreign Service… and this is it.

I've always worked very hard, I'm a workaholic. And then, they were giving me one responsibility after the other, but I never set that as a goal, to become an ambassador. It evolved naturally.

Ambassador, I'd like to thank you for your time and for the very interesting interview. Deeply appreciated.

References

France 24. (2019, April 17). EU, Canada warn of reprisals as US targets foreign interests in Cuba. https://www.france24.com/en/20190417-eu-canada-warn-reprisals-us-targets-foreign-interests-cuba

Wadley, Nicole (2015, October 1). *The truth about gender equality in Cuba.* Berkley Center for Religion, Peace, and World Affairs. Retrieved February 28, 2022, from https://berkleycenter.georgetown.edu/posts/the-truth-about-gender-equality-in-cuba

CHAPTER 8

Interview with Foreign Investment Minister Rodrigo Malmierca Díaz

Rodrigo Malmierca Díaz is Cuba's Minister of Foreign Investment and Trade. The Minister is also the Joint Chairman of the Cuba Initiative Trade and Investment Forum, an event which last took place on June 17, 2019, in Havana (Fig. 8.1).

In this interview, Minister Malmierca offers some insights into the shared priorities of the Cuba–United Kingdom relationship, its new "One-Stop Shop" (VUINEX) for foreign investment, and the challenges of a dual currency economy.

I also found it of prime concern for our readers to ask the Minister how Cuba intends to protect its foreign investors in terms of the recent enactment of the U.S. Helms–Burton Title III regulations.

Prior to the interview, I asked a few preliminary questions to Minister Malmierca to serve as an introduction. I wanted to know where Cuba and the UK's shared investments stand today.

Hernández: Can the Minister please provide the numbers of British foreign direct investment (FDI) into Cuba for 2018 and where British FDI is situated today, year-to-date?

Minister Rodrigo Malmierca Díaz: Cuba has six British companies' investments. Four of them are joint ventures linked to the tourism sector, including hotels and real estate developments. Another important British investment was developed by a joint venture in the energy sector called

T. K. Hernández, *The Cuba Interviews*,
https://doi.org/10.1007/978-3-031-30203-9_8

Fig. 8.1 Rodrigo Malmierca Díaz, Minister of Foreign Investment and Trade (MINCEX) (Photo courtesy of MINCEX)

Biopower S.A. It is a project to build a new 60 MW bioelectric plant, which is expected to be completed in 2019.

The other project in the energy sector is a totally foreign-owned enterprise to install a new 50 MWp solar park in the Special Development Zone of Mariel. His Royal Highness, the Prince of Wales, visited the location where it is being built in March 2019.

Could the Ministry provide the combined exports and imports numbers—Cuba–United Kingdom: 2018 and, if known, for 2019, year-to-date?

Minister Malmierca: At the end of 2018, the United Kingdom occupied the 33rd place in the commercial exchange of Cuba with the world and the 14th position in Europe. Within the European Union, it is ranked in the 11th place.

In 2018, the commercial exchange of goods registered an approximate value of 51 million pesos, which represented a decrease in the order of 33% with respect to the same period of the previous year. This was motivated by a 26% decrease in the volume imported. Among the primary products exported are tobacco, rum, and immunizing agents, while medicines and turbines are the main imports.

There is a lot of potential to increase the commercial exchange in both directions.

What are the priority sectors Cuba is most eager to present to British investors at the Cuba Trade and Investment Mission?

Minister Malmierca: The activities we have identified as prioritized for foreign capital correspond to the strategic sectors defined in the National Development Program until 2030. These include, among others, tourism, the biotechnological and pharmaceutical industries, food production, construction, and the energy sector, with an emphasis on increasing the use of renewable sources of energy.

In my opinion, the priority sectors that could be of interest to UK investors are agriculture and food industries, construction, light industry, mining, tourism, and biotechnology.

The Cuban business community is open to receiving business proposals and assessing their suitability. We have a Portfolio of Opportunities with more than 525 projects identified to develop with foreign capital in over 16 sectors of our economy. We recommend the UK business community review the portfolio for the sake of facilitating the exchanges with the Cuban companies.

I understand there is a delay of bureaucracy and negotiations that still face potential investors. There is a "One-Stop Shop"—Single Window for Foreign Trade (VUINEX) in place at the Special Development Zone of Mariel and there are plans to initiate this throughout Cuba. How advanced is Cuba's progress on hastening the process for foreign investors? What is the expected completion date?

Minister Malmierca: There is a One-Stop Shop in the Special Development Zone of Mariel (ZEDM). That one is not for foreign trade, but to help the users or concessionaries of the Zone to establish themselves there.

In any case, the Ministry of Foreign Trade and Foreign Investment is developing two new One-Stop Shops, one for Foreign Trade (VUCE) and the other for Foreign Investment. We expect that the One-Stop Shop for Foreign Investment throughout Cuba will be in place in January 2020. We are confident it will speed up the assessment process of foreign capital projects as well as facilitate getting all the permits and licenses the investors are required from different Cuban authorities to materialize their investments in my country.

A dual currency economy poses challenges for both Cuba and foreign investors. Will the currency situation be resolved in the near future, or is it to remain as it is? What is the projected timing?

Minister Malmierca: Certainly, the currency and exchange duality causes distortions in the way in which economic facts are measured and in the proper functioning of the national economy. That is why we are determined to complete this process, and we have been working hard for it. Although we cannot define a specific date, I assure you that our will is to achieve it as soon as possible.

This is an extremely complex process. Fundamentally, because of the determination of the Cuban government to minimize the effects on the population.

How is Cuba going to protect foreign investments considering the enactment of Helms–Burton Title III?

Minister Malmierca: Cuba has a legal framework focused on protecting foreign investors. In 1996, after the Helms–Burton Act was passed in the U.S. Congress, Cuba issued a law stating that the law is illegal, unenforceable, and without legal value or effect, so any actions under that U.S. law are worthless here.

This Cuban law states that the government can support foreign investors in different ways. For instance, providing information about the owners of the land or assets nationalized since 1960; helping them to give evidences of the illegitimacy of the claims under the Title III; supporting them in courts of their own countries to get compensations against the prejudices caused by claims, among others measures.

The new Foreign Investment Law of 2014 included in the Guarantees Chapter, the protection against extraterritorial acts, among others. The new Cuban Constitution of April 2019 recognizes in Article 28 those guarantees incorporated in the Foreign Investment Law. It is a very transparent and secure legal framework in this regard.

Other countries also enacted different regulations to protect the investments of their nationals in Cuba. The European Union has a Blocking Statute in the World Trade Organization, which protects European investors in Cuba in the case of claims against them, allowing the investors to ask for compensations in case of any prejudice caused by the claims.

Considering the recent visit by Their Royal Highnesses in March, how do you perceive the Cuba–UK investment climate? Would you like to comment on the relations between Cuba and the United Kingdom?

Minister Malmierca: I perceive the Cuba–UK investment climate very open and with important possibilities to strengthen the bilateral economic relations between both countries. There are many business opportunities in sectors of mutual synergy to increase projects.

These days the Cuba Initiative is being relaunched, which is a joint mechanism to favor bilateral economic relations. A British delegation headed by the Co-Chair of the Cuba Initiative, Lord David Triesman, is in Havana to attend a Business Forum and visit places of interest. We have high hopes on the results of these activities.

Minister Malmierca, I am most honored and grateful that you could speak with me and share your thoughts on the potentials of the Cuba–UK trade relationship and current investment issues and priorities for Cuba.

Follow-up to the Interview: July 2022

In earlier interviews published in the media this year, Minister Malmierca identified several challenges to attracting foreign direct investment in Cuba. These include procedural and structural activities.

What also emerges from the interviews is a more complex issue, more difficult to resolve. This is "prejudices in the mentality of businesspeople, cadres and officials" (Fors Garzon, 2022).[1]

In this update, I asked the Minister those questions and another about FDI regulations for non-state and state-owned businesses. At the present time, both operate under the same laws that govern their activities.

Can you please provide a report for foreign investment in the first six months of 2022? Where does FDI inflow stand compared to the last two difficult years of pandemic and increased sanctions?

Minister Malmierca: In 2020 over 30 businesses with foreign capital were approved, which meant more than $2 billion of committed capital. In 2021 the amount was much lower, only 17 new businesses with foreign capital were approved, due to the global economic crisis that has also affected Cuba, more so considering the tightening of the blockade imposed by the government of the United States against our country. We expect that FDI in Cuba will rise in the following years. In the first

[1] Fors Garzon, E. (2022, January 3). *Cuba will streamline foreign investment flows in 2022.* Prensa Latina News Agency. Retrieved August 26, 2022, from https://www.plenglish.com/news/2022/01/03/cuba-will-streamline-foreign-investment-flows-in-2022/.

half of 2022, nine businesses with foreign capital were approved (one of them in the ZED Mariel), and over 50 others are in negotiation in sectors related to renewable energy, food production, tourism, mining, industry and wholesale trade, construction, and biotechnology, among others.

In recent interviews this year, you identified several challenges, structural and procedural, which Cuba faces in securing foreign investment. You mentioned delays in the negotiation process, file preparation, and the promotion and attraction of foreign capital. What steps is Cuba taking to improve results?

Minister Malmierca: As part of the Economic-Social Strategy to boost the economy and confront the global crisis caused by COVID-19, we are working in a set of issues related to foreign investment, which are aimed at eliminating or making more flexible provisions that may represent obstacles or limit the attraction of foreign capital. One measure adopted to streamline the process of setting up new businesses with foreign investment is the granting to the heads of entities of the Central Administration of the State with the power to approve and authorize International Economic Association contracts whose purpose is productive administration and services.

In addition, the Minister of Justice issued the Instruction No. 8/ 2020, which establishes the procedure for the constitution of businesses via online in exceptional situations, as well as the Decree Laws for the granting of commercial guarantees to businesses with foreign investment (Decree -Law No. 14, "On the Pledge and the Mortgage," and Decree Law No. 15 "On the Guarantee Trust").

Also, we created an online platform to promote our Business Portfolio. On the website inviertaencuba.mincex.gob.cu you can find over 600 projects we want to develop with foreign capital and information about the policies and the framework for doing business in Cuba. We believe that the digital transformation of processes contributes to reducing time and cost, increasing transparency, and improving productivity, which allows us to promote business opportunities more effectively. The operation of the Portfolio is in real time, which allows a constant flow of information from foreign investment, regarding updates of business opportunities, which imply addition, modification, or elimination of opportunity proposals.

Likewise, having the One-Stop-Shop for Foreign Investment (VUINEX) constitutes an incentive for attracting foreign capital, since national or foreign investors can obtain personalized support in each of the stages that the business goes through. It came into operation in January 2020, under Decree No. 15/2020 "VUINEX Regulations". Besides, the implementation of the VUINEX constitutes an indirect incentive for foreign investment, as it speeds up the permits, licenses, and authorizations required by businesses with foreign capital. It also allows foreign investors and nationals residing abroad to consult and manage, via the web, everything related to the permits of foreign investment modalities. In addition, thanks to its interconnection capabilities with organizations, business groups, entities, and territories, it facilitates direct contact between foreign investors interested in doing business in Cuba and Cuban counterparts.

Another challenge you spoke of, and perhaps a more difficult task, is the need to change attitudes toward FDI. You mentioned in earlier interviews a quote by Raúl Castro who said, "we must change our mentality, get rid of false fears." President Diaz-Canel also speaks of this need (Díaz-Canel, 2022).[2] Changing perceptions is difficult anywhere in the world. How will those who understand the necessity of foreign investment for economic development convince those who oppose? For example, China and Vietnam, with similar political systems, both opened to foreign investment and maintain their sovereignty, lifting millions out of poverty and steadily improving GDP.

Minister Malmierca: Our government is working very hard with entities all around the country to promote the advantages of doing business with foreign capital in order to increase our economic development, even a small business in a local community can provide economic growth and well-being to its population. The relevance of foreign investment is expressed in the Conceptualization of the Economic and Social Model, in the National Plan for Economic and Social Development until 2030 and in the Economic-Social Strategy to boost the economy and confront the global crisis caused by COVID-19. Similarly, in Article 28 of the

[2] "Without disregarding the transformations that have taken place, it is necessary to retake the call made more than once by Army General Raúl Castro Ruz to get rid of prejudices and false fears against foreign investment." Speech by Miguel Díaz-Canel Bermúdez, First Secretary of the Central Committee of the Communist Party of Cuba and President, at the Eighth Session of the Ninth Legislature of the National Assembly of People's Power, on December 22, 2021, "Year 63 of the Revolution." https://misiones.cubaminrex.cu/en/articulo/diaz-canel-year-we-have-overcome-and-one-we-are-preparing-overcome-congratulations-cuba.

Constitution of the Republic of Cuba, foreign investment is defined "as an important element for the economic development of the country." The attraction of foreign investment is oriented toward the diversification of export markets, access to advanced technologies, effective substitution of imports, obtaining external financing, creation of new sources of employment, capture of managerial methods, generation of productive chains with the national industry, among other aspects.

The prioritized sectors to develop with foreign capital are agricultural production and the food industry; tourism, including health; development of renewable energy sources; exploration and exploitation of hydrocarbons and mining resources and the construction or improvement of industrial infrastructures. In these sectors, foreign capital has an active and fundamental role for their development.

Also, the experience with the business that are already operating with foreign capital in Cuba is also having an impact on those who oppose to foreign investment. We have presence of foreign capital from more than 40 countries, the most representative are Spain, Germany, Italy, Canada, and Mexico, among others. These businesses provide an important part of the goods offer in the local market and also have a significant weight in the country's exports, both goods and services. Among the latter, exports of nickel and cobalt, zinc and lead concentrates, rum and tobacco stand out. In services, telecommunications and tourism stand out. The country is also opening up to foreign investment in the financial sector, in sugar mills and in the biotech industry, which are practically unexplored by foreign capital in Cuba; and we are doing this without giving up our sovereignty.

With the expansion of the non-state actors in Cuba—recognized as a contributing sector to GDP growth—are there new laws in the works to regulate it that will differentiate between FDI for the entrepreneurs and that of state enterprises?

Minister Malmierca: In 2021 the legal regulations for the improvement of economic actors were published, including decree laws 46/2021 and 47/2021 on micro, small and medium-sized enterprises, and non-agricultural cooperatives, respectively. These provisions establish as legal persons non-state actors, who until then did not have that status.

That allowed them to be considered national investors in a joint venture with a foreign counterpart, or as part of an international economic association contract, under Cuba´s current Foreign Investment Law, "Law No. 118." Therefore, there is no prohibition for a private or state micro, small and medium-sized enterprises or an agriculture or non-agriculture cooperative to be associated with foreign capital and to constitute a modality of foreign investment.

Thank you, Minister Malmierca, for agreeing to a follow-up interview to our conversation of 2019. Indeed, much has changed these last couple of years.

References

Díaz-Canel: For the year we have overcome and for the one we are preparing to overcome: Congratulations to Cuba! CUBADIPLOMATICA. (2021, December 22). Retrieved August 26, 2022, from https://misiones.cubaminrex.cu/en/articulo/diaz-canel-year-we-have-overcome-and-one-we-are-preparing-overcome-congratulations-cuba

Fors Garzon, E. (2022, January 3). *Cuba will streamline foreign investment flows in 2022.* Prensa Latina News Agency. Retrieved August 26, 2022, from https://www.plenglish.com/news/2022/01/03/cuba-will-streamline-foreign-investment-flows-in-2022/

CHAPTER 9

"One Door Closes, Another Opens," Interview with Ambassador José Ramón Cabañas Rodríguez

José Ramón Cabañas Rodríguez is Cuba's First Ambassador of Cuba to the United States, appointed two months after the restoration of diplomatic relations on September 17, 2015. Prior to becoming Cuba's ambassador in Washington, he was Chief of the Cuban Interests Section in that city.

Ambassador Cabañas holds a bachelor's degree in international political science achieved in 1983 from the Raúl Roa García Higher Institute of International Relations in Havana. He has also worked as a senior professor at the university. While he served as Vice Minister of Foreign Relations, he earned his Ph.D. in political science from the University of Havana (Fig. 9.1).

In 1984, he joined the Cuban Ministry of Foreign Affairs where he wrote "Radio Marti: A New Aggression." Following his two years at the Ministry, Ambassador Cabañas transferred to the North America Division.

The Ambassador's former diplomatic roles include the Ambassador to Austria (2001), Director of Document management at the Ministry of Foreign Affairs (2005), the Vice Minister of Foreign Relations of Cuba (2009), Ambassador to various international organizations in Austria, and Third and Second Secretary at the Cuban Embassy in Ottawa, Canada.

During his years as Cuba's Ambassador in Washington, Cabañas has traveled throughout the United States to speak at many organizations' events on business and investment and U.S.–Cuba relations.

T. K. Hernández, *The Cuba Interviews*,
https://doi.org/10.1007/978-3-031-30203-9_9

Fig. 9.1 Dr. José Ramón Cabañas Rodríguez, formerly the Ambassador of Cuba in Washington, D.C. He is now the Director of the Center for International Policy Research (Photo courtesy of Dr. Cabañas)

Ambassador Cabañas is married to Edilia González and has two children.

Ambassador Cabañas currently serves as the Director of the Center for International Policy Research in Havana.

This interview also appeared on the CubaDiplomatica[1] website of MINREX in January 2020.

Hernández: You often mention in your Twitter account "one door closes, another one opens." What are the most important doors opening for Cuba—investment-wise in recent months—and why?

Ambassador José Ramón Cabañas Rodríguez: The United States is the only country that imposes a unilateral system of sanctions against Cuba. Then, it is preventing itself from being part of the many changes

[1] Hernández, T. K. (2020, January 13). *"One door closes, another opens", interview with Ambassador Cabañas*. CUBADIPLOMATICA. Retrieved November 25, 2021, from http://misiones.minrex.gob.cu/en/articulo/one-door-closes-another-opens-interview-ambassador-cabanas.

taking place in our economy. Cuba's legislation doesn't limit American companies from investing or doing trade with Cuban counterparts. That means that the rest of the world is open to doing business with Cuba.

For many years Canada and Spain have been among the largest investors in Cuba, but now you see non-traditional partners of Cuba looking for new opportunities in Tourism, Biotechnology, IT Technologies, and they come forward. Consider that the Mariel Special Economic Zone puts Cuba on the regional map of freight shipping like never before, the way transshipping can be handled in the Caribbean has changed dramatically.

And we have opened doors in the world not only for economic ventures. People come to Cuba to share and learn on how we tackle climate change, to know why we are resilient in the face of natural disasters, how we can afford to provide free and good quality health care and education to our population, how we build a society without violence, without an opioid crisis. Cuban universities respond daily to foreign exchange initiatives, cultural fests welcome artists from many countries, and vice versa.

U.S.–Cuba relations have experienced an enormous setback under the administration of President Trump. Many setbacks occurred—which have included further restriction of U.S. travel to Cuba, limitations on remittances, etc., all of which have hurt the Cuban people. On the business front, can Americans still move forward and invest in Cuba in the current environment?

Ambassador Cabañas: We still have American companies doing business in Cuba, and we have others coming forward with new proposals. American businessmen know how meaningful Cuba could be for their ventures, from agriculture and communications to civil aviation and sea trade. The so-called new policy on Cuba announced in 2017 is actually a recycling of the blockade fiasco. Twelve different American administrations have spent billions of dollars for regime change in Cuba in exchange for nothing, *zero*, *nada*. And we have to say that the impact is on both sides, not only on Cuba. United States federal agencies know that the need to exchange information and coordinate actions with Cuba on alien smuggling, on drug trafficking, on cybercrime, oil spill in the Caribbean Sea, search and rescue at the Florida Straits, tropical diseases, storms, and hurricanes, to mention a few subjects. The fact that you don't like your neighbor doesn't mean that someone has to move.

And there is a large human impact. The majority of more than one million Cuban Americans living in the States want to protect the so-called family agenda: travel, communications, remittances, parcels, mail. American scientists know about the potential outcome of cooperation with Cuba in terms of reducing the rate of cancer, diabetes, heart diseases among the population. Would you exchange all of that for a few votes in Florida? Most people don't think it is wise.

Does Cuba still feel the support of American civil society groups and certain members of Congress in favor of the relaxation of current U.S. government policy, or has the interest and support diminished?

Ambassador Cabañas: Since our fight against Spanish power back in 1868, we have felt solidarity coming from the American people. Remember that even after the U.S. intervention in 1898, Congress passed a Joint Resolution supporting Cuban Independence. Many private people and organizations in the United States still understand what is fair and right in regard to Cuba and what it is not. There is a National Network in Cuba with projects on the Island, and the National Council of Churches defends its links with Cuban churches. Many local governments have passed resolutions against the blockade and still, you have in Congress several initiatives calling to lift sanctions on Cuba, to remove travel barriers, or to support trade. Are all these people "supporting" Cuba, or are they thinking as good Americans on what benefits better their country? And my response is that they are thinking as Americans and not as short-view pretenders trying to escalate in political pyramids for personal benefits.

Would you say, over the last two to three years of the Trump administration, that anything positive has occurred vis-à-vis US–Cuba relations?

Ambassador Cabañas: Absolutely. We need to remember how we got to December 17th, 2014.[2] American people and authorities realized at that time that the blockade against Cuba and the policy of isolation failed. That sentiment is still present among most Americans and Cuban Americans. At every State we visit people ask us, "what is going on? Why do we have this rollback?" Regular people don't understand how the United States benefits from that reversal. And you have hundreds of thousands voting with their feet literally, visiting Cuba for several reasons and

[2] Barack Obama and Raúl Castro announced on December 17, 2014, they would open a path toward normalized relations for the first time in nearly sixty years.

defending their right to do that. In the meantime, most people in the United States understand that all arguments provided by the administration to sever bilateral ties are false and that there is no evidence to sustain them.

What is the present status of the Memorandums of Understanding (MOUs) Cuba and the United States signed during the Obama presidency—healthcare, science, law enforcement, etcetera—are these still in effect?

Ambassador Cabañas: Bilateral official exchange is basically frozen although we have insisted on many initiatives to implement the MOUs. On Law Enforcement, Civil Aviation, and Oil Spill, what is taking place is mainly at the technical level. The rest of the exchange remaining is people to people, NGOs to NGOs, or business-to-business.

Do you have any comments on the future of relations between Cuba and the United States? Can we be optimistic?

Ambassador Cabañas: We have to be optimistic. What we have lived through so far is the incapacity of U.S. governments for 60 years to deal with a new partner, the Cuban Revolution. On December 2014, the reality came to the surface; the United States had to deal in a different way with the Cuban Government. We engaged in negotiations showing mutual respect and reciprocity. We delivered 23 MOUs signed in a year and a half of intense negotiations. We listed those subjects in which we have to agree and those where we have serious disagreements that will last for some time. Those MOUs are the pillars for any future relationship, it is not a dream anymore. The only part missing from the puzzle is that American Democracy works as it is supposed to and really represents the will of the majority which is clearly focused on enhancing bilateral ties. As CNN's motto[3] says, "*this is an apple, anything else is a distraction*" (CNN, 2017).

[3] Ambassador Cabañas used this quote from CNN's "Facts First" initiative launched in October 2017 in the interview.

References

CNN. (2017). *CNN facts first*. CNN Creative Marketing. Retrieved November 25, 2021, from https://www.cnncreativemarketing.com/project/cnn_factsfirst

Hernández, T. K. (2020, January 13). "*One door closes, another opens*", *interview with Ambassador Cabañas*. CUBADIPLOMATICA. Retrieved November 25, 2021, from http://misiones.minrex.gob.cu/en/articulo/one-door-closes-another-opens-interview-ambassador-cabanas

CHAPTER 10

Expanding Political Dialogue and Links Between Cuba–Canada, First Deputy Minister Marcelino Medina González

First Deputy Minister Marcelino Medina González of the Ministry of Foreign Affairs (MINREX) visited Canada in March 2020, leading a delegation to attend the annual political consultations between MINREX Cuba and Global Affairs Canada. The First Minister's visit coincided with the 75th anniversary of the diplomatic relations of the two nations (Fig. 10.1).

Marcelino Medina González, a career diplomat, was appointed First Deputy Minister at MINCEX in 2009.

Deputy Minister Medina began his career as a Specialist at the Europe Division of MINREX in 1984. Between 1986 and 1991, he was Third and Second Secretary at the Cuban Embassy in Germany. He returned to Cuba and, from 1991 to 1993, worked at the Europe Division of the Ministry.

During the years 1994 to 1996, he held positions as Counsellor at the Embassy of Cuba in Bonn, and as Counsellor and Head of the Diplomatic Office in Berlin. In 1996, he became the Deputy Director and later the Director of the Europe Division of the Ministry of Foreign Affairs until 2000.

From 2001 to 2005, Minister Medina was the Cuban Ambassador to Germany. After his post as Ambassador, he served as Deputy Director and then Deputy Minister at the Ministry of Foreign Affairs.

T. K. Hernández, *The Cuba Interviews*,
https://doi.org/10.1007/978-3-031-30203-9_10

Fig. 10.1 His Excellency, Marcelino Medina González, is now the Ambassador of Cuba in Spain (Photo by the editor)

Minister Medina holds a Bachelor of International Relations from the Raúl Roa García Higher Institute of International Relations, and a master's degree from the National Defense College (1993). He speaks Spanish, German, English, and French.

In January 2022, Deputy Minister Medina became Cuba's Ambassador to Spain.

He is married and has two daughters.

Hernández: Welcome to Ottawa, Canada, Minister Medina. Thank you for taking the time to speak with me. How would you characterize the Cuba–Canada relationship in your own words?

First Deputy Minister Marcelino Medina González: Cuba and Canada have enjoyed long-lasting positive relations. Strong people-to-people ties have developed over the years. Our relationship is a good example of the links that can exist between two countries with different political, social, and economic systems at different stages of their development. Relations between Canada and Cuba have historically been an example of mutual respect and mutual benefit. Cuba and Canada maintain a respectful bilateral dialogue even when dealing with issues in which we have different approaches, but which are of common concern. The exchange of visits between the two Foreign Ministers during the last year shows that dialogue is the most effective way to deal with those issues that we do not agree on.

Have you seen a strengthening of the bilateral relationship between Cuba and Canada over recent years?

First Deputy Minister Medina: Cuba–Canada relations have considerably developed in the last years. Diplomatic and commercial ties have grown stronger. Canada is an important partner for Cuba. It has consolidated over the years as our main tourism issuing market, the second investor, and the fourth trading partner. It is also one of our main providers of development cooperation in priority sectors for our country. Cuba is the fifth preferred international destination of Canadians and the second-largest market for Canada in the subregion of Central America and the Caribbean. Several Canadian companies have significant investments in the mining, energy, oil and gas, agri-food, and tourism industries.

The existing high-level dialogue has been strengthened through several government visits in both directions, including those of the Ministers of Foreign Affairs, and with the institutionalization of the annual bilateral consultations four years ago. Three Canadian Prime Ministers, Pierre Trudeau (1976), Jean Chretien (1998), and Justin Trudeau (2016), have visited Cuba.

On strengthening Cuba–Canada relations: is there room to further fortify the relationship? How would you like to see relations develop in the future?

First Deputy Minister Medina: Cuba looks forward to seeing Canada becoming a key player in the development of its economy in the coming years. Cuba hopes to keep counting on Canada's support in the future to continue facing the difficult conditions imposed by U.S. unilateral coercive measures on its economy. At the same time, we would like to go back shortly to a fully staffed Canadian Embassy in Havana, in correspondence with the ties that bind us.

There are conditions for this to happen, given the stability in our bilateral relations and the business opportunities that the Canadian and Cuban markets offer today.

Do you have plans to meet with the Québec government and the province's business groups on this visit?

First Deputy Minister Medina: The relation with the province of Québec has strengthened in the last years. There is a Québec–Cuba Working Group and a Québec office in Havana for the promotion of its culture and mutually beneficial links. Québec companies have a permanent presence in the Cuban market. About 40 cooperation projects funded by the provincial government have been implemented in various fields in the market. The presence of Québec tourists among the Canadians who visit Cuba is overwhelming. That's why I cannot come to Canada without stopping by Québec.

Can you share what you hope to discuss with your Canadian counterparts? What is currently on the table for discussion? Will you, for instance, be speaking about contemporary issues such as Canada's position vis-à-vis Helms–Burton Title III, Latin America, or the Canadian embassy services in Havana?

First Deputy Minister Medina: We intend to exchange with the Global Affairs authorities about the historical links between both countries, which arrive this year to the 75th anniversary. We'll also address various multilateral, regional, and international issues of common interest. I will thank on behalf of my government for the traditional support of Canada to the resolution Cuba presents at the General Assembly of the United Nations calling for the lifting of the U.S. blockade as well as Canada's firm position against the application of Title III of the Helms–Burton Act and in favor of Canadian companies that might be affected. We will discuss the way to expand and strengthen political dialogue and links in various sectors of mutual interest and benefit.

Thank you, Your Excellency, for taking the time to speak with me about the long-standing Cuba–Canada relationship. I hope it has not been too cold for you here and that you have had the chance to see some of the National Capital Region.

CHAPTER 11

Interview with Her Excellency, Berris Ekinci, Ambassador of Turkey in Cuba

Last December I had the delightful opportunity to meet with the Turkish Ambassador to Cuba at the Embassy where we sipped coffee and held a conversation on Turkish business on the Island (Fig. 11.1).

In this interview, yet another taking place during the pandemic, I spoke with Her Excellency, Berris Ekinci, Ambassador of Turkey in Cuba, in late October.

On November 12, the day prior to the publication of this interview, a ceremony was held at the premises of the Ministry of Foreign Trade and Foreign Investments of the Republic of Cuba (MINCEX) with the attendance of Ambassador Ekinci and Mrs. Ana Teresita Gonzalez Fraga, First Deputy Minister of MINCEX, Dr. Aldo Grandal, Director General at the Ministry of Health, and Mr. Ahmet Altintas, representative of Karpowerships, in which a donation from the company was presented to support Cuba's fight against the COVID-19 pandemic.

The donation arrived in Cuba on September 28 on a Turkish Airlines' charter flight included 5,100 surgical face masks, 40,000 surgical gloves, 300 liters of disinfectant, 420 protective suits, 400 surgical face shields, 1,000 COVID-19 CRT rapid tests, and three portable ventilators. This is a demonstration of the solidarity and friendship between Turkey and Cuba, and it is the mutual will of both countries to continue this close relationship.

T. K. Hernández, *The Cuba Interviews*,
https://doi.org/10.1007/978-3-031-30203-9_11

Fig. 11.1 Her Excellency, Berris Ekinci, Ambassador of Turkey in Cuba (Photo by the editor)

Ambassador Ekinci shares with us here the fascinating history of Turkish-Cuban relations that reaches back to the days of the Ottoman Empire in the nineteenth century. We also discussed Turkish business on the Island, its successes, challenges, and prospects for the future.

A new era of business communications has evolved during COVID-19. Many diplomats in overseas postings have not been able to return home for holidays, as was normal in the days before the pandemic. Ambassador Ekinci was one of those who has remained in Havana.

Since 2016, the Ambassador has served as Ambassador Extraordinary and Plenipotentiary of Turkey to Cuba. Her career began in 1994 as an Officer at the Department for the Organization for Security and Cooperation in Europe (OSCE) and following this, as Attaché at the Office of the Special Counselor to the Undersecretary (1995). In 1996, Ambassador Ekinci served as Attaché and Third Secretary at the Turkish Embassy in London, Third and Second Secretary at the Turkish Embassy in Azerbaijan (1999), Second and First Secretary at the Department of Energy (2001), First Secretary and Counsellor at the Permanent Mission of Turkey to the United Nations (2003), Head of the Department of Energy (2007), Consulate General in Marseille (2010), and the Deputy Director General for Energy, Water and Environment (2012).

Ambassador Ekinci has a Bachelor's degree in Economics from Middle East Technical University in Ankara and a Master's in Finance from Boston College in the United States.

Hernández: I understand that Turkey and Cuba have held bilateral relations since 1952. Few people are aware of the length of this relationship. What brought Turkey to Cuba in that year? Can you tell us about the historical evolution of relations?

Ambassador Ekinci: When the historical roots of the Turkish-Cuban relations are examined, it could be seen that various interactions began as early as the second half of the nineteenth century. During the Ottoman time, the Empire opened a Consulate in Havana in 1873. We may ask why? From the readings, we understand it was a period when the view of the Ottoman Empire toward the New World had changed, and furthermore, Cuba's fight for independence had attracted the attention of the Empire.

This was the first interaction.

In 1950, our Embassy in Mexico City was accredited to Cuba to carry out the political relations. Then in November 1952, diplomatic relations between the two countries were formally established. There was an increasing interest from the Turkish Government to open up to the Latin American and Caribbean countries.

Since then, we have had uninterrupted diplomatic relations. Having said that, until the 1990s, there has not been much of an interaction between the two countries. It was only after the dissolution of the Soviet Union that the relationship really took off.

In that aspect, the visit of the Cuban leader Fidel Castro to Turkey for the UN Conference on Human Settlements, HABITAT in 1996, constituted an important step.

Toward the end of the 90s, we witness an acceleration of bilateral visits of high-level representatives, focusing on economic and trade relations, followed up again by a period of slowdown.

A crucial milestone has been the visit of our President of the Republic, H.E. Recep Tayyip Erdoğan in 2015 to Cuba. This was the first visit ever at that level to Cuba. Several ministers accompanied our president. The visit was a great success and paved the way to the deepening of relations.

The most concrete and rapid result which came out of it was the start of the Turkish Airlines flights in December 2016. Since then, Turkish Airlines have been flying to Havana three times a week.

On the political ground, another important visit has been the one of the Cuban Minister of Foreign Affairs H.E. Bruno Rodríguez Parrilla to Turkey in 2017, which as well represented the first ever-official visit of a Cuban foreign minister to Turkey.

Then last year in May, we received our Minister of Foreign Affairs H.E. Mevlüt Çavuşoğlu to Havana, a first at that level following a period of 20 years. It has been a very important and successful visit.

At the political level, I can say, without any doubt, that we have very good relations.

Now, together with our Cuban friends, we are working intensively to increase the level of our economic and trade relations up to the level of our political relations.

In the period of 2018–2019, the Turkey–Cuba Technical Follow-up Committee convened three times in order to work on and deepen the bilateral economic and trade relations. The last one took place in February 2019 in Havana. The Turkish delegation was led by the Deputy Trade Minister, H.E. Gonca Yılmaz Batur, who was accompanied by a large delegation of around 50 people, including representatives of different ministries such as Trade, Transport, Agriculture, Health, and Treasury, as well as representatives of the Turkish private sector.

What are the industry sectors Turkish businesspeople are most interested in?

Ambassador Ekinci: Those that have been prioritized by Turkish business, in consultation with the Cuban side, have been biotechnology, tourism, construction, infrastructure, agriculture, and energy including renewable energy. In the sector of tourism, we have the Turkish company Global Ports Holding that took over the management of the Sierra Maestra Cruise Port in Havana. This is a company that operates 25% of the cruise ports in the Mediterranean.

However, following the decision of the U.S. administration in relation to the cruise ships coming to Cuba, and the halt of journeys to Cuban ports, the activities of Global Ports were hampered. Therefore, if I may say so for now, they are in the waiting room. They are waiting to see what the next step would be.

In agriculture, we have engaged in a chickpeas project. We have donated 100 kilos of seeds to Cuba through the Turkish Cooperation and Development Agency. A technical team came to Cuba last year for the plantation in November. They assisted the Cuban party with the plantation in an area of Sancti Spiritus. They were supposed to come for the harvest in the springtime but unfortunately, because of COVID-19, they were not able to. However, we have been told that the harvest had been a very encouraging one. Hence, the parties intend to continue this cooperation.

We would like to have a bigger and deeper cooperation in the agricultural field with the Cuban side. We have a great experience in this area that we are ready to share.

In addition, in the energy field, we have a Turkish company called Kartet (EMIS, 2021), which has been transforming ships into electricity plants.[1] They are operating in many countries all over the world. They have three ships near Havana in Mariel where they are producing electricity. This is viewed as a trade activity since the company is selling the electricity produced to the Cuban operator.

Turkey is not one of the big players in Cuba, but we can see that there has been a deepening of economic-trade relations and an increased interest from the part of the Turkish companies in the last couple of years. I hope that this will be a start. The presence of these companies in this country may pave the way for other Turkish companies to enter the Cuban market. Consequently, I believe that the experience they will have and share with others will be crucial.

Turkish business signed a contract with BioCubaFarma this year. Can you tell us about the deal?

Ambassador Ekinci: Turkish biopharmaceutical companies are very much interested in the health and biotechnology business in Cuba. In 2018, the Ministries of Health of both countries signed a memorandum of understanding on health and medical sciences.

Then last year, in 2019, the regulatory bodies of both countries signed a memorandum of understanding with the objective of cooperation in areas such as the inspection of medicines, the rational use of medicines, clinical trials, quality control, and scientific evaluation. This

[1] Kartet Karadeniz Toptan Elektrik Ticareti AS. For further details of the company: https://www.emis.com/php/company-profile/TR/Kartet_Karadeniz_Toptan_Elektrik_Ticareti_A_S_en_3328611.html.

was a very important step in relation to the registrations of medicines in the respective countries.

As I already said, there is a great interest on the part of the Turkish pharmaceuticals. Last year during her official visit, a large group of high representatives, CEOs of Turkish pharmaceuticals, accompanied our Deputy Trade Minister.

In the margins of the Technical Follow-up Committee meetings, these companies held a series of meetings with the Cuban representatives of the health sector. It lasted for a week; it was very intense and very helpful. It gave a clear idea for the Turkish companies on how to proceed on potential cooperation areas.

There are already several companies doing business with Cuba in this sphere. I may mention some of them. The first one I can label as "the pioneer" as they established relations with the Cuban side more than 10 years ago, namely Hasbiotech. This company registered in Turkey some Cuban-origin medicines like Heberprot-P intended for diabetes, Leukoplus for strengthening the immune system, Epoplus for kidney failure, and Vaxira for cancer. This company also has taken the rights for the CIGB 500, a Cuban-origin molecule that has the objective to diminish heart attacks. Clinical trials will be initiated in Turkey and, if the results are positive, then production will follow. This is a very important project in line.

The clinical trials are in process now?

Ambassador Ekinci: They will start.

Another company, MomentumCuba has teamed up with BioCuba-Farma to commercialize two of their immune therapies in Turkey and in the neighboring region. They also have been working on some other products with the relevant Cuban companies.

Another one I can mention is the OKAN Group, which signed agreements with Servicios Médicos Cubanos,[2] the University of Havana on Medical Sciences, and the Oncology Center. These documents include provisions such as the exchange of students and medical staff and, as well, joint research on cancer tumors. One of the aims is to establish a joint cancer research center in Istanbul.

Turkey is against the economic sanctions imposed on Cuba by the U.S. embargo and regulations, described by many as a violation of

[2] La Comercializadora de Servicios Médicos Cubanos, (CMSC S.A.).

international law. What is the government of Turkey doing to protect Turkish business which operate or plan to operate in Cuba? We have, for example, in Canada, the FEMA Act[3] (Government of Canada, 2021), **and the EU**[4] **have mechanisms in place** (European Commission, 2018) **to protect their international trading and sovereignty.**

Ambassador Ekinci: As you said, Turkey is against any unilateral sanctions and coercive measures. We believe that instead, the parties should engage into dialogue and try to find some common ground. Those sanctions, primarily, affect the population and in this specific example, we can see how the sanctions are affecting the Cuban people. These unilateral sanctions also hamper the third-party interests with their extraterritorial effects. Turkish companies are also affected by these sanctions.

Other companies that have an interest in engaging with Cuba, on economic grounds, have an increased reluctance to do so because of the U.S. sanctions and Helms–Burton law. These are very unfortunate.

We don't have in Turkey, as in Canada or the EU, a legislation or mechanism in place which would directly protect our companies. Of course, we explain to the companies that Turkey does not recognize those unilateral sanctions. We are trying to assist them (the companies) in any way possible, but there is no concrete mechanism as per se. In addition, even when you look at the concrete mechanisms which exist, you can see they also unfortunately have their limits in the real world.

Turkey has always been among the overwhelming majority of countries which has been supportive of the UN resolution tabled by Cuba each year at the General Assembly for the lifting of the U.S. sanctions against Cuba.

Looking to the future of Turkish-Cuban relations—where does Turkey hope to be with Cuba over the next five years?

Ambassador Ekinci: I believe our political relations will continue to be as fruitful as they are now. I really hope that, as I said in the beginning, we will be able to bring the level of our trade and economic relations to the level of our political relations, as they are lagging much behind their true potential. When we look at the trade volume between the two countries, for example, last year's number, it is around $55 million dollars, which is not representative of the potential which exists.

[3] Foreign Extraterritorial Measures Act (FEMA). (R.S.C., 1985, c. F-29). Canada.

[4] Blocking Statute. (Council Regulation (EC) No 2271/96) November 22, 1996. European Union.

I really do hope that the economic, the investment framework in the country will get better, giving incentives to potential foreign investors, traders. There have been some very promising announcements made on the 16th of July by the Cuban government.[5] Of course, it is the implementation of what had been announced which will pave the way for the increase in interest of the potential investors and businesses from Turkey. The investment environment has to get better for the businesses, as there are difficulties related to both the U.S. sanctions and other factors as well.

One should not forget that Turkey is far away from this region, there is the language barrier, the distance barrier. Turkish businesses are choosing to concentrate on regions neighboring Turkey and for the last years, there has been a growing interest toward Africa and the entry into the African markets. We have to find ways to attract them to the Cuban market. Actually, Cuba itself seems very attractive for the Turkish people. People are interested to come to Cuba, willing to do business with Cuba, so I am always asking our Cuban friends to help us in this endeavor.

And right now, the COVID situation helps nothing.

Ambassador Ekinci: Unfortunately, not. But one good thing has been that even during COVID times, we managed to organize some virtual meetings with the participation of both sides. We learned that in between the physical encounters, there could be virtual meetings to pursue with the negotiations, the discussions. No need to say that physical presence has another dimension, but everyone understands advancements could be possible with virtual meetings. We have some companies, which have during these times finalized negotiations. We will continue our efforts for our companies to stay in touch with their Cuban counterparts and continue their talks virtually up until the opening.

Ambassador, I would like to thank you so much for this interview. It is so nice to see you again.

Ambassador Ekinci: Thank you for this opportunity.

[5] On July 16, 2020, the Minister of Foreign Trade and Foreign Investment, Rodrigo Malmierca, explained on the Mesa Redonda TV program a series of economic reforms. One of the most important measures was the authorization of non-state structures to carry out import/export operations through specialized state companies. At the time of the announcement, 36 companies specialized in import and export services to the non-state enterprises. Those companies are located in Havana and other provinces throughout the island.

References

EMIS. (2021, February 23). *Kartet Karadeniz Toptan Elektrik Ticareti A S.* Retrieved February 25, 2022, from https://www.emis.com/php/company-profile/TR/Kartet_Karadeniz_Toptan_Elektrik_Ticareti_A_S_en_3328611.html

European Commission. (2018). *Blocking statute (Council Regulation (EC) No 2271/96).* Retrieved November 25, 2021, from https://ec.europa.eu/info/business-economy-euro/banking-and-finance/international-relations/blocking-statute_en

Government of Canada. (2021). *Foreign extraterritorial measures act.* Retrieved November 25, 2021, from https://laws-lois.justice.gc.ca/eng/acts/f-29/FullText.html

CHAPTER 12

Interview with Andrei Guskov, Russian Ambassador to Cuba

Since June 2018, his Excellency, Andrei Anatolyevich Guskov has served as the Ambassador of the Russian Federation to Cuba. In October 2018, he was appointed to serve concurrently as the Plenipotentiary Ambassador to the Commonwealth of the Bahamas (Fig. 12.1).

A graduate of the Moscow State Institute of International Relations (1983), Ambassador Guskov is a career diplomat holding various positions at the Ministry of Foreign Affairs' central office and abroad since that year.

In 2005, Ambassador Guskov served as the Minister Counselor of the Russian Embassy in Brazil. He became Deputy Director of the Latin American Department in 2011. Following these appointments, he was assigned as the ambassador to Peru from 2015 to 2018.

As the Ambassador to Cuba, he has overseen several humanitarian donations to the Island, including wheat, cooking oil, and medical supplies during the COVID-19 pandemic.

This interview took place in August 2022.

Hernández: What is the status of trade, economic and investment cooperation between Russia and Cuba today? What are the key commodity items exported to Cuba?

Ambassador Andrei Guskov: Cooperation between our countries continues developing quite dynamically in almost all areas. Our states are fulfilling the bilateral economic agenda, primarily through interaction

T. K. Hernández, *The Cuba Interviews*,
https://doi.org/10.1007/978-3-031-30203-9_12

Fig. 12.1 His Excellency, Andrei Anatolyevich Guskov (Photo courtesy of the Embassy of the Russian Federation in Cuba)

within the framework of the Intergovernmental Russian-Cuban Commission on Trade, Economic, Scientific and Technical Cooperation.[1] Mutual efforts are being made to diversify bilateral trade, the volume of which in 2021 amounted to $145.6 million. Traditionally, in the structure of Russian exports to Cuba, the main portion of supplies are vehicles and equipment, food products, and agricultural raw materials.

Close work is underway to stimulate joint projects in the field of energy, metallurgy, transport, informatization and telecommunications, space research, combating climate change, biotechnology, healthcare, and

[1] The Intergovernmental Russian-Cuban Commission on Trade, Economic, Scientific and Technical Cooperation is a bilateral trade and economic relations agreement signed by Russia and Cuba first signed on November 3, 1992, and updated June 14, 2016. The agreement is renewed every five years. More information can be found at: http://government.ru/en/info/463/.

the pharmaceutical industry, which also contribute to the effective participation of the Russian Federation in the implementation of the Plan for the socioeconomic development of the Republic of Cuba until 2030.

Russian companies are involved in a number of major projects in strategic areas of the Cuban economy. In the energy sector, the construction of four power units by Inter RAO-Export LLC at the Maximo Gomez and East Havana TPPs with a unit installed capacity of 200 MW.

In order to meet the needs of Cuba in profile and construction rolled metal, a two-stage modernization of the metallurgical enterprise "Antillana de Acero Jose Marti" with the participation of the Russian company LLC "Industrial Engineering" is underway.

A major project is the restoration and modernization of the railway infrastructure of Cuba through JSC Russian Railways, together with Union of Railways of Cuba. An agreement and a contract were signed,[2] as well as a Protocol of Intentions between Russian Railways and the Ministry of Transport of the Republic of Cuba. It provides for the repair and re-equipment of more than 1,000 km of railway lines using Russian technologies, training of specialists, and the supply of machinery and equipment.

The Russian vehicles, "Gazelle," "GAZon," "URAL," and "PAZ" buses are now being manufactured in Cuba.

Within the framework of the "Cooperation Agreement between the Ministry of Transport of Russia and the Institute of Civil Aviation of Cuba," joint activities are carried out to restore the airworthiness of the Il-96 and Tu-204 aircraft owned by Cuban partners.[3]

Russian companies are involved in the restoration of the textile industry in Cuba. In 2018, Veya Invest LLC and BK Import signed a contract for the reconstruction and modernization of Cuban textile factories.

The most successful in terms of investment activity is the project to increase oil recovery at the Boca de Jaruco oil field, implemented by

[2] The agreement to upgrade Cuba's railway system was signed in 2019. Deputy Prime Minister Yuri Borisov told a press conference the deal was worth, "slightly less than $1 billion." Source: https://tass.com/economy/1062752.

[3] The agreement between Russia and Cuba was signed in 2016. For more information: https://en.mercopress.com/2016/12/10/cuba-and-russia-sign-defence-cooperation-agreement.

Zarubezhneft JSC and CUPET,[4] the state oil company of the Republic of Cuba. The company plans to develop projects in the field of electric transport and green energy on the island.

Negotiations are underway between the Federal State Budgetary Institution "National Research Center for Epidemiology and Microbiology named after N.N. N.V.Gamalei" of the Ministry of Health of Russia and the BioCubaFarma Group of biotechnological and pharmaceutical companies on conducting joint clinical trials of vaccines "Sputnik V," "Sovereign 02," and "Abdala."

How is cooperation between Russia and Cuba carried out under sanctions?

Ambassador Guskov: Our strategic partnership with Cuba is of a long-term nature and is not subject to the influence of the political situation. Both Moscow and Havana understand that sanctions are aimed primarily at undermining the well-being of ordinary people in the countries against which they are imposed. This was clearly shown by the story of the delivery of 20,000 tons of wheat to Cuba as humanitarian aid. The ship with the cargo spent almost a month in the territorial waters of Cuba, waiting for mooring and unloading. The reason for this was the freezing of freight payment to the shipowner due to Western sanctions against Russian banks. However, we have found a way to resolve this situation and deliver the grain to the Cuban elevators. Thus, sanctions, of course, have to be taken into account when structuring our work. But they will not affect our desire to strengthen the time-tested relations of friendship, mutual understanding, and close cooperation.

How do you assess the reforms carried out in Cuba in 2021 in the context of trade with Russia and the prospects for economic development?

Ambassador Guskov: Russia has always supported Cuba in its efforts to modernize its economy. The main goal is to improve the well-being of its 11 million people who are experiencing the consequences of restrictions related to COVID-19 against the backdrop of an unprecedented increase in the U.S. trade, economic and financial blockade. In this context, we welcome the determination of Havana to move along the path of transformation, while maintaining social and political stability and not allowing external players to interfere in these processes. We are ready

[4] Russia's Zarubezhneft and CUPET signed an agreement in 2011 for oil exploration and recovery for a duration of 25 years: https://tass.com/economy/699577.

to continue to provide our Cuban friends with assistance and support to the extent that they are interested in this.

In an interview[5] **with J. M. Garcia of the Prensa Latina news agency** (Garcia, 2022), **you said that "Cuba is an example of the US policy of putting pressure on unwanted governments that protect their sovereignty and follow their own path of development and impose on them an "order based on rules." Your country is now facing the same thing that Cuba has been dealing with for the past 60 years. Could you comment on this?**

Ambassador Guskov: The Russian Federation is the country with the largest number of illegitimate sanctions imposed on it by Western countries led by the United States. The reason for this, as in the case of Cuba, was our independent policy to protect our own national interests. It was they and nothing else that dictated the start of a special military operation in Ukraine to protect the Russian-speaking population, which has been subjected to genocide for the past eight years. For 30 years after the collapse of the USSR, our attempts to prevent the expansion of NATO to the East were defiantly ignored. From Ukraine, they began to make an openly anti-Russian entity, pandering to local neo-Nazis who staged an anti-constitutional coup d'état in 2014. Against this background and taking into account the unwillingness of the West to reckon with our interests, Russia simply could not remain indifferent to everything that was happening. The special military operation will continue despite the sanctions pressure and Western support for Ukraine. All the goals and objectives set for the defense of Donetsk and Lugansk, the demilitarization and denazification of Ukraine, and the elimination of threats to Russia will be fulfilled.

We understand the Cubans well and are inspired by their example. Sixty years of sanctions have demonstrated the complete failure of such a policy, which grossly violates the fundamental principles of the UN Charter.

Thank you, Ambassador, for your time and this opportunity. I am deeply honored.

[5] "Russia is facing an economic blockade by the West." Interview with Ambassador Andrey Guskov by Juan M. Garcia, in Prensa Latina, published April 25, 2022.

References

Garcia, J. M. (2022, April 25). *Russia is facing an economic blockade by the west*. Prensa Latina Latin American News Agency. Retrieved August 7, 2022, from https://www.plenglish.com/news/2022/04/25/russia-is-facing-an-economic-blockade-by-the-west/

MercoPress. (2016, December 10). *Cuba and Russia sign defence cooperation agreement*. Retrieved August 16, 2022, from https://en.mercopress.com/2016/12/10/cuba-and-russia-sign-defence-cooperation-agreement

TASS. (2013, August 26). *Russia's Zarubezhneft launches drilling at Cuba's Boca de Jaruco oil field*. Retrieved August 16, 2022, from https://tass.com/economy/699577

TASS. (2019, June 7). *Russia, Cuba sign agreement for upgrading Cuban railways, says deputy prime minister*. Retrieved August 16, 2022, from https://tass.com/economy/1062752

The Russian Government. (2013, February 21). *Russia-Cuba trade and economic cooperation*. Retrieved August 16, 2022, from http://government.ru/en/info/463/

PART II

The Economy and Foreign Investment

CHAPTER 13

Interview with Economist Juan Triana

Dr. Juan Triana Cordoví is a senior professor at the Center for the Study of the Cuban Economy, University of Havana. He spoke with us on the eve before voters in Georgia headed to the polls in crucial Senate runoffs in the United States in early January 2021 (Fig. 13.1).

In this interview, Dr. Triana discusses the Cuban economy, the devastating effects of COVID on his homeland, exports, recent regulatory changes, and foreign investment.

Since 1982, Dr. Triana has been an invited professor at the Higher Institute of International Relations of the Ministry of Foreign Affairs of Cuba in Havana.

Dr. Triana holds a bachelor's degree in Economics, a master's degree in Cuban and Latin American Studies, and a Ph.D. in Economy from the University of Havana. He also has a Diploma in Planning Policies and Agricultural Development from the FAO-PROCAPLAN, UN, Buenos Aires.

He is an internationally published author and coauthor of over 25 books and a contributor of many articles on strategy for economic change, opportunities, challenges, perspectives, and reflections on economic matters pertaining to Cuba.

Dr. Triana has lectured at more than a dozen universities outside of Cuba including the University of London, University of Nottingham, Universidad de Barcelona, University of Wolverhampton, Institute of

T. K. Hernández, *The Cuba Interviews*,
https://doi.org/10.1007/978-3-031-30203-9_13

Fig. 13.1 Dr. Juan Triana Cordoví (Photo from the personal collection of Dr. Triana)

the Sorbonne University, Columbia University, University of Minnesota, Kellogg Institute, University of Notre Dame, Florida International University, University of Denver, University of Oviedo, Hankuk University, and Seoul University.

In 1997, Dr. Triana was awarded for his work in Economics by the Ministry of Science, Technology, and the Environment (CITMA). He was a four-time winner as coauthor for "Best Book in Economy" from the National Social Sciences Prize from CITMA. In 2002, Dr. Triana won the Raúl León Torras National Economics Prize from the National Association of Economists of Cuba.

Between 1995 and 2004, Dr. Triana was Director at the Center for the Study of the Cuban Economy, University of Havana. He has also held a variety of positions as a consultant to international corporations, is a member of various committees, a host of the Radio Taino program on the Cuban economy, and a contributor to several online news media websites.

Table 13.1 Year-over-year change in quarterly GDP (2020/2019) (%)

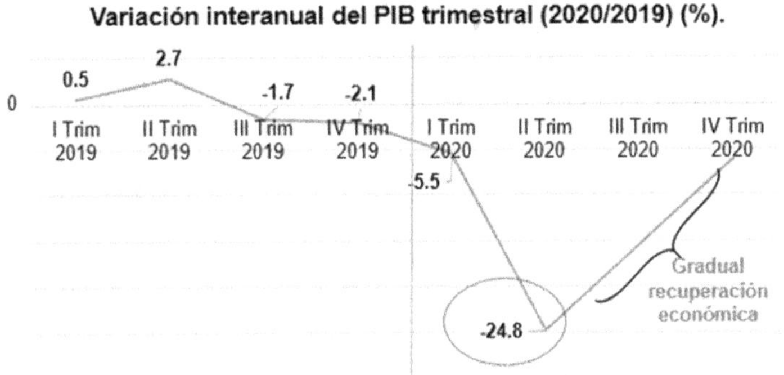

Hernández: The COVID pandemic has had a disastrous effect on the world's economy. The World Bank has predicted a 5.2% contraction in global GDP[1] **this year, and the deepest global recession in decades** (World Bank, 2020). **Can you give us an overall idea of how this pandemic has affected the Cuban economy? What does this reveal about the state of the economy?**

Dr. Juan Triana: As in the rest of the world, the COVID pandemic has hit the Cuban economy very hard. The data on the quarterly behavior of the economy demonstrates this. As of March 2020, the date that Cuba faced the first wave of the disease, the dynamics of the economy plummeted. The graph below shows that drop (Table 13.1).

Cuba had to spend more than 100 million additional dollars on the entire program to contain the disease, while expenditures from the budget also rose, raising the fiscal pressure and deficit.

It must also be understood that the effect of the pandemic was greater because the Cuban economy had already been facing a fall in its economic dynamics since the second quarter of 2019, partly as a result of the increase in the U.S. blockade and partly due to a combination of problems conjunctural and structural, the latter being long-standing.

However, the pandemic also forced a search for new alternatives and revealed important reserves:

[1] COVID-19 to Plunge Global Economy into Worst Recession since World War II. Press Release. June 8, 2020. https://www.worldbank.org/en/news/press-release/2020/06/08/COVID-19-to-plunge-global-economy-into-worst-recession-since-world-war-ii.

The first allowed to verify the solidity of the Cuban health system and the biotechnology pharmaceutical sector. Second, it showed that it was possible to readjust a job and develop teleworking and working from home. Third, it made evident the importance of telecommunications, the network, and developing services associated with it.

It highlighted the strategic importance of the food production system and the profound weaknesses it still suffers. It demonstrated the vitality and creativity of the non-state sector and its capacity to adapt to these new conditions. It confirmed that it is essential to achieve greater complementarity between all economic agents regardless of the form of ownership. It forced the acceleration and deepening of reforms announced years before and highlighted the importance of supporting government measures with the work of the academic and scientific centers.

What impact will the currency unification, which took place on January 1, have on the economy?

Dr. Triana: Like any monetary reform that has at its center the devaluation of the official exchange rate, it has short and long-term effects.

In the short term, it should eliminate monetary distortions that impact the measurement of efficiency, productivity, and profitability of companies. In the short term, its immediate effect will be an upward price readjustment, as well as the cost structures of the economic agents and the spending structure of families.

Also, in the short term, it should have an impact on the reduction of imports and on the preference of Cuban companies to buy domestically produced products. In the same way, it must generate incentives to seek employment.

In the medium and long term, if the devaluation occurs as it should, it should have positive effects on efficiency, labor productivity, and exports. However, other structural factors must be combined for this to occur.

Cuba has made several reforms (including the change to a single currency). What will the impact of these changes be for foreign investors?

Dr. Triana: Cuban authorities have argued that they will prevent these changes from negatively impacting joint ventures and 100% foreign companies operating in the country.

The unification of the exchange rate and the monetary unification has meant a devaluation of the official rate and this should benefit foreign investors:

1. Because a dollar or a euro will yield more, while all payments will be made in CUP at the rate of one USD for 24 CUP. For example, in the case of hiring the workforce, the foreign investor should benefit.

2. Companies can buy national supplies at much more favorable prices than imports. Before, companies had to pay the prices of these inputs one to one.

3. The rates of some services previously paid in dollars will now be paid in national currency. Of course, not everything will be a profit, imports will now cost more.

What are the expectations for trade and investment under the new Biden presidency?

Dr. Triana: I can only speak about my expectations; I don't know what the government's expectations are.

I do not believe that in the first months Cuba occupies a privileged place on the Biden-Harris agenda. Also, keep in mind that the Senate is still undecided, whether the vote in Georgia is pro-Democrat or contrary, should have a significant influence on the breadth and depth of what Biden-Harris will do.

One last consideration. For the Democrats, keeping the seat in the White House in the next term is essential, and for this, Florida continues to be important. This factor will have weight.

However, I believe that the new president will be able to reverse some of the measures adopted by Trump, especially those that have to do with contacts between the Cuban community living in the United States and their relatives in Cuba.

Travel and remittances could be among the first measures to change. Reactivating the visa granting service at the U.S. consulate in Cuba could be another measure.

To facilitate again the tourism of Americans to Cuba, as well as some other measures that do not depend on negotiations between the Executive and Congress. Reversing the measures taken by President Trump against Cuban companies and banks seems more difficult, not only because they are more complex and manipulable by the Republicans but also because today, they constitute a resource to "negotiate" with Cuba.

Promoting trade and investment of American companies in Cuba under specific licenses will depend more on the pressure of these companies and the balance of costs and benefits for the future Democrat in the White House. I'm not that optimistic. But as for the environment for trade and investment in Cuba, undoubtedly a more relaxed relationship between the United States and Cuba will have a positive effect.

What are the strongest sectors that will drive success for the Cuban economy?

Dr. Triana: Right now, medical services are the most powerful of all. Turning Cuba into a destination to receive these services seems possible.

Obviously, tourism, although it is clear it requires profound transformations to adapt not only to a post-COVID world but also to the new conditions of the national economy. Tourism, taking advantage of these new conditions, can significantly increase its multiplier effect on the rest of the economy. It has and will have a very large impact on the non-state sector, both in terms of employment and income.

Biotech pharmaceuticals are among the most powerful of all. Cuba must take advantage of what has been advanced this year in the work of drug production to face COVID. The production of some agricultural products, especially with the Caribbean and Canadian markets in mind, although requires a powerful process of technological improvement and learning in commercial and regulatory terms.

There are other traditional sectors already known, the production of tobacco and Habanos cigars, rums, sugar, nickel, and other metals.

But you also have to think that many small things can build something very large. Cuba has undeniable potential in its citizens. The reform that has begun is opening up opportunities for the creation of small and medium-sized companies, with a greater or lesser degree of complexity that can also, together, become a great engine of economic growth and employment.

Dr. Triana, it was a pleasure speaking with you on Cuba's economy. Thank you for taking this time today.

Reference

World Bank. (2020, June 8). *COVID-19 to Plunge global economy into worst recession since World War II*. Retrieved December 12, 2020, from https://www.worldbank.org/en/news/press-release/2020/06/08/COVID-19-to-plunge-global-economy-into-worst-recession-since-world-war-ii

CHAPTER 14

Day Zero to the Future–Economist Dr. Emily Morris Discusses the Cuban Economy

In this interview, Development Economist Dr. Emily Morris discusses GDP, economic development, and the complicated task of transformation to Cuba's new economy, among other topics.

Dr. Morris is a research associate at the UCL Institute of the Americas. From 1995 to 2008, she was a Senior Editor/Economist in Latin America at the Economist Intelligence Unit (EIU) in London, and later (2014–17) served as the Country Economist for Belize at the Inter-American Development Bank. Her current research is on Cuban macroeconomic management and performance in terms of national income and sustainable development goals (Fig. 14.1).

As well as her role as a research associate at the UCL Institute of the Americas, Dr. Morris is a consultant on Cuban, Caribbean, and Latin American economies and a Director of the Caribbean Research and Innovation for Knowledge Exchange and Transfer (CRICKET) community interest company, which promotes UK–Cuban research collaboration for sustainable development.

Hernández: On the relationship between GDP and economic development. Has it become easier to forecast short and long-term periods of economic growth with all the recent changes announced by the Cuban government?

Dr. Emily Morris: Measuring Cuban GDP is difficult. Estimates of the size of the economy vary widely because of the problem of valuation of

T. K. Hernández, *The Cuba Interviews*,
https://doi.org/10.1007/978-3-031-30203-9_14

Fig. 14.1 Dr. Emily Morris (Photo by Michael Lachmann)

production and incomes when market prices do not prevail. Calculating its growth from one year to the next is particularly challenging, as the structure of the Cuban economy has altered greatly since 1997, which is the base year for Cuba's GDP index. Part of the change in structure has arisen from the series of economic reforms since 1997. An important transformation has been the creation of a new non-state sector, the fortunes of which have frequently diverged from those of the rest of the economy. A large part of this new area of economic activity has been linked to the informal economy, complicating measurement of its impact on trends in real output, consumption, and incomes.

The latest changes have complicated measurement further. Calculating real (that is, inflation-adjusted) economic growth from year to year is always made more challenging when there are sharp changes in relative prices, and 2021 will see extremely sharp changes in Cuba. Starting on January 1st, 2021—"day zero" of the "monetary reordering" process—all prices and incomes are being radically realigned. While the government has some control of nominal state wages and is attempting to cap prices of many basic goods, the process of adjusting other prices will be an iterative one, as the new exchange rate, cost matrices feed through supply chains in the state and non-state sectors.

The extent to which the exchange rate reform and price liberalizations will feed through to an inflationary spiral—and thus exacerbate price instability—will depend on expectations and the strength of the supply response. Expectations are, of course, extremely uncertain, and the supply response depends on the capacity of domestic producers to alter production in the light of new relative prices. This structural adjustment will make the existing relative weights of economic sectors used for calculating real aggregate growth less accurate, further complicating the measurement of real aggregate growth.

Eventually, as relative prices settle into a more stable structure, and that structure more closely reflects market prices, a more accurate measurement of GDP and its annual real growth will become easier. But in the meantime, estimation of real economic performance will have a large margin of error, and the Cuban monetary authorities and statistical office[1] (upon which the government relies for data to inform economic management decisions) will need to keep their systems of measurement under constant review.

Can we determine level of growth more accurately now from what appears to be an increased access to foreign currency (monetary unification, increased access to banking for non-resident Cubans, and the emergence of the MLC stores)?

Dr. Morris: Measuring flows of foreign exchange has always been relatively straightforward because we have a single measure of value: the U.S. dollar (or other foreign currency equivalents at market exchange rates). Official data for these flows—that is, the data provided in Cuba's external accounts—have not been complete or timely, leaving economists to depend on some estimations and guesswork, but nonetheless this has always been easier than measuring the value of domestic production. This has not changed.

Economic restructuring, the new economy, *Tarea Ordenamiento*—do you believe this restructuring will substantially transform the economy?

Dr. Morris: My short answer is yes, definitely.

But we don't know exactly how the economy will be transformed. If everything goes well, with the government able to contain expectations and economic actors responding quickly to the new price signals—investing and reorganizing to exploit new opportunities to boost foreign exchange earnings, increase productivity and reduce import dependence through greater efficiency—then the currency reform and realignment of prices will shift the economy onto a higher growth trajectory. But it is not

[1] National Office of Statistics and Information (ONEI) also known as known as the Oficina Nacional de Estadística e Informacion was created by article 31 of Decree Law No. 281 of February 2, 2011.

possible to achieve such a structural change, in which labor moves from low-productivity to higher-productivity activities, entirely painlessly. Even in this positive scenario, there will be less job security, transformations of work practices that will be resented by some, and more unemployment.

If things don't go so well, the economic disruption could result in a form of "transition recession", as state and private enterprises have to cease production because they are no longer competitive, while new opportunities are created too slowly to compensate for the fall in output.

To avoid the negative scenario, the government has stated that state companies will have a year to adjust, with subsidies and credits to cushion them over the period of restructuring. This has some similarities with a strategy of "fiscally-cushioned big bang" recommended in a 2013 Brookings Institution report.[2] While this approach is feasible in theory and would serve to mitigate the economic and social cost of adjustment, in practice it will need development of sophisticated capacity (among enterprise managers, official authorities, and financial institutions) for highly complex evaluations, coordination, communication, and negotiations.

Let's discuss the business environment for foreign investors. Would you say it has improved with recent changes for foreign investors which include regulatory changes, an update to the annual Portfolio of Opportunities with projects worth $12.01 billion, new platforms (VUCE and VUINEX) to simplify the investment process, currency unification, and the ability for foreign entities to hold a majority share in their investments/joint ventures)?

Dr. Morris: Cuban efforts to attract foreign investors—including the increased portfolio and new platforms indicate that the Cuban authorities are serious about seeking an increase in foreign business partners. It is difficult to assess the success of their efforts to date. The relatively low level of investment has been blamed by both Cuban and foreign analysts on rigidities of the Cuban bureaucracy and/or the Cuban government's ideological suspicion of international businesses (both of which are real), but for as long as U.S. sanctions remain in place, it is unlikely that foreign investors would be significantly more enthusiastic about the opportunities in the Cuban market even if Cuban officials and policy had been more welcoming.

[2] De la Torre, Augusto and Ize, Alain, Exchange Rate Unification: The Cuban Case (January 10, 2014). Available at https://www.brookings.edu/research/exchange-rate-unification-the-cuban-case/.

Currency unification and the recent reforms will simplify the process of negotiating, evaluating, and managing foreign businesses in Cuba, and may make a marginal difference in terms of the foreign investor appetite for the Cuban market, but the potential cannot be realized until U.S. sanctions are lifted to remove the threats to businesses engaging with Cuba.

What are your predictions for the Cuban economy? There are two scenarios—one being the ramifications of an enduring pandemic which continues to affect the entire global economy, and the other, with vaccinations and other precautions in place, the eventual return to global health.

Dr. Morris: In the context of current uncertainties—about the amount of foreign exchange reserves, the behavior of expectations and adjustment speed and costs within Cuba, as well as the prospects for U.S. sanctions—forecasting the Cuban economy is a very hazardous business.

For the two scenarios:

1. If we assume the pandemic endures, Cuba's tourism sector will remain extremely depressed, and the benefit from the expected relaxation of U.S. travel restrictions will be slow to arrive. Cuba's economy is very open, so such an unfavorable external environment will hit its capacity to import essential supplies of inputs and weigh on prospects.

   Having contracted by an estimated 11% in 2020 due to the foreign exchange shock (and this is likely to be an underestimate, as the informal sector's woes, which feed through to household consumption and savings, are not likely to have been fully taken into account in official GDP estimates), the economy will struggle to return to growth in 2021. With external demand weak, prospects will depend upon the capacity to produce goods and services for the domestic market. Potential sources of growth are the relaxation of regulatory restrictions on the private sector and the creation of stronger incentives (through price changes and decentralization of decision-making) for innovation in the public sector.

   On balance, at this stage, my forecast would be for a flat-lining economy at the aggregate level: zero or a further contraction in 2021, albeit a less sharp decline than in 2020.

   Beneath the surface of this national growth figure, we can expect substantial structural transformation, with the monetary reordering and other reforms resulting in some sectors growing and others contracting. This implies the persistence of severe economic hardship, low investment (and some degree of decapitalization), and rising official unemployment. Recovery would begin in 2022, accelerating in the medium term.

2. A return to global health would provide an external boost. Assuming that this is coupled with a relaxation of restrictions on travel to Cuba from the United States, we can expect this to bring swift reanimation of economic activity in some areas, particularly in Havana, with the non-state sector enjoying the most immediate stimulus. Apart from the support to household incomes in the regions that host most international visitors, this would also provide some relief to the wider economy, with the relaxation of the government's foreign exchange constraint enabling a recovery in public investment, including infrastructure improvements, and reforms providing increasing scope for Cuban (state and non-state enterprises) to respond to new opportunities.

   However, given the hazards and complexities of economic restructuring, and the need to replenish foreign exchange reserves after the damage incurred in 2020, growth in 2021 would still be modest. At this stage, more than 2–3% seems unlikely. That is, GDP would remain below its 2019 level, but the new growth industries would at least be able to offer opportunities to offset the contraction of sectors rendered unviable by the withdrawal of subsidies.

   Structural change and rising productivity as a result of reforms should also pave the way for some acceleration of growth in the medium term.

In both these scenarios, I assume that the price instability arising from monetary reform does not spiral out of control in 2021. During this challenging period of adjustment, the fact that the government retains substantial capacity to anchor prices and wages will serve to restrain the inflationary spiral, although it will be much harder to contain price pressures in the private sector which is larger than it was when Cuba last experienced such a severe external shock in the early 1990s. In the final analysis, Cuba's large public sector and relatively robust social safety net should serve to support resilience and provide an adequate underpinning to limit the cost of restructuring. But nonetheless, 2021 will be a testing year.

Thank you, Dr. Morris, for your valuable insight into the challenges facing Cuban economic restructuring presently taking place in the midst of the global COVID pandemic. It is a difficult time for all.

Follow-up to the Interview: June 2022

In our interview of January 2021, you gave an economic forecast for Cuba under two scenarios, both in uncertain times: (1) an enduring pandemic and (2) an end to pandemic conditions. We have witnessed a decrease in global COVID rates, the reopening of tourism in November 2021, economic restructuring, the effects of monetary reforms, and the growth of the non-state sector.

What do you now predict for Cuba's economy, given the perspective of time?

Well, since January 2021 we have seen first Scenario 1, then the beginnings of Scenario 2.

In the first half of 2021, with the twin external shocks of a surge in COVID infection rates and U.S. sanctions biting more deeply than ever, the resumption of economic growth was impossible. In this context, the January exchange rate reform added to economic disruption and difficulties for Cuban families.

As anticipated, the reform produced a one-off price shock. It is impossible to give a single rate of inflation that represents the experience of every Cuban household during such radical realignment of relative prices, and the official consumer prices index showing 44% consumer prices inflation in January certainly understated the impact for some. For those dependent on state employment or benefits, the increase in the cost of living was more than covered by a one-off hike in wage and social security payments introduced in December 2020 in anticipation of this adjustment; but for those dependent on non-state earnings, which were largely linked to the now non-existent tourist trade, there was no automatic adjustment to compensate for inflation. In the following months, with the acute supply shortages precipitated by the external shocks, prices continued to rise, and attempts to control them served to exacerbate shortages and queues, and the diversion of goods to illegal markets fed tensions between Cubans. Widespread alarm reflected everyday frustrations and hardships, and fear of the real danger of an uncontrolled inflationary spiral.

For Cuban producers, the new relative prices that were supposed to have incentivized innovations to improve efficiency failed to do so. Inflation, recession, an acute shortage of foreign exchange, U.S. sanctions, and an underdeveloped financial system together made restructuring all but impossible. During the economic emergency, centralized allocation of resources was needed both to ensure that basic needs were met and to keep state companies operating (with an indefinite extension of the one-year adjustment period), which meant the postponement of the intended drive toward decentralized decision-making in response to less distorted price signals.

However, by the end of the year, a rapid and successful vaccination campaign had radically reduced COVID infections, while the authorities had managed to restrain inflation and international travel was starting to return, albeit very gradually. So, the beginnings of Scenario 2 were coming into view. Also, two further changes—the opening to non-state business, and decentralization of economic planning from central to municipal government level—mean that the economic system that has been emerging from the recession is very different from the pre-COVID one.

What do you expect to see by the end of this year and going into early 2023?

In the first half of 2022, some sort of economic recovery has begun. But how strong and sustained the growth will be depends on domestic, as well as external, conditions.

With a new set of relative prices, along with reforms of business organization and economic management, there is potential for a wave of innovation and growth within the domestic economy. However, still weighing on performance this year are depressed foreign exchange earnings, national income, and living standards; prices distorted by an overvalued official exchange rate and remaining state-controlled, segmented markets; and legacies of the old economic model and habits.

The dearth of published official data prevents close monitoring, making forecasting even more hazardous than it would otherwise be in the context of the changes under way, but there are some indications that efforts to mobilize the country's latent resources to spur innovation, restructuring, and improved living conditions are taking effect.

There seems to have been a swift response to the opening to new forms of private business, with thousands of new micro, small, and medium-sized businesses having been registered. But to flourish, the new entrepreneurs will require all the infrastructure that supports successful business: not only finance for capital investment but also premises, access to reliable suppliers, clear legal frameworks and protections, new management skills, and access to markets. The government appears to be struggling to put these in place, and despite pockets of enthusiasm and innovation, the current surge in emigration indicates that many young people are not yet convinced that the opportunities are worth staying for.

Although external conditions have been improved by the partial recovery of tourism (in January–May 2022 arrivals were around one-quarter of the 2019 pre-COVID level), on the whole, they are not very favorable for Cuban recovery prospects. Growth in tourism source countries remains depressed; high international prices for food and energy, which together absorb around half of the country's import capacity, represent a heavy burden; and despite some small positive changes in terms of travel and remittances, the U.S. administration has not yet indicated any appetite for relaxing the most important sanctions. That said, strengthening bilateral ties with other partners (both U.S. allies such as Canada and the EU, and its rivals including Russia and China) have brought cooperation programs, some debt relief, and much-needed new lines of credit.

Finally, there is still an exchange rate problem. To be economically efficient and internationally competitive, the new businesses as well as the old state enterprises that still dominate large-scale industrial production, need to be able to respond to price signals that are broadly in line with international markets. But this is not going to happen for as long as the exchange rate distortion remains. Due to the recent inflation the overvaluation of the official value of the Cuban peso, at 24 CUP = 1 USD, still fails to provide sufficient incentive for export growth or import substitution. Meanwhile, the black-market rate, which values the Cuban peso at around a quarter of the official rate (around 100 CUP = 1 USD), continues to incentivize informal economic activity that not only evades taxation and perpetuates low-productivity employment, but also encompasses theft from the formal economy.

The authorities are understandably reluctant to further devalue the official rate at the risk of resurgent inflation. Instead, they suggest that as foreign exchange inflows and domestic production improve, the black-market value of the peso will appreciate. But as it is unlikely to reach the official rate any time soon, it looks like the Cuban economy will continue to be encumbered by the exchange rate and price distortions for a while yet.

So, prediction is difficult. The official 4% growth forecast for 2022, leaving GDP still 6% below its 2019 level, seems suitably cautious. In 2023, in the absence of further shocks (a brave assumption given the experience of the past few years), I would expect a stronger and more broad-based recovery stemming from restructuring and reform.

Reference

de la Torre, A., & Ize, A. (2014, January 10). *Exchange rate unification: The Cuban case*. The Brookings Institution. Retrieved November 25, 2021, from https://www.brookings.edu/research/exchange-rate-unification-the-cuban-case/

PART III

The Industrial Zones

CHAPTER 15

ZED Mariel: Interview with General Director Ana Teresa Igarza

Ana Teresa Igarza Martínez is the General Director of the Mariel Special Development Zone Office. She holds a Law Degree, with a Gold Degree and a Diploma in Public Administration. Ms. Igarza has been practicing law for 17 years, working in the Courts as a professional judge and later as a legal advisor in corporate activity. Since March 2018, Ms. Igarza is Deputy to the National Assembly of People's Power for Bauta municipality, Artemisa province (Fig. 15.1).

Hernández: Decree Law 165 of 1995 established four export processing zones (EPZs), built to attract manufacturing, job creation, and boost exports. In 2004, I understand they were renamed as development zones. And then they were closed. It was reported that the reasons for the closure of EPZs were based on two factors: the cost of labor compared to similar markets nearby), the lack of free trade agreements, and, specifically, the closed U.S. market. Economist Richard Feinberg called them a "failed experiment."[1]

[1] In the 2012 Latin America Initiative at Brookings' publication, "*The New Cuban Economy: What Roles for Foreign Investment?*" economist Richard E. Feinberg called Cuba's FTZs, "Free Trade Zones: A Failed Experiment." In updated research for his book, "*Open for Business*" (2016), "Foreign Trade and Development Zones: Learning from Past Mistakes?" it was, indeed, too early to properly assess the success or failure of the FTZ experience.

T. K. Hernández, *The Cuba Interviews*,
https://doi.org/10.1007/978-3-031-30203-9_15

Fig. 15.1 Ana Teresa Igarza, General Director at the Mariel Special Development Zone (Photo by the editor)

In 2013, Decree Law 313 established the Mariel Special Development Zone, which was inaugurated in January 2014. From what I have seen now by visiting ZED Mariel twice this month, there has been incredible development. Would you say that ZED Mariel is on the road to success?

Ana Teresa Igarza: Special development zones are an experience that did not begin in the twenty-first century. The first experience of a special zone was in Ireland, near Shannon airport in 1959 with a cluster for vehicle production. Later, Europe and Asia adopted this model and developed their own according to the conditions of the areas where they were to be established. But they all had four elements in common, the development of infrastructure, the approval of the regulatory framework, a development approach based on these development activities, and the fourth element, government support for these areas to be able to implement special policies and regimes.

It is precisely these four elements that we used to develop the concept of the Mariel Special Development Zone.

In order to define the Mariel Special Development Zone, we also took into account the analysis of the experience of the defunct free trade zones to which you referred, created in compliance with Decree 165.

As you mentioned, Feinberg is right when he says they failed; our assessment is that the experience of those four FTZs was dysfunctional.

That is why, in 2011, when the Party Congress approved the guidelines for updating the Cuban model of economic and social development of the Revolution, among them was one that referred to developing special development zones in the country. From that moment on, we set ourselves the task of studying the international experiences of successful economic zones.

In 2013, two years after studying international experiences, various international regulatory frameworks of these development zones, as well as talking with the managers of the previous free trade zones in Cuba, we came up with the concept of Mariel Special Development Zone.

In these almost nine years since the creation of the Mariel Special Development Zone, we have implemented a regulatory framework that was adopted and which clearly established that the main objective was to attract investments that create value-added goods and services, using innovation and knowledge, as well as clean technologies.

All of these attributes of the Mariel Special Development Zone are related to the national interests of import substitution, export promotion, and job creation.

Normally in the world, what they do is develop the infrastructure in parallel with the drafting of the legislation for the regulatory framework and, once those elements are completed, then they launch the zone and start attracting investment. We, in our case, adopted the legal framework and then, in parallel, developed the infrastructure and attracted investment.

The Mariel Special Development Zone was inaugurated on November 1, 2013. The first infrastructure was the container terminal, which was officially inaugurated on January 27, 2014. It was the first and only infrastructure existing at that time in the Zone.

That was one of the main challenges we had to face at that time: how to attract an investor to establish a company in an area that will be urbanized in the future but is not yet urbanized. That was the main challenge to develop infrastructure and, at the same time, attract foreign investment.

We were defining priorities by economic sectors in this work of attracting investment.

Then, in the process of attracting investments, we needed to do it in an orderly manner so that in the future they would have a structure within the Zone and not improvise by attracting any type of investment and establishing companies here and there, which would then generate an impact in the future. So, we had to structure the development of infrastructure, plan each area and draw up a strategy for attracting it.

At that time, we only had as infrastructure the container terminal and a very, very basic infrastructure around it. With that, we took on the task of hiring a company to make the master plan of this first area to be urbanized, which is sector A, as well as to hire a consulting firm to make a market study of the area.

Hernandez: What a challenge!

Ms. Igarza: Immense.

At that time, it was very difficult because these lands were virgin from the first traffic circle encountered on your way here to the sea, there was nothing. Just vegetation.

We had a map, and, on the map, we would show the investors where we were going to locate their factory or their facilities. At that time, they would ask us to visit the place, to get to that site. And we would say that it was impossible because there was no access. We explained to them that, at the same time, we were working on the design of the infrastructure, including the roads that would give access to those areas. And the most gratifying and challenging thing at that time was that the first potential investors who faced that situation, trusted us. The best reward is that those early investors have been so successful today that they are reinvesting in expanding their facilities and production. Even today, more than two years after the pandemic that has impacted us very seriously and the economic crisis, they are still reinvesting.

This is what I have heard. Despite COVID, there is still foreign investment in Cuba. But perhaps it is calmer because of the situation with the United States.

Ms. Igarza: Yes. In fact, I can tell you that in the last two years, in addition to COVID, there has been increased persecution of our investors, of their financial and banking operations, and that threatens some companies. That is why we have decided to protect them and not to disclose information because they, the United States, have been aggressively pursuing all their operations.

We always consult and there are several companies that don't care. They say we can post any information about their company here.

We do it to protect the origin of the company, the shareholders, and the parent company. But in some cases, they don't care. Others ask for confidentiality.

It is very interesting that early investors reinvest.

Ms. Igarza: They have made several reinvestments. They have reinvested more than once. In the middle of COVID, they presented the proposal to reinvest to expand their activities and with it, the capital. After a year, a year and a half after the first reinvestment, that is, at the beginning of this year, they are going to propose a second reinvestment. For us, these companies are our first and foremost promoters. Because as a company you can make an investment somewhere and it doesn't do badly, or it doesn't do well either, but you say I'm already here; I'll stay.

Now, when companies decide to reinvest their profits and expand the scope of their activities, it is a sign that things are going well for them and that there are conditions to invest in that zone, there is confidence. Apart from the regulatory framework, which is the most attractive compared to the rest of our country and the regional environment, because we, as members of the Free Zone Association of the Americas,[2] have studied and compared the regulatory framework and incentives of all members and we describe the incentives that we offer. In addition to those incentives and the regulatory framework, there are two key elements that distinguish our Zone.

The first is the financial and banking scheme that we apply in the ZED Mariel, which consists of the fact that all companies operating here in Mariel always do so in freely convertible currency. They are not subject to the administrative and exchange control mechanisms, and this facilitates permanent and free access to their currency. This scheme allows companies to have permanent liquidity in their bank accounts at all times.

And the second element that distinguishes us is our One-Stop Shop system. Our office, accompanied by representatives of 14 government entities, channels all applications for licenses, authorizations, and permits.

[2] Cuba is a member of the Free Trade Zones Association of the Americas (AZFA), a non-profit organization representing more than 10,000 tenants in 600 FTZs in 23 countries. It is the most important regional Free Trade Zone Association in Latin America. For more information: https://www.asociacionzonasfrancas.org/es/.

In addition, the office staff provides personalized and permanent assistance to our investors. That means that all requirements, absolutely all requirements of the companies established here, are channeled through our office; they do not have to go to different government offices to process their applications. And for anything they need, they just come to us. And we do it on their behalf.

Has anyone compared the speed between the previous process and the Single Window?

Ms. Igarza: Our office has had that system since we started operating. But, when we started, we reviewed all the procedures of each government office for applications and issuance of licenses, permits. When we were informed of their procedures, we realized that the process took too long, or sometimes there was no time frame established in the rules for issuing a license. And the first definition that we agreed upon between the Bureau and the licensing agencies was that no license application could take more than a month. In addition, working together with those government offices we have reduced the number of documents to be submitted to process a license application. This is an ongoing review process to reduce them to a minimum.

From the very first meetings we have with a potential new investor, we explain the documents to them and give them the guidelines for drafting those documents. It is not a matter of them preparing the documents themselves, but we accompany them in the process of drafting all the documents, making sure they meet the requirements.

Our office has two functions. The first is to manage the Zone and to ensure the coherence of the activities of all those who operate in it, within the political guidelines, the governing bodies, and the government. This is why the office reports directly to the Council of Ministers, precisely to articulate all the structures operating within and outside the Zone and to ensure the development of the Zone itself. The second important function is to accompany our investors because it is not possible to manage the Zone without accompanying and protecting our investors.

Regarding wages for ZEDM workers: What are the established wages? Are there different wage levels for different types of work? What is the tax rate? Does the investor pay wages in CUP? What percentage of the worker's salary goes to the employment agency (contracting entity)?

Ms. Igarza: I believe that before talking about salaries, we must take into account the special policies applicable to those who establish themselves in the ZED Mariel. In order to make that highly qualified labor force available to foreign investors, certain policies had to be established. During the first years of the ZED Mariel and until the implementation of the monetary and exchange unification, we applied particular policies to encourage the labor force to work in the Zone.

The hiring of the labor force is free and its value is negotiated between the investor and the employing entity that is in charge of providing the labor recruitment service.

Today there is satisfaction in recruitment. In the early years, when we entered a recently created province (Artemisa), most of the workforce came from the capital. At the beginning, 70% of the workers came from Havana and only 30% from the province. In the beginning, there were no more than 5,000 indirect workers, mainly linked to the development of infrastructure.

From the work carried out with the (provincial) authorities of Artemisa, linked to the training of the labor force, both workers and technical and professional personnel, the situation is different. Today 70% of the workers come from the province of Artemisa.

As a support, we developed a population settlement. We have a housing construction program to provide housing for workers in the ZED Mariel.

We have continued to work on improving the labor regime and within this, the salary regime of those working in the Mariel Special Development Zone.

The objective is to maintain attractive salaries so that workers prefer to work here. Today there are more than 15,000 workers and the average salary is 11,500. This is also good for the province because this workforce works closer to home and receives higher salaries than the rest of the workers in other companies.

Compared to other zones, for example, Costa Rica, is the salary paid by foreign investors higher in the ZED Mariel compared to industrial zones in other countries?

Ms. Igarza: Well, it depends, because it is relative, if you compare it with other surrounding countries. In Cuba, for example, that salary is paid, and the investor pays in hard currency and the worker receives the salary in Cuban pesos at the official exchange rate, but the type of area and the qualification demanded, among others, must be taken into account.

In Costa Rica, for example, there are areas with high technology, but others are mostly intensive manufacturing areas where the level of knowledge of workers is lower than what is demanded here where we require a higher professional level of the workforce, and obviously, unskilled labor is not paid the same wages as highly skilled labor. So we say that the comparison is relative. We will have to compare jobs in different countries, but we are modeling at the same level.

How does the ZED Mariel contribute to Cuba's sustainable economic development?

Ms. Igarza: The Zone is part of the updating of the Cuban economic model. When it was created, among other things, we carried out a market study that, based on our needs and potential, would allow us to attract foreign investment. We defined three pillar industries to attract investment: biotechnology and the pharmaceutical industry, because of Cuba's strength in that industry; logistics services because they are essential to ensure the flow of incoming and outgoing goods, storage, and processing platforms. The second is advanced manufacturing in general, which includes metal mechanics, food production, construction materials, packaging, chemical products, as well as personal and household consumer goods.

When you evaluate Cuba's economic and social development strategy until 2030, you can see that the main industries that need to be developed in order for us to ensure those goals are present in the ZED Mariel; among others are infrastructure development, logistics, construction materials, renewable energies.

In the strategy until 2030, some of the objectives and programs are aimed at satisfying the needs of our population, developing tourism, and ensuring the local production of the main inputs required by the industry, and developing our own packaging industry, among several others. And when you compare those and relate them to the Zone's Business and Development Program they complement each other.

The amount of investment attracted in the ZED Mariel in these more than eight years exceeds $3 billion, corresponding to the 62 businesses established. That is the amount of investment committed. But we would not be happy if it were only the amount committed. We are happy when investments are made. We are happy when it has been invested. Half of it, that is, one and a half billion dollars has already been invested. So those factories that have already been completed, they are operating and producing, they are supplying the domestic market and they are also exporting part of their products, which is an achievement.

Unlike in the beginning, we now have plots of land, already developed, that we can show to investors.

Ms. Igarza, the Mariel Special Development Zone has come a long way since the early days when it was just a container port and empty fields. Indeed, it is a project with a vision and a future. I would like to thank you and I am very, very grateful for your time.

References

Asociación de Zonas Francas de las Américas. (n.d.). *AZFA—Asociación de Zonas Francas de las américas: AZFA*. Retrieved August 28, 2022, from https://www.asociacionzonasfrancas.org/es/

Feinberg, R. E. (2012). The new Cuban economy: What roles for foreign investment? *Latin America Initiative at Brookings*, 16–18. Retrieved April 15, 2022, from https://www.brookings.edu/wp-content/uploads/2016/06/cuba-economy-feinberg-9.pdf

Feinberg, R. E. (2016). Opening to foreign investment: New portfolio opportunities. In *Open for business: Building the new Cuban economy*. Brookings Institution Press.

CHAPTER 16

Interview with Huong Nguyen, Business Manager, ViMariel

Huong Nguyen, ViMariel's Business Manager, and I, first met at the offices of ViMariel in May 2022. I was grateful for the opportunity to include Vietnam, another international investor in Cuba, in this work (Fig. 16.1).

Ms. Nguyen is a bright and intelligent young woman, possessing an infectious enthusiasm for her work that seems reflected in the spirit of the sign that hangs over the office entrance, "Never Say Tomorrow."

On the day we first met, she gave a presentation on the company's investment in Cuba.

We also hopped in her car for a tour around the ViMariel concession. We drove along the roads, prepped, ready and waiting, for their final coat of asphalt. It's evident there's been incredible progress during the two years of COVID lockdown. The concrete manufacturing plant and the extension to it is up and running. We also passed the site of an upcoming Spanish investment.

Ms. Nguyen's presentation was an eye-opener to Vietnam's dynamic path of economic development known as the *Đổi M'ơi* (renovation) period which began in 1986. By any evaluation, it is an astounding success story. I'm left with the thought; this is how it's done.

Several days later, we held our interview in a secluded corner of the busy lobby of the Habana Libre Hotel.

T. K. Hernández, *The Cuba Interviews*,
https://doi.org/10.1007/978-3-031-30203-9_16

Fig. 16.1 Huong Nguyen, Business Manager at ViMariel (From the personal collection of Nguyen)

Ms. Nguyen first came to Cuba as a student in 2009 to study psychology at the University of Havana. In 2015, she graduated.

This is not Ms. Nguyen's first position at the ZED Mariel. In 2016, she began as an Investment Specialist and later became the Human Resources Manager at another Vietnamese company.

Ms. Nguyen speaks four languages: Vietnamese, Spanish, Portuguese, and English.

Hernández: Please tell us about ViMariel. When did your company sign an agreement with Cuba and the ZEDM to create an economic zone? What were the motivations to build an economic zone in Cuba?

Huong Nguyen: Thank you so much for the question. I would like to say that we come from Vietnam, a country with more than three decades of working on foreign direct investment promotion. Since 1986, to develop a deepened integration into regional and world economies, our government started carrying out many measures with the promulgation of foreign investment law and numerous amendments, alongside other legal-economic reforms on trading rights, the tariffication of non-tariff barriers, etc. As a result, Vietnam has 406 industrial parks, 18 coastal economic zones, and 26 border gate economic zones, attracting over 21,000 domestic and foreign investment projects with a total registered capital of about 340 billion USD. During that period, as a country, we have been researching, studying, and improving our legal framework to turn Vietnam into an increasingly attractive destination for foreign investment inflows. At the same time, it allows Vietnamese enterprises to gain more experience in the real estate field, technical infrastructure development, and FDI inflows promotion.

You asked me why we chose Cuba; I think first we have to mention the solid foundation of relations between Cuba and Vietnam since December 1960. Thanks to that relationship, every year both governments organize many high-level visits to build on the mutual relationship of collaboration, trading, and investment activities. This was also an important element that contributed to our successful installation in the Mariel Special Development Zone as its first and only concessionaire.

In February 2018, our company and the Mariel Special Development Zone signed an agreement to create ViMariel JSC, a company with 100% foreign capital to be responsible for the development of technical infrastructure and attracting foreign investment into the concession area of 156.24 hectares.

In July 2018, we hosted the groundbreaking ceremony and began all the paperwork and requests for sub-licenses including ground leveling and technical infrastructure. To offer better support to investors during the investment process, ViMariel JSC registered with the Ministry of Construction (MICONS) to provide technical consulting, construction, and designing services in the ZED Mariel Zone.

With this project, the first one of its type in Cuba, we hope to bring our experience and administrative methods to Cuba, to share our knowledge in this field, and contribute to the development of the Mariel Zone as a macro project.

What challenges did ViMariel face in its development?

Ms. Nguyen: Our construction activity began in May 2019, six months before the beginning of the COVID-19 era, when the entire world changed. It became impossible to travel or organize in-person meetings. Instead of ceasing all activities, we concentrated on developing the infrastructure and taking advantage in technological development and organizing online events for the promotional purposes.

Did the company use Vietnamese or Cuban workers or a combination of both for the construction?

Ms. Nguyen: We have workers from both nations. Besides, highly experienced personnel from Vietnam, who have been working in different infrastructure development projects in Vietnam, we also hired local employees through Cuban employment agencies to accomplish our commitment as a concessionaire regarding the capacitation and training activities, especially in infrastructure development, such as ground leveling and underground system execution.

That's excellent. You spent the two years of COVID building the infrastructure. That's a spectacular achievement. What does ViMariel offer to investors?

Ms. Nguyen: The first thing that you see when you arrive is the prepared infrastructure. If you make an investment within the Mariel zone, or in another territory of Cuba, you will have to start with a base with no ground leveling, which means time and cost you have to fork out.

If you choose our area to build a factory, this is already complete. Our entire area has been urbanized with technical infrastructure systems such as electricity, water supply, wastewater treatment, telecommunication services, etc. This is a very important element because it is time-saving.

The second element we refer to as the "three-in-one" infrastructure, is the information platform, which provides information to our investors in a shorter period of time. As an investor, we have developed effective networking and relationships with entities from different fields of the Cuban economy which assist us in any research such as information about the local market, the priority level for Cuba, and the possibility of exporting to support the investors in their decision-making process.

Regarding the third platform, we refer to connectivity with different markets all over the world, especially from Asia due to our networking and experience in international commerce. We can connect our investors with their potential partners and suppliers to ensure their productive and commercial activities.

This is quite an achievement. ViMariel's north concession has the installed infrastructure. You have the connection to government entities and the Asian markets, and Cuba has the connections to North and South American markets. What type of information do you

provide to an investor when they first inquire about investing in ViMariel's economic zone?

Ms. Nguyen: When you intend to make business in a new market, you must have information about it, and you must know about the demand, what people need or which kind of market, the local market or foreign market to focus on.

Many investors have told us they face many challenges to get information from some Cuban authorities, delays in gaining that information, or the information isn't complete enough to make decisions.

Once identified as a negative issue, we have been working to fix this problem and now, we have the solution. So, any investor from any sector, when they ask us for information they need, we can get a reply in seven days or less.

You're doing the important legwork for a potential investor with a time frame of only seven days. This is very advantageous for investing. The three-in-one infrastructure, the connectivity, the access, the services are there.

Ms. Nguyen: Yes. This is the one point we talk about the information and, of course, during the investment process. We commit to support our investors, representing them, and tracking the procedures with Cuban authorities.

Are you using the VUINEX One-Stop Shop system?

Ms. Nguyen: We work with the Mariel office One-Stop Shop system instead of VUINEX for two main reasons: First, this one was created especially for investors who develop a project in the Zone to provide direct communication with the organization and presents the proposal to the government entity for approval. During the investment process, the same office tracks the procedure and makes sure that the company is proceeding correctly and on time, all the steps according to the legal norm.

Second, when we started our research on the decision to make the investment in the Special Development Zone, the VUINEX system wasn't established yet.

But even if it was, we would choose Mariel office One-Stop Shop system. We consider it the ideal platform for investors into the Zone.

You took me on a tour of the ViMariel zone today. Can you tell us more about the concrete factory we saw in the concession?

Ms. Nguyen: That is one challenge we had to overcome as a provider of designing and building services to investors. We had to prepare some basic conditions to ensure our accomplishment with the schedule of the construction. One facility was the concrete plant. It helps us become proactive with our plan, instead of depending on other suppliers. One important element is that we work on a non-stop schedule, from Monday to Saturday every week, so guaranteeing all materials on site is the key element to ensure our success.

There is a shortage of precast concrete?

Ms. Nguyen: We did it to avoid any interruption to our schedule and to reduce precast concrete cost as well, so it allows us to offer better prices for construction services.

The other positive point is that the excess amount of precast concrete could be sold to other investors or builders through a sale and purchase agreement.

You also mentioned you will sell this to Cuba.

Ms. Nguyen: Yes. We have the approval to produce and use concrete for our building. The quantities that we don't need, we can sell to other investors inside of the Mariel Zone.

We consider this one of most important elements that allows us to accomplish our schedule, but also contributes to ensuring the construction activities of other investors, and creates conditions to become more competitive in our services fees.

When an investor comes to see you at the ViMariel, what do you need from them? What do investors need to know in the way of information/help from ViMariel?

Ms. Nguyen: At ViMariel, we don't just supply services; we offer solutions.

In order to do that, during the discussions with the investors, our priority is identifying the problem. We can then propose the adequate solution for their decisions and their needs.

Besides meetings, we help our potential investors complete a form called the "*ficha informative,*" an official form created by the Mariel office to capture company information, the core business, the schedule to develop a project, and general data regarding their requirements for technical services, human resources, and residuals of the industry.

This data allows us to identify if the intention meets all requirements to be implemented into ViMariel Economic Zone. If not, we can send it to the Mariel office where they will help them define the adequate area for the project.

For example, the urbanization of our concession doesn't have approval for agriculture activities. We then ask the Mariel office to identify other areas near the economic zone for these objectives, so the industrial activities related to the product of the activity could be installed into our park.

This form will be sent to Mariel offices for their approval. Then the investor could start with the paperwork to request the license to implement their industries.

Can we discuss employment at ViMariel. Can you hire your own workers, or do you have to work with a Cuban employment agency? What are the costs of labor?

Ms. Nguyen: There are five employment agencies available to the investor through which they can discuss prices and salary levels for each position. Except for the percentage of social security and vacation, you can negotiate all elements to meet your budget. As far as the regulation goes, the salary level should be higher than the minimum established amount in the Mariel Zone, which is 3,990 CUP (approximately 310 USD according to official rate between the U.S. dollar and the CUP).

Once you contract with an employment agency, all you have to do is hire the employees, administrating them according to your company procedure. The employment agency ensures the processes of paying salary, social security, and other paperwork.

Can you discuss salaries?

Ms. Nguyen: Yes, of course. I think there is flexibility. We don't negotiate the salary with the worker but with the agency. Different job levels are paid different salaries.

How does the ViMariel concession benefit the surrounding population? Or is it too early to tell at this point?

Ms. Nguyen: The concession contributes to local development from different aspects.

For example, first, employment creation. Despite the variety of industries inside the park and the close distance, the workforce from the surrounding population will be the priority for any company there.

Second, as far as we experienced, near an economic zone, there are many opportunities to create secondary services and logistic platforms for local and foreign personnel, and companies. For example, housing rentals, taxi services, mechanical services, etc. That means additional sources of income for the population and elevated living conditions.

Third, there is the possibility of improving living conditions with better infrastructure and services. The reason is, when a government works to industrialize a zone, they should prepare and enhance the quality of existing infrastructure such as hospitals, schools, residences, banks, etc. As a result, it allows the population easier access to that platform and services.

In summary, there are many elements that can improve the living conditions, employment, and incomes sources, contributing to the development of the surrounding population.

I noticed in the video you presented of Vietnam's industrial zones you had constructed housing for the employees. Is that in the plans for ViMariel?

Ms. Nguyen: Yes, it is. Nowadays, this is one of the biggest difficulties in Cuba, of employees living far away from our Zone. It could affect productivity such as late arrivals because of transportation issues, tiredness from commuting, etc. This problem exists not only in Cuba but in every country. So, to solve this problem in the future, we build housing for employees and experts. That is the solution we solved in our industrial zones in Vietnam.

Is ViMariel pleased with the recent economic reforms beginning with currency unification in January 2021?

Ms. Nguyen: Yes, absolutely. I think it's been one of the best benefits, not only for ViMariel but also for any foreign investor. This is about the unification of the currency. It reduces the investment cost. Why do I say that?

Because before that move, the currency was based on the CUC. The CUP is equal to one dollar. All the activity when you invest is now in CUP. Everything is expensive, especially in the workforce because before the currency unification, if you pay 100 USD to your employee, they will receive 1,000 CUP (with the applied coefficient 10 times for salary payment within the Mariel Zone). However, nowadays, with the 100 USD you pay, the employee will receive 2,400 CUP. In summary, as you can see, we now save $60 to pay the same salary to the employee. We have the opportunity now to create an employee incentive fund program to reward our employees.

With currency unification, the same thing has happened to services and products we purchase from local suppliers.

You're buying materials with the CUP now?

Ms. Nguyen: No. All banking transactions of foreign companies within the ZED Mariel are done in foreign currency.

This concludes our interview, Huong. I thank you so much. It's been a delight to meet you and I'm honored for this opportunity to witness the remarkable progress achieved at ViMariel.

Ms. Nguyen: Thank you so much for having me today and for allowing me to represent ViMariel Economic Zone to share our motivations and reasons to invest in Cuba, especially in Mariel Zone. I am happy to share our products and services, our strengths and benefits we offer to investors when they implement their investment into the ViMariel Economic Zone. Once again, thank you and I hope the best success for your book.

PART IV

Banking

CHAPTER 17

Interview with Minister-President Marta Sabina Wilson González

Minister-President Marta Sabina Wilson González has had an extensive and distinguished career in banking. Beginning in 1988 at the National Bank of Cuba (the former name of the bank until 1997), she has held various positions at the Central Bank of Cuba, Banco Exterior de Cuba, and Banco de Exportación y Comercio, C.A. in Venezuela (Fig. 17.1).

The Minister holds a Bachelor's degree in Economics and a Master's in Finance from the University of Havana. In addition, she has obtained postgraduate diplomas in Banking and Markets, Financial Engineering, Corporate Financial Management, Business Management, Specialization in Central Banking, Commercial Banking Instruments and Mechanisms, and others from the University.

She began her career in banking in 1988, working in foreign exchange, balance of payments operations, macroeconomics and risk analysis. Ms. Wilson has also conducted many studies in monetary and credit policies and international economics.

From 2007 to 2012, she worked at Banco Exterior de Cuba as the Commercial Director. In 2012, she was appointed as Chief Executive Officer at Banco de Exportación y Comercio, C.A. She returned to Banco Exterior in 2018 as vice president and then promoted the same year to president.

T. K. Hernández, *The Cuba Interviews*,
https://doi.org/10.1007/978-3-031-30203-9_17

Fig. 17.1 Minister-President, Marta Wilson González, of the Central Bank of Cuba (Photo by the editor)

Appointed as a member of the Council of Ministers on December 21, 2019, President Miguel Díaz-Canel Bermúdez nominated Ms. Wilson as Minister-President of the Central Bank of Cuba on that date.

I interviewed Minister-President Wilson at the head office of the Central Bank in Old Havana in early June 2022.

Hernández: In a recent article published in Granma,[1] the analysis of the Cuban banking system demonstrated the need for modernization and transformation that "contributes to the economic and social development of the country." This is a great responsibility. What measures are being taken to strengthen and modernize the banking institutions in Cuba?

Minister-President Marta Wilson: The Cuban financial system consists of nine banks, 13 non-bank financial institutions, and 11 representative offices of foreign financial institutions.

The Cuban economy remains in a process of transformations that allow the implementation of the economic model designed for the development of the country, as set out in the components of the National Economic and Social Development Plan until 2030, which determines that the National Banking System develops to respond to the challenges and imperatives of the proposed goals.

The aspects that characterize the strengthening of Cuban banking to date can be summarized as follows:

Raise the technical-professional training of specialists and managers of the banking system, as one of the edges of the financial education strategy designed in the country.

Strengthen control mechanisms for the use of banking services with rigorous compliance with FATF recommendations[2] to combat money laundering, financing of terrorism, and weapons of mass destruction.

Promote electronic banking services with the use of electronic means of payment through the platforms available for this purpose, as well as remote banking, and ways to facilitate non-face-to-face operations in bank branches and provide convenience to customers.

Diversification of banking products and services according to the different players in the economy, particularly local development projects, non-agricultural cooperatives, and micro, small, and medium-sized enterprises.

[1] Granma (2022, April 8). *El país demanda UN Sistema Bancario Moderno y Activo*. Granma.cu. Available at: https://www.granma.cu/cuba/2022-04-08/el-pais-demanda-un-sistema-bancario-moderno-y-activo-08-04-2022-01-04-12.

[2] FATF is the acronym for the Financial Action Task Force, the inter-governmental global organization has established recommendations (standards) to prevent organized crime, corruption, money laundering, and terrorist financing. The banking system in Cuba abides by these recommendations. For more information: https://www.fatf-gafi.org/about/.

Support the growth of the Central Bank of Cuba's Guarantee Fund to back up the riskiest credit operations.

Establish specialized services for strategic sectors, as in the case of agriculture and the sugar agro-industry, for which the treatment of agricultural development banking is introduced for the benefit of producers with more advantageous financing conditions.

Work on the institutional redesign of the system, including the proposed specialization of development banking, with a view to promoting investment processes.

This is a huge task, how are you going to communicate this to people so that they understand it? I would say that about ten years ago people didn't use banks or bank cards or use payment platforms in Cuba. I think it is a culture.

Minister-President: As part of the work mechanisms, macro-programs, programs, and projects have been designed to enable the institutions to comply with the Social Economic Strategy and the National Economic and Social Development Plan through 2030.

Within the Institutionalism and Macroeconomics Macroprogram, the Financial System program was designed to develop a project called the "Financial Inclusion and Education and Development of Payment Systems."

I must point out that, although we do not want to talk about politics in the interview, we cannot fail to mention the effects of the U.S. blockade of Cuba, which has a marked impact on the Cuban financial system in many aspects, including the acquisition of new technologies[3] that allow us to offer a better service to the population. In recent years, a great effort has been made to introduce the use of electronic payments and the use of different means of payment. For example, at the end of April of this year, 12.8 million magnetic cards have been issued, and 43% of the operations carried out by the banking system were made through electronic channels. In addition, the *Enzona* and *Transfermovil* platforms have been created, allowing payments for different services and transfers between accounts, which contribute to the provision of a better service to the population and the rest of the economic actors, as well as to the development of electronic commerce.

[3] The technology regulations can be viewed at: Monjay, R. (2022, April 4). Export Administration Regulations. Bureau of Industry and Security: https://www.bis.doc.gov/index.php/documents/regulations-docs/2336-ccl5-pt1-3/file.

Hence the importance of financial education aimed at the different economic actors and the population to provide them with the necessary knowledge to incorporate these services into their economic and personal lives.

How does the BCC support the growth of the non-state sector, which is expected to contribute to growth and sustainable economic development? What banking services does it provide to the private sector (taxes? bill payments? fund transfers? clarification of banking regulations? etc.) Does it have a "small business banking" department?

Minister-President: The non-state sector in Cuba is not new, it has existed for some years, previously constituted under the figure of the self-employed, so this sector has always had the support and accompaniment of the banking system. Micro, small, and medium enterprises (MSMEs) are a sector of interest in terms of boosting the national economy.[4]

The establishment of these companies has counted from the beginning with the participation of the banking system, so that the Platform of Economic Actors (PAE for its acronym in Spanish), led by the Ministry of Economy and Planning for the processing of incorporation applications, includes the aspects required to facilitate the relations of these new economic agents[5] with the national banking system.

A working style has been developed to accompany MSMEs by the banks, with the purpose of providing them with information about the services provided by the banks, the ways to obtain financing, and its modalities.

MSMEs can access credit in the system's universal banks to finance their current operations and the investments they require for their operations.

They can obtain financing in the form of credit lines, revolving or simple loans, and leases, depending on the characteristics and merit of their businesses.

[4] In a move to stimulate the economy and create employment, Cuba announced the expansion of the non-state sector from 127 to 2,000 types of activities in February of 2021. The application for small business licensing process began in September 2021.

[5] As of August 17, 2022, 4,758 new economic actors have been approved since the process began in September 2021. Of the MSMEs, 4,650 are private, 51 are state-owned and 57 are cooperatives. For more information: http://www.cubadebate.cu/noticias/2022/08/17/ministerio-de-economia-y-planificacion-aprueba-106-nuevas-mipymes-privadas-y-una-cooperativa-no-agropecuaria/.

In order to finance these economic actors, the financial entity FIMELSA was converted into an entity dedicated to this purpose called Financiera de Microcrédito S.A., which together with the entity Financiera Iberoamericana offers financing in foreign currency in accordance with the provisions of the Central Bank of Cuba in this matter.[6]

In this way, the Cuban financial system has created all the conditions to finance and support the development of the new economic actors, of course making the corresponding risk analysis, which allows it to guarantee the return of the borrowed funds.

And of course, we are open to foreign investment to support this sector, which can be carried out through the modality of joint ventures or by creating entities with 100% foreign capital.

Resolution 215 of 2021 determines that the Central Bank of Cuba will issue licenses for virtual asset service providers. Do you see this as a logical option in the face of attacks on the international banking community's ability to transact with Cuban banking institutions in light of continued U.S. sanctions?

Minister-President: The purpose of Resolution 215 of the Central Bank of Cuba[7] is to establish the rules from which the monetary authority, for reasons of socioeconomic interest, regulates the use of certain virtual assets in commercial transactions, as well as the licensing of virtual asset service providers for operations related to financial, exchange, and collection or payment activities, in and from the national territory.

There are examples of swindles with the use of virtual assets that move in wallets through cyberspace and in such sense the Central Bank of Cuba also establishes that natural persons assume the risks and responsibilities that in the civil and criminal order derive from operating with virtual assets and virtual asset service providers that operate outside the banking and financial system, even though transactions with virtual assets between such persons are not prohibited. In such a sense, the resolution establishes

[6] In 1995, Banco Nacional de Cuba granted Banco Sabadell, a Spanish bank, License No. 330, to establish a representative office in Cuba. It shares a 50% joint venture with Grupo Nueva Banca, S.A. in Financiera Iberoamericana. For more information:

Banco Sabadell S.A. Banco Central de Cuba. (n.d.)., from https://www.bc.gob.cu/institucion/oficina/12.

[7] For further information, Resolution 215 of 2021 can be viewed here in the Official Gazette: https://www.gacetaoficial.gob.cu/sites/default/files/goc-2022-o43pdf.pdf.

that natural persons may carry out transactions with crypto assets, but not through financial institutions.

In order for an institution providing virtual services to operate in Cuba, it must apply for a license from the BCC, and the BCC, having complied with the requirements established for this purpose, may grant the license if it is in the country's interest.

It is good to remember that in this modern world, most countries' central banks do not accept cryptocurrencies as legal currency because they are too risky; there is a tendency to prohibit commercial banks to carry out these types of operations and many are studying the possibility of issuing their own virtual currency.

Can you share the latest regulations regarding banking for investors. What are, in your opinion, the most promising and encouraging reforms for investors to come to Cuba?

Minister-President: There are many reasons why foreign investors may choose Cuba to make their investments, among them being a politically stable and safe country, in addition to having a wide portfolio of investment projects in different sectors that could be attractive.

Foreign investment in the Cuban financial system can be established through a mixed or a 100% foreign capital entity. The Central Bank promotes foreign investment in the banking and financial sector and to meet this objective has created a negotiating group composed of specialists with a high level of training and banking experience to carry out the analysis and accompany investors throughout the negotiation process.

The establishment of a totally foreign capital financial institution under the Foreign Investment Law is conditioned to the interested parties being subject to consolidated supervision and located in a country where the Superintendence of the Central Bank of Cuba can sign agreements that ensure adequate coordination and exchange of information with the supervisory authorities of the country of origin, and that they submit the application to the Central Bank of Cuba, accompanied by the required documents.

Documents submitted to the Central Bank of Cuba drafted in a foreign language must be accompanied by their corresponding translations into Spanish.

Certifications of validity and validity issued by the Mercantile Registries are exempted from the legalization and notarization process since they are considered subject to expiration.

For the creation of financial institutions in the country as established in Decree Law 362 of September 14, 2018, "On the Institutions of the Banking and Financial System," the authorization of the Central Bank of Cuba is required through the granting of the corresponding license, and the registration in the Registry of Financial Institutions and Non-Financial Entities within the term set forth in the license.

The license of the Central Bank of Cuba is the administrative authorization for the creation, modification, and dissolution of financial institutions.

In order to obtain a license from the Central Bank of Cuba, a written application must be submitted together with a set of documents.

Once the application is submitted in due form and the procedures in force have been complied with, the President of the Central Bank of Cuba grants or denies the license and issues the corresponding Resolution, within a term of up to 60 working days.

It should also be noted that the procedure for requesting licenses to the Central Bank of Cuba to operate bank accounts in freely convertible currency is governed by the provisions of Resolution 76 of December 26, 2000, while the procedure related to the deposit of funds for the subscription of shares of commercial companies incorporated in the national territory is regulated by Resolution 46 of April 16, 2014.

What are the first steps in obtaining a business bank account?

Minister-President: The Decree Law addresses all the requirements to be taken into account by a foreign investor to invest in the Cuban financial system. We consider that the first thing to do is to identify the modality and investment he/she is willing to make, prepare a project and present it to the negotiating group of the Central Bank, which will analyze the proposal and carry out the required negotiations until it authorizes or not the project presented.

The procedure to request Licenses to the Central Bank of Cuba to operate bank accounts in freely convertible currency is governed by the provisions of Resolution 76 of December 26, 2000; while the procedure related to the deposit of funds for the subscription of shares of commercial companies incorporated in the national territory is regulated by Resolution 46 of April 16, 2014.

Thank you, Minister Wilson. That brings us to the conclusion of this interview. I am very grateful, very honored to meet you.

Annex 1A

The documents required for the establishment of a wholly foreign-owned financial institution under the Foreign Investment Law, as applicable, are as follows:

1. Legal structure of the Group or of the shareholder institution, and the way in which the parent company plans to direct and control the management of the financial institution.
2. Certification from the parent company stating the authorization of the regulatory or supervisory body of the country of origin, for the incorporation of a financial institution in the national territory.
3. Certification of the parent company where the approval of the bylaws and the shareholding structure of the financial institution is evidenced.
4. Draft internal control and operations manual.
5. Any other document that may be established by Cuban law and the Central Bank of Cuba.

In the case of institutions that are subsidiaries, it must express in the corporate name, the evidence of the existing relationship with the parent company.

Annex 1B

To obtain a license from the Central Bank of Cuba for the creation, modification, and dissolution of financial institutions, the application must be submitted in writing, accompanied by at least the following documents, as applicable:

1. Type of institution applying and activity they intend to perform.
2. Duly legalized document accrediting the incorporation of the applicant institution or entity.
3. Duly legalized certification of the Bylaws of the applicant institution or entity.
4. Copies of the financial statements of the applicant institution or entity for the last three (3) fiscal years, certified by external auditors, recognized, and accepted by the Central Bank of Cuba.
5. Feasibility study and business plan.

6. General shareholders' equity and the capital to be subscribed and paid.
7. Organizational structure for the financial institution to be created.
8. Name of the proposed president or highest executive authority of the financial institution for which a leave of absence is requested, as well as of the directors who will occupy higher level positions, accompanied by the curriculum vitae, which accredits the most important activities in the field of economy, banking, and finance that they have carried out and the results achieved with their management.
9. Name, denomination, or corporate name that will identify the financial institution for which a license is requested from the Central Bank of Cuba, a name that cannot coincide with that of another existing institution, and in the case of representative offices, the name of the parent company is added.
10. Commitment to comply with international standards to prevent and combat money laundering, terrorist financing, and the proliferation of weapons of mass destruction.
11. Approval or conformity of the regulatory and supervisory authorities of the country of origin, if applicable, in accordance with the legislation of the country of origin.
12. Any other document established by Cuban law and the Central Bank of Cuba.

Annex 2

Main legislative changes in recent years:

- Resolution 147 of April 20, 2021: states the banking procedure for the management of the financing of Local Development Projects, according to their classification, holders, and sources of financing.
- Resolution 212 of August 16, 2021: states the rules on bank account services applicable to Non-Agricultural Cooperatives (CNA) and Micro-, small-, and medium-sized enterprises (MSMEs).
- Resolution 213 of August 16, 2021: states the general principles and procedures that regulate credits and other banking services for NACs and MSMEs.

- Resolution 249 of September 22, 2021: states that financial institutions may grant credits in foreign currency, to CNAs and MSMEs, prior approval of the Central Bank of Cuba/Microcredits.
- Resolution 89 of April 12, 2022: states the specific requirements for the authorization, operation, regulation, supervision, oversight, corrective mechanisms, and cancelation of licenses for virtual asset service providers operating in and from the national territory.
- Compendium of Resolutions 177 to 183 of November 26, 2020: states the rules for individuals and legal entities related to the monetary and exchange unification, derived from the monetary order process carried out in the country.

References

Banco Sabadell S.A. Banco Central de Cuba. (n.d.). Retrieved July 18, 2022, from https://www.bc.gob.cu/institucion/oficina/12

Central Bank of Cuba (BCC). (2021, August 27). *Resolución 215 de 2021 de Banco Central de Cuba*. Gaceta Oficial. Retrieved April 5, 2022, from https://www.gacetaoficial.gob.cu/es/resolucion-215-de-2021-de-banco-central-de-cuba

Granma. (2022, April 8). *El país demanda un sistema bancario moderno y activo*. Granma.cu. Retrieved April 14, 2022, from https://www.granma.cu/cuba/2022-04-08/el-pais-demanda-un-sistema-bancario-moderno-y-activo-08-04-2022-01-04-12

FATF-GAFI. (n.d.). *Who we are*. Financial Action Task Force (FATF). Retrieved August 16, 2022, from https://www.fatf-gafi.org/about/

Ministerio de Economía y Planificación Aprueba 106 nuevas mipymes privadas y una cooperativa no agropecuaria. Cubadebate. (2022, August 18). Retrieved August 22, 2022, from http://www.cubadebate.cu/noticias/2022/08/17/ministerio-de-economia-y-planificacion-aprueba-106-nuevas-mipymes-privadas-y-una-cooperativa-no-agropecuaria/

Monjay, R. (2022, April 4). *Export Administration Regulations*. Bureau of Industry and Security. Retrieved August 18, 2022, from https://www.bis.doc.gov/index.php/documents/regulations-docs/2336-ccl5-pt1-3/file

PART V

The Lawyers and the Law

CHAPTER 18

The What's-next Scenario for Helms–Burton Claimants—Daniel R. Zim, Attorney

On May 2, 2019, the U.S. government reactivated Title III of the Cuban Liberty and Democratic Solidarity (Libertad) Act of 1996 (known as Helms–Burton) (Fig. 18.1).

As expected, the move opened the door to lawsuits filed in U.S. federal courts where plaintiffs could demand payment for property nationalized or expropriated by post-revolutionary Cuba.

By November, approximately 26 cases[1] had been filed by persons, mostly Cuban Americans from Florida, against U.S. companies not actually operating in Cuba (Bellinger, 2020).

I approached Daniel Zim with a handful of questions on the "what's-next scenario" for Helms–Burton Title III claimants. A lively discussion led to an invitation to interview for publication in the Cuba Business Report.

Mr. Zim is the principal attorney at Zim Travel Law, PLLC, a firm specializing in travel law located in Fairfax County, Virginia. He is also the author of several essays on the U.S.– Cuba relations.

Mr. Zim's published works include an academic paper titled: "Straining the Special Relationship: British and U.S. Policies Toward the Cuban

[1] Bellinger, John B. "The First Year of Helms Burton Lawsuits," www.lawfareblog.com/first-year-helms-burton-lawsuits.

T. K. Hernández, *The Cuba Interviews*,
https://doi.org/10.1007/978-3-031-30203-9_18

Fig. 18.1 U.S. attorney Daniel R. Zim (From the personal collection of Mr. Zim)

Revolution, 1959–1961."[2] The essay examines a new perspective of the U.S.–Cuba relationship and discusses why Britain was able to remain both an ally of the United States and pursue its own interests in Cuba (Zim, 2002). He also wrote an important opinion piece to the editor of the Washington Post,[3] "Luis Posada Carriles was a terrorist, not just a 'militant'" (Zim, 2018).

A part of Mr. Zim's practice involves giving presentations to travel agents and lawyers on the restrictions imposed on American citizens by

[2] Zim, Daniel Rubiera. "*Straining the Special Relationship: British and U.S. Policies toward the Cuban Revolution, 1959–1961.*" Cuban Studies, vol. 33, University of Pittsburgh Press, 2002, pp. 71–94, http://www.jstor.org/stable/24487786.

[3] Zim, Daniel Rubiera (2018) *Luis Posada Carriles was a terrorist, not just a 'militant'*. Washington Post. [Online] June 1, 2018. Available from: https://www.washingtonpost.com/opinions/luis-posada-carriles-was-a-terrorist-not-just-a-militant/2018/06/01/a9d4a79c-637c-11e8-81ca-bb14593acaa6_story.html.

the U.S. government vis-à-vis Cuba. "It's not even a drop in the bucket, but it is what I can contribute," he told me. "Policymakers are the ones who need to make things right."

Mr. Zim is an Active Member in Good Standing with the Virginia State Bar and the Cuban American community.

A frenzy of cases hitting the media inspired this interview. It was like a wild-west shootout in the justice system and the press. The continuous explosion of articles on Helms–Burton claims gave the impression everybody had jumped on the bandwagon. They filed cases against hotels, CUPET, CIMEX, cruise lines, travel companies, and operators of the ports. There was even a claim by a man who believes he is the owner of José Martí International Airport.

Hernández: Daniel, let's discuss the current rash of Helms–Burton Title III court cases that have made headlines recently. You are an attorney in the United States. What is involved for those unfamiliar with the legal process in the U.S.? My general thought is that they have not considered the "what's next?" scenario.

Let's say one of these people suing under Helms–Burton Title III is successful in obtaining a judgment. What's the next step? Would the company being sued then appeal the decision?

Daniel R. Zim: The only reason there would be a judgment in a Helm-Burton action is if the parties cannot settle before or during the trial or if the defendants fail to get the case dismissed. The defendant has a number of options if that occurs. Most immediately, the defendant can file post-trial motions such as a motion to reconsider or a motion to set aside the verdict. Those types of actions rarely succeed, but they could be used strategically to delay the entry of a judgment.

Regardless of whether or not the defendant decides to file post-trial motions, he or she certainly has a right to appeal the verdict to a federal appeals court. If Defendant–Appellant fails at the federal appellate level, he or she can appeal to the U.S. Supreme Court.

Earlier you said that the defendant can file post-trial motions as a delay tactic. What is the advantage for the defendant of delaying and creating obstacles for the plaintiff? In that case, the defendant would be accused of delaying justice that is 60 years in the making, would he not?

Mr. Zim: Getting back to the delay strategy, time is really on the defendant's side. But time, unfortunately, is not on the side of the plaintiff or the Trump administration in these lawsuits because the next president, whether he or she is elected next year or in five years, has the power to suspend Helms–Burton lawsuits.

This is not only hypothetical, but also not without precedent. In 1981, a case came before the U.S. Supreme Court which involved nearly the same facts as the Helms–Burton litigation, only it involved property claims against Iran to recover debts purportedly owed by the government of Iran.

The dispute in Dames & Moore vs. Regan[4] arose when the Reagan administration reached an agreement with the government of Iran to terminate legal proceedings in U.S. courts involving claims by U.S. nationals against Iran, to nullify attachments against Iranian property entered by U.S. courts to secure any judgments against Iran, and to transfer such claims from U.S. courts to a new arbitration tribunal.

The Reagan administration took this action by executive order without the approval of Congress arguing that the Executive Branch has plenary power in the area of foreign policy which supersedes the need to seek Congressional approval for the suspension of the Iran property claims in litigation and the creation of a new arbitration panel to deal with the property claims.

The U.S. Supreme Court agreed and found that the administration's actions were authorized under the International Emergency Economic Powers Act (IEEPA).[5] It further ordered the suspension of claims filed in U.S. courts (Cornell University, n.d.).

So, theoretically, the next president could suspend Helms–Burton litigation or judgments on the basis that the president is supreme in its authority to conduct foreign policy. By the way, the same rationale—presidential power—was originally used to enact the ban on travel to Cuba when it first came into force.

Since time is not on the side of the Helms–Burton plaintiffs and these cases can drag on for five to ten years, they would have a strong incentive to settle even for a very small fraction of the damages they are originally requesting. Defendants also have powerful incentives to settle for various other reasons, but the ball is really in the plaintiff's court because they

[4] Dames & Moore v. Regan, 453 U.S. 654, 101 S. Ct. 2972 (N.Y. Sup. Ct. 1981). https://www.law.cornell.edu/supremecourt/text/453/654.

[5] The International Emergency Economic Powers Act (IEEPA) was enacted October 28, 1977 and signed by President Jimmy Carter on December 28, 1977.

need a satisfying victory as fast as possible. Therefore, because of the relatively more desperate position the plaintiffs are in, I believe defendants have the upper hand in this litigation.

Let's imagine, for example, that the appeal is denied. Is a judgment then made against Cuba? Cuba has, in the past, said that it does not honor decisions obtained in a U.S. court. Added to this potential scenario, let's suppose, the company in question is European or Canadian, both of which have statutes in place. Canada, for example, has the Foreign Extraterritorial Measures Act (FEMA) legislation. And much like the Canadian blocking statute, the European Union has come out swinging, issuing its own statement on the decision of the United States to further activate Title III, saying:

> In the light of the United States Administration's decision to not renew the waiver related to Title III of the 1996 Helms–Burton (LIBERTAD) Act, the European Union reiterates its strong opposition to the extraterritorial application of unilateral Cuba-related measures that are contrary to international law. This decision is also a breach of the United States' commitments undertaken in the EU-US agreements of 1997 and 1998, which have been respected by both sides without interruption since then. In those agreements, the US committed to waive Title III of the Helms–Burton Act and the EU, inter alia, suspended its case in the World Trade Organization against the US.
>
> The EU will consider all options at its disposal to protect its legitimate interests, including in relation to its WTO rights and through the use of the EU Blocking Statute. The Statute prohibits the enforcement of U.S. courts' judgements relating to Title III of the Helms–Burton Act within the EU and allows EU companies sued in the US to recover any damage through legal proceedings against US claimants before EU courts. (European Commission, 2019)[6]

Could you comment on the purpose of the blocking statutes?

Mr. Zim: Yes. Let me first explain the Canadian legislation. FEMA was enacted with the intention of protecting Canadian sovereignty, including Canada's international trading and commercial interests, by allowing the Canadian government to respond to extraterritorial assertions of foreign

[6] Joint Statement by High Representative/Vice President Federica Mogherini and Commissioner for Trade Cecilia Malmström, April 17, 2019. Available at: ec.europa.eu/commission/presscorner/detail/en/STATEMENT_19_2171.

jurisdiction which are allowed by the U.S. government under Helms–Burton.

According to FEMA, judgments issued under Title III of the Helms–Burton Act will not be recognized or enforced in Canada. In addition, the Canadian blocking statute allows Canadians to use Canadian courts to sue the person who has instituted an action under the Helms–Burton Act, even while proceedings are ongoing in the United States. This will allow Canadians to claim any amounts that have been obtained against them, including legal expenses, and losses or damages incurred.

Regarding the EU legislation, you very correctly note that Federica Mogherini and Cecilia Malmström, both top trade officials in the EU, came out with a very terse statement on the decision of the United States to further activate Title III of the Helms–Burton Act. They did not mince words. They basically said that U.S. sanctions are illegal. They violate international law, and the EU will do everything in its power to prevent any Helms–Burton plaintiff from recovering even a dime from this litigation.

Could you further comment on what effect the Canadian and EU blocking statutes will have on any pending or future litigation?

Mr. Zim: Yes. It would be a long time before the Canadian and European blocking statutes are invoked, if ever, as a consequence of Helms–Burton litigation. And they really illustrate the futility and extreme complexity of bringing Helms–Burton claims really are.

In addition to the significant legal hurdles based on the merits of bringing a colorable claim that is 60 years old on behalf of a distant ancestor, these cases, if not settled, can really drag on for years involving the courts of multiple countries. So, yes, a court in a foreign country can effectively nullify a verdict in U.S. courts that has fully run its course through the appellate process.

In international law, the nations are bound by the concept of comity, which is similar to the "full faith and credit" clause of the U.S. Constitution requiring legal reciprocity. In other words, a judgment by a foreign nation's court must be respected and enforced by a U.S. court.

The scenario you have depicted creates a conflict of law issues, the likes of which we have never seen. A valid U.S. verdict that results in a loss for the defendant and a foreign verdict that results in a win for that same person or corporate entity—which verdict trumps the other is anyone's guess. You could literally go around in circles with this question forever and ever.

Then what do the plaintiffs' attorneys hope to achieve through this litigation if recovery seems so distant to you?

Mr. Zim: That's a good question. I'm not quite sure I know how to answer it. Maybe they hope to sustain their respective practices for the next four to five years?

Look, I'm not out here to disparage attorneys or their clients. But the reality is that there are now literally dozens of opportunistic lawyers in South Florida bringing these cases to a federal court whom I don't believe are setting realistic expectations for their clients as to the likely outcome of these suits.

Their clients feel robbed, cheated, and they are mad as hell. Many of them have earnestly invested their energy, their life's work, and their ingenuity in Cuba's version of the American Dream. That dream dissipated practically overnight when the Cuban government nationalized their property. And, unfortunately, one of the longest international conflicts the world has ever endured, precluding any chance of a settlement between the United States and Cuba for more than a generation, began.

I can't get into these peoples' heads and read their minds, but they probably feel that there is no way the Cuban government with its bankrupt economy will never be able to compensate them. They know the American government will not compensate them. So, who is left? The hundreds of firms that are "trafficking" on their land, the land that they built with their own hands. How dare they? So, the claimants have placed their hopes in a long-shot litigation strategy that is their last great hope of forgetting what was theirs.

What would you advise them if they consulted with you about their claims?

Mr. Zim: I would advise them. I would implore them to not go down this path. It's good money and good energy after bad.

Daniel, thank you for taking the time to answer these questions.

References

Bellinger, J. (2020, April 23). *The first year of Helms Burton lawsuits*. Lawfare. https://www.lawfareblog.com/firstyear-helms-burton-lawsuits

Dames & Moore. (1981). *Petitioner, v. Donald T. REGAN, Secretary of the Treasury, et al.* https://www.law.cornell.edu/supremecourt/text/453/654

European Commission. (2019). *Joint Statement by High Representative/Vice President Federica Mogherini and Commissioner for Trade Cecilia Malmström on the decision of the United States to further activate Title III of the Helms Burton (Libertad) Act*. https://ec.europa.eu/commission/presscorner/detail/en/STATEMENT_19_2171

International Emergency Economic Powers Act, 50 U.S.C. § 1701 (1977). https://uscode.house.gov/statviewer.htm?volume=91&page=1626

Zim, D. R. (2002). Straining the special relationship: British and U.S. policies toward the Cuban Revolution, 1959–1961. *Cuban Studies, 33*, 71–94. http://www.jstor.org/stable/24487786

Zim, D. R. (2018, June 1). Luis Posada Carriles was a terrorist, not just a 'militant.' *Washington Post*. Retrieved June 28, 2020, from https://www.washingtonpost.com/opinions/luis-posada-carriles-was-a-terrorist-not-just-a-militant/2018/06/01/a9d4a79c-637c-11e8-81ca-bb14593acaa6_story.html

CHAPTER 19

Interview with Hermenegildo Altozano, Partner, Bird & Bird, Spain

Spanish lawyer Hermenegildo Altozano is a leading world expert on matters involving foreign investment with Cuba. Since 2011, Mr. Altozano is a partner at the Bird & Bird law firm in Madrid where he heads the Energy and Infrastructures practice.

At Bird & Bird, Mr. Altozano advises leading global market players in the energy, natural resources, aviation, agribusiness, tourism, food, and infrastructure sectors.

Mr. Altozano is co-director of the Energy and Regulation Forum of the *Fundación para la Investigación sobre el Derecho y la Empresa* (FIDE), former Director of the Energy Law program at the *Instituto de Empresa* and former Associate Professor of Private International Law at *Universidad Francisco de Vitoria*. He regularly participates in the radio broadcast *La Gran Tertulia de la Economía* on Capital Radio broadcast from Madrid (Fig. 19.1).

He has given lectures at some of the most important investment conferences in Cuba.

I have had the pleasure of meeting and listening to him at two of these conferences in Havana.

Most recently, Mr. Altozano gave a presentation at the CUPET Oil and Gas conference in November 2019, where he spoke to a captive audience on legal matters for investors concerning the Helms–Burton Act.

T. K. Hernández, *The Cuba Interviews*,
https://doi.org/10.1007/978-3-031-30203-9_19

Fig. 19.1 Spanish attorney, Hermenegildo Altozano, CUPET Conference, 2019 (Photo by the editor)

This interview with Mr. Altozano took place in the context of the COVID-19 pandemic and covers several current issues on Cuba. He spoke to me on the recent banking reforms,[1] the complexity of the due diligence process related to Helms–Burton cases, and the impact of COVID-19 on foreign investment.

I spoke with Mr. Altozano in Madrid, via Zoom, in June 2020.

Hernández: Good morning. I'd like to start off this interview with a personal question. At what point in your career did you decide to work on cases involving Cuba and Latin America? I'm trying to understand how you ended up as a one of the most known legal experts for foreign investment matters related to Cuba. Did you choose Cuba or did Cuba choose you?

[1] Resolution 73/2020 published in the Official Gazette of the Republic of Cuba regarding Central Bank of Cuba allows citizens to open foreign currency accounts.

Hermenegildo Altozano: My first trip to Cuba was the result of the invitation of Luis Callejón, a Spanish hotel entrepreneur and outstanding character who had an extensive relationship with the Cuban tourism industry. He invited me to give a lecture on timesharing, which was then a fashionable new industry. Cuba was looking for new alternatives to develop the tourism industry and Luis Callejón organized a series of lectures that were held at the Palacio de Convenciones. I had the opportunity to give a lecture on how timesharing was helping to develop the tourism industry in some areas of Spain, particularly the Canary Islands, which had some similarities with Cuba. And then, you know, it's like falling in love; I felt that Cuba was a land of opportunity. I thought that there were a tremendous number of opportunities to be pursued.

Luis Callejón invited me for a second trip and I had the opportunity to travel through the Island. We went to Camagüey where I had the opportunity to give a lecture. We met a number of government officials in the tourism industry and then I started to develop a number of relationships in Cuba. In 1996, one of our clients was invited to participate in a joint venture to develop the first office building in Havana (*La Lonja del Comercop*). The client asked the law firm where I was working at the time to assist in the negotiations.

That was the first significant Cuban deal I was involved with. From there, this is like a "cherry situation" where one deal brings another deal and you start building a consistent practice and reputation.

So, Cuba found you.

Mr. Altozano: Well, I would not say that. It could have been a mutual discovery, but I can say that I found Cuba.

Can you discuss the impact of COVID-19 on foreign investment with Cuba?

Mr. Altozano: As you can imagine there are a number of legal issues involving COVID-19 and particularly there is sort of a "resurrection" of hardship clauses, *force majeure* clauses, change of law clauses impacting different contracts in various industries. It's impacting the flow of foreign investments because many countries are adopting protective measures to control the flow of foreign investments. And that's making everything much more difficult.

In addition, the access to financing is becoming difficult due to the uncertainties created in some industries as a result of the *pandemia*. The increasing difficulties in securing financing may adversely impact the capacity to invest although it has to be taken into account that the end of the *pandemia* will revive the appetite for foreign investments.

In these days of COVID-19, one of our clients, Panterra Gold,[2] has been able to complete a joint venture with the Cuban entity GeoMinera S.A. in the mining sector (Antilles Gold, 2020). We are currently also assisting another client in completing an important deal in the food industry. So there's a continuous flow of investment and of interest in Cuba.

Obviously, the world tourism industry is severely impacted by COVID-19 as you can imagine, and their contracts with the main tour operators and hotel operators have been or are in the process of renegotiation.

In this same context, Cuba has announced, and it is not a surprise, its will to restructure its existing debt obligations. Financial institutions are eager to consider the restructuring of the existing financial agreements due to the fact that everyone is aware that this is an extraordinary situation. If you are driven by common sense, you will have to find a way through in order not to harm both parties—the debtor and the creditor—in the equation.

We've seen a number of cases filed under the Helms–Burton Title III legislation which have resulted in dismissal. My question is, have these plaintiffs received poor legal advice or do you believe there's an attention-seeking strategy behind these cases? Are they show trials?

Mr. Altozano: I think there was a big expectation on the part of the potential claimants when the suspension of Title III was lifted. It is my belief that many of those potential claimants were thinking that the defendants were going to simply sit down and enter into a settlement agreement.

I think that most of them were on the advice of telling them, "We will file a Title III lawsuit. This is going to be enough to bring them to the negotiation table. Sit down and we will settle. We'll get your money." And they have not taken into account the reaction of the defendants. I mean there's just been a miscalculation by the plaintiffs.

First of all, the defendants are sophisticated people. Secondly, the defendants have taken this matter very seriously. They have hired some of the major U.S. law firms, and they have created very capable legal teams across the world.

[2] PanTerra Gold Limited is now known as Antilles Gold Limited. The corporate name change took place November 6, 2020.

They have also minimized a very important element of Title III of Helms–Burton, which is that these lawsuits have to be filed before federal judges. A judge or a federal court is someone that is on top of the hierarchy. He or she is someone very sophisticated, with a serious legal background and practise. Serious persons that have been appointed because of their prestige as a legal professional with a long-standing professional career behind them.

If you have a look at the motions to dismiss, the cases that have been filed already by the defendants, you will see that there is serious legal work behind them, carried out by very serious lawyers. I will not say that the plaintiffs had poor legal advice. I think those advisors were not anticipating properly what was going to be the reaction of the defendant.

When the decisions were taken, for example, the Amazon[3] and Melia Hotels' cases,[4] the cases were dismissed based on very basic facts. For example, the person was not a U.S. resident in 1996. It is almost as if the plaintiff's lawyer completely missed important elements.

Mr. Altozano: I think some of the plaintiffs have been led to believe that Title III lawsuits would be a very straightforward exercise: "If you just send a little claim letter you will get the defendant to the table" and that was not the case. And they have not taken care of some basic elements such as evidence of the ownership of a claim or response to the very basic question of "where is the title of your property?".

If you go to a court you need to evidence a number of issues: your legitimacy to litigate (*standi*) which includes the evidence that you have a claim, etcetera. And in some of these cases they simply said, "I was born in Cuba, I owned a property, or my father owned a property, and the communists stole the property."

What should an investor plan prior to a decision to invest in Cuba. What's the most important first step, for example, something such as due diligence.

[3] Analysis of dismissal by a Southern District of Florida court of Gonzalez v. Amazon: Amazon Seizure Case May Limit Title III's Reach–Analysis: June 4, 2020: law360.com/articles/1279954/dismissal-of-amazon-seizure-case-may-limit-title-iii-s-reach.

[4] Melia Hotel's corporate press release on the first decision taken by a European court on Helms–Burton matters which determined the court of Palma de Mallorca had no jurisdiction to decide whether nationalization by a Cuban government in 1960 was lawful or not. meliahotelsinternational.com/en/newsroom/our-news/Courts-close-case-lawsuit-Sanchez-Hill-against-Melia-Hotels-International. September 3, 2019.

Mr. Altozano: That simple question claims a complex answer. The foreign investment process in Cuba is a complex process that involves a number of authorities. It's a very regulated process. You cannot simply go to Cuba and invest. You need to go through an authorization process. And the counterparty normally has to be authorized to negotiate with the foreign investor, even though, as you know, the Cuban foreign investment legislation contemplates the possibility of a 100% foreign company.

The fact is that the foreign investment process takes some time and obviously, when you are investing in Cuba and you are a foreign investor in Cuba, you only have to take into account two sets of rules: the Cuban laws and the laws of your jurisdiction. Helms–Burton Act is an extraterritorial legislation which interferes with the investment process. You must take that into account if you are a European Union, Canadian or Mexican investor—you cannot comply with the Helms–Burton Act without breaking your own regulations, and you cannot also comply with the Helms–Burton without breaching Cuban regulations.

For instance, imagine that a non-European Union investor would like to invest in Cuba, and he says, well, I would like to set up a company in Spain that will, in turn, invest in Cuba, because that way I will benefit from the protection of the European Union Regulation 2271/1996,[5] and I will be able to show that I have a shield *vis-à-vis* any potential plaintiff under Helms–Burton. Although there is a claim registry with the Foreign Claims Settlement Commission of the U.S. Department of Justice that shows 5,913 U.S. national claims as a result of the nationalizations process carried out by the Cuban Government from January 1, 1959, there is no such registry for Cuban American claimants: this fact makes it virtually impossible to carry out a due diligence to learn whether there is a claim in relation to any specific property.

On the recent news of banking reform, Resolution 73/2020 (Gaceta Oficial, 2020)**, in the last couple of weeks. Do you think this will have positive benefits for investors?**

[5] Council Regulation (EC) No 2271/96 of 22 November 1996 protecting against the effects of the extra-territorial application of legislation adopted by a third country, and actions based thereon or resulting therefrom. eur-lex.europa.eu/legal-content/EN/TXT/?uri=CELEX%3A31996R2271.

Mr. Altozano: My opinion is that Resolution 73/2020[6] is moving forward to the direction of resolving the double currency situation. I think that it's a resolution which is driven obviously to the purpose of not spending more than you have. So it brings a kind of a control over the flows of currency. I think it is going to have a positive impact in the medium and long term for foreign investment.

And for the long term?

Mr. Altozano: Particularly the perception of stability in the currency flows and the ability to have a single currency.

It was nice to talk with you, someone who is actively involved with Cuba. Thank you so much.

Mr. Altozano: Thanks so much to you for your time and for your kindness. I'm looking forward to the publication of the interview. A real pleasure.

Annex

Gaceta Oficial de la República de Cuba -2020–382-EX28
RESOLUCIÓN No. No. 73/2020 (GOC)

Gaceta Oficial No. 28 Extraordinaria de 22 de mayo de 2020
BANCO CENTRAL DE CUBA

RESOLUCIÓN No. 73/2020

POR CUANTO: La Resolución 275 de 15 de octubre de 2019 de la ministra presidente del Banco Central de Cuba, dispuso que las cuentas bancarias de las personas naturales residentes permanentes en el país, reciben fondos mediante transferencias bancarias del exterior en cualquier moneda libremente convertible; transferencias bancarias desde otras cuentas en moneda libremente convertible que operan en bancos cubanos; transferencias

de FINCIMEX S.A. por concepto de remesas, y depósitos en efectivo en dólares estadounidenses, euros, libras esterlinas, dólares canadienses, francos suizos, pesos mexicanos, coronas danesas, coronas noruegas, coronas suecas y yenes japoneses.

POR CUANTO: La Resolución 117 de 26 de marzo de 2020 del ministro de Comercio Exterior y la Inversión Extranjera precisa las

[6] See Resolution 73/2020 of the Central Bank of Cuba, published in the Official Gazette of the Republic of Cuba.

regulaciones que rigen las relaciones comerciales en las operaciones de importación, para la nomenclatura de productos que se autoricen a comercializar en moneda libremente convertible, a las entidades importadoras aprobadas con las personas naturales incluidas en sus carteras de clientes.

POR CUANTO: La experiencia práctica en la aplicación de la citada Resolución 275 de 2019 hace necesario adecuar sus disposiciones y en consecuencia derogar esa Resolución.

POR TANTO: En el ejercicio de las atribuciones conferidas en el artículo 25, inciso d), del Decreto-Ley No. 361 "Del Banco Central de Cuba" de 14 de septiembre de 2018,

RESUELVO

PRIMERO: Disponer el uso de dólares estadounidenses en las operaciones de ventas minoristas en divisas, así como en las de importación que realizan las personas naturales a través de las entidades importadoras autorizadas por el ministro de Comercio Exterior y la Inversión Extranjera.

SEGUNDO: Para la realización de sus cobros y pagos, las entidades importadoras autorizadas por el Ministerio de Comercio Exterior y la Inversión Extranjera, solicitan Licencia Específica al Banco Central de Cuba para abrir cuenta bancaria en dólares estadounidenses en el Banco Financiero Internacional S.A., teniendo en cuenta las regulaciones y procedimientos vigentes sobre esta materia. 308 GACETA OFICIAL 22 de mayo de 2020

TERCERO: Las personas naturales para la realización de los pagos que por la presente Resolución se autorizan, abren cuentas bancarias en dólares estadounidenses en el Banco Metropolitano S.A.; Banco Popular de Ahorro y Banco de Crédito y Comercio, teniendo en cuenta las disposiciones jurídicas vigentes sobre esta materia.

CUARTO: Las cuentas bancarias de las personas naturales sujetos de esta Resolución son operadas mediante tarjetas magnéticas, las que pueden ser utilizadas para efectuar transacciones en dólares estadounidenses, pesos cubanos y pesos convertibles en cajeros automáticos, terminales de punto de venta, y otros canales de pago.

QUINTO: Las cuentas bancarias en dólares estadounidenses de las personas naturales reciben fondos mediante transferencias bancarias del exterior en cualquier moneda libremente convertible; de transferencias bancarias desde otras cuentas en moneda libremente convertible que operan en bancos cubanos; transferencias de FINCIMEX S.A. por concepto de remesas, y mediante depósitos en efectivo de dólares estadounidenses, euros, libras esterlinas, dólares canadienses, francos suizos, pesos mexicanos, coronas danesas, coronas noruegas, coronas suecas y yenes japoneses. En el caso del depósito de dólares estadounidenses en efectivo, se aplica el gravamen del 10%.

SEXTO: Las personas naturales, desde sus cuentas bancarias en dólares estadounidenses pagan por las operaciones de ventas minoristas en divisas, y la importación de mercancías a las cuentas en dólares estadounidenses de las entidades importadoras autorizadas por el ministro de Comercio Exterior y la Inversión Extranjera. Desde estas cuentas bancarias pueden realizar, además, todas las operaciones establecidas para los titulares de Tarjeta RED con cuentas bancarias en pesos cubanos y pesos convertibles.

DISPOSICIONES FINALES

PRIMERA: Se mantienen vigentes la Resolución 65 de 16 de julio de 2003 y la Resolución 80 de 23 de octubre de 2004, ambas del Banco Central de Cuba, salvo en lo que se oponga a lo dispuesto en la presente Resolución.

SEGUNDA: Se deroga la Resolución 275 de 15 de octubre de 2019 de la ministra presidente del Banco Central de Cuba.

DESE CUENTA a la Secretaría del Consejo de Ministros, a los ministros del Comercio Exterior y la Inversión Extranjera, de Industrias, de las Comunicaciones, de Turismo y a la ministra de Ciencia, Tecnología y Medio Ambiente.

COMUNÍQUESE a los presidentes de la Corporación CIMEX S.A., de la Cadena de Tiendas Caribe y de Servicios Automotores S.A., así como a los presidentes del Banco Financiero Internacional S.A., Banco Metropolitano S.A., Banco Popular de Ahorro y el Banco de Crédito y Comercio, al vice presidente primero, a los vice presidentes, al superintendente y a los directores generales, todos del Banco Central de Cuba.

PUBLÍQUESE en la Gaceta Oficial de la República de Cuba.

ARCHÍVESE el original en la Secretaría del Banco Central de Cuba.

DADA en La Habana, a los dieciocho días del mes de mayo de dos mil veinte.

Marta Sabina Wilson González
Ministra Presidente
Banco Central de Cuba

References

Antilles Gold. (2020, August 7). Panterra Gold Signs Joint Venture Agreement for La Demajagua Gold/Silver Project in Cuba. https://www.investi.com.au/api/announcements/aau/80c451b4-397.pdf

EUR-Lex. (1996, November 22). *Consolidated text: Council Regulation (EC) No 2271/96 of 22 November 1996 protecting against the effects of the extra-territorial application of legislation adopted by a third country, and actions based thereon or resulting therefrom*. European Union. Retrieved July 7, 2020, from https://eur-lex.europa.eu/legal-content/EN/TXT/?uri=CELEX%3A01996R2271-20180807

Freyre, P., & Sosa, L. (2020, June 4). *Dismissal of Amazon Seizure Case may limit title iII's reach retrieved*. Law 360. Retrieved March 20, 2020, from https://www.law360.com/articles/1279954/dismissal-of-amazon-seizure-case-may-limit-title-iii-s-reach

Meliá Hotels International. (2019, September 3). *The Spanish Courts decide to close the case regarding the lawsuit filed by the Sanchez-Hill family against Meliá Hotels International*. Meliá Hotels International. Retrieved July 7, 2020, from https://www.meliahotelsinternational.com/en/newsroom/our-news/Courts-close-case-lawsuit-Sanchez-Hill-against-Melia-Hotels-International

Wilson Gonzalez, M. S. (2020, July 23). *Gaceta Oficial No. 28 extraordinaria DE 2020*. Gaceta Oficial. Retrieved March 15, 2022, from https://www.gacetaoficial.gob.cu/es/gaceta-oficial-no-28-extraordinaria-de-2020

CHAPTER 20

Protecting Foreign Investors–Interview with Déborah Rivas, Vice Minister, MINCEX

Déborah Rivas Saavedra is the Vice Minister at the Ministry of Foreign Trade and Foreign Investment (MINCEX) of the Republic of Cuba (Fig. 20.1).

Minister Rivas holds a degree in International Economic Relations from the University of Havana. Over the years, she has continued studies in development cooperation, project management, investment, and multilateral negotiations in Sweden, Chile, Peru, Spain, and Italy.

Her early career history includes a research position at Cubazucar and as president of the Panamericana Corporation, Inc. She has also served in diplomatic positions at the Embassies of Cuba in Mexico and Peru.

Ms. Rivas began her career at MINCEX as the Director of Promotion and Evaluation of Joint Business in 1998.

In 2010, she became the Director of the Foreign Investment Division. Three years later, Ms. Rivas was promoted to Director General.

She was appointed Deputy Minister of MINCEX in 2020. In this capacity, she leads the Cuban delegations in trade negotiations and is active in the promotion of foreign investment in Cuba.

The Minister is currently doing a Ph.D. in Economic Development at the University of Havana.

In this interview, conducted by email in April 2021, Minister Rivas discussed the legal protections Cuba offers to investors.

T. K. Hernández, *The Cuba Interviews*,
https://doi.org/10.1007/978-3-031-30203-9_20

Fig. 20.1 Déborah Rivas Saavedra, Vice Minister from the Ministry of Foreign Trade and Foreign Investment (MINCEX) (Photo by the editor)

An update to the first interview took place with the Minister at the offices of MINCEX in Havana in May 2022.

Hernández: I would like to ask about the protections Cuba provides to foreign investors and their investments?

Vice Minister Déborah Rivas: Law No. 118 "Law of Foreign Investment" and its complementary legislation of facilities, guarantees, and legal security, encourages the attraction and use of foreign capital. It offers new incentives and explains the three modalities in which a foreign investor can be established in Cuba.

Foreign investments enjoy full protection, legal security and cannot be expropriated, except for reasons of public utility or social interest under the Constitution, international treaties signed by Cuba, and current legislation, with due compensation for its commercial value established by mutual agreement.

On the other hand, the investor can sell or transfer his rights to the State, to the parties in the association, or to a third party, with prior governmental authorization. The State guarantees the foreign investor the free transfer abroad, without payment of taxes or other related encumbrance, of the dividends or benefits that he obtains from the exploitation of the investment. Foreign citizens who provide services to a joint venture, to the parties in any form of international economic association, or to a totally foreign capital company, provided that they are not permanent residents, may transfer abroad the assets received within the amount and under the other regulations issued by the Central Bank of Cuba.

Foreign investment is subject to the special tax regime provided by Law until the expiration of the term for which it was allowed. Among the tax benefits offered to investors, mention can be made of the exemption from payment of personal income tax, for the income from dividends or business profits; the exemption from income tax for eight years from incorporating the business; the bonus of 50% in the tax rate on wholesale sales for the payment of sales tax–which is exempted from its payment in the first year of operation—and taxes for the use of the beaches, for the approved dumping of wastewater in hydrographic basins, for the use and exploitation of bays, for the use of forest resources and wildlife, and for the right to use terrestrial waters during the recovery period—exemption from payment of customs tax in the investment process and land tax for local development during the recovery of the investment.

A particular case is represented by foreign investors who are parties to international economic association contracts whose purpose is hotel, production, or service management and the provision of professional services since they are exempt from sales and service tax.

In the search for ways to provide new commercial guarantees, in 2020 two decree laws were approved[1] to support the granting of external financing related to foreign investment. These laws allow the consolidation of Cuba's credibility in international economic relations, employing the strict fulfillment of commitments and they increase the participation

[1] Decree Law No. 14/2020, "De La Prenda y la Hipoteca", and Decree Law No. 15/2020 "From the Guarantee Trust," were approved on October 23, 2020.

of FDI[2] as an important source for the development of the country in certain sectors and economic activities.

In general, Cuba guarantees political and social stability and high levels of security, which represent the major advantages for attracting investors; and it should continue to be the premise to maintain foreign investment, thus contributing to economic and social development. Sustainable development is achieved through the diversification and expansion of export markets, access to advanced technologies, import substitution, and the generation of productive chains that spread the positive effects of capital to the rest of the economy.

With the new digital platform, the Single Window for Foreign Investment (VUINEX), and other changes, how much time is saved in the process from the first application to invest until the completed approval?

Vice Minister Rivas: The creation of VUINEX fulfills the purpose of making processes more efficient and eliminating bureaucratic obstacles to carrying out business with foreign investment. Its primary objectives are to provide information and advice on investment; promote business opportunities and facilitate the constitution of foreign investment modalities, the realization of its investment processes, and the processing of permits, licenses, and authorizations. It has an "online" computer system, which is currently in the implementation stage,[3] as a way of approaching a non-face-to-face exchange.

VUINEX speeds up the time needed to complete the dossier to be presented for the approval of the business with foreign capital and to get all the licenses, permits, and authorizations for its operation. Such aspirations to reduce terms were included in Decree No. 15/2020 "Regulation of the One-Stop Shop for Foreign Investment," issued in September 2020. Likewise, it has been a positive response mechanism to proposals from national and foreign investors, relating to the cumbersome procedures for the approval, constitution, and operation of businesses.

[2] See "Publica Gaceta Oficial Decretos Leyes Sobre Garantías Mercantiles Para respaldar La Inversión Extranjera" on CubaDebate: http://www.cubadebate.cu/noticias/2020/10/23/publica-gaceta-oficial-decretos-leyes-sobre-garantias-mercantiles-para-respaldar-la-inversion-extranjera/.

[3] The VUINEX online system went live on March 10, 2021 and is available at https://vuinex.mincex.gob.cu/web/login.

There has already been experiences of directing a business from the first investment intention to approval showing the efficiency of VUINEX. Investors have said it's easier and has sped up the process. Now they just go to VUINEX to get the licenses, permissions, and authorizations that are required to set up in Cuba. At the end of 2021, more than 284 procedures were carried out. In addition, over 169 inquiries were received from potential investors related to the industry sectors of construction, transportation, renewable energy, food production, tourism, professional services, health, culture, and mining.

Implementing VUINEX is an indirect incentive for foreign investment, as it provides a free service that allows speeding up and facilitating the procedures because the interested parties only have to access a single place where representatives of the different organizations and authorities can be found. Based on its interconnection capacities with organizations, business groups, entities, and territories, it favors contacts between interested companies and the Cuban counterparts in each case. We are continuing to work to improve the climate for foreign investment, and today VUINEX represents a step forward.

Would you say that Cuba is becoming a more "business-friendly" environment and what is it like?

Vice Minister Rivas: In the last two years, decisions were taken, and actions implemented in order to make the processes of foreign investment more flexible and streamlined. Among those with the greatest impact, the following stands out:

1. Updating of some complementary norms of Law 118, "Law of Foreign Investment."
2. Incorporation and/or modification of general and sectoral policies associated with investment, as part of the updating of the Portfolio of Foreign Investment Opportunities published each year. Since the first edition of the Portfolio of Foreign Investment Opportunities was published in 2014 after the approval of Law 118, it has been an essential tool for promoting the attraction of foreign capital. The Portfolio of Opportunities 2021–2022 has 678 projects for a total investment of 12.5 billion USD. Its distinctive features include 175 newly incorporated projects and has 43 more, worth over 320 million USD compared to the previous one. Also, it should be noted that the Portfolio has projects in all sectors that have approved policies.

3. The incidence of the pandemic in processes related to foreign investment has encouraged actions to reduce its impact on existing businesses and those that are in the process of approval and constitution.

Agreement No. 8937 of the Executive Committee of the Council of Ministers (CECM) was issued which automatically extended those businesses with an expiration date of June 1 to June 30, 2021. The Ministry of Justice (MINJUS) issued provisions that allow the realization of commercial acts of an associative nature through video conferencing or any other technical means that has image and sound, with the virtual presence of the parties connected with the notary, in response to the current exceptional situation.

Thank you for taking the time to clarify, in depth, the protections in place for foreign investors and their business activities in Cuba.

Follow-up to the Interview: May 2022

The following is an update by the Vice Minister to the interview of April 2021. It was conducted in person in a boardroom at the offices of MINCEX in May 2022. I sat down with the Vice Minister to review the original interview, and we discussed the current legislation for protecting investors and what has evolved. After we met, she invited me to visit the new VUINEX office in Vedado.

We last communicated in 2021. What has evolved in the foreign investment scenario in Cuba over the last year?

Vice Minister Rivas: Now, with the end of the pandemic in sight, new investors are visiting Cuba again, and connecting with Cuban partners. New businesses are starting up.

The blockade is still a hindrance to development.

We Cubans are very optimistic about FDI in Cuba. The business is coming back.

We have many opportunities in different sectors, and now we have the private sector, the Micro, Small, and Medium Enterprises (MSMEs). The MSMEs can associate with foreign investors because they are enterprises under Cuban investment law. They have the possibility to associate with foreign capital. There are now many more independent businesses. It is a tremendous change. These small businesses will contribute a percentage to increase Cuban GDP.

The U.S. blockade constitutes the main obstacle to doing business under normal international terms in Cuba. Our legislation protects the foreign investors from U.S. sanctions and responds to the unilateral measures of the United States. The legislation would be different if it did not exist. This is difficult for foreigners to understand. For example, over 100 banks ceased operations with Cuba because of the measures of the Trump administration.

An investor in Cuba has to adopt different business policies and practices to protect his project compared to other countries. Anyhow, the opportunities are here, and the businesspeople come to take advantage of them.

Is Cuba moving forward to present a more business-friendly climate?

Minister Rivas: Cuba's latest Portfolio of Investment Opportunities 2021–2022 is no longer in PDF format but on a new website at inviertaencuba.mincex.gob.cu. An investor can now search by sector, province, dollar amounts for the investment, view the legal framework, public policies, FAQ section, and sign up to the VUINEX system. There is also a direct link to the ZED Mariel website.

VUINEX has made the entire application process quicker and easier for investors. From the original application to investment completion now takes approximately six months when before, it could often take as long as two years. We have trained specialists in the VUINEX office that provide information to their specific portfolio of sectors. These specialists are there to help investors with the process. There are also three large meeting rooms equipped with audiovisual equipment where the investor can hold meetings.

Annex

GACETA OFICIAL
DE LA REPÚBLICA DE CUBA
MINISTERIO DE JUSTICIA

EXTRAORDINARIA LA HABANA, VIERNES 23 DE OCTUBRE DE 2020 AÑO CXVIII
Sitio Web: http://www.gacetaoficial.gob.cu/—Calle Zanja No. 352 esquina a Escobar, Centro Habana
Teléfonos: 7878-4435 y 7870-0576

Número 58 Página 471
ISSN 1682-7511

CONSEJO DE ESTADO

GOC-2020–669-EX58

JUAN ESTEBAN LAZO HERNÁNDEZ, Presidente de la Asamblea Nacional del Poder Popular.

HAGO SABER: Que el Consejo de Estado ha considerado lo siguiente:

POR CUANTO: La hipoteca y la prenda son derechos reales de garantía para asegurar

el cumplimiento de obligaciones principales, en virtud de créditos financieros.

POR CUANTO: La Ley No. 59 "Código Civil," de 16 de julio de 1987, en el capítulo III, título I, libro Tercero, regula lo relativo a la prenda y a la hipoteca naval, aérea o inmobiliaria

como formas para el cumplimiento de las obligaciones.

POR CUANTO: El Decreto-Ley No. 214 "Constitución de hipotecas sobre bienes inmuebles," de 24 de noviembre de 2000, regula la constitución de hipotecas sobre bienes inmuebles propiedad de empresas y entidades económicas con personalidad jurídica propia existentes en Cuba, cuyas actividades económicas estén dedicadas al desarrollo inmobiliario.

POR CUANTO: El Decreto-Ley No. 226 "Del Registro Mercantil," de 6 de diciembre de 2001, establece en su artículo 20 los asientos registrales susceptibles de inscripción por las sociedades mercantiles.

POR CUANTO: La experiencia en la aplicación de las disposiciones señaladas en los Por Cuantos anteriores, y con el objetivo de propiciar la utilización de la prenda por las personas naturales y jurídicas en el ámbito de sus relaciones económicas, extenderla a los derechos, así como posibilitar la prenda de acciones y ampliar el uso de la hipoteca inmobiliaria, como garantía real, a otros sectores y actividades, resulta necesario modificar las regulaciones antes mencionadas, al igual que la Ley No. 7 "Ley de Procedimiento Civil, Administrativo, Laboral y Económico," de 19 de agosto de 1977, para incorporar un nuevo título de crédito que genera ejecución y derogar el Decreto-Ley No. 214 "Constitución de hipotecas sobre bienes inmuebles," de 24 de noviembre de 2000.

POR TANTO: El Consejo de Estado, en el uso de la atribución que le confiere el inciso c), del artículo 122 de la Constitución de la República, acuerda dictar el siguiente: 472 GACETA OFICIAL 23 de octubre de 2020.

DECRETO LEY No. 14.

"DE LA PRENDA Y LA HIPOTECA"

Artículo 1. Modificar los artículos desde el 270 al 277 y el 288 de la Ley No. 59 "Código Civil," de 16 de julio de 1987, los que quedan redactados de la manera siguiente:

"Artículo 270.1. El derecho de prenda faculta al acreedor a satisfacer su crédito, preferentemente a cualquier otro acreedor, con cargo al valor del bien mueble o derecho prendado del deudor.

2. Puede constituirse prenda con desposesión o sin desposesión del bien o derecho.

3. La garantía de la prenda se extiende a los gastos, los intereses y la indemnización o

sanción pecuniaria.

4. La constitución de la prenda requiere siempre la forma escrita y no puede ser oponible a terceros, si no consta en instrumento público o privado de fecha cierta, cualquiera que sea el valor del crédito.

5. Si el bien o derecho prendado genera frutos o intereses, el acreedor debe percibirlos e imputarlos al pago de la deuda, primero a gastos e intereses y, posteriormente, al capital; es válido el pacto en contrario.

Artículo 271. La prenda, además, puede constituirse sobre bienes y derechos propiedad de un tercero si este lo consiente.

Artículo 272. Los bienes y derechos inembargables no pueden ser objeto de prenda.

Artículo 273. En el documento constitutivo de la prenda se debe consignar:

a) El nombre y domicilio de las partes y, en su caso, del tercero dueño del bien o derecho pignorado;
b) la descripción de dicho bien o derecho;
c) la estimación de su valor, expresada en dinero;
d) el lugar donde se encuentra;
e) la obligación garantizada con la prenda; y
f) el término de su vencimiento.

Artículo 274.1. El acreedor no puede usar los bienes y derechos que recibió en prenda y está obligado a conservarlos en forma adecuada y a responder por su pérdida o deterioro frente al deudor, si no prueba que ocurrió por culpa de este.

2. Si se trata de prenda sin desposesión, el deudor puede usar los bienes y derechos según su destino o cambiarlos de lugar con el consentimiento del acreedor.

3. El incumplimiento a que se contraen los apartados anteriores da derecho al deudor a:

a) Dar por extinguida la garantía y exigir que el bien o derecho le sea restituido;
b) pedir que el bien se ponga en depósito a costa del acreedor; y
c) reclamar daños y perjuicios.

Artículo 275.1. El acreedor a quien no se le haya pagado su crédito puede enajenar el bien o derecho en subasta pública.

2. Si en la subasta no se presenta comprador, o el precio ofrecido no cubre el valor del bien o derecho dado en prenda, este se adjudica al acreedor, quien está obligado a dar al deudor un recibo del pago de la totalidad del crédito.

3. Enajenado el bien o derecho, se entrega al deudor el producto de la venta, descontándole el importe de su deuda y el de los gastos causados.

Artículo 276.1. El derecho de prenda se hace efectivo mediante la venta de los bienes o derechos, por el valor que tengan en ese momento, por cualquiera de las vías legales. 23 de octubre de 2020 GACETA OFICIAL 473.

2. Efectuada la venta, el acreedor debe rendir cuenta al deudor, quien puede impugnarla, sin que ello afecte la validez de la enajenación.

Artículo 277. En la obligación garantizada con prenda el acreedor solo puede satisfacer su crédito con el bien o derecho gravado.

Artículo 288.1. Las hipotecas aérea, naval e inmobiliaria se rigen por disposiciones especiales.

2. El derecho sobre la hipoteca inmobiliaria faculta al acreedor hipotecario a ejercer crédito preferente a cualquier otro acreedor, con cargo al valor del bien recibido del deudor."

Artículo 2. Modificar el inciso e), del artículo 20.2, del Decreto-Ley No. 226 "Del Registro Mercantil," de 6 de diciembre de 2001, el que queda redactado como sigue:

"e) las emisiones de acciones, expresando la serie y número de los títulos de cada emisión, su interés, rédito, amortización y prima; y cuando así lo requieran, la cantidad total de la emisión y los bienes, obras, derechos y obligaciones que se afecten a su pago, incluida la constitución de prenda de acciones autorizadas;"

Artículo 3. Modificar el artículo 486 de la Ley No. 7 "Ley de Procedimiento Civil, Administrativo, Laboral y Económico," de 19 de agosto de 1977, en el sentido de adicionar un apartado, que será el 7), con el texto siguiente:

"7. Las garantías derivadas de los contratos."

Artículo 4. Las organizaciones superiores de dirección empresarial, las empresas estatales,

las sociedades mercantiles de capital totalmente cubano y las modalidades de inversión extranjera pueden prendar sus bienes y derechos, previa autorización del Consejo de Ministros.

Artículo 5.1. Las organizaciones superiores de dirección empresarial, las empresas estatales, sociedades mercantiles de capital totalmente cubano y las modalidades de inversión extranjera pueden constituir hipotecas sobre bienes inmuebles u otros derechos reales con que cuenten, con el fin de garantizar el cumplimiento de las obligaciones contractuales crediticias contraídas.

2. También pueden constituir hipotecas a esos fines los propietarios en desarrollos inmobiliarios.

Artículo 6. El régimen legal de la hipoteca inmobiliaria es el establecido en la Ley Hipotecaria, de 14 de julio de 1893 y su Reglamento, sus normas legales complementarias y este Decreto-Ley.

DISPOSICIONES ESPECIALES

PRIMERA: La constitución de hipotecas sobre bienes inmuebles y otros derechos reales, con los fines dispuestos en este Decreto-Ley, está dirigida a negocios de especial interés económico y requiere la autorización previa y expresa del Consejo de Ministros.

SEGUNDA: El Estado tiene derecho preferente para la adquisición de títulos hipotecarios, mediante el pago de su valor, para lo que los sujetos interesados lo informan de forma previa y oportuna al Consejo de Ministros.

DISPOSICIONES FINALES

PRIMERA: Derogar el Decreto-Ley No. 214 "Constitución de Hipotecas sobre Bienes Inmuebles," de 24 de noviembre de 2000, y cuantas otras disposiciones se opongan al cumplimiento de lo que por este se establece.

SEGUNDA: El presente Decreto-Ley entra en vigor a los treinta días posteriores a su publicación en la Gaceta Oficial de República de Cuba.
474 GACETA OFICIAL 23 de octubre de 2020

PUBLÍQUESE en la Gaceta Oficial de la República de Cuba.

DADO en La Habana, a los 24 días del mes de septiembre de 2020.

Juan Esteban Lazo Hernández.

GOC-2020–670-EX58

JUAN ESTEBAN LAZO HERNÁNDEZ, Presidente de la Asamblea Nacional del Poder Popular.

HAGO SABER: Que el Consejo de Estado ha considerado lo siguiente:

POR CUANTO: El Decreto-Ley No. 361 "Del Banco Central de Cuba," de 14 de septiembre de 2018, faculta al Banco Central de Cuba para autorizar, mediante el otorgamiento de licencias, la creación de instituciones financieras y el establecimiento de oficinas de representación de instituciones financieras extranjeras y, en correspondencia con ello, fijar el alcance y las operaciones que pueden realizar, que incluye al fideicomiso como actividad de intermediación financiera.

POR CUANTO: Resulta necesario regular el uso del fideicomiso de garantía como herramienta financiera que permita captar financiamiento, con el fin de impulsar el desarrollo económico y social del país.

POR TANTO: El Consejo de Estado, en uso de la atribución que le confiere el inciso c), del artículo 122, de la Constitución de la República, acuerda dictar el siguiente:

DECRETO-LEY No. 15.

"DEL FIDEICOMISO DE GARANTÍA"

Artículo 1. El fideicomiso de garantía es una operación de intermediación financiera formalizada mediante contrato escrito, en virtud del cual una persona natural o jurídica denominada fideicomitente, transfiere la custodia de bienes y derechos a una entidad, que actúa como fiduciario, para asegurar el cumplimiento de una obligación en su provecho o el de un tercero, denominado beneficiario o fideicomisario.

Artículo 2.1. El fideicomiso se constituye sobre bienes y derechos del fideicomitente, presentes o futuros, que están dentro del comercio y son de lícita procedencia.

2. En el contrato de fideicomiso se designa, de ser necesario, a la persona natural o jurídica beneficiaria y se define el acreedor de la deuda garantizada con los bienes o derechos fideicomitidos.

Artículo 3.1. Actúan como fiduciarios las entidades que hayan sido expresamente autorizadas, mediante licencia expedida por el Banco Central de Cuba.

2. Los fiduciarios solo pueden aceptar la constitución de un fideicomiso, una vez efectuada la debida diligencia para determinar el origen y el beneficiario de los fondos, así como la valoración de los riesgos asociados, en particular los correspondientes al lavado de activos, el financiamiento al terrorismo, la proliferación de armas y el movimiento de capitales ilícitos.

3. De conocerse por alguna de las partes una nueva información durante la vigencia del fideicomiso sobre la realización de las actividades citadas en el apartado anterior, el contrato es nulo.

Artículo 4.1. Los bienes y derechos fideicomitidos conforman un patrimonio de afectación, separado e independiente de los patrimonios del fideicomitente, del fiduciario y del beneficiario. 23 de octubre de 2020 GACETA OFICIAL 475.

2. Los bienes y derechos en fideicomiso solo son afectados al fin consignado en el contrato por el cual fueron transmitidos.

3. El fiduciario en ningún caso responde por las obligaciones contraídas en la ejecución del fideicomiso, las que solo son satisfechas con los bienes y derechos fideicomitidos.

Artículo 5. La custodia sobre el patrimonio en fideicomiso se traslada al fiduciario, quien actúa diligentemente con vistas al cumplimiento de lo establecido en el contrato, ejerciendo las acciones que correspondan para la defensa de los bienes fideicomitidos, tanto ante terceros como frente el beneficiario.

Artículo 6.1. El fideicomiso es remunerado mediante una comisión, cuyo monto y forma de pago la determinan las partes.

2. Salvo estipulación en contrario, el fiduciario tiene derecho al reembolso de los gastos incurridos en beneficio del patrimonio que integra su dominio fiduciario y al pago de una comisión por sus servicios.

Artículo 7.1. El fiduciario desarrolla sus cometidos y cumple con prudencia y diligencia las obligaciones pactadas por el negocio de fideicomiso, sobre la base de la confianza depositada en la institución.

2. Responde por el incumplimiento de sus obligaciones ante el fideicomitente y el beneficiario por los daños y perjuicios que resulten de su acción u omisión.

3. El fiduciario rinde cuenta al beneficiario sobre el estado de los bienes o derechos fideicomitidos y del cumplimiento de sus deberes con una periodicidad no mayor a un (1) año, sin perjuicio de lo dispuesto en el contrato.

Artículo 8.1. El contrato de fideicomiso recoge expresamente la declaración del fideicomitente que garantiza al fiduciario la inexistencia de situaciones tales como:

a) Quebrantamiento de otras relaciones contractuales que tenga el fideicomitente al momento de constituirse el fideicomiso;
b) separación de fondos en fraude de terceros; y
c) encubrimiento de problemas contables del fideicomitente.

2. En caso de incumplimiento el fideicomitente responde por los daños y perjuicios ocasionados al fiduciario.

Artículo 9.1. El fideicomiso es considerado válido, siempre que su fin sea lícito, posible y determinado; a falta de estipulación expresa o en el caso de faltar el fideicomisario designado, se tiene como beneficiario al fideicomitente.

2. Concluido el fideicomiso, los bienes y derechos fideicomitidos que queden en custodia del fiduciario se entregan a quien corresponda, según lo pactado en el contrato.

Artículo 10.1. Son causas de extinción del fideicomiso:

a) El cumplimiento total de sus fines o la imposibilidad absoluta de cumplirlos;
b) el cumplimiento del plazo o condición resolutoria a que se hubiese sometido; si no se dispuso plazo alguno, el máximo legal es de un (1) año;
c) el acuerdo entre fideicomitente y beneficiario, sin perjuicio de los derechos del fiduciario;
d) la revocación del fideicomitente, si se hubiere reservado expresamente esa facultad en el negocio de fideicomiso;
e) la muerte o incapacidad judicialmente declarada del fideicomitente o del fideicomisario o beneficiario, excepto que en el contrato de

fideicomiso se haya designado sustituto; 476 GACETA OFICIAL 23 de octubre de 2020

f) la extinción de la entidad fiduciaria, salvo que en el contrato de constitución del fideicomiso se haya designado fiduciario sustituto;
g) el cambio en las condiciones pactadas en el instrumento de constitución del fideicomiso por parte del fideicomitente; y
h) cualquier otra causa establecida expresamente en el instrumento de fideicomiso.

2. Extinguido el fideicomiso, el fiduciario está obligado a entregar los bienes o derechos fideicomitidos al fideicomitente o a sus sucesores, salvo que otra cosa se hubiera establecido en el contrato.

3. En el supuesto regulado en el inciso f) del apartado Primero del presente artículo, de no ser designado sustituto, la entrega opera de pleno derecho.

4. El fiduciario no puede adjudicarse los bienes o derechos recibidos en fideicomiso.

DISPOSICIÓN ESPECIAL

ÚNICA:

En los casos en que se pretenda constituir en fideicomiso bienes o derechos que conformen el patrimonio de un negocio instituido al amparo de la inversión extranjera, se requiere la aprobación previa del Consejo de Estado o del Consejo de Ministros, según lo dispuesto en la legislación vigente.

DISPOSICIÓN FINAL

ÚNICA: El presente Decreto-Ley entra en vigor a los treinta días posteriores a su publicación en la Gaceta Oficial de la República de Cuba.

PUBLÍQUESE en la Gaceta Oficial de la República de Cuba.

DADO en La Habana, a los 24 días del mes de septiembre de 2020.

Juan Esteban Lazo Hernández

References

CubaDebate. (2020, October 23). *Publica Gaceta Oficial Decretos Leyes Sobre Garantías Mercantiles Para respaldar La Inversión Extranjera*. Cubadebate. Retrieved October 30, 2022, from http://www.cubadebate.cu/noticias/2020/10/23/publica-gaceta-oficial-decretos-leyes-sobre-garantias-mercantiles-para-respaldar-la-inversion-extranjera/

General policies. MINCEX. (n.d.). Retrieved May 21, 2022, from https://inviertaencuba.mincex.gob.cu/en/

VUINEX. Vuinex. (n.d.). Retrieved May 21, 2022, from https://vuinex.mincex.gob.cu/web/login

PART VI

Business

CHAPTER 21

Felix Chevalier on the Houston Trade Mission to Havana

In September 2016, I interviewed Felix Chevalier, a U.S. attorney from Houston, Texas, who had just returned from a three-day trade mission to Cuba.

The trade mission was led by Houston's Mayor Sylvester Turner, Jamey Rootes, Chairman, and Bob Harvey, President of the Greater Houston Partnership (Fig. 21.1).

We wanted to hear what Mr. Chevalier had to say about the Houston trade mission and asked him a few questions about the trip.

Mr. Chevalier is a partner of the Chevalier Law Firm, PLLC based in Houston, Texas, United States. He is an experienced business and government affairs attorney representing Fortune 500 Companies in various industries, including transportation, development, telecommunications, manufacturing, engineering, and finance. He is adept at facilitating commercial transactions and structuring public–private partnerships deals. Mr. Chevalier represents major corporations seeking to do business in Cuba by navigating them through the intricate process.

Felix's civic activities include serving as a member of Engage Cuba, the leading coalition of private companies and organizations working to end the travel and trade embargo on Cuba.

He received his Juris Doctorate from St. John's University School of Law. Felix is a native New Yorker, speaks Spanish, and is the son of Cuban parents.

T. K. Hernández, *The Cuba Interviews*,
https://doi.org/10.1007/978-3-031-30203-9_21

Fig. 21.1 U.S. attorney, Felix Chevalier and Jeffrey DeLaurentis, Chargé d'affaires ad interim of the Embassy of the United States, Havana, 2017 (Photo from the personal collection of Mr. Chevalier)

Hernández: Do you feel the Houston Trade Mission was a success? What did the trade delegation to Havana achieve? Any signed deals?

Felix Chevalier: The objective of the trip was to build upon the existing relationship the City of Houston shares with Cuba. Houston, primarily through the Port of Houston, has engaged in exempt embargo exchanges for decades. I believe Mayor Sylvester Turner, Jamey Rootes, Chairman of the Greater Houston Partnership, and Bob Harvey, President of the Greater Houston Partnership, who led our delegation, facilitated the mission's objective successfully.

We were able to reinforce our interest in building stronger ties between our city and the Island. Commissioners from the Port of Houston, City Council Members, Chair of the Texas Medical Center, City Council Members, Director of the Houston Airport System, corporate executives from major corporations such as Siemens, United Airlines, Halliburton, and other delegation members shared how their respective expertise can help Cuba as it seeks foreign investment, training, and goods and services.

No deals were signed as all trade of goods and services are contingent upon the U.S. Congress lifting the embargo or obtaining a special license from the Office of Foreign Assets Control of the U.S. Department of Treasury.

Are the Texas businesses who want to invest in Cuba further ahead today after the trade mission? In what ways?

Mr. Chevalier: I believe business that engages earlier has a slight head start because, as with most business relationships, it starts with an introduction. However, there's plenty of opportunity for other U.S. firms. To provide you some context, the most recent refinery built in Cuba was in the 1970s by the Russians and the last refinery was built by the Americans in the 1950s. The refinery built by the Americans has better technology than the 20 years younger Russian refinery. Cuba has many needs, from overhauling their entire power grid, construction, engineering, updated technology, energy exploration, training, and other resources to developing a robust energy sector. That's just the energy sector. There are comparable opportunities in all other sectors including, but not limited to, transportation, tourism, healthcare, education, technology, sports, construction, and engineering.

If a U.S. business wishes to invest in Cuba, what would you recommend as a first step?

Mr. Chevalier: I advise companies interested in doing business in Cuba to focus on developing a relationship, understand the culture, adhere to Cuba's protocols, and focus on what the Cubans need. The Cubans operate differently than many Americans are accustomed. The Cubans place an emphasis on relationships because they are focused on the long term.

If a businessperson goes to Cuba with you on a trade mission, what are the next steps for these executives after they return from the trip?

Mr. Chevalier: The initial step is to assess if they can provide the goods and/or services the Cubans are requesting. Secondly, the company needs to evaluate the potential return on their investment. Lastly, if they are planning to move forward, they should understand it may take significant time and patience because they'll either have to get a special license to do business in Cuba via the Office of Foreign Assets Control (OFAC) or wait for the U.S. Congress to lift the trade embargo. Given the momentum and increasing demand, I think the lifting of the trade and travel embargo is a matter of time. The companies that are proactive in pursuing opportunities in Cuba early are likely to have a competitive advantage.

Thank you, Felix, for sharing this with us and those considering doing business in Cuba. It's a great perspective on what participation in a trade delegation to Cuba can offer.

CHAPTER 22

The Quiet Optimism in the American Business Community

A month after the election of Donald Trump in November 2016, I talked with some members of the American business community.

There was still a quiet optimism in the business community despite what then-President-elect Donald Trump might or might not do as far as the Cuba–U.S. relationship was concerned. Nobody was certain if he would step back in time and reverse the progress made or, follow a more pragmatic approach. Some Cuba experts we spoke to agreed; there remained a quiet optimism in the business community, albeit a cautious one.

The optimism was demonstrated by the increase in trademark registration by American companies at the Cuban Industrial Property (OCPI) office[1] in Havana. Corporate giants such as Google and General Electric (GE) were pushing for signed contracts before Trump entered office in January.[2]

I posted a couple of questions to some leading experts involved in the U.S.–Cuba relationship and/or advancing business interests in Cuba. I

[1] Cuban Industrial Property Office (OCPI), Ministry of Science, Technology and Environment. The website is available at: https://www.ocpi.cu/

[2] White House Pushing Cuba on Deals for GE, Google. Carol E. Lee and Felicia Schwartz https://www.wsj.com/articles/white-house-pushing-cuba-on-deals-for-ge-google-1480546325. December 1, 2016.

T. K. Hernández, *The Cuba Interviews*,
https://doi.org/10.1007/978-3-031-30203-9_22

spoke with James Williams of Engage Cuba[3] in Washington, Felix Chevalier of the Chevalier Law firm in Texas, and Judy Kruger of Kruger International in Michigan to get their feedback on the current mood of the business community at that time.

The questions I asked these experts were as follows: **Based on the undeniable, continuing interest of American business and agriculture groups in doing trade and investment with Cuba and the increase of U.S. trademark registrations with the OCPI office, do you think there's a "quiet optimism" in the American business community? Do you think the U.S. President-elect will turn back the hands of time?**

Judy Kruger, growth strategist at Kruger International outlined her take on the reasons for optimism in the community. She said, "There's continued interest in doing business with Cuba because this is not the time to stall out on good efforts. Recent and significant game changers are good for U.S.-Cuba business."

Ms. Kruger saw Fidel Castro's passing as relieving Cuba from its hard line against making concessions with the United States. She said, "In the past few years, President Raúl Castro has been a softer and more approachable leader. This is evidenced by the generous incentives and new foreign investment laws that have passed under Raúl's leadership."

Like many others, she believes "the next president of Cuba is Miguel Díaz-Canel,[4] who is known to be tech-savvy and business friendly." Ms. Kruger said, "No doubt there will be changes when President Castro retires from his leadership position."

Ms. Kruger added, "President-elect Trump's continued harsh dialogue is shaking U.S.-Cuba relations up and this may be a very good thing to push pass stalled agreements between the countries. Trump is known as an astute businessman and will perhaps be perceived as leading businesses to Cuba, not away from Cuba. This may involve some unique regulatory changes that fit Trump's style."

[3] Engage Cuba, established in 2015, was a non-profit advocacy group working to end the travel and trade embargo of the United States against Cuba. The organization was based in Washington, D.C. The website for Engage Cuba is no longer in existence and appears to have been inactive since 5 June 2021.

[4] Miguel Díaz-Canel Bermúdez was elected as Cuba's president on April 18, 2018, and sworn into office the following day. He was the president of the Council of State of Cuba from 2018 to 2019 and first vice president from 2013 to 2018.

She concluded by saying, “There’s an attraction factor to Cuba unlike any other emerging country. That won’t stop and companies ahead of the game will get a larger slice of the pie.”

We spoke with Houston attorney Felix Chevalier who advises U.S. companies seeking to enter the Cuban market. He described his clients as “cautiously optimistic.”

“My clients are cautiously optimistic, but still vocal in their support of lifting the trade and travel embargo. There are entire U.S. industries that can grow by entering the Cuban market. Companies, political leaders, and trade associations will continue to lobby the new administration and Congress to not only continue the ongoing negotiations with Cuba, but to also work towards normalized relations.”

Mr. Chevalier explained, “Clawing back all the advancements that we’ve made in U.S.-Cuba relations may be easier said than done. President-elect Trump has been very vocal on the subject of human rights in Cuba, but he is businessman who is also looking to strengthen trade agreements and boost the U.S. economy. Hopefully, he’ll support opportunities for American businesses to expand into the Cuban market while seeking ways to improve human rights.”

Speaking on the same issue, James Williams of Engage Cuba said, “We have witnessed a strong optimism in the business community across the country. Just yesterday, we saw the announcement of two new cruise lines—Royal Caribbean Cruises and Norwegian Cruise Line—that are planning to sail to Cuba next year.”

Mr. Williams continued, “We’re also enthused by the robust support from American agriculture to open a market 90 miles off our shore. And just last week, several major U.S. airlines began direct flights into Havana,[5] signaling their long-term commitment to operate in the country. Mr. Trump, a businessman, has long recognized the economic benefits of engaging with Cuba. No business in the world, including a Trump company, would continue to pursue a strategy that has failed for 55 years, and I would imagine that Mr. Trump would expect nothing less from the U.S. government.”

[5] U.S. airlines began commercial flights to Cuba in 2016 under the Administration of President Barack Obama. https://www.nytimes.com/2016/09/01/world/americas/cuba-us-first-flight-jetblue.html.

On December 10, 2019, the Trump administration barred flights to all destinations in Cuba except for Havana.

References

Lee, C. E., & Schwartz, F. (2016, December 1). *White House pushing Cuba on deals for GE, Google*. The Wall Street Journal. Retrieved August 21, 2021, from https://www.wsj.com/articles/white-house-pushing-cuba-on-deals-for-ge-google-1480546325

Oficina Cubana de la Propiedad Industrial (n.d.). *Oficina Cubana de la Propiedad Industrial*. Retrieved May 23, 2022, from https://www.ocpi.cu/

Robles, F. (2016, August 31). *Scheduled flights to Cuba from U.S. begin again, now with Jet Engines. The New York Times*. Retrieved November 26, 2021, from https://www.nytimes.com/2016/09/01/world/americas/cuba-us-first-flight-jetblue.html

CHAPTER 23

"Facts and Knowledge Are the Antidote to Threat" Mark Entwistle, Former Ambassador to Cuba

Mark Entwistle was the Canadian ambassador to Cuba from 1993 to 1997. Today, he is co-founder and co-managing director of Acasta Cuba Capital Inc. in Toronto, Canada. Acasta Cuba is an advisory and specialist business development firm which enables clients to understand the Cuban market and pursue commercial opportunities (Fig. 23.1).

Mr. Entwistle has been involved in Cuban affairs for over 25 years and travels to the Island frequently.

I first spoke with Mr. Entwistle in August 2019. This interview includes an update from April 2022 in which he analyzes the expectations vs. results of the Biden presidency.

Hernández: Tell us about your years as the Canadian ambassador to Cuba from 1993 to 1997. How was the experience in Havana during that time? Was it considered a "charmed" posting?

Mark Entwistle: The unbroken relationship between Canada and Cuba as two fellow countries of the Americas has been special for a long time, dating from well before the Cuban Revolution. It has been deep and multifaceted, both at the personal, individual level and between governments. Given the long-standing bilateral relations as well as the absence of the United States in Cuba until the historic opening engineered by former Presidents Raúl Castro and Obama in 2014, the role played by Canada in Cuba was often unique. In that sense, it was a fascinating assignment for me as a professional career Canadian diplomat.

T. K. Hernández, *The Cuba Interviews*,
https://doi.org/10.1007/978-3-031-30203-9_23

Fig. 23.1 Mark A. Entwistle, former Canadian Ambassador of Canada to Cuba, co-founder of Acasta Cuba (Photo by Juanita Montalvo)

When I first arrived in Havana in July 1993, the so-called "Special Period" was in full effect, triggered by the collapse of the Soviet Union and the former socialist world's global trading system. Economic conditions were harsh, and it was an extremely tough time for Cubans. Almost permanent power outages, food shortages, few cars, no gas, and bicycles everywhere. At the same time, it was a challenging experience. On behalf of the Canadian people, I was very involved in many aspects of Cuban life and society. But, by the time I departed Havana officially as Ambassador four years later, the Cubans had clawed their way back from the precipice, a telling demonstration of the broad social resilience and determination characteristic of the Cubans. A lesson that I never forgot. Cubans should never be underestimated, in any circumstances.

Do you think the U.S. embargo against Cuba is effective? I mean, we have countries such as Russia, China, Vietnam, Spain, Italy, and the United Kingdom investing in Cuba? If the embargo worked, it would not be worth anyone's effort to trade with Cuba.

Mr. Entwistle: What we call generally the U.S. embargo against Cuba is a mash-up of laws, regulations, and executive orders. Taken in its totality, it is one of the most comprehensive and aggressive instruments of coercion in world economic history, launched against a developing Caribbean nation and hemispheric neighbor. This is not a political position on my part, but a statement of fact that is hard to perceive in any other way.

Over the span of decades, the core aim was to prevent U.S. businesses, entities, and persons from having contact with Cuba. Given that effectively no other country in the world supports the unilateral American embargo,[1] foreign companies were encouraged by their own governments to conduct legal business in Cuba. And, generally, foreign businesspeople have tried to be reasonably informed and respectful of the interests of holders of claims for compensation for properties expropriated in the early 1960s from U.S. nationals.

However, the driving ethos of the embargo changed fundamentally in April of this year with the decision of the Trump administration to fully implement Title III of the so-called Helms–Burton Law,[2] after 23 years of being suspended by successive U.S. Presidents and Secretaries of State.[3] In confirming extraterritorial design directly and explicitly, there is now a

[1] On June 23, 2021, a total of 184 nations voted in favor of a resolution to demand the end of the U.S. economic blockade on Cuba for the 29th year in a row, three countries abstained (Brazil, Colombia, Ukraine). The United States and Israel voted against. UN General Assembly calls for United States to end Cuba embargo for 29th consecutive year. https://news.un.org/en/story/2021/06/1094612. June 23, 2021.

[2] On April 17, 2019, the U.S. government announced the implementation of Title III of the Cuban Liberty and Democratic Solidarity (LIBERTAD) Act of 1996 (the Helms–Burton Act). The United States indicated on that same day it will be enacting the application of Title IV of this legislation.

[3] See Under Helms–Burton Act, entities with business ties to Cuba now at risk of lawsuits: Insights: Skadden, arps, slate, meagher & flom LLP. Insights|Skadden, Arps, Slate, Meagher & Flom LLP: https://www.skadden.com/insights/publications/2019/05/under-helms-burton-act.

clear intent to do harm to third parties and render them unintentional agents of subsequent damage to the Cuban economy. This is now a qualitatively different phase.

The extraterritoriality of the U.S. embargo, a legal concept that is widely rejected by friends and allies of the United States, is really an attempt to offload to third parties the responsibility to seek solutions to issues that are bilateral matters between Cuba and the United States. The prospect of compensation for expropriated property is something that needs to be negotiated directly between the U.S. and Cuban governments, in the same way that the governments of Canada, Spain, and many other countries settled years ago on behalf of their companies and citizens that had claims for compensation.[4] The process of dialogue with Cuba began in the Obama administration, included a bilateral working group on claims, which is where this matter belongs, rather than trying to weaponize companies from third countries that have every right to conduct legal business in Cuba.

The U.S. embargo has an additional purpose—to cast enough of a shroud of doubt and concern about exposure to distracting and possibly expensive lawsuits in American courts to dissuade potential foreign and American businesspeople from participating in the Cuban economy. To muddy the waters. In that sense, it has an undeniable effect.

But understanding what the embargo does and can do, and what it cannot, is key. There is a business that can certainly be done in Cuba regardless of the U.S. embargo.

What are the implications of the recent enactment of the Helms–Burton regulations by the United States on Canadian business investments on the Island? Are Canadians still able to do business in Cuba?

Mr. Entwistle: Yes, without doubt, Canadians can do business in Cuba. The government of the United States or the American courts of course have no jurisdiction over Canadians, and, in any case, nothing in the U.S. embargo says that a Canadian company or national cannot do business in Cuba.

[4] Five countries negotiated settlements with the Republic of Cuba: Switzerland (1967), Spain (1967), France (1967), the United Kingdom (1978), and Canada (1980). Feinberg, R. E. (2015). "*Reconciling US property claims in Cuba*" https://www.brookings.edu/wp-content/uploads/2016/07/Reconciling-US-Property-Claims-in-Cuba-Feinberg.pdf.

Business people make decisions based on a range of considerations. Capital inexorably follows returns, even a type like socially responsible impact investing, and constantly weighs the relative costs and benefits of each competing global opportunity. Provided the structure of a deal in Cuba makes business sense, if there is the chance to participate fully with the possibility of seeing sustainable longer-term value, there is no shortage of opportunity in the Cuban economy for Canadian business in different sectors.

Is there an antidote to the Helms–Burton regulations? How can investors protect their investments in Cuba?

Mr. Entwistle: The U.S. embargo adds an extra category of risk to be considered by businesses and investors. Serious global business people are not afraid of risk per se because it is everywhere. But they need to understand it and be able to factor that risk into the mix of decision-making. The recent implementation of Title III of Helms–Burton suggests another level of risk, but it is all about knowledge.

The lever at the heart of everything is property, pure, and simple.

Part of the reasonable response to potential embargo risk is, therefore, to know and understand the antecedents of property title. This is not always easy to do, and it creates an additional layer of diligence. But, armed with knowledge, it may be that possible risk from Title III lawsuits is manageable and can be mitigated. I am certainly not a lawyer and would never give legal advice. But it is clear that potential action under Title III in U.S. courts is a right of private action that could, in theory, be privately settled without needing to be licensed by the Office of Foreign Assets Control (OFAC) of the U.S. Department of the Treasury and that a putative claimant must meet a documentary burden of proof that the claim is bona fide. There is also precedent for U.S. courts to have determined that they lack jurisdiction over a foreign entity. There is not an insignificant fee to file such a lawsuit.

I only mention these several aspects to underscore that there are many considerations, and that facts and knowledge are the antidote to threat.

What do you think about Canada's response to Helms–Burton? Was the Canadian government's response adequate for protecting Canadian businesses against the extraterritorial reach of the American legislation?

Mr. Entwistle: I think that the Canadian government's response to the recent ratcheting up of Helms–Burton and its extraterritorial reach has been correct.[5]

In 2019 there has not been the level of political intensity in expressing the need to protect Canadian sovereignty and the global rules-based trading system that we saw when Helms–Burton was first adopted back in 1996. It was then a galvanizing issue that seemed to reach beyond the arcane subject matter of the U.S. embargo against Cuba.

I remember well that period in 1996 because I was Ambassador in Havana during the shoot down of two small private planes from the Cuban American activist group Brothers to the Rescue, who had been repeatedly warned against violation of Cuban airspace,[6] and the subsequent signing into law of Helms–Burton. The loud opposition to the extreme extraterritoriality represented by Title III of the law by Canada, the European Union and others contributed to the decision of the Clinton administration to waive implementation of that section, a position which held until the period of President Trump.

But we are in a different time now. And the dynamics are different.

Despite their best behind-the-scenes lobbying efforts in Washington, D.C., Canada, along with others including the U.S. Chamber of Commerce, was unable to change the single-minded view of the Trump administration. So, the reality is what it is.

However, the Canadian government has made it abundantly clear that the full weight of Canada's national antidote legislation against such extraterritoriality, the so-called Foreign Extraterritorial Measures Act

[5] On April 17, 2019, Chrystia Freeland, former Minister of Foreign Affairs, announced Canada's official position on the United States' decision not to suspend Title III of the Cuban Liberty and Democratic Solidarity (Libertad) Act of 1996. She said she met with U.S. Secretary of State, Mike Pompeo, to register Canada's concerns and stated, "Canada is deeply disappointed with today's announcement. We will be reviewing all options," and that, "we will fully defend the interests of Canadians conducting legitimate trade and investment with Cuba.": www.canada.ca/en/global-affairs/news/2019/04/government-of-canada-will-defend-interests-of-canadians-doing-business-in-cuba.html.

[6] Brothers to the Rescue, founded in 1991 by Jose Basulto and Bay of Pigs veteran Bill Shuss, was an activist non-profit organization based in Miami. On February 24, 1996, two of their planes were shot down by the Cuban air force after repeated violation of Cuba's airspace and other provocations. The incident was condemned internationally, while the Cuban government defended the decision claiming the planes were there to destabilize the government. See author Keith Bolender's book, "Cuba Under Siege: American Policy, the Revolution and Its People" published by Palgrave Macmillan, 2012.

(FEMA), will be made available to Canadian companies and applied by the Department of Justice. There are various elements to the Canadian law, but, in short, Canadians are prohibited by law from even participating in a Helms–Burton action against them, and the Canadian courts can be used to reciprocally claw back from the U.S. claimant's corresponding damages. The message has been clear to any potential American claimant—if you have assets in or connections to Canada, reconsider and proceed with caution.

The importance of knowledge is a refrain throughout this interview. In the same light, U.S. lawyers will be advising their American clients interested in launching Title III processes that there is Canadian antidote legislation that could pose significant risks for them as well.

What could the Cubans be doing to increase foreign investment in Cuba?

Mr. Entwistle: Over the years, I have noticed a sea of change in the attitude to direct foreign investment in Cuba from past ambivalence to a recognition that such investment, and a role for foreign participation in the economy is a pillar of economic development policy reflected in Foreign Investment Law 118.

I learned a long time ago to decline to provide advice to the Cuban government on their policy decision-making, partly because it is not my place as a guest in the country and because there are always many considerations, some little known or understood outside Cuba, that go into the policy mix. There is a strong and understandable desire in Cuba to protect Cuban sovereign ownership of strategic national assets to the greatest extent possible, especially in the context of Cuban economic and political history over the past two hundred years. This is not something wholly unique to Cuba.

I think that there are important forces that cannot be overlooked—relationships are critically important, but, at the same time, capital has its own behavior and cost. The greatest flexibility possible in terms of deal structure acceptable to the Cuban side is always helpful because foreign investors generally want to be able to participate actively in the creation of value for both themselves and the Cuban people in equal measure. Structure is important to encourage and facilitate such involvement.

Additionally, the full implementation of Title III has changed the landscape by introducing the unknown. It would certainly be helpful to serious foreign investors and businesses committed to building long-lasting partnerships with Cuba, that the relevant Cuban authorities facilitate legitimate diligence needs to understand historic property title by making available the necessary documentation as required.

Do you have a vision of Cuba moving forward?

Mr. Entwistle: The overarching answer is whatever vision Cubans have for their future is synonymous with my own.

Cuba faces challenges and problems, of that there is no dispute. And all Cubans would agree. As is the case in many countries, including Canada, governments must try to find the balance between creating enough growth and prosperity in the national economy to be able to reinforce social justice, while at the same time ensuring that their own citizens receive the benefits of that prosperity. A country like Canada relies heavily on taxation and the transfer of financial resources internally to maintain as much equality and fairness as possible in society through access to health care, education. The mechanics and fiscal tools in Cuba are different and expensive social programming is delivered more directly to citizens.

Cuba's experience also differs from that of virtually every other country in one important way—on top of the various challenges, it must cope with the overt hostility of arguably the most powerful country on earth. Without question, all economic and fiscal policy decisions of the Cuban government have effects and implications, but it would be willful blindness to suggest that the embargo does not do serious harm to the Cuban people themselves in its attempt to cripple the Cuban economy.

Cuba is a market of well over 11 million people that dwarfs the rest of the Caribbean basin and can be a regional economic power. Illiteracy is almost non-existent. The Cuban people are smart, resilient, dynamic, and not passive, engaged, talented, and patriotic. The country continues to evolve, too quickly for some and too slowly for others. But I believe Cuba will continue to surprise and defy expectations.

Mr. Entwistle, I'd like to thank you for agreeing to speak with me. Very deeply appreciated.

Follow-up to the Interview: April 2022

Mr. Entwistle, we last spoke in August 2019 before the election of President Biden. It was hoped, based on his fleeting campaign promises, he would roll back Trump's sanctions on Cuba. We now witness, two years into his presidency, that he has failed to live up to those promises and continues with the U.S.–Cuba policies of his predecessor. Can we discuss his lack of action on Cuba policy? Is it a

situation of "the more things change, the more they stay the same"? In defense of his time in office, though, he's been very occupied with pressing domestic and international issues.

Mr. Entwistle: For people who follow the U.S.–Cuba relationship, there was certainly an expectation created by Mr. Biden in his statements about Cuba during the 2020 election campaign that there would be a return to a dialogue with the Cuban government. Whether it would look like the bold initiative of President Obama was unclear, but Mr. Biden at the time had left the impression that he would lessen at least some of the torqued embargo measures put in place by President Trump. That has not happened.

The explanation lies in the entrenched context of U.S. policy toward Cuba—it is a domestic political issue in the United States and not a foreign policy matter. That remains the same for President Biden as it was for President Trump. Just different party politics.

The political considerations for President Biden are multiple in my estimation.

First, the same statements about Cuba made by Mr. Biden during the election campaign became a cudgel for Republican opponents in a key battleground state like Florida, where the margins to secure victory are tight. The Trump campaign was successful in painting these rational instincts about the advantage of a more normal relationship with Cuba as meaning he was "soft on Communism." This provided much-needed ammunition for the Republicans to shore up support in the hardline Cuban American community in South Florida that had been waning recently. In a way, President Obama had been liberated to pursue the opening with Cuba in 2014 precisely because he was not running for reelection. A U.S. election campaign is a risky place to talk about Cuba.

Secondly, when the results in Florida did not go well for the Democrats in the 2020 election, key voices in the Florida Democratic Party laid the blame for losing various House seats they believed were theirs to win squarely at the doorstep of the Biden campaign's handling of the Cuba issue. This diminished the Democratic majority in the House. The implication was that they had been outplayed by the Trump team using Mr. Biden's comments on Cuba. If the local Democratic Party was to rebuild that machinery in key electoral districts in South Florida in time for the 2022 mid-terms, the message was that the Biden White House had to cease and desist in pursuing any reset with Cuba.

Thirdly, the powerful Chairman of the Senate Foreign Relations Committee and a senior ranking member of Congress, Senator Bob Menendez, is himself the son of Cuban immigrants to the United States and a quite hardline opponent of any rapprochement with Cuba without preconditions. On this issue, he is indistinguishable from outspoken Florida Republican members of Congress. President Biden needs the support of Senator Menendez on so many foreign policy issues of import that it would be impolitic to press him on the Cuba issue.

In a Biden White House where there are real political needs to both mollify the Democratic Party machinery in South Florida and reassure Senator Menendez that the administration will not undertake any measures on Cuba with which he does not approve, and in the absence of a clear internal champion of rapprochement with Cuba, it is no wonder that there is no appetite to take on the Cuba issue, even if the foreign policy determinants that propelled the Obama team might still hold. There is no political upside to a distracting battle that would have to be fought on various fronts, both in Congress and internally, with crucial mid-term elections looming.

Lastly, the Russian invasion of Ukraine has doubtless sucked up all available policy bandwidth and created in the administration a mood unsympathetic to other countries perceived to be "soft on Russia," or "friends of Russia," which would certainly include Cuba.

Annex

Gaceta Oficial de la Republica de Cuba—Ley No. 118, Ley de la Inversión Extranjera.

ACTUALIZADA: 7 de febrero de 2020.

La presente es la versión actualizada de la Ley No. 118, "Ley de Inversión Extranjera," de 28 de marzo de 2014, publicada en la Edición de la Gaceta Oficial Extraordinaria No. 20 de 16 de abril de 2014.

JUAN ESTEBAN LAZO HERNÁNDEZ, Presidente de la Asamblea Nacional del Poder Popular de la República de Cuba.

HAGO SABER: Que la Asamblea Nacional del Poder Popular de la República de Cuba, en su Primera Sesión Extraordinaria de la VIII Legislatura, del día 29 de marzo de 2014 ha aprobado lo siguiente:

POR CUANTO: Nuestro país ante los desafíos que enfrenta para alcanzar un desarrollo sostenible puede, por medio de la inversión extranjera, acceder a financiamiento externo, tecnologías y nuevos mercados, así como insertar productos y servicios cubanos en cadenas internacionales de valor y generar otros efectos positivos hacia su industria doméstica, contribuyendo de esta manera al crecimiento de la nación.

POR CUANTO: Los cambios que tienen lugar en la economía nacional como consecuencia de la actualización del modelo económico cubano regido por los Lineamientos de la Política Económica y Social del Partido y la Revolución, aconsejan revisar y adecuar el marco legal de la inversión extranjera que establece la Ley No. 77, "Ley de la Inversión Extranjera," de 5 de septiembre de 1995, para ofrecer mayores incentivos a esta y asegurar que la atracción del capital extranjero contribuya eficazmente a los objetivos del desarrollo económico sostenible del país y a la recuperación de la economía nacional, sobre la base de la protección y el uso racional de los recursos humanos y naturales y del respeto a la soberanía e independencia nacionales.

POR CUANTO: La Constitución de la República establece entre otras formas de propiedad, la de las empresas mixtas, sociedades y asociaciones económicas y prevé, con respecto a la propiedad estatal, la transmisión total o parcial de objetivos económicos destinados a su desarrollo, con carácter excepcional, si ello resultare útil y necesario al país.

POR TANTO: La Asamblea Nacional del Poder Popular, en uso de las atribuciones que le están conferidas en el artículo 75, inciso b) de la Constitución de la República, acuerda dictar la siguiente:

LEY No. 118.

Ley DE LA INVERSIÓN EXTRANJERA

CAPÍTULO I

DEL OBJETO Y CONTENIDO

ARTÍCULO 1.1. Esta Ley tiene por objeto establecer el marco legal de la inversión extranjera en el territorio nacional sobre la base del respeto a la ley, la soberanía e independencia de la nación y el beneficio mutuo, para contribuir a nuestro desarrollo económico en función de una sociedad socialista próspera y sostenible.

2. La presente Ley y su legislación complementaria establecen un régimen de facilidades, garantías y seguridad jurídica al inversionista que propicia la atracción y el aprovechamiento del capital extranjero.

3. La inversión extranjera en el país se orienta a la diversificación y ampliación de los mercados de exportación, el acceso a tecnologías de avanzada, la sustitución de importaciones, priorizando la de alimentos. Del mismo modo a la obtención de financiamiento externo, la creación de nuevas fuentes de empleo, la captación de métodos gerenciales y la

vinculación de la misma con el desarrollo de encadenamientos productivos, así como al cambio de la matriz energética del país mediante el aprovechamiento de fuentes renovables de energía.

4. Las disposiciones que contiene esta Ley incluyen las garantías a los inversionistas, los sectores destinatarios de inversiones extranjeras, las modalidades que pueden adoptar estas, las inversiones en bienes inmuebles, los aportes y su valoración, así como el régimen para su negociación y autorización. También establecen el régimen bancario, el de exportación e importación, el laboral, el tributario, el de reservas y seguros y el de registro e información financiera; las normas relativas a la protección del medio ambiente, el uso racional de los recursos naturales, la protección a la innovación científica y tecnológica; instituye las acciones de control a la inversión extranjera y el régimen de solución de conflictos.

CAPÍTULO II

DEL GLOSARIO

ARTÍCULO 2. En esta Ley y su Reglamento se utilizan con la acepción que en cada caso se indica, los términos siguientes:

a) Asociación económica internacional: unión de inversionistas nacionales y extranjeros dentro del territorio nacional para la producción de bienes, la prestación de servicios o ambos, con finalidad lucrativa, que comprende las empresas mixtas y los contratos de asociación económica internacional.

b) Autorización: título habilitante expedido por el Consejo de Ministros o por el jefe del organismo de la Administración Central del Estado en el que se delegue, para la realización de alguna de las modalidades de inversión extranjera previstas en esta Ley.

c) Capital Extranjero: capital procedente del extranjero, así como la parte de los dividendos o beneficios pertenecientes al inversionista extranjero que sean reinvertidos a tenor de esta Ley.

d) Cargos de dirección superior: cargos de miembros de los órganos de dirección y administración de la empresa mixta y de la empresa de capital totalmente extranjero, así como de los representantes de las partes en los contratos de asociación económica internacional.

e) Concesión administrativa: título habilitante que otorga, con carácter temporal, el Consejo de Ministros para la gestión de un servicio público, la realización de una obra pública o la explotación de un bien de dominio público, bajo los términos y condiciones que se establezcan.

f) Contrato de asociación económica internacional: acuerdo entre uno o más inversionistas nacionales y uno o más inversionistas extranjeros para realizar actos propios de una asociación económica internacional sin constituir persona jurídica distinta a las partes.

g) Empresa de capital totalmente extranjero: entidad mercantil con capital extranjero sin la concurrencia de ningún inversionista nacional o persona natural con capital extranjero.

h) Empresa Mixta: compañía mercantil cubana que adopta la forma de sociedad anónima por acciones nominativas en la que participan como accionistas uno o más inversionistas nacionales y uno o más inversionistas extranjeros.

i) Entidad empleadora: entidad cubana con personalidad jurídica facultada para concertar con una empresa mixta o de capital totalmente extranjero, un contrato mediante el cual facilite a solicitud de esta los trabajadores necesarios, quienes conciertan sus contratos laborales con dicha entidad.

j) Haberes: salarios, ingresos y demás remuneraciones, así como los incrementos, compensaciones u otros pagos adicionales que perciban los trabajadores cubanos y extranjeros, con excepción de los provenientes del fondo de estimulación económica, si este existiere.

k) Inversión extranjera: aportación realizada por inversionistas extranjeros en cualesquiera de las modalidades previstas en la Ley, que implique en el plazo por el que se autorice, la asunción de riesgos en el negocio, la expectativa de obtener beneficios y una contribución al desarrollo del país.

l) Inversionista extranjero: persona natural o jurídica, con domicilio y capital en el extranjero, que participa como accionista en una empresa mixta o participe en una empresa de capital totalmente extranjero o figure como parte en un contrato de asociación económica internacional.

m) Inversionista nacional: persona jurídica de nacionalidad cubana, con domicilio en el territorio nacional, que participa como accionista en una empresa mixta, o sea parte en un contrato de asociación económica internacional.

n) Zona Especial de Desarrollo: zona en la que se establecen un régimen y políticas especiales, con el objetivo de fomentar el desarrollo económico sostenible a través de atracción de inversión extranjera, la innovación tecnológica y la concentración industrial, con vistas a incrementar las exportaciones, la sustitución efectiva de importaciones y la generación de nuevas fuentes de empleo, en una constante articulación con la economía interna.

CAPÍTULO III
DE LAS GARANTÍASA LOS INVERSIONISTAS

ARTÍCULO 3. El Estado cubano garantiza que los beneficios concedidos a los inversionistas extranjeros y a sus inversiones se mantienen durante todo el período por el que hayan sido otorgados.

ARTÍCULO 4.1. Las inversiones extranjeras dentro del territorio nacional gozan de plena protección y seguridad jurídica y no pueden ser expropiadas, salvo que esa acción se ejecute por motivos de utilidad pública o interés social previamente declarados por el Consejo de Ministros, en concordancia con lo dispuesto en la Constitución de la República, los tratados internacionales suscritos por la República de Cuba en materia de inversiones y la legislación vigente, con la debida indemnización por su valor comercial establecido de mutuo acuerdo, pagadero en moneda libremente convertible.

2. De no llegarse a acuerdo sobre el valor comercial, la fijación del precio se efectúa por una organización de prestigio internacional en la valoración de negocios, autorizada por el Ministerio de Finanzas y Precios y contratada al efecto por acuerdo de las partes que intervienen en el proceso de expropiación. De no existir acuerdo entre ellos con respecto a la selección de la referida organización, a su elección, se realizará un sorteo para determinarla o se acudirá a la vía judicial.

ARTÍCULO 5. Las inversiones extranjeras son protegidas en el país, contra reclamaciones de terceros que se ajusten a derecho o la aplicación extraterritorial de leyes de otros estados, conforme a las leyes cubanas y a lo que dispongan los tribunales cubanos.

ARTÍCULO 6.1. El plazo de la autorización otorgada para el desarrollo de las operaciones de una empresa mixta, de las partes en un contrato de asociación económica internacional o de la empresa de capital totalmente extranjero, puede ser prorrogado por la propia autoridad que lo otorgó, siempre que se solicite por las partes interesadas antes del vencimiento del plazo fijado.

2. De no prorrogarse el plazo a su vencimiento, se procederá a la liquidación de la empresa mixta, del contrato de asociación económica internacional o de la empresa de capital totalmente extranjero, según lo acordado en los documentos constitutivos y lo dispuesto en la legislación vigente. Lo que corresponda al inversionista extranjero, será pagado en moneda libremente convertible, salvo pacto expreso en contrario.

ARTÍCULO 7.1. El inversionista extranjero parte en una asociación económica internacional puede, previo acuerdo de las partes, vender o transmitir en cualquier otra forma al Estado, a un tercero o a las partes en la asociación, previa Autorización, total o parcialmente, sus derechos en ella, recibiendo en moneda libremente convertible el precio equivalente, salvo pacto expreso en contrario.

2. El inversionista extranjero en una empresa de capital totalmente extranjero puede, vender o transmitir en cualquier otra forma, al Estado o a un tercero, previa Autorización, sus derechos en ella, total o parcialmente, recibiendo en moneda libremente convertible el precio equivalente, salvo pacto expreso en contrario.

ARTÍCULO 8. El importe que corresponda recibir al inversionista extranjero en los casos a que se refieren los artículos 6 y 7 de esta Ley se de- termina por acuerdo entre las partes. De ser necesario acudir en cualquier momento del proceso a un tercero para establecer el importe, se selecciona una organización de prestigio internacional en la valoración de negocios, autorizada por el Ministerio de Finanzas y Precios.

ARTÍCULO 9.1. El Estado garantiza al inversionista extranjero la libre transferencia al exterior en moneda libremente convertible, sin pago de tributos u otro gravamen relacionados con dicha transferencia, de:

a) los dividendos o beneficios que obtenga por la explotación de la inversión; y

b) las cantidades que deberá recibir en los casos a que se refieren los artículos 4, 6 y 7 de esta Ley.

2. Las personas naturales extranjeras que presten sus servicios a una empresa mixta, a las partes en cualquier otra forma de asociación económica internacional o a una empresa de capital totalmente extranjero, siempre que no sean residentes permanentes en la República de Cuba, tienen derecho a transferir al exterior los haberes que perciban dentro de la cuantía y conforme a las demás regulaciones dictadas por el Banco Central de Cuba.

ARTÍCULO 10. Las empresas mixtas y los inversionistas nacionales y extranjeros partes en los contratos de asociación económica internacional, son sujetos del régimen especial de tributación que dispone esta Ley, hasta el vencimiento del plazo por el que fueron autorizadas.

CAPÍTULO IV

DE LOS SECTORES DESTINATARIOS DE INVERSIONES EXTRANJERAS Y DE LA CARTERA DE OPORTUNIDADES

ARTÍCULO 11.1. La inversión extranjera puede ser autorizada en todos los sectores, con excepción de los servicios de salud y educación a la población y de las instituciones armadas, salvo en sus sistemas empresariales.

2. El Consejo de Ministros aprueba las oportunidades de inversión extranjera a promocionar y las políticas generales y sectoriales para la inversión extranjera, las que se publican en la Cartera de Oportunidades de inversión extranjera por el Ministerio del Comercio Exterior y la Inversión Extranjera.

3. Los órganos, organismos de la Administración Central del Estado y entidades nacionales patrocinadoras de la inversión extranjera tienen la obligación, conforme a las políticas aprobadas, de identificar y presentar al Ministerio del Comercio Exterior y la Inversión Extranjera las propuestas de negocios con inversión extranjera.

4. El Ministro del Comercio Exterior y la Inversión Extranjera informa anualmente al Consejo de Ministros el estado de conformación y actualización de la Cartera de Oportunidades por los órganos, organismos de la Administración Central del Estado y entidades nacionales patrocinadoras de la inversión extranjera.

CAPÍTULO V

DE LAS INVERSIONES EXTRANJERAS

SECCIÓN PRIMERA

De las modalidades de la inversión extranjera.

ARTÍCULO 12. La inversión extranjera definida en la presente Ley, puede manifestarse como:

a) inversión directa, en las que el inversionista extranjero participa como accionista en una empresa mixta o de capital totalmente extranjero o con aportaciones en contratos de asociación económica internacional, participando de forma efectiva en el control del negocio; y

b) inversiones en acciones o en otros títulos-valores, públicos o privados, que no tienen la condición de inversión directa.

ARTÍCULO 13.1. La inversión extranjera adopta alguna de las modalidades siguientes:

a) empresa mixta;

b) contrato de asociación económica internacional; o

c) empresa de capital totalmente extranjero.

2. Como contratos de asociación económica internacional clasifican, entre otros, los contratos a riesgo para la exploración de recursos naturales no renovables, para la construcción, la producción agrícola, la administración hotelera, productiva o de servicios y los contratos para la prestación de servicios profesionales.

SECCIÓN SEGUNDA
De la empresa mixta.
ARTÍCULO 14.1. La empresa mixta implica la formación de una persona jurídica distinta a la de las partes, adopta la forma de compañía anónima por acciones nominativas y le es aplicable la legislación vigente en la materia.

2. Las proporciones del capital social que deben aportar los inversionistas nacionales y los inversionistas extranjeros, son acordadas por los socios y establecidas en la autorización.

3. El convenio de asociación es el acuerdo suscrito entre los socios y contiene los pactos fundamentales para la conducción del negocio que pretenden desarrollar.

4. La constitución de una empresa mixta requiere la forma de escritura pública como requisito esencial para su validez y a la misma se incorporan los estatutos sociales y se adjuntan la Autorización y el convenio de asociación.

5. Los estatutos sociales incluyen disposiciones relacionadas con la organización y operación de la sociedad.

6. La empresa mixta adquiere personalidad jurídica cuando se inscribe en el Registro Mercantil.

7. Creada una empresa mixta, pueden cambiar los accionistas, por acuerdo entre estos, previa aprobación de la autoridad que otorgó la Autorización.

8. Las empresas mixtas pueden crear oficinas, representaciones, sucursales y filiales, tanto en el territorio nacional como en el extranjero, así como tener participaciones en entidades en el exterior.

9. La Disolución Y Liquidación De La Empresa Mixta Se Rige Por Lo Dispuesto En Sus Estatutos Sociales, Sujeto a Lo Previsto En La Legislación Vigente.

SECCIÓN TERCERA
Del contrato de asociación económica internacional
ARTÍCULO 15.1. El contrato de asociación económica internacional tiene, entre otras, las características siguientes:

a) no implica la constitución de una persona jurídica distinta a la de sus partes;

b) puede tener por objeto la realización de cualquier actividad contenida en la Autorización;

c) las partes tienen libertad para estipular todos los pactos y cláusulas que entiendan convenir a sus intereses, con tal de que no infrinjan el objeto autorizado, las condiciones de la Autorización o la legislación vigente; y

d) cada parte contratante hace aportaciones distintas, constituyendo una acumulación de participaciones de las cuales son propietarios en todo momento y aunque sin llegar a constituir un capital social, les es dable llegar a formar un fondo común, siempre y cuando quede determinada la porción de propiedad de cada uno de ellos.

2. En los contratos de asociación económica internacional cuyo objeto sea la administración hotelera, productiva o de servicios o la prestación de servicios profesionales, no se acumulan participaciones ni se crea un fondo común y tienen las características descritas en los apartados 3 y 4 de este artículo.

3. Los contratos de asociación económica internacional para la administración hotelera, productiva o de servicios tienen como objetivos lograr mejores servicios al cliente o producciones con mayor calidad, beneficiarse con el uso de una marca internacionalmente reconocida y con la publicidad, así como la comercialización y pro- moción internacionales del inversionista extranjero. Los mismos poseen entre otras, las características siguientes:

a) el inversionista extranjero actúa a nombre y en representación del inversionista nacional, en lo que respecta al contrato de administración firmado;

b) no se comparten utilidades; y

c) el pago al inversionista extranjero se condiciona a los resultados de su gestión.

4. Los Contratos De Asociación Económica Internacional Para La Prestación De Servicios Profesionales Tienen, Entre Otras, Las Características Siguientes:

a) se suscriben con compañías extranjeras consultoras de reconocido prestigio internacional; y

b) tienen por objeto la prestación conjunta de servicios de auditoría, asesoría contable, servicios de avalúos y finanzas corporativas, servicios de reingeniería organizacional, mercadotecnia y gestión de negocios e intermediación de seguros.

5. El contrato de asociación económica internacional requiere para su validez la forma de escritura pública y entra en vigor al momento de su inscripción en el Registro Mercantil.

6. Otorgado un contrato de asociación económica internacional no pueden cambiar sus partes, salvo por acuerdo entre ellas y con la aprobación de la autoridad que concedió la Autorización.

7. La terminación del contrato de asociación económica internacional se rige por lo dispuesto en el mismo, sujeto a lo previsto en la legislación vigente.

SECCIÓN CUARTA

De la empresa de capital totalmente extranjero.

ARTÍCULO 16.1. En la empresa de capital totalmente extranjero, el inversionista extranjero ejerce la dirección de la misma, disfruta de todos los derechos y responde por todas las obligaciones prescritas en la Autorización.

2. El Inversionista Extranjero En Empresas De Capital Totalmente Extranjero, Previa Inscripción En El Registro Mercantil, Puede Establecerse Dentro Del Territorio Nacional:

a) Como persona natural, actuando por sí mismo;

b) como persona jurídica, constituyendo una filial cubana de la entidad extranjera de la que es propietario, mediante escritura pública, bajo la forma de compañía anónima por acciones nominativas; o

c) como persona jurídica, estableciendo una sucursal de una entidad extranjera.

3. Las empresas de capital totalmente extranjero constituidas como filial pueden crear oficinas, representaciones, sucursales y filiales, tanto en el territorio nacional como en el extranjero, así como tener participaciones en entidades en el exterior.

4. La disolución y liquidación de la empresa de capital totalmente extranjero bajo la forma de filial cubana, se rige por lo dispuesto en sus estatutos sociales, sujeto a lo previsto en la legislación vigente.

5. La terminación de las actividades autorizadas a la persona natural y a la sucursal de compañía extranjera se rige por lo dispuesto en la Autorización y en lo que al efecto se establezca en la legislación vigente.

CAPÍTULO VI

DE LAS INVERSIONES EN BIENES INMUEBLES

ARTÍCULO 17.1. De conformidad con las modalidades establecidas en la presente Ley, pue- den realizarse inversiones en bienes inmuebles y obtener su propiedad u otros derechos reales.

2. Las Inversiones En Bienes Inmuebles a Que Se Refiere El Apartado Anterior Pueden Destinarse a:

a) viviendas y edificaciones, dedicadas a domicilio particular o para fines turísticos;

b) viviendas u oficinas de personas jurídicas extranjeras; o

c) desarrollos inmobiliarios con fines de explotación turística.

CAPÍTULO VII

DE LOS APORTES Y SU VALORACIÓN

ARTÍCULO 18.1. A los fines de esta Ley se consideran aportes los siguientes:

a) aportaciones dinerarias, que en el caso del inversionista extranjero lo es en moneda libremente convertible;

b) maquinarias, equipos, u otros bienes tangibles;

c) derechos de propiedad intelectual y otros derechos sobre bienes intangibles;

d) derecho de propiedad sobre bienes muebles e inmuebles y otros derechos reales sobre estos, incluidos los de usufructo y superficie; y

e) otros bienes y derechos.

Los aportes que no consistan en moneda libre mente convertible se valoran en esa moneda.

2. La transmisión a favor de los inversionistas nacionales de la propiedad o de otros derechos reales sobre bienes de propiedad estatal, para que sean aportados por aquellos, se efectúa bajo los principios establecidos en la Constitución de la República y previa certificación del Ministerio de Finanzas y Precios, oído el parecer del órgano, organismo o entidad correspondiente y con la aprobación del Consejo de Ministros o su Comité Ejecutivo, según proceda.

En lo que respecta a los aportes de derechos de propiedad intelectual y otros derechos sobre bienes intangibles, se estará sujeto a lo dispuesto en la legislación que regula esta materia.

3. Las aportaciones dinerarias en moneda libremente convertible se tasan por su valor en el mercado internacional y a los efectos del cambio en pesos cubanos, se aplican las tasas de cambio del Banco Central de Cuba. La moneda libremente convertible que constituye aporte de capital extranjero, se ingresa al país a través de una institución bancaria autorizada a realizar operaciones en el territorio nacional y se deposita en esta según las regulaciones vigentes en esta materia.

4. Los aportes de la parte extranjera que no sean aportaciones dinerarias, que estén destinados al capital social de empresas mixtas, de empresas de capital totalmente extranjero o que constituyen aportaciones en contratos de asociación económica internacional, se valoran a través de

los métodos que acuerden libremente los inversionistas siempre que sean los generalmente aceptados por las normas internacionales de valoración, acreditándose su valor por el correspondiente certificado pericial extendido por entidades que posean autorización del Ministerio de Finanzas y Precios y son transcriptos en la escritura pública que se otorgue.

CAPÍTULO VIII

DE LA NEGOCIACIÓN Y AUTORIZACIÓN DE LA INVERSIÓN EXTRANJERA

ARTÍCULO 19.1. Para la creación de una asociación económica internacional, el inversionista nacional debe negociar con el inversionista extranjero cada aspecto de la inversión, incluida su factibilidad económica, los aportes respectivos, según corresponda, la forma de dirección y administración que tiene esa asociación, así como los documentos jurídicos para su formalización.

2. Si se tratase de una empresa de capital totalmente extranjero, el Ministerio del Comercio Exterior y la Inversión Extranjera indica al inversionista, la entidad cubana responsable de la rama, subrama o de la actividad económica en la que pretende realizar su inversión, con la que debe analizar su proposición y obtener la correspondiente aprobación escrita.

ARTÍCULO 20. El Estado cubano autoriza inversiones extranjeras que no afecten la defensa y seguridad nacional, el patrimonio de la nación y el medio ambiente.

ARTÍCULO 21.1. La aprobación para efectuar inversiones extranjeras en el territorio nacional se otorga atendiendo al sector, la modalidad y las características de la inversión extranjera, por los órganos del Estado siguientes:

a) el Consejo de Estado;

b) el Consejo de Ministros; y

c) el jefe del organismo de la Administración Central del Estado autorizado para ello.

2. El Consejo De Estado Aprueba La Inversión Extranjera, Cualquiera Que Sea Su Modalidad, En Los Casos Siguientes:

a) cuando se exploren o exploten recursos naturales no renovables, excepto al amparo de contratos de asociación económica internacional a riesgo que se aprueban y autorizan según el apartado 3 inciso d) del presente artículo; y

b) cuando se realicen para la gestión de servicios públicos, tales como transporte, comunicaciones, acueductos, electricidad, la realización de una obra pública o la explotación de un bien de dominio público.

Aprobada la inversión extranjera por el Consejo de Estado, en los casos anteriormente previstos, se dicta la Autorización por el Consejo de Ministros.

3. El Consejo De Ministros Aprueba Y Dicta La Autorización De La Inversión Extranjera, Cuando Se Trate De:

a) desarrollos inmobiliarios;

b) empresas de capital totalmente extranjero;

c) la transmisión de la propiedad estatal u otros derechos reales sobre bienes estatales;

d) los contratos de asociación económica internacional a riesgo para la explotación de recursos naturales no renovables y su producción;

e) la intervención de una empresa extranjera con participación de capital público;

f) el uso de fuentes renovables de energía;

g) el sistema empresarial de los sectores de la salud, la educación y de las instituciones armadas; y

h) otras inversiones extranjeras que no requieran la aprobación del Consejo de Estado.

4. El Consejo de Ministros puede delegar en jefes de los organismos de la Administración Central del Estado, la facultad de aprobar y autorizar inversiones extranjeras en los casos de su competencia y atendiendo a su modalidad o sectores destinatarios.

ARTÍCULO 22.1. Para la constitución de una empresa mixta o empresa de capital totalmente extranjero, así como para la celebración de un contrato de asociación económica internacional, corresponde presentar la solicitud ante el Ministro del Comercio Exterior y la Inversión Extranjera, de conformidad con lo previsto en el Reglamento de la presente Ley.

2. Si el objetivo de la inversión aprobada es la gestión de un servicio público, la realización de una obra pública o la explotación de un bien de dominio público, el Consejo de Ministros, una vez aprobado por el Consejo de Estado, otorga la correspondiente concesión administrativa, bajo los términos y condiciones que establezca, de conformidad con lo previsto en la legislación vigente.

3. La decisión que deniega o autoriza la inversión extranjera por la autoridad competente, se dicta dentro del plazo de sesenta días naturales,

contados a partir de la fecha de presentación de la solicitud y debe ser notificada a los solicitantes.

En los casos de las modalidades de inversión extranjera sujetas a la aprobación de jefes de organismos de la Administración Central del Estado la decisión se dicta dentro del plazo de cuarenta y cinco días naturales, contados a partir de la fecha en que fue admitida.

ARTÍCULO 23. Las modificaciones a las condiciones establecidas en la Autorización requieren aprobación de la autoridad competente conforme establece el artículo 21 de la presente Ley.

ARTÍCULO 24. Las condiciones establecidas en la Autorización pueden ser aclaradas, por medio del Ministerio del Comercio Exterior y la Inversión Extranjera, a instancia de los inversionistas.

CAPÍTULO IX

DEL RÉGIMEN BANCARIO

ARTÍCULO 25.1. Las empresas mixtas, los inversionistas nacionales y los inversionistas extranjeros partes en contratos de asociación económica internacional y las empresas de capital totalmente extranjero, abren cuentas en cualquier banco del Sistema Bancario Nacional, por medio de las cuales efectúan los cobros y pagos que generan sus operaciones según el régimen monetario vigente. Asimismo, podrán acceder a los servicios que ofrecen las instituciones financieras establecidas en el país.

2. Las empresas mixtas y los inversionistas nacionales partes en contratos de asociación económica internacional, previa autorización del Banco Central de Cuba y con arreglo a las regulaciones vigentes, pueden abrir y operar cuentas en moneda libremente convertible en bancos radicados en el extranjero. Así mismo pueden concertar operaciones crediticias con instituciones financieras extranjeras de acuerdo con las regulaciones vigentes en esta materia.

CAPÍTULO X

DEL RÉGIMEN DE EXPORTACIÓN E IMPORTACIÓN

ARTÍCULO 26.1. Las empresas mixtas, los inversionistas nacionales y los inversionistas extranjeros partes en contratos de asociación económica internacional y las empresas de capital totalmente extranjero tienen derecho, de acuerdo con las disposiciones establecidas a tales efectos, a exportar e importar directamente lo necesario para sus fines.

2. Las empresas mixtas, las partes en los contratos de asociación económica internacional y las empresas de capital totalmente extranjero adquirirán, preferentemente bienes y servicios en el mercado nacional,

ofrecidos en iguales condiciones de calidad, precios y plazos de entrega a las del mercado internacional.

CAPÍTULO XI

DEL RÉGIMEN LABORAL

ARTÍCULO 27. En la actividad de las inversiones extranjeras se cumple la legislación laboral y de seguridad social vigente en la República de Cuba, con las adecuaciones que figuran en esta Ley y su Reglamento.

ARTÍCULO 28.1. Los trabajadores que presten sus servicios en las actividades correspondientes a las inversiones extranjeras serán por lo general, cubanos o extranjeros residentes permanentes en la República de Cuba.

2. No obstante, los órganos de dirección y administración de las empresas mixtas o de las empresas de capital totalmente extranjero o las partes en los contratos de asociación económica internacional pueden decidir, que determinados cargos de dirección superior o algunos puestos de trabajo de carácter técnico, se desempeñen por personas no residentes permanentes en el país y en esos casos determinar el régimen laboral a aplicar así como los derechos y obligaciones de esos trabajadores.

3. Las Personas no Residentes Permanentes En El País Que Sean Contratadas Están Sujetas a Las Disposiciones Legales De Inmigración Y Extranjería Vigentes En La Nación.

ARTÍCULO 29.1. Las empresas mixtas, las partes en los contratos de asociación económica internacional y las empresas de capital totalmente extranjero pueden ser autorizadas por el Ministerio del Comercio Exterior y la Inversión Extranjera a crear un fondo de estimulación económica para los trabajadores cubanos y extranjeros residentes permanentes en la República de Cuba que presten sus servicios en actividades correspondientes a las inversiones extranjeras. Las contribuciones al fondo de estimulación económica se hacen a partir de las utilidades obtenidas.

2. Se exceptúan de la creación del fondo de estimulación previsto en el apartado que antecede, los contratos de administración hotelera, productiva o de servicios y los contratos para la prestación de servicios profesionales.

ARTÍCULO 30.1. El personal cubano o extranjero residente permanente en la República de Cuba que preste servicios en las empresas mixtas, con excepción de los integrantes de su órgano de dirección y administración, es contratado por una entidad empleadora a propuesta del Ministerio del Comercio Exterior y la Inversión Extranjera y autorizada por el Ministerio de Trabajo y Seguridad Social.

Los miembros del órgano de dirección y administración de la empresa mixta son designados por la junta general de accionistas y se vinculan laboralmente a la empresa mixta en los casos que corresponda.

Solo por excepción, al otorgarse la Autorización, puede disponerse que todas las personas que presten sus servicios en la empresa mixta puedan ser contratadas directamente por esta y siempre con arreglo a las disposiciones legales vigentes en materia de contratación laboral.

2. Los trabajadores cubanos o extranjeros residentes permanentes en la República de Cuba que presten sus servicios a las partes en los contratos de asociación económica internacional son contratados por la parte cubana, con arreglo a las disposiciones legales vigentes en materia de contratación laboral.

3. En las empresas de capital totalmente extranjero, los servicios del personal cubano o extranjero residente permanente en la República de Cuba, con excepción de los integrantes de su órgano superior de dirección y administración, se prestan mediante un contrato que suscribe la empresa con una entidad empleadora propuesta por el Ministerio del Comercio Exterior y la Inversión Extranjera y autorizada por el Ministerio de Trabajo y Seguridad Social.

Los miembros de los órganos de dirección y administración de la empresa de capital totalmente extranjero son designados y se vincularán laboralmente a esta en los casos que corresponda.

4. Los Pagos a Los Trabajadores Cubanos Y Extranjeros Residentes Permanentes En La República De Cuba Se Efectúan En Pesos Cubanos.

ARTÍCULO 31.1. La entidad empleadora a que se refiere el artículo anterior, contrata individualmente a los trabajadores cubanos y extranjeros residentes permanentes en la República de Cuba, los que mantienen con ella su vínculo laboral de acuerdo con lo dispuesto en la legislación vigente en la materia.

2. Cuando las empresas mixtas o las empresas de capital totalmente extranjero consideren que un determinado trabajador no satisface sus exigencias en el trabajo, pueden solicitar a la entidad empleadora que lo sustituya por otro. Cualquier reclamación laboral se resuelve en la entidad empleadora de conformidad con el procedimiento establecido en la legislación específica.

ARTÍCULO 32. No obstante lo dispuesto en los artículos precedentes de este Capítulo, en la Autorización que apruebe la inversión extranjera, a modo de excepción, puede establecerse regulaciones laborales especiales.

ARTÍCULO 33. Se reconocen conforme a lo previsto en la legislación vigente, los derechos de los trabajadores cubanos que participen en la obtención de resultados tecnológicos u organizativos consistentes en innovaciones que aporten beneficios económicos, sociales o medioambientales.

CAPÍTULO XII

DEL RÉGIMEN ESPECIAL DE TRIBUTACIÓN

ARTÍCULO 34. Las empresas mixtas y los inversionistas nacionales y extranjeros partes en contratos de asociación económica internacional, en cuanto al cumplimiento de las obligaciones tributarias y sus derechos como contribuyentes se regirán por lo establecido en las disposiciones vigentes sobre la materia, con las adecuaciones que se disponen en los artículos siguientes.

ARTÍCULO 35. Se exime del pago del impuesto sobre los ingresos personales, a los inversionistas extranjeros socios en empresas mixtas o partes en contratos de asociación económica internacional, por los ingresos obtenidos a partir de los dividendos o beneficios del negocio.

ARTÍCULO 36.1. El impuesto sobre utilidades, se paga por las empresas mixtas, los inversionistas nacionales y extranjeros partes en contratos de asociación económica internacional aplicando un tipo impositivo del quince por ciento sobre la utilidad neta imponible.

2. Se exime del pago del impuesto sobre utilidades a las empresas mixtas y partes en los contratos de asociación económica internacional por un período de ocho años a partir de su constitución. El Consejo de Ministros podrá extender el período de exención aprobado.

3. Se exime del pago del impuesto sobre utilidades, por la utilidad neta u otros beneficios autorizados a reinvertir, en los casos en que sea aprobada la reinversión de estos en el país por la autoridad competente.

4. Cuando concurra la explotación de recursos naturales, renovables o no, puede aumentarse el tipo impositivo del impuesto sobre utilidades por decisión del Consejo de Ministros. En este caso puede elevarse hasta en un cincuenta por ciento.

ARTÍCULO 37.1. Las empresas mixtas y los inversionistas nacionales y extranjeros partes en contratos de asociación económica internacional pagan el impuesto sobre las ventas con una bonificación del cincuenta por ciento en el tipo impositivo a aplicar sobre las ventas mayoristas.

2. Se exime del pago de este impuesto a las empresas mixtas y a los inversionistas nacionales y extranjeros partes en contratos de asociación

económica internacional, durante el primer año de operación de la inversión.

ARTÍCULO 38.1. Las empresas mixtas y los inversionistas nacionales y extranjeros partes en contratos de asociación económica internacional pagan el impuesto sobre los servicios con una bonificación del cincuenta por ciento en el tipo impositivo a aplicar.

2. Se exime del pago de este impuesto a las empresas mixtas y a los inversionistas nacionales y extranjeros partes en contratos de asociación económica internacional, durante el primer año de operación de la inversión.

ARTÍCULO 39. Se exime del pago del impuesto por la utilización de la fuerza de trabajo a las empresas mixtas y a los inversionistas nacionales y extranjeros partes en contratos de asociación económica internacional.

ARTÍCULO 40. Las empresas mixtas y los inversionistas nacionales y extranjeros partes en contratos de asociación económica internacional pagan los impuestos por el uso o explotación de las playas, por el vertimiento aprobado de residuales en cuencas hidrográficas, por el uso y explotación de bahías, por la utilización y explotación de los recursos forestales y la fauna silvestre y por el derecho de uso de las aguas terrestres, con una bonificación del cincuenta por ciento durante el período de recuperación de la inversión.

ARTÍCULO 41. Se exime del pago del impuesto aduanero a las empresas mixtas, los inversionistas nacionales y extranjeros, partes en contratos de asociación económica internacional, por las importaciones de equipos, maquinarias y otros medios durante el proceso inversionista, de acuerdo con las normas establecidas al respecto por el Ministro de Finanzas y Precios.

ARTÍCULO 42. Son sujetos pasivos de la contribución territorial para el desarrollo local, las empresas mixtas, los inversionistas nacionales y extranjeros partes en contratos de asociación económica internacional y las empresas de capital totalmente extranjero.

Se eximen del pago de la contribución territorial para el desarrollo local, durante el período de recuperación de la inversión, a las empresas mixtas, así como a los inversionistas nacionales y extranjeros partes en contratos de asociación económica internacional.

ARTÍCULO 43.1. Se excluyen de lo establecido en los artículos precedentes a los inversionistas nacionales y extranjeros partes en contratos de asociación económica internacional que tengan por objeto la administración hotelera, productiva o de servicios y la prestación de servicios profesionales, que tributan con arreglo a lo dispuesto en la Ley del Sistema Tributario y las normas que la complementan.

2. Los Inversionistas Extranjeros Partes En Los Contratos a Que Se Refiere El Apartado Precedente Están Exentos Del Impuesto Sobre Las Ventas Y El Impuesto Sobre Los Servicios.

ARTÍCULO 44. Las empresas de capital totalmente extranjero están obligadas durante su plazo de vigencia, al pago de los tributos con arreglo a la legislación vigente, sin perjuicio de los beneficios de carácter fiscal que se establezcan por el Ministerio de Finanzas y Precios, siempre que sea de interés para el país.

ARTÍCULO 45. A los fines de esta Ley, la Aduana General de la República puede conceder a las personas naturales y jurídicas a que se refiere el presente Capítulo, facilidades especiales en cuanto a las formalidades y al régimen aduanero, en correspondencia con lo establecido en la legislación vigente.

ARTÍCULO 46. El pago de tributos y demás derechos recaudables en aduanas, se realiza conforme a la legislación vigente en la materia, excepto los casos que establezca el Consejo de Ministros en ocasión de autorizar la modalidad de inversión.

ARTÍCULO 47. El Ministerio de Finanzas y Precios, oído el parecer del Ministerio del Comercio Exterior y la Inversión Extranjera, teniendo en cuenta los beneficios y la cuantía de la inversión, la recuperación del capital, las indicaciones que se dispongan por el Consejo de Ministros para los sectores de la economía priorizados, así como los beneficios que pueda reportar a la economía nacional, puede conceder exenciones totales o parciales, de manera temporal o permanente, u otorgar otros beneficios fiscales de conformidad con lo establecido en la legislación tributaria vigente, para cualesquiera de las modalidades de inversión extranjera reconocidas en esta Ley.

CAPÍTULO XIII

DE LAS RESERVAS Y SEGUROS

ARTÍCULO 48.1. Las empresas mixtas, los inversionistas nacionales y extranjeros partes en los contratos de asociación económica internacional y las empresas de capital totalmente extranjero, constituyen con cargo a sus utilidades y con carácter obligatorio, una reserva para cubrir las contingencias que pudieran producirse en sus operaciones.

2. El Procedimiento Para La Formación, Utilización Y Liquidación De La Reserva Prevista En El Apartado Anterior, Es Regulado Por El Ministerio De Finanzas Y Precios.

ARTÍCULO 49. Sin perjuicio de la reserva a que se refiere el artículo anterior, las empresas mixtas, los inversionistas nacionales y extranjeros partes en los contratos de asociación económica internacional y las empresas de capital totalmente extranjero, pueden constituir reservas con carácter voluntario con sujeción a las regulaciones del Ministerio de Finanzas y Precios.

ARTÍCULO 50.1. Las empresas mixtas, los inversionistas nacionales y extranjeros partes en los contratos de asociación económica internacional y las empresas de capital totalmente extranjero están obligados a contratar el seguro de los bienes de cualquier tipo y las responsabilidades. Las aseguradoras cubanas tendrán el derecho de primera opción bajo condiciones competitivas a escala internacional.

2. Las instalaciones industriales, turísticas o de otra clase o los terrenos, que sean cedidos en arrendamiento por empresas estatales u otras organizaciones nacionales, son aseguradas por el arrendatario a favor del arrendador, en correspondencia con las condiciones previstas en el apartado anterior.

CAPÍTULO XIV

DEL RÉGIMEN DE REGISTRO E INFORMACIÓN FINANCIERA

ARTÍCULO 51. Las empresas mixtas, los inversionistas nacionales y extranjeros partes en los contratos de asociación económica internacional y las empresas de capital totalmente extranjero antes del comienzo de sus operaciones, cuentan con treinta días naturales a partir de la fecha de notificación de la Autorización para el otorgamiento.

De los documentos públicos notariales necesarios y dentro de los treinta días siguientes a este acto, se inscriben en el Registro Mercantil.

ARTÍCULO 52. Las empresas mixtas, las partes en los contratos de asociación económica internacional y las empresas de capital totalmente extranjero están sujetas al cumplimiento de las Normas Cubanas de Información Financiera dictadas por el Ministerio de Finanzas y Precios.

ARTÍCULO 53.1. Los sujetos referidos en el artículo anterior, presentan al Ministerio del Comercio Exterior y la Inversión Extranjera el informe anual de sus operaciones y cualquier otra información que se requiera, de conformidad con lo previsto en el Reglamento de la presente Ley.

2. La presentación del informe anual dispuesto en el apartado anterior se realiza con independencia de sus obligaciones informativas con el Ministerio de Finanzas y Precios, la administración tributaria correspondiente, la Oficina Nacional de Estadísticas e Información, así como la

información exigida por las normativas metodológicas y de control del Plan de la Economía Nacional.

CAPÍTULO XV

CIENCIA, TECNOLOGÍA, MEDIO AMBIENTE E INNOVACIÓN

ARTÍCULO 54. La inversión extranjera se estimula, autoriza y opera en el contexto del desarrollo sostenible del país lo que implica que, en todas sus fases, se atenderá cuidadosamente la introducción de tecnología, la conservación del medio ambiente y el uso racional de los recursos naturales.

ARTÍCULO 55. El Ministerio del Comercio Exterior y la Inversión Extranjera somete las propuestas de inversión que reciba a la consideración del Ministerio de Ciencia, Tecnología y Medio Ambiente, el que evalúa su conveniencia desde el punto de vista ambiental y decide si se requiere la realización de una evaluación de impacto ambiental, así como la procedencia del otorgamiento de las licencias ambientales pertinentes y el régimen de control e inspección, conforme a lo dispuesto en la legislación vigente.

ARTÍCULO 56.1. El Ministerio de Ciencia, Tecnología y Medio Ambiente dicta las medidas que se requieran para dar solución adecuada a las situaciones que ocasionen daños, peligros o riesgos para el medio ambiente y el uso racional de los recursos naturales.

2. La Persona Natural O Jurídica Responsable Del Daño O Perjuicio Está Obligada Al Restablecimiento De La Situación Ambiental Anterior Y a La Correspondiente Reparación O Indemnización, Según El Caso.

ARTÍCULO 57. El Ministerio del Comercio Exterior y la Inversión Extranjera, presenta a la consideración del Ministerio de Ciencia, Tecnología y Medio Ambiente la propuesta de inversión que reciba, este último, evalúa su factibilidad tecnológica y las medidas para la protección y gestión de la propiedad intelectual necesarias para garantizar la soberanía tecnológica del país.

ARTÍCULO 58. Los derechos sobre los resultados logrados en el marco de cualesquiera de las modalidades de inversión extranjera, susceptibles de ser protegidos por la vía de la propiedad intelectual, se rigen por lo acordado en los documentos constitutivos en correspondencia con la legislación vigente en esta materia.

CAPÍTULO XVI

DE LAS ACCIONES DE CONTROL

ARTÍCULO 59.1. Las modalidades de inversión extranjera están sujetas a las acciones de control establecidas en la legislación vigente y se realizan por el Ministerio del Comercio Exterior y la Inversión Extranjera, así como por otros órganos, organismos de la Administración Central del Estado o entidades nacionales rectoras en las diferentes actividades con competencia para ello.

2. Las Acciones De Control Tienen El Propósito De Evaluar, Entre Otros, El Cumplimiento De:

a) las disposiciones legales vigentes; y

b) las condiciones aprobadas para la constitución o instrumentación de cada negocio.

CAPÍTULO XVII

DEL RÉGIMEN DE SOLUCIÓN DE CONFLICTOS

ARTÍCULO 60.1. Los conflictos que surgen de las relaciones entre los socios de una empresa mixta o entre los inversionistas nacionales y extranjeros partes en contratos de asociación económica internacional o entre los socios de una empresa de capital totalmente extranjero bajo la forma de compañía anónima por acciones nominativas, se resuelven según lo acordado en los documentos constitutivos, salvo los casos previstos en este Capítulo.

2. Igual Regla Se Aplica Cuando El Conflicto Se Produce Entre Uno O Más Socios Y La Empresa Mixta O La Empresa De Capital Totalmente Extranjero a La Que Pertenecen.

3. Los conflictos surgidos con motivo de la inactividad de los órganos de gobierno de las modalidades de inversión extranjera previstas en la Ley, así como de la disolución o terminación y liquidación de estas, serán resueltos en todos los casos por la Sala de lo Económico del Tribunal Provincial Popular que corresponda.

4. Los conflictos que surgen de las relaciones entre los socios de una empresa mixta o de una empresa de capital totalmente extranjero bajo la forma de compañía anónima por acciones nominativas o entre los inversionistas nacionales y extranjeros partes en contratos de asociación económica internacional, que han sido autorizados para llevar a cabo actividades vinculadas a los recursos naturales, servicios públicos y ejecución de obras públicas, son resueltos por la Sala de lo Económico del Tribunal Provincial Popular que corresponda, excepto disposición contraria prevista en la Autorización.

La regla anterior se aplica cuando el conflicto se produce entre uno o más socios extranjeros y la empresa mixta o la empresa de capital totalmente extranjero a la que pertenecen.

ARTÍCULO 61. Los litigios sobre la ejecución de contratos económicos que surgen entre las distintas modalidades de inversión extranjera previstas en la Ley o entre ellas con personas jurídicas o naturales cubanas, pueden ser resueltos por la Sala de lo Económico del Tribunal Provincial Popular que corresponda, sin perjuicio de someterlo a instancias arbitrales conforme a la ley cubana.

DISPOSICIONES ESPECIALES

PRIMERA: Las empresas mixtas, los inversionistas nacionales y extranjeros partes en contratos de asociación económica internacional y las empresas de capital totalmente extranjero, están sujetas a las regulaciones que se establezcan en la legislación vigente en materia de reducción de desastres.

SEGUNDA: Las disposiciones de esta Ley, su Reglamento y las normas complementarias, son de aplicación a la inversión extranjera que se establezca en las zonas especiales de desarrollo con las adecuaciones que dispongan las normas especiales que para ellas se dicten y siempre que no se opongan a su funcionamiento. Sin perjuicio de lo anterior, los regímenes especiales concedidos en la presente Ley serán de aplicación a estas inversiones, cuando les resulten más beneficiosos.

DISPOSICIONES TRANSITORIAS

PRIMERA: Esta Ley es de aplicación en lo sucesivo a las asociaciones económicas internacionales, a las empresas de capital totalmente extranjero existentes y a las que están en operaciones a la fecha de su entrada en vigor.

Los beneficios concedidos al amparo del Decreto-Ley No. 50 "Sobre asociación económica entre entidades cubanas y extranjeras," de 15 de febrero de 1982 y de la Ley No. 77 "Ley de la Inversión Extranjera," de 5 de septiembre de 1995, se mantienen durante todo el plazo de vigencia de la asociación económica internacional o de la empresa de capital totalmente extranjero.

SEGUNDA: Esta Ley se aplica a las solicitudes de autorización de inversión extranjera que estén en tramitación a la fecha de su entrada en vigor.

TERCERA: Las disposiciones complementarias dictadas por los distintos organismos de la Administración Central del Estado para la mejor aplicación y ejecución de las normas de la Ley No. 77, de 5 de septiembre de 1995, en lo concerniente a cada uno, continúan aplicándose en lo que no se opongan a la presente Ley. Los organismos implicados, en un plazo no mayor de tres meses, contados a partir de la entrada en vigor de esta Ley, revisarán las mencionadas normas y, oído el parecer del Ministerio del Comercio Exterior y la Inversión Extranjera, las armonizarán conforme a las prescripciones de esta Ley.

CUARTA: Las empresas mixtas, las partes en los contratos de asociación económica internacional y las empresas de capital totalmente extranjero, pueden ser autorizadas excepcionalmente por el Consejo de Ministros, para realizar determinados cobros y pagos en pesos cubanos.

QUINTA: Para proceder al pago en pesos cubanos que se establece en el apartado 4 del artículo 30, debe obtenerse previamente dichas cantidades con pesos convertibles.

SEXTA: El pago de los tributos y demás derechos recaudables en aduanas por los inversionistas se realiza en pesos convertibles, aun en aquellos casos en que su importe se exprese en pesos cubanos.

SÉPTIMA: Lo regulado en las Disposiciones Cuarta, Quinta y Sexta que anteceden, mantienen su vigencia hasta que se disponga en el país la unificación monetaria, a partir de lo cual, los sujetos obligados en esta Ley se regirán por las normas que a tales efectos se establezcan.

DISPOSICIONES FINALES

PRIMERA: El Consejo de Ministros dictará el Reglamento de la presente Ley dentro de los noventa días siguientes a su aprobación.

SEGUNDA: Se derogan la Ley No. 77 "Ley de la Inversión Extranjera," de 5 de septiembre de 1995; el Decreto-Ley No. 165 "De las Zonas Francas y Parques Industriales," de 3 de junio de 1996; y los acuerdos No. 5279, de 18 de octubre de 2004; No. 5290, de 11 de noviembre de 2004; No. 6365, de 9 de junio de 2008, adoptados por el Comité Ejecutivo del Consejo de Ministros y cuantas otras disposiciones legales se opongan a las prescripciones de esta Ley.

TERCERA: La presente Ley entra en vigor a los noventa días siguientes de su aprobación.

CUARTA: Publíquese, junto a su Reglamento y demás disposiciones complementarias en la Gaceta Oficial de la República para su conocimiento general.

DADA en la sala de sesiones de la Asamblea Nacional del Poder Popular, Palacio de las Convenciones, en la ciudad de La Habana, a los 29 días del mes de marzo de 2014.

Juan Esteban Lazo Hernández.

Presidente de la Asamblea Nacional del Poder Popular de la República de Cuba.

References

Bershteyn, B., Boucher, J. L., Fisch, E. J., Kwok, S., Nelson, T. G., & Robertson, E. (2019, May 9). *Under Helms-Burton Act, entities with business ties to Cuba now at risk of lawsuits: Insights:* | Skadden, Arps, Slate, Meagher & Flom LLP. Retrieved March 14, 2022, from https://www.skadden.com/insights/publications/2019/05/under-helms-burton-act

Bershteyn, B., & et al. (2019, May 9). *Under Helms-Burton Act, entities with business ties to Cuba now at risk of lawsuits: Insights: Skadden, arps, slate, meagher & flom LLP*. Insights | Skadden, Arps, Slate, Meagher & Flom LLP. Retrieved December 30, 2019, from https://www.skadden.com/insights/publications/2019/05/under-helms-burton-act

Bolender, K. (2012). *Cuba Under Siege: American policy, the revolution and its people*. Palgrave Macmillan.

Feinberg, R. E. (2015, December). *Reconciling US property claims in Cuba*. Brookings Institution. Retrieved March 14, 2022, from https://www.brookings.edu/wp-content/uploads/2016/07/Reconciling-US-Property-Claims-in-Cuba-Feinberg.pdf

Global Affairs Canada. *Government of Canada will defend interests of Canadians doing business in Cuba*. Retrieved January 8, 2021, from https://www.canada.ca/en/global-affairs/news/2019/04/government-of-canada-will-defend-interests-of-canadians-doing-business-in-cuba.html

Lee, C. E. & Schwartz, F., (2016, December 1). *White House Pushing Cuba on deals for GE, Google*. The Wall Street Journal. Retrieved August 21, 2021, from https://www.wsj.com/articles/white-house-pushing-cuba-on-deals-for-ge-google-1480546325

CHAPTER 24

"Cuba's Day in the Sun Will Come"—Fred Wade, President, Fireworks FX

In early October 2019, a ship set sail destined for the Port of Mariel loaded with over 13 tons of fireworks and equipment. Fireworks FX Inc, a small Canadian company from the Annapolis Valley in Nova Scotia, had been tasked with one of the most exciting events of the century about to take place in Havana in November of that year (Fig. 24.1).

Fred Wade, the company's president, spoke to me in a telephone interview about this once-in-a-lifetime event, the staging of the Habana 500 fireworks display. We discussed how his company came to Cuba, his experiences working on the Island, and the company's future road map.

There are few people in the world who have been up to the "lantern dome" which sits on the cupola of the Capitolio building, but Fred Wade has been there. His company staged the fireworks displays that took place in two locations in Havana, one at El Capitolio and the other at El Morro Castle that November for the 500th anniversary of Havana.[1]

Hernández: How long has your company been doing business in Cuba?

Fred Wade: Our first exploratory meeting regarding the Cuban market took place in 2011 with Arturo Mena, who was working for Nova Scotia Business Inc. as a consultant for the Latin America market.He now owns

[1] Havana was founded on November 16, 1519, in the Villa of San Cristóbal de La Habana. For more information visit: https://www.wmf.org/blog/celebrating-500th-anniversary-havana-cuba.

T. K. Hernández, *The Cuba Interviews*,
https://doi.org/10.1007/978-3-031-30203-9_24

Fig. 24.1 Fred Wade, president of Fireworks FX, at the top of the lantern dome of the Capitolio, 300 feet above the streets of Havana (From the collection of Mr. Wade)

his own consulting firm in Halifax, M & C Latin Trade Consulting. In 2012, I attended my first FIHAV (*la Feria Internacional de Cuba*) as part of the trade delegation from Atlantic Canada organized by the Atlantic Canada Opportunities Agency. I haven't missed one since.

Tell us about your company. Why and how did Fireworks FX ended up working in Cuba?

Mr. Wade: Our company first expanded into the Caribbean in Barbados in 2006, and it turned out to be very successful. We are now present on several islands in the Caribbean. In Barbados we created a local base of trained technicians by teaching the "Canadian Fireworks Certification" to the Barbados Defense Force, Fire, and Polices services.

I had never been to Cuba. I thought the Island offered real potential. Cuban has not used fireworks historically for celebrating, as do the other Caribbean islands. Seeing the potential with the growth in tourism, developments grew from there.

I see our future business in Cuba with the hotel industry that plays host for special events such as destination weddings and other celebrations such as New Year's Eve. Then there are corporate, cultural and sporting events, etc.

Do you see the U.S. embargo against Cuba as a hindrance to business?

Mr. Wade: No. I see it as an opportunity for Canadian business and foreign investors. Once the embargo is lifted, Cuba will be flooded with U.S. trade. For us, if the Americans were already in Cuba, there would be no chance for a company like ours, a small rural company from Nova Scotia to get a foothold, a chance to succeed in the Cuban market. One day the embargo will go away, it is a question of not "if" but "when."

At that time, the floodgates will open with an explosion of U.S. tourism and business. Then it will be Cuba's time in the sun. But right now, the embargo is a great opportunity for Canadian companies and foreign investors.

The bulk of tourists are Canadian, it's been that way now and forever. Cuba and Canada have a good relationship which goes a long way back from the days when schooners from Nova Scotia set sail to Cuba, loaded up with salt fish, lumber, and potatoes that would then return with loaded with molasses and rum.

You know, we Nova Scotians have a special relationship with Cuba that goes way back to 1903. Cuba's first president opened a consulate up on Main Street in Yarmouth (Nova Scotia). Cuba used to import their codfish from Spain, but after Cuba's independence from Spain in 1898, it changed and Cuba started getting their cod fish from us. Nova Scotia's relationship with Cuba goes back more than a century.

Tell us what you have learned about Cubans and doing business in Cuba?

Mr. Wade: Cuba is not like any other market. It takes more work to get your name out there, to meet the people and organizations that you need to, and things do not happen quickly, patience is required.

Relationships are very important to Cubans, as they are for us. Once you establish a relationship, trust will follow and this connection with your Cuban partners will give you an advantage over someone completely unknown. But they are not naïve and will always be aware of what other vendors are offering. Respect is the key.

Let's discuss the fireworks displays your company is doing in Havana for the 500th anniversary. Tell us how Fireworks FX is going to light up the city skies.

Mr. Wade: The first shows will take place at the El Morro Castle on November 15. This is a traditional fireworks display. The display on the next night at El Capitolio is a gala event, with thousands of seated guests in the plaza in front of the newly restored building. This show is a pyro-musical where the fireworks are choreographed in exact timing with the music.

We have a team of eight technicians from Canada to prepare the two shows, and we will have 15 Cuban assistants at each site as well.

How are you going to do the Capitolio fireworks show?

Mr. Wade: We will be using the entire Capitolio building which is massive, pyrotechnics from ground level at the front of the building, the entire length of roof, the giant dome of the cupola, and the lantern dome on the very top. Almost a ton of pyrotechnics fired in four minutes!

That's impressive! This has never been done before.

Mr. Wade: It is. It's never been done before. We're very excited.

How did you win the contract to stage the fireworks display for the 500th Anniversary of the City of Havana?

Mr. Wade: They selected us from our reputation, the quality of our work, and the fact that we were known in Cuba.

Did you present to President Díaz-Canel? How did you demonstrate what you had to offer the Havana 500th anniversary celebration? What format? What did he say?

Mr. Wade: They required us to provide a computer video simulation of both shows to the authorities for review and approval. We were told by the composer of the music for the Capitolio show, Frank Fernandez, that the president viewed it. He said it was in perfect rhythm with his music, and our designer has music in his blood! After viewing the video, the President stated he liked it very much.

Have you done any other fireworks display in Cuba before this one?

Mr. Wade: Yes, we did the 500th anniversary celebrations for Santiago de Cuba, which took place on July 26, 2015. The fireworks display was a stellar success and broadcast live in Cuba, and we received praise from the highest Cuban authorities.

The 500th anniversary celebrations in Santiago established our company's name in Cuba. The show was paid for by the Italian company ITALSAV[2] as a gift to Cuba for the 500th anniversary celebrations. ITALSAV operates a chain of stores in Cuba which sell household items.

ITALSAV had sponsored earlier pyrotechnical shows in Cuba and had used Italian and Spanish companies in the past. When these companies became too expensive, they looked for other providers; they found our company.

We have done three other shows in Santiago de Cuba, including the July 25 "*Santiago de las Luces*," 2018 Anniversary of the Revolution, and last New Year's Eve celebrations 2018 for the city.

We have also done something for the Caravan of Freedom which travels from Santiago de Cuba to Havana each year retracing the path of Fidel Castro's victorious army march to the Capital. This was in July last year, with a launch of red and white streamers which covered the Caravan.

The city of Cienfuegos has also used Fireworks FX to light up their skies for the city's 200th birthday last April. Cuba Cooperation France sponsored this. This a non-profit organization representing the French descendants of those who once lived in Cienfuegos.

What's in store for Fireworks FX in the future?

Mr. Wade: Our road map for development includes training courses in Cuba to develop a base of trained Cuban technicians so that eventually we will not have to send experts from Canada. We will need to establish storage for both inventory and equipment in Cuba because, at present, each show must be shipped by sea container, which is a significant expense.

Fred, I'd like to thank you for speaking to us about one of the most exciting events in Havana's history. Fireworks FX is going to be putting on the most amazing show the night skies of Havana and the citizens of the City have ever seen. This is truly marvelous!

[2] Italsav S.r.l. was founded in 1994. The Company's line of business includes the wholesale distribution of non-durable goods. Available at https://www.bloomberg.com/profile/company/4348709Z:IM.

References

Barbacci, N. (2019, December 31). *Celebrating the 500th anniversary of Havana, Cuba*. World Monuments Fund. Retrieved October 20, 2019, from https://www.wmf.org/blog/celebrating-500th-anniversary-havana-cuba

Bloomberg, n.d. *Italsav Srl*. Bloomberg. Retrieved December 6, 2020, from https://www.bloomberg.com/profile/company/4348709Z:IM#-1

PART VII

Oil and Energy

CHAPTER 25

Is Energy Self-Sufficiency in the Cards for Cuba? Peter Stickland, CEO, Melbana Energy

In 2012, Melbana Energy Limited (ASX: MAY, formerly known as MEO Australia) was looking for new ventures with large resources in under-explored onshore settings. Cuba fits the requirements. Errol Johnstone, Chief Geo-scientist of the company, said that only a handful of places onshore in the world show the kind of conventional oil potential Cuba demonstrates (Fig. 25.1).

In December 2016, the company announced its corporate name change from MEO Australia to Melbana Energy Limited. Chief Executive Officer and Managing Director Peter Stickland said of the change, "The MEO Board believes the relaunching of MEO as Melbana Energy Limited will better reflect the company's focus on its high-potential Cuba Block 9 Production Sharing Contract and other Cuban business development activities. We look forward to continuing all the company's exploration activities under the Melbana Energy banner in the future" (Cuba Business Report, 2016).

I met with Peter Stickland, the former Chief Executive Officer and Managing Director of the company in Toronto in the summer of 2016. We discussed Melbana's oil exploration project in Block 9.

One of the most interesting revelations to come from our conversation was the fact that Cuba could one day attain oil self-sufficiency and has the potential to become a net exporter.

T. K. Hernández, *The Cuba Interviews*,
https://doi.org/10.1007/978-3-031-30203-9_25

Fig. 25.1 Peter Stickland, Non-Executive Director at Australia's Melbana Energy Limited (Photo courtesy of Mr. Stickland)

In 2012, Melbana executives began looking at Cuba. A year later, the company was working through the prequalification process with Petro Australis, a private company with expertise in Cuba. When the prequalification process was completed, direct negotiations with CUPET, the national oil company, began.

Negotiations concluded in September 2015 when Melbana signed a Production Sharing Contract (PSC) for what is known as Block 9. Block 9 is an onshore location about 2,300 square km or 1/2 million acres in size, not far from Varadero. The signed PSC with CUPET has a duration of 25 years consisting of an exploration period of 8.5 years in four subperiods. Melbana can start production earlier if a commercial discovery is made.

The first assessments by Melbana of Block 9 demonstrated that one of the three identified petroleum plays on Block 9 contains potentially 8,183 billion barrels of Oil-in-Place with prospective recoverable volumes of 395 million barrels. Significant oil potential is also expected to be identified in the shallower plays.

Mr. Stickland summed it up as, "it looks good and better than we expected. To identify almost 400 million of potentially high-quality light oil, recoverable in conventional onshore oil play is extraordinary."

An independent American assessment of the entire Cuban oil province recorded a potential of 4.6 billion barrels (U.S. Geological Survey North Cuba Basin Assessment Team, 2008).[1] Domestically, Cuba produces approximately 80,000 barrels of oil a day, about half of what is needed for national use. Although the oil is chiefly heavy oil with a high sulphur content, Melbana believes they may find a lighter, higher quality oil than what is produced now.

Will these findings significantly impact Cuba's energy sector?

Mr. Stickland: If the potential we are seeing so far is borne out by drilling results, then there is the possibility for Cuba to become self-sufficient, but that's not going to happen overnight, of course. There might be a five or ten-year period but the potential is there, and that's from the resource assessment we've done so far, not the entire assessment—as I think there's still more to come in the block we have. Eighty thousand barrels a day is a lot of oil obviously, but if we can find a couple of hundred million barrels or the 400 million barrels that's suggested, an unrisked potential outlook, then 80,000 barrels per day of production is not impossible.

Could we then assume that Cuba will become self-sufficient one day?

Mr. Stickland: It's natural that Cuba has an ambition to be self-sufficient for energy. It's a core ambition for most countries to be self-sufficient for energy. Cuba has affinities with the Gulf of Mexico petroleum system which has huge resources. If you look at Louisiana, Texas onshore and offshore, and Mexico onshore and offshore, and you add all that, it's of the order of 100 billion barrels. Cuba is part of that arc of the Gulf of Mexico, but it's been under explored for the last 50 years. The opportunity presents itself to look at it afresh, and certainly for us it's very exciting.

I'd like to think that Cuba has the potential to go beyond self-sufficiency and, in an upside case, be able to become a net exporter of energy. That would be very exciting.

How was the investment experience with the Cubans?

[1] U.S. Department of the Interior U.S. Geological Survey estimated a mean of 4.6 billion barrels of undiscovered oil, USGS. Fact Sheet. February 2005.

Mr. Stickland: There have been limitations with the American embargo. Melbana is not allowed to import U.S. technology into Cuba and Melbana respects that. Working around this limitation, Chinese and European companies have offered their expertise.

Overall, the Cubans were reasonable to negotiate with and very professional in the way they negotiated the Block.

References

Cuba Business Report Staff. (2016, December 7). *Business update Melbana Energy—MEO Australia*. Cuba Business Report. Retrieved November 20, 2021, from https://www.cubabusinessreport.com/business-update-melbana-energy-meo-australia/

Schenk, Christopher J. et al. (2004). *Executive summary—Assessment of undiscovered oil and gas resources of the jurassic-cretaceous composite total petroleum system in the North Cuba Basin, Cuba*, (2004). U.S. Geological Survey (USGS). Retrieved September 3, 2020, from https://pubs.usgs.gov/dds/dds-069/dds-069-m/

CHAPTER 26

Interview with the Chief Representative of Greatwall Drilling, China

This interview took place in December 2019, just before the world was hit with the outbreak of the COVID-19 pandemic. When I started reviewing the transcript, the Chinese New Year had begun on January 25. Many people were left stranded because of the closing of airports and the cessation of travel to and from countries under lockdown. It was the beginning of a very tough year (Fig. 26.1).

The interview here is special for me personally and professionally for many reasons. It is with an executive I have known for more than two years. We first met at the CUPET conference's tour of the oil fields in 2017. It is always good to meet again, like greeting an old friend from far away one hasn't seen in a while.

This interview signifies the substance of what Cuba Business Report is. Because it takes place with the head of a Chinese company active in Cuba, it represents the publication's views on international participation in foreign investment on the Island. And China is one of the biggest players in Cuba.

Mr. Xiangzhong Kong is Chief Representative of Greatwall Drilling Company of China. The interview took place in the offices of Greatwall Drilling at the Miramar Trade Center complex in Havana on December 5, 2019, after the last CUPET Energy Oil and Gas Conference.

T. K. Hernández, *The Cuba Interviews*,
https://doi.org/10.1007/978-3-031-30203-9_26

Fig. 26.1 At the Greatwall Drilling site near Matanzas with Kong Xiangzhong (From the personal collection of the editor)

Hernández: How long has Greatwall Drilling of China been present in Cuba?

Kong: Actually, Greatwall Drilling Company came to Cuba in 2005. Almost 15 years ago. We are working with CUPET.

Do you work with any other companies here? For example, the Russians (Zarubezhneft) and Melbana Energy of Australia are both present on the Island.

Kong: We have been working with Sherritt International, a Canadian company, which is now the biggest oil and gas production company here and also we worked with Peberco, a joint venture company from Canada and France. Peberco left Cuba almost two years ago. We worked with them for almost two or three years. We drilled one well for them. Also, we worked with PetroVietnam. So in the last 13 years we worked with many oil and gas companies.

Have you been working in Cuba since 2005?

Kong: Since 2008.

How many drilling projects does Greatwall have in Cuba and where are they located?

Kong: Actually, since 2005 we have drilled a lot of wells, near to 100 wells in different blocks for different projects. Most of the wells were drilled for CUPET (Cuba Petróleo) and a few wells for Sherritt and the other oil production companies. All the blocks which are producing oil and gas, we drilled in the last 15 years.

We have the main production blocks such as Varadero, Seboruco (near Matanzas), Santa Cruz, Habana del Este, Guanabo, and Bacuranao.

Nowadays we have four heavy drilling rigs with different service teams, mud service, mud logging service, and directional drilling.

We provide integrated and turnkey services and all services around the well hole.

Does your company foresee great potential in the oil industry here in Cuba?

Kong: Yes, I'm sure. There is very great potential in Cuba because right now, the Cuban Blocks are not well-developed. There is not so much exploration activity right now.

So that's the reason CUPET is auctioning off the blocks now?

Kong: Yes. Last year CUPET did some seismic surveys. In the few years, they did seismic surveys offshore and onshore and have very good analysis and results from the Chinese company BGP data research[1] and also the French company CGG. So there's very great potential.

Also, the wells we drilled in the different blocks have shown very good production. Some wells produce 350 cubic meters of oil daily.

Normally, the main production is heavy crude oil in Cuba. In the last two years we also cleared a well which produces the good quality oil, light oil.

That ties in with my next question. Is Greatwall still drilling at all projects or are some of the locations now producing heavy and light oil?

[1] In November of 2016, BGP Marine, a division of BGP Inc., the China National Petroleum Corporation and the CUPET, announced the signing of contract for 2D multi-client acquisition in offshore Cuba. At that time, the areas were largely unexplored. The aim of the agreement was to identify and evaluate areas for possible for future hydrocarbon exploration.

Kong: Yes, now we are drilling in Bacuranao. In that area we drilled one well, which is producing around 300 cubic meters a day of light oil. About 2,000 barrels a day.

That's good.

Kong: Yes, it's very good.

Now we are drilling in Varadero, which is also producing oil, approximately 700 to 1,000 barrels a day from one well. We are also drilling at Varadero West and Varadero North. We are working in Santa Cruz.

Is Greatwall involved in drilling only or is the company also involved in production?

Kong: Actually, our Company is a service company and not involved in the production, but we provide integrated service. Greatwall Drilling has the ability to provide oil and gas companies solutions to produce better oil and gas to solve the complicated problems.

On a personal level, do you like working here in Havana?

Kong: Yes. I like Havana, I like the Cuban people very much. Also, I like to work with our friends from CUPET and different companies.

What do you like best about your time in Cuba? What's the thing you enjoy the most being here?

Kong: I like to drink Cuban coffee and I enjoy a good time with colleagues from CUPET. Sometimes we have a barbecue with roasted pork and black beans with rice (frijoles). Also, I like to drink Mojitos, lemonade, and piña coladas especially on the Bacunayagua bridge on the way to Varadero. There is a restaurant there with a very beautiful view.

I would like to thank you very much for the time we spent together today. It has been a pleasure to meet with you and your staff. I wish you and Greatwall Drilling continued success in Cuba.

Reference

BGP. (2016). *BGP announces new 2D multi-client acquisition offshore Cuba*. BGP Multi-Client. Retrieved March 17, 2022, from http://www.bgpmulticlient.com/e/action/ShowInfo.php?classid=52&id=36

CHAPTER 27

Melbana CEO Announces New Partnership with Sherritt: "The Best Opportunity We Have for Delivering the Best Outcome"

In this interview, my second with Melbana Energy's board of directors, CEO Andrew G. Purcell announces the company's new partnership. And the news is big in the oil world (Fig. 27.1).

Since 2015, Melbana Energy Limited (ASX: MAY) has been conducting oil exploration in the area known as Block 9 on the north shore of Cuba. The company recently announced the signing of a farm-in agreement with Angola's Sonangol and the commencement of drilling early next year at the Alameda and Zapato high-potential sites.

Mr. Purcell became a member of the board at Melbana in 2015.

His background expertise is in investment banking at Macquarie Bank and Credit Suisse (financial structuring, capital raising, and business development). He served as a public company director for over 20 years in companies in several countries of the Asia–Pacific region. He founded Teknix Capital in Hong Kong in 2005, a company specializing in the development and management of engineering and resource projects in emerging markets.

Mr. Purcell holds an engineering degree from the Queensland University of Technology and an MBA from the University of Queensland.

In our conversation, Mr. Purcell revealed for the first time, Melbana's new partnership with Sherritt International, a Canadian corporation involved in the business of oil and gas exploration, mining, and electricity generation in Cuba.

T. K. Hernández, *The Cuba Interviews*,
https://doi.org/10.1007/978-3-031-30203-9_27

Fig. 27.1 Melbana Energy's CEO, Andrew G. Purcell (Photo courtesy of Mr. Purcell)

Hernández: Can you give us an overview of Melbana's portfolio of projects in Cuba?

Andrew G. Purcell: Of the portfolio of projects we have in Cuba, our current focus is the onshore Block 9 production sharing contract that we were awarded in 2015. We have commenced preparations to drill two exploration wells early next year and are working hard to ensure that now happens as soon as possible and within budget.

Could you update us on Melbana's activities over the last year in Cuba?

Mr. Purcell: In December of last year, we entered a farm-out arrangement with Sonangol with respect to our Block 9 license area in Cuba.

That arrangement with Sonangol saw them take a 70% interest in the licensed area in return for agreeing to fund 85% of the cost of a two-well drilling program.

So our work this year has been in advancing the formality of that agreement, advancing and receiving the permitting we needed in Cuba to undertake this drilling program, updating our estimates of the cost, and undertaking international tenders for the supply of tubulars and accessories as well as for various contractors we will need to support us in this drilling program.

In December Melbana signed a farm-in agreement with the Angolan oil company Sonangol. What was the rationale behind the agreement with Sonangol, one of Africa's largest oil companies?

Mr. Purcell: As a small Australian oil and gas explorer, we don't have the financial resources by ourselves to undertake work programs of the magnitude as the one we have put together and identified as an attractive opportunity in Cuba.

Our business model and one that we have successfully done many times over the years is to use our technical capability to license and then analyze an early stage opportunity, gather all the data, put together an exploration thesis and a work program proposal, and then to present it to larger, better-funded parties who can come in and help us execute what it is we think we have identified.

We've done that with international oil companies over the last decade for projects all over the world. So finding a partner to help us do this again for our acreage in Cuba is business as usual for us, but having a national oil company as a partner is particularly welcome.

Sonangol is already operating in Cuba?

Mr. Purcell: Indeed. They have their own acreage already in Cuba; however, it is an offshore block that is in deepwater Gulf of Mexico, in Cuban waters. It is a very different cost proposition even for a large well-resourced national oil company undertaking deep water drilling in the Gulf of Mexico or indeed anywhere offshore deepwater. It is a much more expensive proposition than operating onshore.

So given where the oil and gas world has gone these past few years, the increased volatility, the tendency of large oil and gas companies to limit their exploration budgets and focus more on higher "bang for buck" opportunities that may exist onshore, I think Sonangol was of that mind as well, and they were looking to continue to build on the knowledge they had accumulated operating in Cuba for a number of years. They were looking for a more cost-effective way forward which our onshore Block 9 provided for them.

Has work been hindered on the Melbana drilling sites since the onset of COVID-19?

Mr. Purcell: Not as much as you might think. Cuba—being an island state—means it's very dependent on shipping supplies to the Island. That hasn't really missed a beat throughout this whole pandemic.

Cuba has also had a very responsible, rapid response and management plan for COVID. It has impacted the ability of senior managers like myself to spend as much time in-country as we would have liked over the past year. But we are very fortunate to have a good team already in Cuba, a very experienced team and they have decent international communications as well so we've been managing to do everything reasonably well despite all the border restrictions and quarantine requirements that have been in place these past six or so months.

We would hope that changes, though, as we get closer to drilling because we will need to have some of our project management team on the ground as drilling operations get closer to commencing, but I'm happy to see that things in Cuba seem to be headed in the right direction now.

Melbana's latest press release stated that negotiations are advanced and a "contract award is imminent" with a preferred drilling contractor. Are there any updates on this? Can you reveal the company's name at this point in time?

Mr. Purcell: Well, the documentation has been completed, subject to the review of the contractor's legal team. Once we have their final comments, and assuming those final comments are acceptable to us, then the process will be to seek Sonangol's approval, but they've already seen an advanced draft so I don't imagine that's going to be anything too contentious (if there are no further material approvals or changes). Then once the JV has approved it, given the amount involved in the award of this contract, we have to also get the approval of the administration committee for the Block 9 PSC (which is the JV participants plus CUPET).

So there are a couple of formal stages to go through but the drilling contractor that's been selected is Sherritt International.

Sherritt, as you know, has had many decades of experience in drilling oil and gas wells in Cuba and has a very established presence in-country having drilled hundreds of wells there. It's a good relationship we have built up over the years, helped by a common language and a similarity of styles between Australians and Canadians as to how we go about doing business.

I'm very pleased and excited about having this opportunity to work with them and I think it's going to be the best opportunity we have for delivering the desired outcome in the minimum amount of time.

That's big news!

Mr. Purcell: It will be big news when we make the announcement.[1]

Do you foresee drilling at Alameda-1 to begin any earlier than the mid-Quarter One, 2021 projection date (equipment delivery occurring on schedule and COVID-related travel restrictions easing?

Mr. Purcell: Probably not. It mostly depends on the manufacturing and shipping times of tubulars, and they are the critical part for the commencement of drilling operations. We may go a month earlier if everything goes swimmingly. But given the COVID world, given the end-of-year holidays which people tend to take between Christmas and New Year's in our cultures at least, allowing for the noise around all that, my gut feeling is that it is unlikely that we will improve significantly on that date but it would be welcome if we could and we are ready.

Why is Block 9 a major opportunity for Melbana investors?

Mr. Purcell: Well, the northern production zone of Cuba is a prolific producer of hydrocarbons. It extends a little from the west of Havana all the way to Varadero, and that production zone extends into Block 9. And in Block 9 there has been evidence of oil in place. There is the Motembo oil field in Block 9, which was the first oil field discovered in Cuba back in the late 1800s. In fact, the tar from the Motembo oil fields is what paved the streets of Manhattan. It's a long-established oil zone.

There are also previous exploration wells that have been drilled, several of which have discovered hydrocarbons and flowed them to the surface. Just as importantly, Cuba typically has a reputation for producing a heavier type of crude because it produces in very shallow zones. These wells in Block 9 that were drilled deeper recovered a much lighter crude so the opportunity for our investors participating in this program is not only are we going into a proven hydrocarbon zone that has had previous discoveries and evidence of oil being in place, but there is the potential from previous evidence to find a much lighter oil which would be far

[1] Melbana announced the news of its partnership with Sherritt International on March 17, 2021, the date of the publication of this interview in Cuba Business Report.

more valuable and far easier to recover than the heavier crude typically found in Cuba.

When do you see that "eureka day?".

Mr. Purcell: Well, that first well is designed to test three different targets, so from the moment we commence drilling, there is the potential to intercept hydrocarbons. To reach the total depth and the primary target will take, we estimate, about 75 days.

So perhaps one month after we have been drilling, we will be in that first zone that we wish to test and that may be the earliest time at which we will be able to say something about what it is we found.

Thank you so much for this opportunity to see you and speak with you again.

PART VIII

Healthcare, Biotechnology and Medical Tourism

CHAPTER 28

Cuba's Medical Tourism Business—Its Past, Present, and Future, Dr. Osvaldo Héctor, Servicios Médicos Cubanos

Dr. Osvaldo Héctor Ardisana from the Comercializadora Servicios Médicos Cubanos (CSMC S.A.)[1] was in Canada meeting with Services Santé International, a medical tourism company with offices in Montreal, Trois-Rivières, and Québec. I spoke to him in the Montreal office and had the opportunity to ask about CSMC and Cuba's medical tourism program. The interview took place in April 2017 (Fig. 28.1).

Dr. Héctor, an integral medicine specialist, has worked with the CSMC since 1997. At the present time, he is responsible for the markets of Canada and the English–French-speaking Caribbean countries in the International Academic and Medical Services division.

Founded in 1987, CSMC offers medical alternatives to foreign patients seeking healthcare in Cuba. It was formerly known as Servimed. In 2011, it merged with Servicios Médicos Cubanos, the current name of the company.

[1] Comercializadora Servicios Médicos Cubanos (CSMC S.A.) is known by the abbreviations CSMC, SMC, and SMC Salud. The acronyms/terms have been used interchangeably over the years and on their website, social media, and company's publications. See https://www.smcsalud.cu/en/.

T. K. Hernández, *The Cuba Interviews*,
https://doi.org/10.1007/978-3-031-30203-9_28

Fig. 28.1 Dr. Osvaldo Héctor from SMC in Montreal with Services Santé International President, Alain Leclerc

CSMC offers health services to patients coming from overseas. The company is an umbrella organization overseeing the Henry Reeve Medical Brigade which has served in over 80 nations. It also manages the medical training program for foreign students, pharmaceutical products, and other services addressing health care and well-being.

Hernández: When did Cuba first offer medical care to tourists at its hospitals and clinics?

Dr. Osvaldo Héctor Ardisana: Healthcare for Cuban citizens is universal and free in every medical institution.

During the 1970s and 1980s, foreign residents in Cuba, most of them refugees from Latin American countries, received these services during their stay and enjoyed the quality of the treatments. In the 1990s, some returned to their homelands where they, unfortunately, did not always find the same. When they needed qualified medical services and the only alternatives were the United States or Europe, they thought, why not to come to Cuba?

In the 1960s and 1970s, Cuba did not charge foreigners for medical care. It was at the end of the 1980s, in 1987, Cuba began charging for medical services through its company Servimed. Cuba could not continue providing free medical care to everyone because of the internal economic situation during the 1990s.

Because of the opening to international tourism in the 1990s, thousands of foreign visitors (mainly Canadian and European) went to the Island as tourists and eventually needed medical care for unexpected conditions. They realized the Cuban health system had something to offer not only for emergencies but also for some diseases or conditions that were treated in Cuba with high success rates using treatments sometimes not available in their own countries. So, health tourism was born as an answer to the international request of these services.

How can a potential patient know that he/she is dealing with a legitimate company offering medical tourism services to Cuba?

Dr. Héctor: Nowadays, CSMC has contracts with about 150 international companies or agencies in 30 countries. All these companies presented their legal documents to the Cuban embassies or consulates where they are officially legalized. Every year there's a procedure of validation and update of services, programs, conciliation, etc.

CSMC is open to new opportunities of commercial relationship with universities, medical institutions, insurance companies, and any kind of private or public healthcare providers to fulfill health requests in Cuba or abroad.

In Canada there are several companies with valid agreements with CSMC, all of them in Ontario and Québec at present. The pioneer of these companies is Services Santé International in Québec City, which celebrated its tenth anniversary of successful collaboration with CSMC this year.

What are the most common procedures patients travel to Cuba for?

Dr. Héctor: It depends on the region or country where the patient comes from. Canadians demand treatments for cancer using a monoclonal antibody vaccine which is a state-of-the-art product of Cuban biotechnology industry with high rates of success in lung cancer. They also request treatment for orthopedic surgeries (lumbar spine, hip replacement, knee prosthesis) because of the waiting list for some of these treatments; ophthalmology (treatment to stop the progression of symptoms of retinitis pigmentosa using a Cuban method); skin conditions as vitiligo and psoriasis (using Cuban unique products obtained from placental tissues); treatments to heal diabetic foot ulcers with Heberprot-P (another Cuban Biotechnology product); and cosmetic surgery with high standards, high quality, and excellent pricing. Dental care is also much appreciated.

People from other countries have different priorities, but these are the most frequently requested.

Currently, what region/country sends the most patients seeking medical services to Cuba?

Dr. Héctor: At the beginning there were mostly Latin American patients because of the reasons explained before. Also, the geographic and cultural bonds were additional reasons to encourage patients from Argentina, Mexico, Chile, Peru, etc., to visit Cuba.

African countries are equally an important source of patients because of the historical links between this continent and Cuba, as well as the lack of basic health programs in most of these countries. A large number of African students that went to Cuba are now engineers, doctors, professionals in their own countries but kept the remembrance of those days on the island. They don't hesitate to recommend their comrades to go to Cuba to be healed.

And last but not at least, people from Canada and Europe found a solution in Cuba for medical issues that are not available there, not covered by the insurance programs, very expensive in private care or unfortunately delayed due to a long waiting list. Since 2010 Canada is one of the top three countries sending patients to Cuba.

What is the future direction for CSMC Health and how is the company going to be marketing its services to the world?

Dr. Héctor: CSMC has some principles that will remain invariable: the respect for the patient and relatives, the priority of medical subjects over commercial or lucrative interests. We are not competitive but cooperative with the medical institutions of each country.

We do not offer medical services to foreign citizens which are not 100% guaranteed for the Cuban population.

CSMC incorporates innovations, new techniques, and equipment coming from the most advanced sources of knowledge worldwide, but always places the human being over everything else. We offer personalized care, focused on the prevention and the enhancement of the quality of life.

The list of agencies and countries signing contracts with CSMC grows each day. The Middle East, Asia, East Europe are new interest areas and, of course, U.S. patients are, no doubt, among the challenges that CSMC has to face in the current scenario.

Reference

Servicios Médicos Cubanos. SMC Salud. (n.d.). Retrieved September 30, 2017, from https://www.smcsalud.cu/en/.

CHAPTER 29

The Future Direction of CSMC, Dr. Yamila De Armas Águila, President, Comercializadora De Servicios Médicos Cubanos

Dr. Yamila de Armas Águila, is the president of Comercializadora de Servicios Médicos Cubanos (CSMC S.A.). She was kind enough to provide me some time from her hectic schedule for a brief interview. I first met with Dr. de Armas at the offices of CSMC in Miramar in July of 2018. In 2022, we met again at her office for an update to the first interview (Fig. 29.1).

Dr. Osvaldo Héctor Ardisana, chief medical specialist at CSMC and responsible for the markets of Canada and the English–French-speaking Caribbean countries, acted as translator for our first conversation.

Founded in 1987, CSMC is an entity which falls under the Ministry of Health.

CSMC manages seven departments which market medical services on the Island and abroad. It is responsible for the delivery of medical tourism, academic and postgraduate education programs, Cuba's international medical services program (Henry Reeve Medical Brigade), well-being and quality-of-life programs for Cubans, medical services for foreign residents, management of the country's network of pharmacies and optical services, and the organization of health science congresses and events.

T. K. Hernández, *The Cuba Interviews*,
https://doi.org/10.1007/978-3-031-30203-9_29

Fig. 29.1 Dr. Yamila de Armas, President of the CSMC at our interview (Photo by the editor)

CSMC maintains strategic business alliances with the Ministry of Tourism, the business group BioCubaFarma, the National Institute of Sports, Physical Education and Recreation (INDER), the Ministry of Higher Education and the Ministry of Public Health, to provide specialized health services.

Hernández: What is the future direction for CSMC?

Dr. Yamila de Armas Águila: The first priority and the most important goal of CSMC for the next year will be to increase the amount of people coming to Cuba for medical reasons to resolve their health problems. To achieve that goal, we have made a huge investment in technology to improve the quality and the type of services we are offering.

We have high technology services that are very important in unique places probably, one-of-a-kind services internationally. This could be, for example, the use of some vaccines for various types of specific cancers. We are also putting together this kind of facility with the other advantages of coming to Cuba as a complete tourist destination.

We are also developing a health and quality-of-life services initiative to promote thermal and seaside spas. We hope to develop a close alliance between medical and ecotourism combining the natural qualities of the country.

Not only will there be the possibility of sun and beaches tourism but also the enormous natural wellness, the safety that you have here in Cuba, and the charm of the Cuban population, the high possibility of making friends in Cuba, together with the possibility of better health. So we are quite sure that this will increase the happiness of people coming to Cuba.

The translation was provided by Dr. Osvaldo Héctor Ardisana.

Follow-up to the Interview: May 2022

Experts predict the global market size of health tourism will expand in the coming years after the impacts of the pandemic. Can you provide Cuba's medical tourism stats for the last five years, countries of origin, services, number of visitors?

Dr. Yamila de Armas: Indeed, everything predicts that after the crisis generated by the pandemic, health and quality of life will be better valued by individuals and families. Some have even said that it is the new luxury, after the years of social isolation and loss of human lives. The perception and weight people place on their health is undoubtedly important. This could generate a greater demand for these services and even the selection of tourist destinations is highly conditioned by their general safety and health safety and proven response capacity for the contingencies experienced and those that may continue to occur. People need to travel safely, and this lesson has been very well learned. The coverage of vaccinated populations, including children, is one of these indicators that becomes an attribute in tourist destinations, as well as evidence of the robustness of the health system and its preventive vision.

It is up to those of us who offer services to adjust in correspondence to this scenario, which is sufficient for the populations that have emerged from the pandemic and are seeking alternatives to live longer and better, and for us as providers to ratify our commitment to life.

Regarding health tourism statistics, we begin by saying that they result from these two years in totally abnormal conditions of closed borders and total depression of the tourism sector, from which health tourism and its components, medical tourism, and quality-of-life tourism, do not escape. The fundamental causes are related precisely to the health, economic, and social phenomena. In our case, it has also allowed us to enter a process of revision and adjustment in the way of collecting the primary data. This allows us to separate, with greater precision, medical tourism itself, from the medical attention to tourism and these two, from the quality-of-life services. These adjustments will allow the best comparability with international statistics, so the data published this year will have the results of this improvement.

In 2019, 7,000 medical tourists who traveled to Cuba to solve their health problem were reported. The main issuing countries and regions were Canada, Central America, and the Caribbean, and we observed growth from Turkey and Europe.

The most interesting medical programs are related to the use of Cuban biotechnology products to address cancer and other chronic non-communicable diseases, skin disorders, esthetic treatments, and rehabilitation in its broadest concept.

We have a wide network of institutions that offer world-class treatment that includes, first, the participation of professionals of high caliber and proven human quality, in addition to protocols of action that have documented results over several decades of use and are continually updated.

Cuba, like many other countries, has made a commitment to the development of general tourism and specialized health tourism as a source of income for our economy. And above all, we are determined to continue consolidating it.

There is no table/data today with all these elements, but at the end of the year, it will be published in the official statistics.[1] All this information, with the three kinds of tourists we are receiving, the ones that travel to improve their quality, their health, those that receive medical treatment when they are here, and those that receive a proposal for quality-of-life treatments.

The Ministry of Health is delivering the attention, the health care to the people that come because it is not only in the hospitals but also in the tourism centers. But that is not medical tourism. Over 45,000 people have received medical care in that area. You can go to Cira Garcia

[1] These statistics will be published by the Office of National Statistics of the Republic of Cuba (ONEI) at year end 2022.

or La Pradera. You can get the same person and maybe you receive three medical services. The number one thing is the medical community themselves. They do that intending to treat their disease.

As for general numbers, when you see the numbers of the official statistics published, there will be a difference because the system of collecting information has changed. But the numbers are similar. That's why data and the collection of the information at this point is adjusted to the international concepts so that you can compare it with other countries. It cannot be compared if you do not provide the correct information.

The National Statistics Office is the one that will provide this official information. We cannot compare the numbers I have mentioned with tourism statistics because they are health statistics. They only say the medical care to foreign persons but that doesn't help promote medical tourism. For example, the statistics of patients who have been taken care of through telemedicine are not included. We have that service as well. It is a medical service that is being developed and is now functioning very well. Then, we can add this information to the statistics that we collect during the year.

How will the CSMC promote to the potential market composed of Central/Latin America, Canada, and the United States? Cuba has various advantages over global competitors, for example, location, bilateral relationships, safety as a tourist destination, health indicators, well-trained doctors. As well, its ability to handle pandemic conditions, evidenced by research and development of five vaccinations despite adverse conditions imposed by U.S. sanctions.

Dr. de Armas: We want to be seen as a safe destination, committed to improving the health of people who decide to travel. The slogan of our campaign is "Feel safe," identifying us with the services that give hope of life to patients. For example with cancer, by extending their life expectancy or curing it with the use of immunological therapies to build the body's own defenses against cancer. For this purpose, we have monoclonal antibodies against specific localizations such as non-small cell lung cancer, head, and neck.

The programs we offer are directly aimed at health problems from which no population in the world escapes. As well important demographic phenomena such as aging, treatment for Alzheimer's disease, or other alternatives for the control of diabetes mellitus and to avoid such dreaded complications as amputations. There are over 250 medical programs that are personalized because there are patients, not diseases. To accomplish this task, CSMC also can integrate the services offered in various health institutions according to the medical program for a patient. It is a whole system for those who choose us to improve their health.

We offer a new quality-of-life programs carried out in the hotels' own facilities that integrate traditional aesthetic treatments, anti-stress, innovative techniques to improve sleep, nutrition, take advantage of the benefits of sea water, in the privileged nature that we have. Combining nature and the best of our specialists to generate the best experience for individuals and families.

A unique offer is the successful programs for the rehabilitation of those patients who have had COVID-19. With this, we return once again to what the pandemic has left us, because millions of people now live with some sequelae, and we intend to accompany them in their solution.

For those who face harsh winters, a stay in our warm winter mixed with our beaches, trails, and even swimming with dolphins can certainly leave an imprint on these people's lives. This is a project for seniors that we have worked on with Canadian companies in the past.

Cuba needs to promote this because few people know about Cuba's medical tourism products and quality-of-life programs.

Dr. de Armas: I completely agree with you. We have been busy in surviving and helping many to survive. Now we are going all out in communicating what we are ready to give. Our truths collide with the walls that are raised so that they are not seen. We have an imperfect reality, but we have undeniable truths and opportunities to develop for all. We are tenacious and we will continue to do so. We have to find the paths that are none other than those of the contemporary world to which are added the challenges of our own reality, but we trust and work to achieve it.

We have a communication strategy for different audiences. We have been present at the most important national and international fairs this year. Our campaign has started. In October we will hold the first International Medical Tourism and Wellness Fair.

Is this in collaboration with Meliá **Hotels?**

Dr. de Armas: With Meliá Hotels, we first worked together conceiving a product adjusted to their standards and customers. We signed a working alliance as we also have with Iberostar, Cubanacan Group Hotels, Gran Caribe, and all the entities of the Ministry of Tourism. It is a comprehensive development strategy that has the highest priority of the country, to achieve a true articulation that allows the design of products adjusted to the markets and a correct use of the sales channels. This will allow covering an important space in the diversification of the Cuban tourist product and, in particular, the services of well-being and quality of life.

Cayo Largo del Sur, Ciénaga de Zapata, and vacation dialysis projects are highlighted, as well as the development of the tourist poles of Trinidad and Viñales.

First, to merge traditional markets, expansion is closely linked to the recovery of connectivity. Ease of travel in the Cuban case is an important condition considering our island status. Geographical proximity for medical tourists will have an important specific weight, so the Caribbean has priority. We also plan actions in the Asian and African markets in another dimension because of the distance that separates us.

What we offer has, as you have well expressed, advantages in relation to the offerings in the world.

The warmth of our people and our professionals who have accumulated prestige, first for their high professionalism and excellent training, accompanied by the best in human values, makes them people who are committed to solving the health problems of those they serve. That is our best wealth we offer with the utmost humility.

Because of our geographical location, we have been called the key to the Gulf. We offer our beaches and nearby hot springs, mountains, heritage cities, history, and culture. Finally, the exemplary performance in an unprecedented exercise in confronting the pandemic showed the ability to align all the forces of a country to ensure the lives of its people, even in conditions of extreme limitations. Its response also includes the production of its own vaccines and a group of biotechnology products to integrate successful protocols that together allowed us to achieve better mortality rates than a large group of countries, although for us the life of a single human being is more important than an indicator.

Integration is the only strategy for the development of health tourism. It is also a sign of the country's willingness to join forces to enhance the competitive advantages we have.

The Portfolio of Investment Opportunities lists three investment projects, two IEAs and one joint venture for a combined total of \$54.14 million. Can you tell us more about these projects and how will CSMC promote to potential investors?

Dr. de Armas: Since its origins, Cuban legislation on foreign investment has included the participation of the health sector, mainly directed to exportable services and, more recently, to the improvement of the infrastructure in logistics.

The sector has a business portfolio that includes the reconstruction and exploitation of thermal centers based on the enormous natural wealth available in the country. Cuba registers more than a thousand springs of thermal mineral-medicinal waters throughout the island. We were first recognized for our hot springs before being known as a tourism destination of sun and beaches. Many of our spas were the first in the world. That is why we have decided, as part of the diversification of the tourist product, to invest in them. Emblematic names such as San Diego de Los Baños, San Miguel de Los Baños, Menéndez, and Elguea, just to mention a few, treasure not only the certified natural resource studied but also a history that goes back to centuries of use, accompanied by beautiful stories and rituals.

In San Diego, for example, we have known the use of its waters since the eighteenth century. It has the capacity to attend 500 tourists at the same time and has maintained in its history indicators to ensure the sustainability of its use, such as the volume of liters of water per minute, chemical composition, as well as the microbiological quality.

San Miguel gave rise to a peculiar community of the same name that has developed an original architecture and typical craftsmanship. Besides being a heritage site reminiscent of the Monte Carlo spa in Europe, under a proposal for restoration, it was the first place in the world where medicinal waters were brought to the bathtubs of the Hotel.

Menéndez has unique qualities. Its 38 springs have different characteristics in terms of temperature and some variations in chemical composition. Besides providing table water, its charms are many and it is undoubtedly an important opportunity for investors who decide to expand.

In addition to the spas, there are other business opportunities that include clinics and health centers dedicated to international medical tourism and other alternatives linked to health system sustainability projects.

The people that come as tourism reopens, how will they know about these services?

Dr. de Armas: There is a group of them that remains in the market and who traditionally prefer us. But we are very excited about our new offers, especially those we believe will attract and provide excellent experiences to people who enjoy them and then become part of the life projects. Especially for improving the quality of life of those who have had to live through such difficult times.

That's why we are also changing our way of communicating to a more contemporary, digital, light way that makes it easier to find us and choose us.

Our international sales management is focused on simplifying and personalizing each request to make it easier, more reliable, and secure. There you will find medical specialists 24 hours a day, available to build a proposal that fits the needs of the people who identify and prefer us. For that, we have a perfectly integrated network of services that allows us to bring together professionals of the highest qualification to the program. This is the strength of a whole system with one goal: the satisfaction of those who visit us. This integration includes the hotel and extra-hotel offers.

CSMC launched its upcoming conference, the first edition of the International Health and Wellness Tourism Fair (in October) last week at the Hotel Nacional de Cuba. Can you share with us the CSMC plans for participants and attendees?

Dr. de Armas: Indeed, for the first time we will meet within the framework of an event that already has a history, the *Salud Para Todos* fair, which for over 20 years has brought together executives from the world's health systems, suppliers of medical technologies, medicines, prominent Cuban producers, our biotechnological sector, and, of course, our entity in charge of exporting medical services.

On this occasion, the first Medical and Wellness Tourism fair is born with the need to communicate to the world our offer and to exchange with operators, facilitators, insurance companies, media—the value chains of this type of specialized tourism. It is a tremendous opportunity for commercial and academic exchange because it will also coincide with an event called the International Seminar with a confirmation of delegations and entrepreneurs from the countries with whom we have commercial relations. Our sales network will have plenty of time to exchange and update our products.

To update the sector's foreign investment business portfolio, the second Foreign Investment Forum will be held on this date, which will include business roundtables that we hope will bring potential partners closer and allow us to close deals that are already underway.

Thank you, Dr. de Armas, it is wonderful to meet with you again. There has been so much development in the health tourism industry since we last met. It will be very interesting to see the outcomes of Cuba's first Salud Para Todos event.

Dr. de Armas: Thank you for giving us the opportunity to tell you about the roads we walk.

CHAPTER 30

A US Journalist Reports on Health from Havana, Gail Reed, MEDICC

In this chapter, I interviewed MEDICC Review's Executive Editor, Gail Reed, who shares her experiences as a foreign journalist in Havana, MEDICC's activities as a non-profit organization in Cuba,[1] U.S.–Cuba health cooperation, and the Cuban health care system (Fig. 30.1).

Hernández: Tell me a bit about yourself. When did you first arrive in Cuba? Were you working at the time for MEDICC? Why did you come to Cuba? Did you visit first as a tourist?

Gail Reed: I first went to Cuba as a student. Those were the years of Civil Rights and the Vietnam War, and I think it was natural that many of us were curious to see the different society Cubans were attempting to create. I went on to do graduate studies in journalism at Columbia in New York, where I had the privilege of meeting professor Phyllis Garland, who became my friend and mentor and encouraged me to open my eyes further to society's challenges. I remember that my graduate thesis was an original and very long article on violence against a Black family in Rosedale, Queens. I also began writing about Cuba's role in Southern Africa.

[1] Founded in 1997, MEDICC is a non-profit organization based in California. MEDICC Review is a peer-reviewed journal that works to promote U.S.–Cuba health collaboration and highlight its public health contributions towards global health equity and universal health. For more information: http://mediccreview.org/about-us/mission/ .

T. K. Hernández, *The Cuba Interviews*,
https://doi.org/10.1007/978-3-031-30203-9_30

Fig. 30.1 Gail Reed, Executive Editor at MEDICC Review, at home in Havana (Photo by the editor)

But it wasn't until several years later that I made Havana a second home with a Cuban partner. We had a child together, and even after we separated, I decided to stay on with my son as a temporary resident and journalist. Then, in 1993–1995, I returned to my first love: public health. Because when I was young, I had always wanted to be a doctor, but in those days, scholarships for women to study medicine just weren't available. Returning to public health first meant working with UNICEF to jump start U.S. NGO collaboration with Cuba's health sector during the very difficult time of the 1990s. That was after the collapse of the socialist bloc, when the United States also reinforced the embargo (or as Cubans call it, the blockade) with the Torricelli legislation.[2] Then came a foundation request to lead a study to determine if the embargo violated the human rights of Cuba's 11 million people. The research was the result of a Washington, D.C. law firm's allegation to this effect presented to the OAS Human Rights Commission—to which the Commission basically replied, "prove it."

With local support in Havana, our small team took 18 months to dig into the files of medical importers and an array of healthcare institutions; interview patients, care providers, and international agencies; and finally produce a 300-page report published by the American Association of World Health: Denial of Food Medicine: The impact of the U.S. embargo on Health Nutrition in Cuba.[3] The Executive Summary by Kai Bird and Julia Sweig was translated into several languages, and was used in Congress to make the case for allowing food exports to Cuba, still with significant restrictions.

The report also turned out to be the foundation stone for our non-profit (Medical Education Cooperation with Cuba). The idea and the first board members came from the blue-ribbon, bipartisan commission that visited Cuba to validate the study's methodology. As I did my research, I kept running into U.S. doctors and other health professionals who had visited Cuba at one time or another but had no way of continuing to collaborate—much less communicate—with their Cuban colleagues. By then, the Cuban health system, its universal nature and outcomes, had drawn the attention of the U.S. medical and public health communities. So MEDICC was founded to provide a bilateral institutional bridge between these medical and health professionals—always looking for best practices that improve the health of individuals and populations as a whole.

[2] The Torricelli legislation known as the Cuban Democracy Act was a bill presented by U.S. Congressman Robert Torricelli. It was passed in 1992 during Cuba's Special Period. The legislation prohibited foreign-based subsidiaries of American companies from trading with Cuba, travel to Cuba by American citizens, and family remittances to Cuba: www.congress.gov/bill/102nd-congress/house-bill/5323.

[3] American Association of World Health, March 1997 study: https://medicc.org/ns/documents/The_impact_of_the_U.S._Embargo_on_Health_&_Nutrition_in_Cuba.pdf.

Was life in Cuba easy or difficult for you to adapt to?

Ms. Reed: When I first became a temporary resident, I was housed in the Alamar district, a bedroom community of some 100,000 residents in eastern Havana. Each building had 30 apartments, most destined for those who had participated in the construction. As an antidote to the obvious housing shortage, "micro-brigades" had been set up in a number of workplaces, where employees would volunteer to pitch in to raise the new structures under the guidance of experienced builders, while others took their place at the office, factory, or wherever they worked. The building where I lived was built by cigar workers. And that turned out to be fascinating. As you may know, these folks are enormously talented, rolling cigars by hand. But they also have a decades-old tradition: the reader who reads fragments of news, novels, all sorts of things, throughout the day. So, no matter their formal education, these craftsmen and craftswomen are full of knowledge. They were also full of curiosity and solidarity when it came to the *norteamericana* who suddenly appeared in the fifth-floor walkup.

So I never felt alone, even at first. And Cuba is such a child-friendly place, that I was lucky in that respect, too. "It takes a village" became real to me whenever I would hear a neighbor calling down to my son to "be careful!" or to "stop throwing the ball there! You're going to hit somebody!" The most difficult thing for me was language. I barely spoke Spanish, and I had to make my way to the grocery store, learn to use my ration card, to get in line, to just get along with daily life. But there is nothing like total immersion to put you to the test! My second challenge had nothing to do with Cuba: I always thought I would have a daughter. I only knew girls, after all, since all my cousins were girls and I was an only child. So when I had a boy, I knew that both my son and I were in for a mutual learning experience. He is still the joy of my life.

You've been running a series of conferences in Cuba focused on health, and your next one is coming up soon. Have these been successful? How have the response and participation been? Are attendees solely American?

Ms. Reed: We have actually had only two conferences—one in 2017 and one in 2018. The rest have been opportunities for mainly (but not solely) U.S. health professionals to make the trip to Cuba, see the island and the health system for themselves, and in many cases establish long-term relations of cooperation. Our mission at MEDICC is to foster cooperation among the United States, Cuban, and global health communities that leads to improved health and health equity.

MEDICC was founded in 1997, at first organizing electives and rotations in Cuba for medical, nursing, and public health students. By the time former President George W. Bush limited student exchanges in 2004, over 1,000 had taken advantage of MEDICC electives to earn credits from 118 U.S. universities.

Then, we changed direction to involve health professionals, policymakers, and others who could still legally travel to Cuba. We must be nearing 2,000 by now. The response has been extraordinary, as a result, I think, of Cuba's continuing impressive population health outcomes on a shoestring budget and its outsized role in strengthening health systems worldwide.

In 2018, there was a downturn after the current administration's announcements of new travel restrictions and the whole "sonic" affair but the trend is, once again, upward in 2019.

I also think enormous credit is due to the U.S. medical, health, and scientific communities, which have never stepped back, but maintained their interest in cooperation, against even the fiercest headwinds. We saw that very clearly in the spring of 2018, when our journal MEDICC Review published a special issue, The Path to U.S.–Cuba Health & Science Cooperation.[4] Not only did we have prestigious American and Cuban guest editors, but virtually all the articles had U.S. and Cuban coauthors and the issue was launched both in Havana and at the American Association for the Advancement of Science (AAAS) in Washington, D.C.

One of our key messages was that U.S.–Cuba cooperation is good for the health of Americans, as well as Cubans, providing examples such as Cuban biotech's lung cancer vaccine now in clinical trials at Roswell Park Comprehensive Cancer Center in Buffalo, New York.

What is it like for you as a foreign journalist working in Cuba?

Ms. Reed: I've worked as a teacher of journalists on the Cuban end, and also for U.S. media such as Cuba Update, NBC News, and Business Week. An assignment in Havana is a complicated one for any U.S. journalist. First, because the two social and economic systems are so

[4] The Path to U.S.-Cuba Health & Science Cooperation. Drs. Jon Kim Andrus, Pastor Castell-Florit, C. William Keck and Gail Reed. Special Edition. Vol 20, No. 2. April 30, 2018.

different—it makes it almost impossible to understand the dynamics in Cuba for those who "parachute in."

For those who are accredited on a more long-term basis, I think the biggest challenge is to dump your baggage—and get your editors to do the same—to keep from repeating the tired old notions of "communist Cuba." That doesn't mean there isn't a Communist Party that plays a formidable role. It does. But Cuba is far from communist. Its system is socialist, and it's very much "Cuban socialism." What that means, how it has evolved, the changes going on right now (for some, too fast and for others too slow), all these are very hard to grasp for any outsider.

And of course, now it's not just Cuba's official press: as in many other countries, a journalist in Cuba has to keep informed through blogs and other social media, as well as on-the-street experiences, interviews, and old-fashioned research. How to ascertain what is balanced, who has an axe to grind, what are the "legitimate concerns," and in what context? All these are more difficult in Cuba, I think, because reading people in such a different society as the United States is a major challenge. There is also the challenge of the Cuban bureaucracy, its snail's pace, and multiple levels of authority. These can be frustrating, to say the least.

What's your take on health care in Cuba?

Ms. Reed: They have done an impressive job on health and healthcare, with seriously limited resources. That's not my opinion. It is the opinion of the United Nations, Pan American Health Organization (PAHC), World Health Organization (WHO), UNICEF, and even the former head of the World Bank. Their infant mortality at four per 1,000 live births is well under that in the United States, and other indicators match or better those in many of the richer countries. Importantly, their indicators also reflect fewer disparities. Cuba is a very robust primary healthcare system, a condition deemed internationally to be the cornerstone of any health system worth its salt. And care is truly universal and free to patients.

Yet, they are also terribly challenged by the lack of resources, complicated by the U.S. embargo. Equipment is expensive, training is expensive, research is expensive. And most expensive is to maintain this universal access to quality care for 11 million people. During the frightening recession of the 1990s, keeping people healthy was like balancing on a fraying tightrope. I witnessed health professionals in tears when they had to bend a protocol, to extend the amount of time between mammograms or other important preventive tests. The health indicators made it through, but not without enormous sacrifices.

Today, the situation is complicated by some younger health professionals' decision to work permanently abroad because of the admittedly quite low salaries they earn in Cuba—or who are turning to other jobs in Cuba itself. This is a problem that, in my view, begs urgent attention, but also solutions that can also be applied to other public-sector workers. And how do you enact major salary raises across the board when the economy is growing so slowly?

There are several ways they're now working at sustainability for this universal public health system: increasing health tourism from Latin America, Canada, and Europe (taking advantage of the prestige of Cuba's health professionals); exporting biotech and other pharmaceutical products developed in Cuba to address important health issues (such as Heberprot-P for diabetic foot ulcers, studies showing it decreases amputation risk by over 70%); and, of course, the export of health professionals.

The latter has received some criticism from abroad, since where a foreign government pays significant salaries to Cubans serving in their country, the Cuban government heavily taxes these salaries to fund the health system at home. The taxes can run as high as three-fourths of the salaries paid.

However, those working abroad (and thousands continue to volunteer) make about ten times what they do in Cuba itself and return with all manner of goods for their families.

In other cases, where Cuban assistance is to a very poor country, the Cuban government doesn't expect the host nation to pay salaries. So Cuban health professionals staff the public health system (mainly in underserved areas, as determined by the host country), receiving housing and a small stipend (paid by either Cuba or the host government). In all cases, Cuban volunteers abroad receive their regular salaries in full, as if they were working in Cuba itself.

Of course, Cuba has invested not only in the education of its own health professionals—with over 90,000 physicians, for example—but also in talented students from low-income families in over 100 countries. The Latin American School of Medicine, which celebrates its 20th anniversary this year, has graduated nearly 30,000 physicians from and for the world's poorest communities. This is an unprecedented contribution to extending health care globally.

What does American healthcare have to learn from the Cuban healthcare system?

Ms. Reed: I remember years ago sitting in the waiting room in my doctor's office in the States, reading the "Patient's Bill of Rights." By then, I had spent a lot of time in Cuba. I got to the end of the poster and realized that one right was missing: the right to health care. So, that would be the first thing to learn, not only from Cuba but from many other countries: in the richest country in the world, health care should be a fundamental right for everyone.

The second thing of course is a conceptual difference that I'm not sure can be learned. That is, viewing medicine as a public service rather than a business, making health services free to patients. In the United States, patients' health expenses are bloated by insurance companies, big Pharma and often tethered to being employed. So it's difficult to imagine it any other way. But some are actually beginning to, and that's where the Medicare for All movement is coming from, which also enshrines the idea that quality health care is, first and foremost, the responsibility of government.

I think we also must learn to collaborate more effectively with a country like Cuba, with which we may have many differences, but where cooperation can make a great contribution to global health. The Ebola epidemic in West Africa is one example: there was last-minute joint activity. But how much more could have been done, how many more lives could have been saved, if the United States (with its technology and logistics) and Cuba (with its trained emergency doctors) could have counted on such collaboration from the outset?

The U.S. embargo, as I mentioned, also tends to hurt American patients who suffer from diseases where Cuban biotech may offer novel, proven solutions, such as diabetic foot ulcers (DFU). Some 70,000 DFU amputations are carried out on American patients every year. Most disabilities, hardships, and expenses could be avoided, if U.S. law provided our companies with more assurances that positive trial results and FDA approval of Cuba's Heberprot-P would result in permits to import and use this medication to treat the tens of thousands of Americans suffering from DFU.

It is axiomatic now to point out that comprehensive primary care is the basis for good health outcomes since 70 to 80% of prevention and treatment happen at this level. That is something we could learn from in the United States, where our system is overburdened with a reverence for high tech at the expense of simpler tests and overstocked with subspecialists at the expense of internists, pediatricians, OB/GYNs, and family physicians.

And we have a medical education system that is sorely in need of reform, in which grads are forced into these subspecialties just to pay off their student loans, a personal debt running at about $200,000 by graduation time. It's interesting to see schools like that of Kaiser Permanente and New York University offering free or lower-cost medical education. Let's see what happens with that in terms of heading off the 15,000 to 50,000 shortage of primary care physicians by 2030, predicted by the AAMC, and a more serious shortage of physicians who are people of color. (Just six percent of physicians are African Americans, Hispanics, or Native Americans, while they are some 32% of the U.S. population).

In the end, you have to ask yourself: how is it possible that Bloomberg's 2019 Healthiest Country Index rates Cuba higher than the United States (Miller & Wei, 2019), when it spends one tenth of what we do per capita on health care? That alone would indicate we have something to learn.

Gail, thank you so much for this opportunity to speak with you and learn of your experiences as a foreign journalist in Havana, the country's healthcare system, and your very valuable work with MEDICC.

References

Andrus, J., et al. editors. MEDICC, (2018). *The path to US–Cuba health and Science Cooperation*, https://medicc.org/ns/us-cuba-health-science-cooperation-medicc-review-special-issue/. Accessed 23 Mar. 2020.

H.R.5323–102nd Congress (1991–1992): *Cuban democracy act of 1992.* (1992, October 1). https://www.congress.gov/bill/102nd-congress/house-bill/5323.

Lee, J. M., & Wei, Lu. (2019). *These are the WORLD'S Healthiest Nations.* BloombergQuint. Retrieved March 4, 2022, from https://www.bloombergquint.com/onweb/spain-tops-italy-as-world-s-healthiest-nation-while-u-s-slips

MEDDIC. (n.d.). *Mission.* MEDICC ReviewHome. Retrieved July 10, 2022, from http://mediccreview.org/about-us/mission/

Reed, G., & Frank M. (1997, March). *The impact of the U.S. embargo on health and nutrition in Cuba.* http://medicc.org/ns/documents/The_impact_of_the_U.S._Embargo_on_Health_&_Nutrition_in_Cuba.pdf.

CHAPTER 31

VP of BioCubaFarma Discuss Partnerships, COVID-19, and the Future of the Company—Dr. Mayda Mauri Pérez

As the COVID-19 pandemic gripped the world in 2020, face-to-face contact and business travel became a thing of the past as everything shut down. In this chapter, I interviewed BioCubaFarma's Vice President, Dr. Mayda Mauri Pérez in late June via the WhatsApp application (Fig. 31.1).

We covered a variety of topics that included Cuba's current COVID-19 protocol, BioCubaFarma's partnerships/joint ventures with the Roswell Park Cancer Center, China, Russia, and the future direction of the company.

The pharmaceutical and biotechnology industries in Cuba have a history of over 35 years. In 2012, the Pharmaceutical and Biotechnology Industries Group (BioCubaFarma) was created. Dr. Mauri played an important role in the commercial business development of the industry as General Manager of Heber Biotec S.A. from 2000 to 2012. Heber Biotec is a company of the Center for Genetic Engineering and Biotechnology (CIGB), an industry leader in biotechnology, with internationally recognized prestige.

Dr. Mauri has more than 27 years of experience working in the Cuban biotech sector. In 2012, as one of the founders of the BioCubaFarma group of companies, she began her career as Director of Business, Commercial, and International Cooperation.

From July 2017 to the present time, Dr. Mauri is Vice President in charge of Commercial and Business Development.

T. K. Hernández, *The Cuba Interviews*,
https://doi.org/10.1007/978-3-031-30203-9_31

Fig. 31.1 Dr. Mauri in her office at BioCubaFarma (From the personal collection of Dr. Mauri)

Since 2013, Dr. Mauri is the coordinator of the Cuba–China Working Group on Biotechnology.

In 2019, Dr. Mauri was a member of the Cuban delegation attending the 72nd World Health Assembly with the Minister of the Public Health Department, Dr. José Ángel Portal Miranda to present Cuba's role in primary care.[1]

Dr. Mauri studied International Economic Relations at the Raúl Roa García Higher Institute of International Relations. She holds a Master of Business Administration and a Ph.D. in Economic Science from the University of Havana.

[1] The Seventy-second World Health Assembly is held annually in Geneva, Switzerland. www.who.int/about/governance/world-health-assembly/seventy-second-world-health-assembly.

Hernández: Let's discuss the challenges and successes BioCuba-Farma has faced during the COVID-19 pandemic. There are reports that the CIGB-258 vaccine[2] has shown great promise (Hernandez-Cedeño et al., 2021). **What is the treatment protocol for patients now? Have any other countries requested to export any of Cuba's COVID-19 drugs?**

Dr. Mayda Mauri Pérez: Yes, the use of the drug initially called CIGB-258 had an impact on the treatment of Cuban patients with COVID-19 in serious or critical condition.

Recently, the Cuban Regulatory Authority (CECMED) released the Emergency Use Authorization for this drug, with the trademark name Jusvinza.

Jusvinza is an immunoregulatory peptide discovered and developed by the Center for Genetic Engineering and Biotechnology (CIGB) of Cuba. This immunoregulatory peptide has been demonstrated to induce regulatory mechanisms of inflammation in different experimental systems associated with autoimmune diseases and in clinical investigation in patients with rheumatoid arthritis.

Currently, a phase II clinical trial with this immunoregulatory peptide is ongoing in patients with rheumatoid arthritis in which 187 patients have been treated with the peptide with a remarkable safety profile outcome.

These results supported the use of Jusvinza to control SARS-CoV-2-induced hyper-inflammation. Initially, Jusvinza was used in critical patients under compassionate use. The results were astonishing, incredible even for the medical doctors that used it in the intensive care units. These results led to including Jusvinza in the Cuban national protocol to treat severe and critically ill patients with COVID-19. Sixty Cuban patients were treated with Jusvinza. The survival rate of critically ill patients is 73% and in severe patients, 92%. There is no doubt the use of Jusvinza has contributed to reducing the lethality of patients with COVID-19 in Cuba.

About the treatment protocol, critically ill patients (with mechanical ventilation) are treated with 1 mg of Jusvinza every 12 hours until they

[2] "CIGB-258, a peptide derived from human heat-shock protein 60, decreases hyper-inflammation in COVID-19 patients," National Center for Biotechnology Information (NCBI), accessed September 30, 2021, https://www.ncbi.nlm.nih.gov/pmc/articles/PMC7904296/.

are extubated. They continued therapy with Jusvinza for another 72 hours after extubation, and the seriously ill patients are treated with 1 mg of Jusvinza every 24 hours. The drug is administered intravenously.

Worldwide, 80% of patients with mechanical ventilation died. In Cuba, it is quite the contrary, with over 80% surviving. We are proud of these results and ready to share them with every country and every patient that needs them. In fact, we are discussing clinical trial protocols with several nations and companies. Modestly, we can assure you we already have the drug to save the lives of those patients in severe and critical conditions because of COVID-19.

Can you update us on the status of the BioCubaFarma joint venture "Innovative Immunotherapy Alliance S.A." with Roswell Park Cancer Center in the Mariel Special Development Zone?

Dr. Mauri: The joint venture company Innovative Immunotherapy Alliance, incorporated in Mariel Special Development Zone in 2018, continues to be a successful cooperation project between The Center of Molecular Immunology in Havana and Roswell Park Comprehensive Cancer Center in Buffalo, New York. The collaboration is focused on making the novel immunotherapies, previously developed in Cuba, available to U.S. cancer patients as a part of the innovative clinical research at Roswell Park.

CIMAvax-EGF is a cancer drug, developed by the Center of Molecular Immunology and used in the treatment of lung cancer in Cuba for several years. Roswell Park is running a Phase I/II clinical trial in U.S. cancer patients with CIMAvax-EGF in combination with an anti-check point antibody, one of the leading cancer therapies in the U.S. market.

This combination has proved safe for the patients according to the Phase I results published last April at the annual conference of the American Association for Cancer Research.[3] Phase I data also indicated preliminary encouraging results that this new combination could benefit some patients (Dy et al., 2019), which requires further investigation. The clinical trial is now enrolling patients in Phase II, where other combinations and tumor localizations could be included.

[3] Final results of the Phase I study of nivolumab in combination with CIMAvax, an epidermal growth factor (EGF)-depleting immunotherapy in patients (pts) with advanced non-small cell lung cancer (NSCLC): Focus on biomarker analyses 10.1158/1538–7445.AM2019-CT088 Published July 2019.

The JVC is planning to make other Cuban immunotherapies available to U.S. cancer patients in the future, as part of comprehensive research collaboration between both centers, pioneers in cancer research. The Company, as a joint team, has also taken part in recent events organized by Cuba to discuss the results in dealing with the COVID-19 pandemic. They are evaluating the current information to understand if some Cuban medicines could also help cancer patients infected by the new coronavirus.

BioCubaFarma has developed many international partnerships to export pharmaceuticals and conduct joint research, for example, with China. In recent months, this partnership was demonstrated through donations, collaboration (for example, the biotech development between Guangxi Fukang and BioCubaFarma in the Fangchenggang Development Zone). What progress has been made in the partnership? Are there other agreements in the works for biopharma research and development with China?

Dr. Mauri: BioCubaFarma promotes cooperation and business with Chinese companies and institutions in the biotechnology and the pharmaceutical industry in China under different cooperation models. The relationship is formed to advance product development and finally gain faster registration approval of the products in China. As a result of close to 20 years of cooperation, we have settled three joint ventures in the territory, registered three products, and brought in 10 technologies to date. The Centers of Cuban Biotechnology have incorporated to these companies, established in the People's Republic of China, very new products and technologies to treat diseases with high incidence in the population like cancer and hepatitis, among others.

Two of the three registered products are Nimotuzumab (produced by the JV Biotech Pharma Co. Ltd), a humanized monoclonal antibody for the treatment of nasopharyngeal cancer which is included within the Chinese National Health Reimbursement List, has led to the treatment of over 50,000 patients so far and is seeking approval for two other tumor indications (head & neck and esophagus); and the human recombinant Interferon alpha 2b (produced by the JV Changchun Heber Biological Co., Ltd), which upon request of China's National Health Commission, was used in the COVID-19 pandemic in several provinces of China. The product was successfully administered intramuscularly to boost immunity against the virus, especially in medical staff and in patients through nebulization.

There is also a BioCubaFarma's Business Portfolio of ongoing products and projects, which cover most of the core therapeutic areas of interest for China, to share, aiming at conducting partnerships with Chinese companies in the biotechnology and pharmaceutical sector. Such a portfolio comprises global patents for unmet medical needs and underserved patients worldwide.

One example of this sort of cooperation is Guangxi Fukang, a Chinese company with which BioCubaFarma and its designated companies have signed a Licensing and Co-development Agreement. Under this agreement, several innovative Cuban biotech products will be co-developed and introduced into the Chinese market through their establishment in the International Pilot Medical Development Zone of Fangchenggang, in the south of Guangxi province. China and Cuba decided to accelerate this project that will lead to the first joint biotech park to research, develop, produce, and market drugs obtained by Cuban biotechnology, of proven safety and efficacy in Cuba and overseas. The results derived from this cooperation will have an impact not only for China but also for the rest of the countries from the Association of Southeast Asian Nations (ASEAN).

BioCubaFarma is also working with local Chinese governments of Chengdu, Yongzhou, Changchun, and Shanghai, as well as universities and institutions (University of Science and Technology of Shanghai, Institute of Materia Medica of Shanghai, Institute of Neurosciences of Shanghai, University of Science and Electronic of Chengdu) to foster innovation in the biotech field, through the setting up of R&D Centers and joint laboratories to bring jointly developed Cuban proprietary technologies to the Chinese market, of utmost priority for the bilateral cooperation in the sector.

Another prominent partner of BioCubaFarma is Russia. In 2016, BioCubaFarma signed an agreement with the Skolkovo Innovation Center in Moscow to provide Cuban pharmaceuticals to Russians. Can you update us on the biopharmaceutical collaboration with Russia?

Dr. Mauri: We believe that partnerships with Russian companies and institutions can enhance our own results and support the programs undertaken by the Russian government to solve the major health problems of its population.

In this sense, for a few years, several of our companies' products have been registered in Russia. Among these, we can highlight the Heberprot-P, an innovative product for the treatment of diabetic foot ulcers to avoid amputation, and Hebermin for burn treatment, in collaboration with a Russian company. Currently, there are several companies also interested in promoting these products in the Russian market and the Commonwealth of Independent States (CIS).

In June 2019, the representative office of the BioCubaFarma Group was registered with the Russian authorities. This representative office is based in Moscow.

Really, there are several other products of our companies (CIMAvax-EGF, Heberferon, Jusvinza, Ateromixol, Melagenina, Coriodermina, Proctokinasa, Trofin, Iolizumab) that are in different stages of negotiation with around 15 Russian companies. Some of these products have more than one interested Russian company. There are also over 20 Russian companies that are interested in promoting their products in the Cuban and Latin American markets in collaboration with our companies and using our services and experiences to register and market their products in these markets.

Alliances and agreements for collaboration with several Russian institutions have also been established. In the Skolkovo Innovation Center, there are already two start-up companies created by Russian partners (Bioneuropharma and Neyros) with two of our companies (CNEURO and CIDEM) in the field of neurological diseases for the co-development of innovative projects.[4]

Additionally, there are two of our companies that are in the final stage of the process of joining the Bioorganika Consortium, created within the framework of the National Technological Initiative of Russia and coordinated by the Institute of Bio-organic Chemistry of the Russian Academy of Sciences.

MOUs have also been established with several Russian government and research institutions: St. Petersburg Medical and Ecological Equipment and Biotechnology Cluster, Center for Fundamental Research in Biotechnology, the Committees for the Development and Innovation of the Nizhny Novgorod and Mordovia regions.

Exchanges have intensified in recent years. Participation in events and fairs has been organized to promote scientific, business, and medical exchange. We consider the collaboration has great potential and will be very productive for both nations.

[4] See the interview in Chapter 32, "NEYROS CEO Discusses Joint Research with Cuba on New Parkinson's Medication.".

What does the future hold for BioCubaFarma?

Dr. Mauri: The future of BioCubaFarma is very promising.

Our strategy as a company is to consolidate ourselves as a strategic sector in Cuba, with high social and economic impact.

The Cuban biopharmaceutical sector has a worldwide reputation, thanks to its high standards of innovation and quality. BioCubaFarma comprises 32 companies, with over 20,000 employees.

BioCubaFarma has a consolidated international presence with exports to more than 40 countries. The main products in its portfolio are biopharmaceuticals for the prevention and treatment of different diseases, such as cancer, infectious diseases, cardiovascular diseases, diabetes, as well as diagnostic reagents and medical equipment.

In addition, it has a wide portfolio of projects in different stages of development, both for human health, as well as animal and agricultural use.

The high scientific level of human resources in the Cuban biopharmaceutical industry guarantees the quality and competitiveness of its projects. It currently has 425 innovative projects in its portfolio, which represent great potential for the future of our business group.

The Mariel Special Development Zone (ZEDM) should contribute significantly to the growth of the sector through its regulatory framework, favorable for those international companies wishing to invest in research-production facilities with high added value. The Portfolio of Opportunities for Investment offers several options to be inserted as an investor in the companies of the new biopharmaceutical hub of that Special Zone.

The Cuban Biotechnology and Pharmaceutical Industry is ready to introduce its projects and products in the countries with the highest economic development. Its portfolio of products and intangible assets provides the basis for an open and flexible approach to collaboration with external partners through several business models.

Dr. Mauri, thank you for speaking with me today. You have provided a wealth of information on BioCubaFarma's achievements in the industry, its international partnerships, and the COVID-19 global crisis. I wish you and the Company much success in the future. The world needs this kind of independent innovation in the sector.

References

Dy et al. (2019, July). *Abstract CT088: Final results of the Phase I study of nivolumab in combination with CIMAvax, an epidermal growth factor (EGF)-depleting immunotherapy in patients (pts) with advanced non-small cell lung cancer (NSCLC): Focus on biomarker analyses. CT088-CT088.* https://doi.org/10.1158/1538-7445.SABCS18-CT088. *ResearchGate. Retrieved October 23, 2020, from* https://www.researchgate.net/publication/334210617_Abstract_CT088_Final_results_of_the_Phase_I_study_of_nivolumab_in_combination_with_CIMAvax_an_epidermal_growth_factorEGF-depleting_immunotherapy_in_patients_pts_with_advanced_non-small_cell_lung_cance/

Hernandez-Cedeño et al. (2021). *CIGB-258, a peptide derived from human heat-shock protein 60, decreases hyperinflammation in COVID-19 patients. Cell stress & chaperones*, 26(3), 515–525. https://doi.org/10.1007/s12192-021-01197-2, 515–525. Retrieved December 4, 2021, from https://doi.org/10.1007/s12192-021-01197-2

World Health Organization. (2019, May 20–28). *Seventy-second World Health Assembly.* https://www.who.int/about/governance/world-health-assembly/seventy-second-world-health-assembly. Retrieved 30 September 2021.

CHAPTER 32

Wrong Conclusions from Incomplete Science: Dr. Mitchell Valdés-Sosa Discusses the NASEM Report on the "Havana Syndrome"

In early December, Cuba Business Report published a story on the Cuban Academy of Sciences' rejection of the National Academies of Sciences, Engineering, and Medicine (NASEM) report on the "Havana Syndrome." The NASEM report concluded that radio frequency wave exposure (microwaves) was the most plausible explanation for symptoms experienced by American and Canadian diplomats in Havana (Relman & Pavlin, 2020) (Fig. 32.1).[1]

Cuban scientists called this conclusion "a very unlikely hypothesis," and "speculation not established science (Academy of Sciences of Cuba,

[1] Unbeknownst to the scientists of the National Academy at the time was a secret report by the JASON group in 2018 which concluded the cause of injuries was "highly unlikely" to have been microwave weapons or ultrasound beams but more likely to be mating calls of crickets and mass psychogenic effects. The declassified report was obtained in September 2021 by BuzzFeed reporter Dan Vergano, via a Freedom of Information Act request. See: https://www.buzzfeednews.com/article/danvergano/havana-syndrome-jason-crickets.

T. K. Hernández, *The Cuba Interviews*,
https://doi.org/10.1007/978-3-031-30203-9_32

Fig. 32.1 Dr. Mitchell Valdes-Sosa (From the personal collection of Dr. Valdes-Sosa)

2020)."[2] The NASEM Report[3] is a U.S. government-sponsored report that consulted a panel of mainly U.S.-based scientists.

That a report produced by one scientific institution contains a conclusion declared by another to be "a very unlikely hypothesis" undoubtedly demands further investigation. Scientific investigation is even more pertinent when the report is one sponsored by an administration which was probably not impartial.

[2] Cuban Academy of Sciences' initial assessment of the Standing Committee report. http://www.academiaciencias.cu/en/node/1069.

[3] National Academies of Sciences, Engineering, and Medicine. 2020. *An Assessment of Illness in U.S. Government Employees and Their Families at Overseas Embassies*. Washington, D.C.: The National Academies Press. https://doi.org/10.17226/25889.

In pursuit of "both sides of the story," and truth in reporting, I contacted Dr. Mitchell Valdés-Sosa, Director of the Center for Neuroscience in Havana. I originally asked Dr. Valdés-Sosa only to comment on a few items from the NASEM report. This fascinating conversation turned into a full-length interview over the phone, presented here.

Dr. Valdés is an internationally respected MD and Senior Researcher, specializing in Cognitive Neurosciences. He holds a Ph.D. in Physiological Sciences from the University of Havana, and is a Member Emeritus of the Cuban Academy of Sciences, as well as head of the committee to study the "Havana Syndrome."

Hernández: Could you comment on the need for scientific collaboration between scientists in matters like these?

Dr. Mitchell Valdés-Sosa: There is this false story of the so-called "Havana Syndrome" that goes as follows: a large group of U.S. and Canadian diplomats and families were attacked with a mysterious energy beam, and all suffered brain damage as a consequence of the alleged "attacks." After extensive examination I can say that every part of that story is unsubstantiated and false. True, some people that were in Havana became ill, probably due to different causes, but they were definitely not attacked. A large part of the confusion remaining on this issue is because it has been shrouded in mystery, assessments have been very biased, and the story was useful for political purposes for those wanting to roll back the improvement in relationships between the United States and Cuba that occurred during Obama's administration. Voices that should have been heard were ignored or silenced.

It's inconceivable that a health crisis (like the one involving the U.S. diplomats) occurred in a city and that the scientists from that city/country were not adequately involved in the assessment of the problem. Scientists belonging to the Cuban expert committee—created to study the health complaints—were invited to meet in Washington with the medical staff of the State Department (not the doctors treating the diplomats) for one session of conversation. The only information shared was what had already been published in a medical journal. During that visit we offered to collaborate more deeply to uncover the nature of the complaints. We also offered our collaboration directly to the leaders of the U.S. National Academies of Sciences, Engineering, and Medicine (NASEM) and also to the American Association for the Advancement of Science. Unfortunately, communications were cut off and no further exchange carried out. Artificial (politically motivated) barriers for communication between the U.S. and Cuban scientists were created. When NASEM announced the creation of a Standing Committee to study the health complaints of the diplomats, we immediately wrote to its chairman offering to give our input, who said he would get back to us, but never did.

In fact, the U.S. scientists we contacted to discuss the issue have been visited by government agencies and have been discouraged to exchange with us. And we know that U.S. scientists—who are government employees—that have opinions different from what was expressed in the report have been told to shut up. They've been muzzled. So, there's not been a climate of listening to whatever information Cuban scientists have, or to listen to voices in the United States that do not agree with the official version, or should we say, versions because the story has changed drastically over time. Discrepant scientific opinions in the United States have not been heard.

It's good that the Biden administration says it is going to listen to science. It is going to heed what is said about climate change and rejoin the Paris Agreement. They are going to take a different approach on the coronavirus epidemic because science suggests urgent actions are needed to save lives. They should also heed the full science on the case of the so-called "Havana Syndrome," not only the biased reports that are full of internal contradictions.

They have to listen to all sides in the United States, in the United Kingdom, in Europe, in Cuba, and around the world, because there are scientists that have very strong opinions, and they have not been listened to.

We had a meeting here in Havana with the topic "Is There a Havana Syndrome?" This was held in March 2020, and we invited American, Canadian, European scientists and a colleague from New Zealand. We even invited one of the U.S. people that proposed the radiofrequency idea to join in by teleconference. But unfortunately, other scientists were invited, and they were discouraged or limited from attending by American officials. In fact, one of the people who did come said that the FBI visited him and told him he would have trouble in Cuba. Many are willing to speak out about this harassment, but I prefer they tell their own story when it is the right time. This is the situation where there is a lack of collaboration with Cuba and the silencing of differing opinions within the Western world and specifically in the United States.

Really frightening. It's very interesting to hear this. Could you comment further on this paragraph? The following statement comes

from the highlights of the Cuban Academy of Science response to the NASEM report.

> This claim is not supported by direct evidence, nor by a critical examination of the available literature, nor that by the main body of the report itself and also exhibits intrinsic contradictions.[4]

Dr. Valdés: Yes, this refers to the final claim of the NASEM report, the conclusion that microwaves caused symptoms described by American diplomats and their families during their stay here in Havana. NASEM published a report that is full of internal contradictions.

This microwave claim had been made months ago. It was completely debunked by many scientists. If you look carefully at the report, they recognize in the main text there's no evidence for this idea. But despite this, they opted to make this claim in the conclusions. We have consulted about the report with experts on microwaves (who have been studying their effects on the human body and on animals for decades). They do not agree with this conclusion and, in fact, are jointly writing a detailed technical rebuttal with us. What is the evidence for this microwave hypothesis? Zero evidence. The scientific articles they cite are very contradictory. And even some authors of the articles they cite say this is not possible. The only argument they have is that some other U.S. employees heard sounds coming from a certain direction. And they tried to involve the Canadians, but we've spoken to Canadian scientists involved with this. Dr. Alon Friedman states that the majority of Canadian cases did not report this directional phenomenon (Friedman et al., 2019).[5] This is very flimsy, not convincing.

Note that the NASEM report is well written and uses a serious scientific approach in its sections, however, the conclusion that microwaves were involved comes out of the blue. I think they retrofitted the analysis to conform to the story that I mentioned before and that's been peddled by certain people in the U.S. government, that a mysterious energy beam affected the diplomats and their families, and that this caused

[4] Cuban Academy of Sciences' initial assessment of the Standing Committee report 2020. Available at: http://www.academiaciencias.cu/en/node/1069.

[5] "*Havana Syndrome Among Canadian Diplomats: Brain Imaging Reveals Acquired Neurotoxicity*," medRxiv, accessed September 30, 2021, https://www.medrxiv.org/content/10.1101/19007096v1.full-text.

brain damage. This is absurd. The evidence presented to implicate brain damage is not supported by science, as the corresponding section of the NASEM report concludes. The NASEM report and a buried two-year-old CDC report[6] recognize that the people labeled as suffering from the Havana Syndrome are not a homogenous group. It is probably a collection of people with different disorders that have been lumped together (Centers for Disease Control and Prevention, 2019). Thus, the NASEM report in its sections debunks all the elements of the energy beam/brain damage story, but bizarrely jumps to the conclusion that microwaves were plausibly involved in its summary. And some reporters and politicians with an agenda pounced on the summary but ignored the rest of the report.

How would this "weapon" not strike the hundreds of Cubans and Canadians who visit the the Canadian embassy almost every day of the week?

Dr. Valdés: That is a good question. It is implausible for that to have happened at the embassies because other people would have been harmed or it would have been detected. I think the claim is that people were "attacked" in their homes and hotel rooms. The problem is that to harm the brain, microwaves would first burn the skin. This will require some kind of energy source that goes against the laws of physics. It would have to be very strong, and this would have produced malfunction in electronic devices. It makes no sense.

I googled microwave weapons and saw an image of a kind of vehicle with huge, round antenna (Hambling, 2009).

Dr. Valdés: I know little about these weapons. We have been told by U.S. experts that these microwave weapons are not useful against people but could be used to interfere with drones. They are large. The logistics problem of maneuvering such a weapon into the sites where they alleged attacks were supposed to take place is enormous. And impossible to go unnoticed. There has not been one report of someone in Havana seeing something (a vehicle) of this type anywhere on the streets. And they would have "fried" electronic equipment in the houses or hotel rooms.

From the scientific point of view, this is absurd. It's part of the many claims that have been hyped in the media and have no basis on facts.

[6] The "Havana Syndrome" outbreak of mysterious injuries among U.S. diplomats in Cuba can't be explained by their medical records. Cuba Unexplained Events Investigation. CDC Report. 2019.

It is interesting that the NASEM report recognizes that psychogenic factors could have played a role in propagating and exacerbating many of the symptoms. I will say this simply, if your government, your State Department, your doctors, all say that you are under attack, you have to be worried. And this can really make you feel ill.

You know, it's strange that this disease/ infection/ hysteria targeted only Americans and Canadians.[7]

Dr. Valdés: Yes, of all the other diplomats I've talked to here, no one reports anything like this. Because of our international collaboration programs, I have met with some ambassadors from other countries, and they don't believe this story of the attacks. They find it ridiculous.

This quote is from the highlights of the Cuban Academy of Sciences document. Let me read it to you:

> The lack of sufficient evidence was considered in the report as a reason to strongly doubt pesticide poisoning and infectious origin or a psychological trigger is a cause of symptoms. However, the same logic was not applied to the microwave hypothesis, for which there is even less evidence.[8]

Do you want to talk about that?

Dr. Valdés: I really doubt that an infectious agent explains what truly happened, that there could be some kind of virus or something we don't know. The Canadian scientists recruited by their government have presented evidence that part of the symptoms could be due to pesticide intoxication. They reasoned that a massive anti-Zika public fumigation program[9] was being carried out in Cuba. At the time, the Canadian Embassy was also applying the pesticides themselves in their buildings and homes. It's known that pesticides can produce a dysfunction or injuries in the brain at high concentrations. This hypothesis has led to joint research between Canadian and Cuban scientists looking at possible pesticide intoxication in Cuban citizens. We are examining this although we do

[7] Quite the contrary. The so-called "Havana Syndrome" has been spotted around the world. As of mid-year 2021, there were reports of cases in Colombia, Kyrgyzstan, and Uzbekistan and later in Washington, D.C., "*Vienna Is the New Havana Syndrome Hot Spot*," The New Yorker, accessed September 30, 2021.

[8] Cuban Academy of Sciences' initial assessment of the Standing Committee report.

[9] "Forani, J. (2019). *Zika virus fumigation may have caused 'Havana Syndrome': Leaked study*,". CTV News. https://www.ctvnews.ca/health/zika-virus-fumigation-may-have-caused-havana-syndrome-leaked-study-1.4601242.

not think it explains all the health complaints. But it is a testable hypothesis. The NASEM report does not completely dismiss the possibility of pesticide poisoning, but it concludes that there's not enough evidence to accept it. But there is some evidence (Forani, 2019). But then we don't understand how the NASEM report accepts the microwave explanation for which there's absolutely zero evidence.

To summarize what I think of the so-called "Havana Syndrome attacks": There is no plausible weapon for the alleged attacks. Everything suggested about the mysterious energy weapons (sound, microwaves) goes against the laws of engineering and physics. As recognized by the NASEM panel, there is no direct evidence for brain damage in all the subjects and, if present, could be because of preexisting conditions or unrelated diseases. Several cases where the reports of attacks investigated by Cuban authorities by request of the diplomats were shown to be without basis. The FBI concluded something similar (Hitt, 2019).[10] There is important evidence that there were psychogenic factors at play. And finally, there is no motive for Cuba to take part in attacks or allow the attacks to take place and no possibility that it would escape Cuban police surveillance. Cuba has taken this very seriously and investigated thoroughly wherever an avenue of inquiry has been possible. If any similar notion were claimed about foreign diplomats living in the United States, with so little evidence, they would have been dismissed immediately.

Thank you, Dr. Valdés, for speaking with me. I am very honored. What you have said is that crucial scientific evidence is obviously lacking in the NASEM report to support a microwave explanation of the health complaints of the American diplomats. This further contributes to the rejection of the idea that alleged attacks on diplomats took place in Havana.

References

Centers for Disease Control and Prevention. (2020, December 15). *Cuba unexplained events investigation—Final Report*. DocumentCloud. Retrieved December 5, 2021, from https://www.documentcloud.org/documents/20444983-foia-21-00330-final-report1

[10] Hitt, J. (n.d.). *The Real Story Behind the Havana Embassy Mystery*. [online] Vanity Fair. Available at: https://www.vanityfair.com/news/2019/01/the-real-story-behind-the-havana-embassy-mystery.

Cuban Academy of Sciences. (2020, December 15). *Statement by the Cuban academy of sciences* | Cuban Academy of Sciences. Retrieved December 5, 2021, from http://www.academiaciencias.cu/en/node/1069

Entous, A. (2021, July 16). *Vienna is the new Havana Syndrome hot spot*. The New Yorker. Retrieved September 30, 2021, from https://www.newyorker.com/news/news-desk/vienna-is-the-new-havana-syndrome-hotspot

Forani, J. (2019, September 19). *Zika virus fumigation may have caused 'Havana Syndrome': Leaked study*. CTVNews. Retrieved September 30, 2021, from https://www.ctvnews.ca/health/zika-virus-fumigation-may-have-caused-havana-syndrome-leaked-study-1.4601242

Friedman, A. et al. (2019, September 29). *Havana Syndrome Among Canadian Diplomats: Brain Imaging Reveals Acquired Neurotoxicity*. medRxiv. Retrieved September 19, 2021, from https://doi.org/10.1101/19007096

Hambling, D. (2009, July 22). *Microwave weapon will rain pain from the Sky*. New Scientist. Retrieved December 4, 2021, from https://www.newscientist.com/article/mg20327185-600-microwave-weapon-will-rain-pain-from-the-sky/

Hitt, J. (2019, January 6). *The real story behind the Havana Embassy Mystery*. Vanity Fair. Retrieved September 30, 2021, from https://www.vanityfair.com/news/2019/01/the-real-story-behind-the-havana-embassy-mystery

Relman, D. A., & Pavlin, J. A., National Academies of Sciences, Engineering, and Medicine (2020). *An Assessment of Illness in U.S. Government Employees and Their Families at Overseas Embassies*. Retrieved December 4, 2021, from https://doi.org/10.17226/25889.

Vergano, D. (2021, September 30). *A secret state department report says Microwaves didn't cause "Havana Syndrome"*. BuzzFeed News. Retrieved July 12, 2022, from https://www.buzzfeednews.com/article/danvergano/havana-syndrome-jason-crickets

[illegible]

CHAPTER 33

NEYROS CEO Discusses Joint Research with Cuba on New Parkinson's Medication

NEYROS, a company of the Russian Federation, is a research institution in the SKOLKOVO Innovation Center of Moscow. The Company conducts research and development for new pharmaceutical drug candidates to treat neurodegenerative disorders such as age-related Dementia, Parkinson's disease, Alzheimer's, cerebrovascular ischemia, and melanoma (NEYROS, 2011).

NEYROS, a start-up company, shares a collaboration agreement to study neurological diseases with Cuba's Center for Research and Development of Medicines (CIDEM), an institution under the umbrella of BioCubaFarma.

I spoke with Dr. Dmitry Chelovskiy, the CEO of NEYROS, in March 2021.

Hernández: Can you tell me a little about your background?

Dr. Dmitry Chelovskiy: After graduating from the Medical Faculty of Novosibirsk State Medical University in 1987, I started as a doctor in the emergency medical unit in a large hospital. In the 2000s, I began working in Public Health and implemented a number of projects in this sphere. Besides this work, I started cooperating with pharmaceutical companies producing drugs for the hospital sector.

Four years ago, after my first visit to Cuba, I found interesting research projects. One of them was developed by CIDEM (Center for Pharmaceutical Research and Development), in Havana. The project focuses on

T. K. Hernández, *The Cuba Interviews*,
https://doi.org/10.1007/978-3-031-30203-9_33

the creation of a new pharmaceutical drug for the treatment of Parkinson's disease. This project is supported by Skolkovo Innovation Center, Moscow. Preclinical studies are underway for the third year.

As an introduction, can you share with us a brief company profile of NEYROS?

Dr. Chelovskiy: NEYROS was created in 2019 as part of a joint project with CIDEM. The project is aimed at conducting preclinical studies of a new candidate drug for the treatment of Parkinson's disease. It is a serious illness among the elderly, affecting one of every 100 people over the age of 75.

Many famous people suffered from this disease—boxer Muhammad Ali, President Ronald Reagan, etc. Actor Michael J. Fox also suffers from this condition, and even founded the Parkinson's Foundation. I also have a personal motivation—my dad suffered from this disease for over 10 years.

In Russia, a network of research institutes receiving state funding has been created to distribute grants for scientific research. The leading one is Skolkovo, of which NEYROS is a resident.

Can you tell us about the history of your partnership with Cuba's CIDEM?

Dr. Chelovskiy: Our cooperation with CIDEM began by chance during my visit to Cuba in 2017 as part of a Russian delegation of pharmaceutical companies. Then I met Dr. Idania Caballero Torres, Dr. Adolfo Castillo, and Dr. Alejandro Saul Padron (General Director of CIDEM). Subsequently, this grew into friendship.

What Attracted NEYROS to Cuba's pharmaceutical industry and research efforts?

Dr. Chelovskiy: I knew that Cuba has a high level of education, but I had never heard the achievements of Cuban scientists in medicine and pharmaceuticals. I was amazed when I learned about their research and success. Of course, the level of equipment of Cuban laboratories is not as modern as in Europe, but this is compensated for by the top class of Cuban scientists and enthusiasm.

NEYROS has three projects ongoing at the present time. (Parkinson's Disease, Ischemia, Dementia). You mentioned have a fourth project to treat melanoma? Is Cuba collaborating in research with NEYROS for all of these?

Dr. Chelovskiy: The Dementia research project will start after the completion of the preclinical research on the Parkinson's disease project because it will use a significant part of the scientific material received.

The project on a new drug candidate to treat melanoma called IL-2 has been approved by the Skolkovo Foundation and will start in May this year.

Is NEYROS testing Cuba's pharmaceuticals in this research? Are you running clinical trials? And if the trials are taking place and result in successful outcomes, will NEYROS **import Cuban drugs to Russia for Russian patients?**

Dr. Chelovskiy: The NEYROS project is exclusively research and is not related to the testing of Cuban drugs and their supply to Russia. But our other company, AFK—engaged in the distribution of drugs, is now negotiating the registration of Cuban generics in Russia, and their subsequent import.

Has the COVID-19 pandemic impacted your company's research projects with Cuba?

Dr. Chelovskiy: It didn't significantly affect the current projects because all our communication is going online. But it influenced the development of other projects because it is not yet possible to come to Cuba for personal negotiations.

Dr. Chelovskiy, thank you for agreeing to speak with me on the NEYROS and CIDEM collaborative research projects which, if successful, will have a great impact on the health and quality of life of our aging populations.

Update to This Interview

Following the success of the Parkinson's disease project discussed in this interview of April 2021, Dr. Chelovskiy, as general director of the company ALPHANIL, signed a new co-development agreement for the development of a Cuban cancer drug with BioCubaFarma in December 2021. The Center of Molecular Immunology will lead the project in Havana. Development begins in 2022, with plans to commence clinical trials by 2025 (Cubadebate, 2021). The new project will study the cancer immunotherapy, Mutein IL-2 non-alpha, a recombinant, bioinformatics-designed variant of human IL2.

References

Cubadebate. (2021, December 2). *Rusia y cuba firman acuerdo para ampliar La Investigación de un producto innovador contra El Cáncer*. Cubadebate. Retrieved March 18, 2022, from http://www.cubadebate.cu/noticias/2021/12/01/rusia-y-cuba-firman-acuerdo-para-ampliar-la-investigacion-de-un-producto-innovador-contra-el-cancer/

NEYROS—NEYROS—*Development of pharmaceutical candidates for the treatment of neurodegenerative disorders*. (n.d.). Retrieved March 5, 2021, from https://neyroresearch.com/en/

PART IX

Tourism

CHAPTER 34

"No One Remembers the Silver Medalist," Interview with Desmond Taljaard, London & Regional Properties Ltd.

This interview was the first interview to appear on Cuba Business Report. It perfectly expressed the wave of optimism and enthusiasm felt by the world after Presidents Raúl Castro and Barack Obama made the stunning announcement to move forward with U.S.–Cuba relations. In February 2016, Cuban flags fluttered on the *Champs-Élysées* as President François Hollande welcomed Castro on his first visit to the French capital (Horobin, 2016). Websites were launched, Cuban "experts" appeared out of the woodwork, and everybody loved, loved Cuba. Everybody wanted "in" to the Cuban market, but some were already there, building hotels and golf courses. L&R Properties[1] was one of these (London + Regional Properties, 2015).

Anyone who's traveled to Cuba might have thought, at least once, it would be the ideal location to transform into a golfer's paradise. Its climate, topography, and geographical proximity to the United States make it the perfect candidate. To date, there are only two golf courses in Cuba, one in Varadero and the other in Havana.

[1] L&R acquired the Carbonera Resort in Cuba on October 28, 2015, and planned to invest $500 m in the luxury resort development. http://lrp.co.uk/lr-acquires-carbonera-resort-cuba/.

T. K. Hernández, *The Cuba Interviews*,
https://doi.org/10.1007/978-3-031-30203-9_34

I interviewed Desmond Taljaard, Managing Director at London & Regional Properties Ltd., an international global investment and development firm, by telephone at his London office in July 2016.

In April 2022, I again spoke with Mr. Taljaard for an update to this interview on the status of the golf resort project in Carbonera.

L&R holds property stakes in hotels that span the globe, from London to Monaco to Panama. The company's property portfolio stood at about £9 billion at the time. We discussed the progress of L&R's Carbonera Golf & Beach Resort in Cuba.

In 2002, realizing the potential for golf tourism and hoping to drive inward investment to the sector, Cuba's Ministry of Tourism set out to identify locations ideal for developing golf resorts. They came up with 10 premier sites for golf course development. One of the identified properties is on the coast near a small village named Carbonera, in the province of Matanzas. The town is situated between Havana and Cuba's resort hub, Varadero, with quick access to the airport.

The plan for the location at Carbonera was expanded in 2007 to include a mixed-use resort development. Britain's Esencia Group originally held the property. In February 2014, L&R bought out Esencia's interest in the project. It became a joint venture with Cuba's Grupo Extrahotelero Palmares.

Approvals of the master plan were finalized in 2015 by the Cuban government agency UTITT. The Carbonera Golf & Beach Resort was to be the first of its kind in Cuba. At the time of this interview, the project was underway and moving forward. It generated a lot of excitement not only with the L&R group but also for the Cuban government.

The project was to be delivered in three phases with projected development costs estimated at $500 million. This amount would only be confirmed once the soil movement studies were received later in 2016.

Mr. Taljaard said that L&R's ambitious plan for the high-end development was twofold. It aimed to capture "the essence of the Island;" and to "ensure the future sustainability of the environment and tourist economy of Cuba."

There was another aspect to the project which was predicted to generate a lot of excitement around the globe. It would be a first-class resort and golf course and offer freehold residential villas and apartments to foreign buyers.

L&R obtained the right to develop residences on the site. This real estate will not come at a bargain-basement price. The plans included

1,000 high-end residential units comprising 202 villas and 798 apartments. It would feature a five-star luxury hotel and an 18-hole championship golf course. Other amenities at Carbonera Resort included a lagoon, beach, and country club with tennis courts, retail and leisure facilities, and an adventure garden.

Situated on 395 acres (160 hectares) of prime coastal property, the project broke ground in Quarter Three of 2016. At the time of this interview, it was in the pre-construction phase of land surveying and site testing. Those working on the development included Cubans, Cuban subcontractors, and international professionals. The target date for the first Deliveries of Phase One was early 2020.

Owners of the villas were to receive the title for the purchased property from the Cuban government and insurance from an international title insurance company. U.S. companies were not expected to take part.

L&R's development was not dependent on the outcome of the negotiations between the United States and Cuba. The size and scale of the project will succeed with or without an influx of American tourists and buyers.

"Without a doubt, normalization would be a boon to the project but," Taljaard said, "it's not dependent on it."

Interesting to note were the experiences of L&R working with the Cuban government on the project development up to the point where it stands today. Mr. Taljaard described the experience as a "satisfactory one".

It was not a straightforward project not because of the project size, but because it had never been done before. Mr. Taljaard said, "it will be easier for the second guy, but no one remembers the silver medalist."

I was curious to know whether there had been any delays due to "government bureaucracy." Mr. Taljaard said that he found "the Cubans willing to cooperate and work together to come up with solutions. L&R worked with the Cuban authorities to develop standards where none had existed before."

Of his experiences working with the Cubans, Mr. Taljaard said, "I admire the pioneering spirit of the Cubans. The speed at which the project moves is not really a bureaucratic issue. If a process appears slow, it's easy to point to government bureaucracy, but the actual truth of the matter is that certain standards are still being developed or refined. For example, international buyers need international property insurance. International property insurance requires standards such as the 'hurricane storm surge standards' because we are designing and building houses for the international buyer. To come up with solutions, the Cuban and L&R teams sat down together and developed the standard."

He added, "Everything that the project has needed, the Cubans have worked hard to provide. For example, there was a highway that dissected the resort. The authorities agreed to relocate the road. The Cubans 'get it' and have a vested interest in the successful completion of the resort. Senior ministers of the government are keenly interested in this very exciting project and monitor the progress of the project."

"The Carbonera Golf & Beach Resort will put Cuba on the list of the world's most exclusive golf resorts. For Americans, Cuba is seen as the forbidden fruit," said Mr. Taljaard.

One could only imagine how many of the 23.82 million American golfers (Lange, 2021) would be eager to play the greens at Carbonera right from the "get-go." Members of Congress who continue to resist the removal of the embargo but are passionate about golf might have a change of heart when they read this.

Follow-up to the Interview: April 2022

In early April 2022, I again spoke by telephone with Mr. Taljaard at the offices of L&R Properties in London for an update on the status of the Carbonera Golf Resort.

What happened with the Carbonera resort since we first talked in 2016?

Mr. Taljaard: Further development has been paralyzed by the U.S. government's increasing and broadening embargo restrictions on trade and investment in Cuba and then exacerbated by the pandemic. The dialogue is still continuing between L&R Properties and the Cuban authorities, but it will take many months to recover from those two major impacts.

Where does it stand today?

Mr. Taljaard: We will not be able to progress in the current structure in the near future, given embargo restrictions.

Is there a chance this project will recommence at some distant time in the future?

Mr. Taljaard: Yes, for sure, but it may be years rather than months before confidence comes back to develop such a bold, but much-needed, scheme.

References

Horobin, W. (2016, February 1). *France seeks closer ties with Cuba during Castro visit*. The Wall Street Journal. Retrieved July 5, 2016, from https://www.wsj.com/articles/france-hosts-state-dinner-for-cuban-president-1454331794

L&R acquires Carbonera Resort, Cuba - L + R: London and regional properties. L + R | London and Regional Properties. (2017, April 20). Retrieved March 5, 2022, from http://lrp.co.uk/lr-acquires-carbonera-resort-cuba/

Lange, D. (2021, March 10). *Golf: Number of participants U.S. 2019*. Statista. Retrieved December 6, 2021, from https://www.statista.com/statistics/191907/participants-in-golf-in-the-us-since-2006/

CHAPTER 35

Travel to Cuba—A New Era Dawns, Tom Popper, President, InsightCuba

In April 2019, the Trump government announced it would tighten restrictions on travel to Cuba for American citizens. Several months later, on June 5 to be exact, the U.S. Administration banned cruises and people-to-people trips. In consideration of these changes, I held a telephone interview with insightCuba's president, Tom Popper (Fig. 35.1).

Although a new era has emerged with yet another set of rules for American tourists who wish to travel to Cuba—there are still possibilities. Legal travel has not ended, Mr. Popper explained, but there are significant changes. Options remain to allow any American to visit Cuba. Many are not aware, and this must be emphasized: the recent modifications are not an all-out prohibition on travel.

InsightCuba was the first company in the United States to offer people-to-people travel in 2000 under President Clinton. The company also delivers Support for the Cuban People travel for small group specialized tours.

Hernández: What did the opening of U.S. travel to Cuba signify over the last few years (since 2015), for Americans and Cubans? What happens when Americans meet Cubans?

Tom Popper: President Obama's détente with Cuba in 2015 and the resulting loosening of travel restrictions, the most significant since 1961, quickly made Cuba the Number One destination to travel to for U.S. citizens. Over 50 years of pent-up demand to visit our island neighbor was

T. K. Hernández, *The Cuba Interviews*,
https://doi.org/10.1007/978-3-031-30203-9_35

Fig. 35.1 Tom Popper, now CEO, 82° West Consultants at the Special Development Zone of Mariel in 2022 (Photo from the personal collection of Mr. Popper)

released. Tour operators like insightCuba grew four times overnight, and others quickly started offering the destination for the first time. Big names in the travel industry, including Marriott and Airbnb, started operating on the island. For the first time in five decades, U.S. commercial airlines began offering flights to Cuba. Later, the cruise industry was permitted to sail from Florida to ports in Cuba. The more options that travelers had, the more Americans wanted to visit Cuba.

The normalization of relations between the U.S. and Cuban governments coupled with the deluge of American visitors to the Island created a strong sense of optimism in Cuba. Overwhelmingly, the Cubans rejoiced. I personally hadn't seen such an outpouring of affection toward the United States since 9/11. After traveling to Cuba for those 15 years prior to the détente, the one thing every Cuban I met wanted to see in their lifetime, was the United States and Cuba to become friends again.

On December 17, 2014, Cubans got their wish when President Obama and President Castro announced the normalization between the two countries. American flags hung out of many windows, and Cubans welcomed their American brethren with open arms.

In the years that followed, American travelers came, and they brought more than optimism. They brought dollars, creating and supporting a fledgling wave of private enterprise on the island. Opportunities to independently earn a living became a reality. Americans were greeted with Cuban warmth and introduced to their culture. Most Americans were amazed by what they experienced, that Cuba wasn't the dark, militarized country they had been led to believe existed for decades. They learned that Cubans, despite economic hardship, valued family, culture, and happiness. They embraced knowledge, education, the arts, and an entrepreneurial spirit—values that most Americans espouse.

What's your opinion/sentiment of the latest crackdown by the Trump administration against American citizens' right to travel to Cuba?

Mr. Popper: The return to tougher travel restrictions by the administration runs contrary to our own best interest as well as that of the Cuban people. Whatever your brand of politics, left, right, or center, Americans travel, it's a freedom we expect and one we exercise. According to the U.S. National Travel Tourism Office, in 2018, 93 million U.S. citizens traveled outside the United States (U.S. Citizen Travel to International Regions, 2018).[1] Cuba remains the only country where decades of travel restrictions remain. Except for a recent moratorium on travel to North Korea, Americans are free to travel to any country on the planet, including those where we are fighting wars. However, for decades U.S.–Cuba policy has been driven by presidential electoral politics trying to satisfy what has now become a fractured Cuban American community, with more Cuban Americans wanting closer ties with their homeland.

Despite the Trump administration's announcement on June 5, there is a silver-lining, in that most of the 12 permissible categories of travel remain intact, and any American can still legally travel to Cuba. By way

[1] The U.S. National Trade and Travel Office reported a total of 93,038,257 American citizens traveled to international destinations in 2018 at https://travel.trade.gov/view/m-2018-O-001/index.html. The original webpage is no longer available but can be viewed on the internet archive at https://web.archive.org/web/20190402161434/https://travel.trade.gov/view/m-2018-O-001/index.html

of history, and since 1963, travel restrictions on U.S. travel to Cuba have been in place. While President Obama significantly loosened those restrictions in 2015, Americans have had to travel under one of the 12 license categories issued by the U.S. Department of the Treasury.

While Trump's new restrictions issued on June 5 eliminate large cruise ships leaving from the U.S. sailing to Cuba, Americans may travel under the Support for the Cuban People license category. This category simply requires a full-time schedule of activities that promote direct contact with the Cuban people and prohibits leisure travel, which includes spending time on the beach. Companies like insightCuba will continue to provide incredible experiences, meeting regular Cuban people in real-life settings. Travelers overall have been seeking more meaningful and transformative experiences when visiting destinations. The travel industry in general, including hotels and online travel agencies, is trying to adapt to this trend. Visiting Cuba provides the type of experiences travelers are seeking, and they can do so legally.

Let's discuss this "new era" of travel for Americans who wish to visit Cuba. How is travel to Cuba going to change? What new type of travel do you envision? Can you give us some travel options?

Mr. Popper: Travel to Cuba has always been special for U.S. citizens. The opportunity to go after decades of being told they couldn't, is exciting within itself. Under the new rules, tour operators will focus entirely on providing engaging experiences, which are harder to curate, transformative for the traveler, and rewarding for the residents they meet.

On an insightCuba tour, guests will visit uplifting community projects in both the city and countryside; visit with inspiring artists and musicians; meet with career-oriented university students; and get to know the people that give Cuba its spark. With fewer options for Americans to travel to Cuba, traveling there will feel a little more exclusive.

Do you think the cruise ships and the small-ship cruises will come back to Cuba? It is, after all, a favorite method of travel for many people.

Mr. Popper: For now, the large ships that originate in Florida's ports are prohibited from cruising to Cuba. However, small-ship cruises that start and end in Cuba are permitted to operate if passengers follow the Support for the Cuban People requirements once they disembark the ship. InsightCuba offered small-ship cruises from 2013 through 2018 in connection with Group IST.[2]

Will these new regulations affect your business to Cuba? Do you think this will be for the long term?

Mr. Popper: We are quite optimistic that the current regulatory landscape will boost business for insightCuba and other tour operators and have a positive effect on the local Cuban economy throughout the country. With future cruise bookings prior to June 5, estimated at 800,000 passengers and other land-based travel, the U.S. travel market to Cuba swelled to more than 1 million travelers. This is five times what it was only a few years ago. While we anticipate the overall market to contract without the cruise ships, many tour operators will regain a larger market share, albeit of a smaller market, which will result in a net gain for operators, and more jobs in both the United States and Cuba.

Are you optimistic that American travelers' desire and curiosity to know Cuba will continue to grow?

Mr. Popper: With almost 60 years of pent-up demand, American desire to travel to Cuba will remain strong for years to come. Cuba is safe, culturally rich, only 90 miles from the United States, and has inexpensive non-stop service from numerous hubs in the United States. People can go for a long weekend in Havana or spend two weeks touring the country and experiencing this incredible destination. Travel creates a positive affinity. It is not a bad thing. Appreciation and love. We will adjust. It is a new era.

Thanks for talking with me today. It's been good meeting you and learning your impression of the recent changes in travel for the Americans who want to visit the Island.

Follow-up to the Interview: April 2022

In April 2022, I spoke again with Tom Popper after he had returned from a business trip to Cuba, his second since the reopening of borders in November 2021. There have been a massive number of regulatory changes on the Island since the outbreak of the pandemic. We talked about the status on Americans' ability to travel to the Island, and where life has taken him since we last spoke. Our conversation also covered

[2] Group IST https://www.groupist.com/ produced original travel programs for groups to Cuba, and other destinations.

Cuba's new class of small business entrepreneurs, food shortages, the agriculture sector, his visit to the Special Development Zone of Mariel, and, of course, a little politics.

Let's do a quick update of our earlier interview back in June 2019. Can Americans still travel to Cuba?

Tom Popper: Yes, Americans can still legally travel to Cuba under the 12 categories of permissible travel, which still exist today.

While many of those categories are narrow in scope, most Americans can legally travel under a general license category, called Support for the Cuban People. However, there are some limitations that were enacted by the Trump administration. Most notably, a provision that bars Americans from staying in hotels that have been placed on the U.S. Department of State's prohibited list, which currently includes most hotels. However, access to Cuba's wealth of private homes continues to be a popular option.

Given the complexities of travel to Cuba, I advise people to use an experienced tour operator or their travel agent when considering traveling to Cuba. Travel professionals will take care of the many details and will provide access to the country travelers can't often find on their own.

Unfortunately, most Americans believe that the Trump administration ended legal travel to Cuba, which is not the case. This misconception has, in part, impeded Cuba's tourism recovery as it reopened in November of 2021 due to the pandemic.

Over the years, it's become clear that the U.S. traveling public looks at traveling to Cuba as a binary choice. You either can travel or you can't. All the regulations and its nuances that many of us study and talk about are lost on the general traveling public. It's very black and white for them.

For example, when Trump announced at a rally in June of 2017 in Miami, that he was ending Obama's policy of engagement with Cuba, travel to Cuba hit the brakes. This despite Trump not changing any policy until later into his term. Alternatively, if President Biden were to announce that he was allowing Americans to stay in Cuban hotels, removing Cuban hotels from the prohibited list, it's likely that this would send a signal to travelers that Biden reopened travel. But until Biden makes a change in policy, I'm afraid U.S. travel to Cuba will remain dampened.

I see you are still involved with Cuba. What are you doing now?

Mr. Popper: After being in the Cuba travel business for 20 years, I decided to take my knowledge of U.S. regulations, my relationships in Cuba, and my experience doing business in Cuba, and help other companies enter the Cuba market. So, I founded 82° West Consultants dedicated to helping companies explore and execute strategies related to foreign direct investment, market entry, trade, and private small business investment in Cuba.

While U.S. sanctions impact trade with Cuba, there are lots of legal opportunities for U.S. companies in Cuba, notably in the medical field and agriculture.

Cuba is also making substantial changes to its economic system and trade regulations and is becoming increasingly business friendly.

You recently returned from Cuba. What has changed since your pre-pandemic visits?

Mr. Popper: So much has changed, but on the other hand, so much remains the same. Cuba is still this vibrant and lively cultural epicenter. Cubans love life and it rubs off on you easily.

On a positive note, there are many more independent businesses than there were a few years ago. However, and unfortunately, many are struggling because of the lack of tourism and the overall poor economic situation.

Also notable, nearly everyone has a mobile phone. Data costs have come down drastically, which has led to greater access to the internet.

On a less positive note, the Trump sanctions starting in 2017 combined with the pandemic have had a severe impact on Cuba's economy. Unfortunately, and to date, Biden has opted to keep all the Trump administration sanctions in place, despite the impact they have on the lives of Cubans. While the United States was helping other countries around the globe economically and medically to get through the pandemic, we did the opposite to Cuba.

A friend of mine said something very profound one morning as we were talking about the situation. He said, "U.S. policy during the pandemic was different than ever before. It was simply cruel." That's the general sentiment in Cuba. It's something Cubans find hard to understand.

What about the Non-state sector (MSMEs)?

Mr. Popper: There is some movement in this area. MSMEs are starting to have a presence and contribute to the economy and daily life of Cubans, but more needs to happen in this area. Unfortunately, and because of U.S. sanctions, funding for these types of business from the United States and outside comes with risk and concern. It would go a long way if the Biden administration loosened U.S. sanctions to help promote independent business in Cuba, which they have vocally supported in the administration.

Yes, the non-state sector can be a significant contributor to GDP recovery. I have looked at the statistics from other countries and the sector contributes a large percentage to GDP. It's a viable sector. Some complain about the bureaucracy and the regulations, but regulations are everywhere.

Mr. Popper: The acceptance and encouragement of independent business in Cuba is a relatively new concept. The economy has been mostly run by the state since the early sixties. The level of awareness and knowledge about how to start and operate a business isn't ingrained in the population yet. Also, government processes and procedures aren't always clear or well defined. This type of change comes slowly in Cuba; however, new businesses continue to be created.

I spent the day recently with Marta Deus, an entrepreneur who started three successful businesses in Cuba, including an accounting firm, a digital publication, and a food delivery service called Mandao. She is currently opening a restaurant. She's learned how to operate within the new economic model and often meets with budding entrepreneurs, helping them navigate regulations and point them down a path of success. Her digital newsletter provides similar information.

Did you make it to ZED Mariel Development Zone?

Mr. Popper: After hearing about the ZED Mariel special development zone for the past five or so years, I finally visited the area. I met with the main representative from ViMariel, a Vietnamese company which has a special concessionaire's license in the Zone. I also met with representatives from ZED Mariel to learn about current and future investments into the zone.

Currently, they have signed agreements with 62 companies to operate in the zone and an additional 90 companies with MOUs. Now that COVID infection rates have fallen, they are restarting their efforts. Of the 62 companies, 32 are 100% FDI, 12 are 100% Cuban capital, and 16 are joint ventures. Spain is the dominant investor.

I also toured the Zone. It's a picturesque and impressive area and poised to grow. However, until U.S. sanctions are reduced or lifted, it's uncertain if the zone will reach its full potential.

You are focusing on consultancy now and foreign investment opportunities for Americans, even in this political climate of aggressive sanctions?

Mr. Popper: There is a lot of need in Cuba and there is a lot of opportunity. While doing business in Cuba isn't necessarily easy, there are many legal ways for companies to invest in Cuba. Helping them navigate this landscape with experience and knowledge is paramount. Not only can these ventures be profitable, but they will help society. It's a win for everyone.

For example, and most recently, Cuba's been experiencing milk shortages. They need to import much of it, which comes at a great expense, and U.S. sanctions limit their options. Currently, their best option is to import from South Africa and as you can imagine, transportation costs are high and, as with the rest of the world, supply chain issues create their own set of challenges. As a result, supply isn't meeting demand.

Interestingly, there's no shortage of fertile land and farmers. This translates into an opportunity for dairy farmers and dairy producers to help Cuba not only produce enough milk for the population but become a net exporter to the region.

There's so much fertile land. The reasons I understand are the embargo, antiquated equipment, equipment shortages, parts supplies for equipment, but there are farmers and the cooperatives, the need to rely less on imports, and become more self-sufficient and build on food security.

Food security and the prospect of being a net exporter of food in the region is an important economic component for Cuba moving forward. U.S. sanctions impact not only the importation of food, but investment in needed agricultural technology, processing, and packaging. However, agriculture is one area where U.S. or other international companies can legally invest in Cuba. There just isn't enough awareness of this fact.

Do you think Biden will change U.S. policy toward Cuba?

Mr. Popper: I think if you look at the history of U.S. presidents, including Carter, Clinton, Bush, and Obama, all made positive policy decisions at the end of their term of office.

Many people expected Biden to make significant changes in his first year despite having a 50/50 split in the U.S. Senate and a big domestic policy agency. I didn't think this was realistic. Cuba's always been a political lightning rod, so I don't expect Biden to make any changes till the last year or two of his term. But we'll welcome a nice surprise.

Cruise lines, airlines, travel agencies, Marriott International, and other U.S. businesses all had permission to do business in Cuba. Now, because of the activation of Helms–Burton, there may be legal repercussions. I think that, even if Biden does something dramatically positive in relation to Cuba, businesses might still be wary.

Mr. Popper: The Helms–Burton's Title III provision was originally written to discourage investment in Cuba. However, since 1996 when it became law, no president until Trump activated it because of potential legal and political issues with non-U.S. companies and the host country.

As litigation on Title III cases moves forward in the courts, an additional layer of risk has been added to the calculus of doing business in Cuba. The lawsuit between Havana Docks and the cruise lines will most likely have an impact on the future of the cruise industry in Cuba, regardless of the outcome of the case.

Have you had any recent experience with clients and new projects since the pandemic and could you comment on the ease of doing business with Cuba now?

Yes, I'm working with two clients currently that are highly motivated to make market entry work. Cuba has been very supportive in our efforts. More so than ever before, which is wonderful to see. As always, it's a process that takes time and a lot of due diligence must be afforded to make sure the final product is legal, beneficial for both sides, and the deal can cross the finish line.

References

Group IST. (n.d.). *Cuba: A magical journey by Land & sea*. Retrieved March 18, 2022, from https://www.groupist.com/

U.S. Citizen Travel to International Regions. (2018). Monthly departures to international destinations. (2019). https://web.archive.org/web/20190402161434/https://travel.trade.gov/view/m-2018-O-001/index.html

CHAPTER 36

"Start as You Intend to Go on," says CEIBA Investments Portfolio Manager, Sebastiaan Berger

In this interview of November 2019, CEIBA Investments Portfolio Manager Sebastiaan Berger discusses the strategy behind 18 years of building up a successful portfolio in Cuba. The company is currently partnering with Spain's Meliá Hotels International, S.A. in projects underway in Trinidad, Varadero, and Havana (Fig. 36.1).[1]

Sebastiaan began working for CEIBA Investments Limited in 2001 as an independent adviser. From 2002 until 2013, he was the founding executive director of CEIBA International Management Ltd. Upon the internalization of management, he became Chief Executive Officer of the Company in May 2013.

In 2019, after having led the £30 million capital raise and listing of CEIBA on the Specialist Fund Segment of the London Stock Exchange, Sebastiaan was hired by Aberdeen Standard Investments to act as the portfolio manager for CEIBA Investments Limited. Being a "reverse-brexiteer," Sebastiaan and his family moved to London in September 2019.

[1] "... the pace of construction of the Meliá Trinidad Península Hotel is expected to be increased substantially as from May 2021 with a view of opening the hotel by the end of the third quarter of 2022, ahead of the start of the peak season for Cuban tourism." Update from investment manager Sebastiaan Berger, April 1, 2021, https://www.ceibalimited.co.uk/en/latest-article/.

T. K. Hernández, *The Cuba Interviews*,
https://doi.org/10.1007/978-3-031-30203-9_36

Fig. 36.1 Sebastiaan Berger from CEIBA investments in London (Photo by Charles Sturge)

Sebastiaan is also a non-executive director of Adelante Exotic Debt Fund Ltd., a fund specialized in the trade in non-performing indebtedness. He is the coauthor with Cameron Young of "Cuba—The Regulation of Foreign Investment,"[2] and coauthor with Andreas Winkler and Julio Maldonado of the book "Cuba—Contemporary Art."[3]

He graduated from the University of Leiden, The Netherlands, in 1990, with a degree in civil law and has worked in New York, Washington, Rotterdam, Brussels, and Havana. In June 2019, Sebastiaan passed his CFA U.K. Level 4 Certificate Investment Management exam. His primary experience is in the areas of mergers and acquisitions, finance, and foreign investment.

[2] Young, Cameron, Maldonado, J. and Sebastiaan Berger. *Cuba The Regulation of Foreign Investment*. CEIBA Publications Ltd., 2008.

[3] Winkler, Andreas, and Sebastiaan Berger. *Cuba Contemporary Art*. Overlook Books, 2012.

Sebastiaan and his wife, Xantha, are renowned collectors of Cuban contemporary art.

Description of CEIBA Investments Limited and Meliá Hotels International Construction Projects

On 22 October 2018, CEIBA Investments Limited ("CEIBA" or the "Company") added £30 million (approximately US $39 million) to its capital and listed its shares on the Specialist Fund Segment of the London Stock Exchange. Its 2018 audited financial statements show that the Company has total net assets in excess of US $200 million.

The Company's stated investment objective is to provide a regular level of income and substantial capital growth in Cuban real estate and other assets directly related to Cuba. It is the largest and most successful of foreign investors on the Island. Its operational assets include interests in the Miramar Trade Center, the Meliá Habana, Meliá Las Américas, Meliá Varadero en Sol Palmeras hotels (in Varadero).

CEIBA can be seen to be one of the boldest of foreign investors in Cuba. The decision to upgrade and expand its four operational hotels in Havana and Varadero is evidence of this and was made in the middle of Donald Trump's presidency.

CEIBA is in good company. All its hotels are operated by Meliá Hotels International S.A., a leading hotel brand in Spain. Meliá manages over 30 properties in Cuba, predominantly as operator and not as co-owner. Meliá's equity interests in Cuba are in the hotel properties of which CEIBA is the principal foreign shareholder.

CEIBA's secrets? Its seasoned foreign and Cuban managers, its strategy to focus on outstanding assets that make profits today and that may increase in value tomorrow, and its respect for, and at-arms-length dealings with its Cuban partners. As Mr. Berger once stated: "never underestimate your Cuban counterparts because they are twice as smart as you are!"

Hernández: I'm guessing you are passionate about Cuba. Tell us of your first visit to the Island. Were you a tourist?

Sebastiaan Berger: You are absolutely right that I am passionate about Cuba and the Cuban people! That passion started in 1996 when I first set foot on the island, and although it has had its ups and downs and has been severely tested by many U.S. Presidents over the years, it has grown in parallel with my friendships with many Cuban colleagues, artists, entrepreneurs, and others.

The greatest assets of Cuba are its people and their creativity, and if you add to that a coastline of 6,000 kilometers and all the other good things the country has to offer, you may get infected…

When I arrived in Cuba in May 1996, Cuba started to open up to foreign investment and adopted a new foreign investment law[4] (that replaced Cuba's first foreign investment act of 1980).

Conquering Cuba in a 1958 Chevy with a driver, a briefcase, a huge Nokia mobile telephone, a small apartment on the 13th floor of a building that often lacked a functioning elevator. President Clinton had just enacted the Helms–Burton Act. I was a (Dutch) lawyer and my mission was to set up an office for my law firm and to have sufficient clients so we could run a profitable operation.

Within six months, we received a license to open our offices and were the first international law firm to do so since 1959. Business was booming and changes were coming.

In 2001, I started to head the management of CEIBA, which during the period between 2001 and 2019 we have been able to grow from approximately US $19 million to over US $200 million—while distributing over US $85 million in dividends since 2004.

A good friend of mine once taught me that it is important in life to start as you intend to go on! When I started to manage CEIBA's investment portfolio, our basic rule was to invest in assets and businesses that make money today and that are worth a lot more tomorrow. In my opinion, that simple rule has been one of the principal foundations of our success.

How did Meliá Hotels International become your strategic partner? Did it take a long time to negotiate with CEIBA's other partners?

Mr. Berger: Our business relationship with Meliá Hotels International S.A. goes back to 2009 when we took our first small stakes in the Meliá Habana, the Meliá Las Americas, the Meliá Varadero, and the Sol Palmeras hotels. When we expanded our interests in these hotels, we also invited Meliá to partner with us in our Trinidad beach resort hotel (the

[4] Law No. 77, the Foreign Investment Act" was passed on September 5, 1995.

Meliá Playa Trinidad) and jointly developed plans to upgrade and expand the hotels in Havana and Varadero.

Like most relationships, it took a bit of time to get to know each other and fully appreciate what each side was bringing to the table. We came to the conclusion that we share the same values. The end result is that we greatly respect each other and that we are both committed and extremely well-placed to play a role in building up Cuba's tourism sector.

It is good news that CEIBA is investing in the first joint venture beach hotel in Trinidad. Can you tell us how that is going?

Mr. Berger: I think the best news that I can give you today is that we are making great progress with constructing the 400 room Meliá Playa Trinidad hotel, which should be completed by the end of 2020,[5] and is going to be spectacular!

Being the pioneer joint venture carrying out a serious hotel construction in Central-South Cuba is not easy—and especially in the beginning, was quite nerving. But with the (Italian-Cuban) international construction consortium, our team, the managers of the joint venture, Meliá, and last but not least our Cuban partners, we are all putting in lots of energy and efforts, it proves to be entirely feasible, with excellent quality and–so far so good—closely within time and budget.

It is wonderful news to hear that CEIBA will invest in the Meliá Las Americas hotel—especially because of its spectacular golf course, a beautiful beach, and the Xanadu mansion, restaurant, and bar. Why were the other two hotels (Meliá Varadero and the Sol Palmeras) chosen to be a part of this deal with Meliá and the Cubans?

Mr. Berger: Plans to upgrade and modernize the Meliá Las Americas, the Meliá Varadero, and the Sol Palmeras hotels in Varadero are being developed to maintain the leading position these hotels have and to fully benefit from the privileged position and spectacular location.

In parallel, we are analyzing how we can optimize the use of the plot of 28 hectares on which the hotels are situated, which could very well imply that we will add rooms and facilities in the future. All three hotels are

[5] The COVID pandemic and the later emergence of the Omicron variant delayed construction projects throughout Cuba. CEIBA Investments reported the status of the Meliá Trinidad Peninsula hotel in its latest article on its website on February 2022. A "soft opening" of the hotel is planned for the first quarter of 2023. The grand opening will follow Cuba's Feria del Turismo (FITUR) in May 2023 - Berger, S. (2022, February 22). An update from our investment manager, Sebastiaan Berger. CEIBA Investments Limited. https://www.ceibalimited.co.uk/en/latest-article.

located next to the spectacular 18-hole golf course of Varadero and previously belonged to the CUBANACAN joint venture (Cubanacan, n.d.), with which we merged at the end of 2017 with Miramar S.A. (the owner of the Hotel Meliá Habana).

Can you tell us about CEIBA's "Other Cuban Assets may include, but are not limited to, Cuba-related businesses in the construction or construction supply, logistics, energy, technology, and light or heavy industrial sectors?"

Mr. Berger: That is wording from our Prospectus (CEIBA Investments Limited, n.d.) that sets out that—alongside investments in Cuba's real estate sector—we may invest in other asset classes. At present, the focus of CEIBA is 100% on Cuban real estate and that is not likely to change in the near future.

When we pursue and make substantial investments in other sectors, it is likely that a separate investment vehicle will be set up. Given our team, our combined experiences, track record, and contacts (in and outside Cuba), I do believe that we are pretty well positioned to participate and accelerate new foreign direct investment ventures in Cuba.

Is CEIBA Investments, with its headquarters in Guernsey concerned about U.S. sanctions against Cuba (Helms–Burton Title III) or is the company more confident because of the position taken by the United Kingdom and the European Union vis-à-vis sanctions? Can you discuss this?

Mr. Berger: Our Company, and we as managers, keep abreast of all existing U.S.–Cuba embargo legislation and do everything possible so that CEIBA does not act in conflict with the legislation—except for the fact that we do something that U.S. investors presently cannot do, which is invest in Cuba. We carry out proper legal due diligence; we do not use U.S. banks or intermediaries; we do not make any transfers in U.S. dollars. We even prohibit U.S. investors to hold shares in our Company, although Guernsey or U.K. legislation doesn't prohibit Amercian investors to invest in CEIBA.

We are not more or less concerned because of the fact that the European Union—including the United Kingdom—have condemned the U.S.–Cuba embargo legislation and its extraterritorial effects and have adopted counter legislation. In my personal opinion, the European Union and its member states could and should step up their efforts to at least get the highly controversial Helms–Burton Act off the table. However, we are definitely encouraged by the stepped-up efforts from the EU which has condemned the U.S. embargo, has tripled its cooperation with Cuba in the last two years, and has stressed its support for Cuba and its commitment to help Cuba develop its economy!

Personally, I believe that the present U.S. policy regarding Cuba is wrong and that a strategy of engagement and respectful dialogue is the only way to go. And it is sad to notice that the "international" U.S. policy and economic sanctions regarding Cuba continue to be part of "internal" politics and reelection campaigns and that the Cuban people are the unintended ones that suffer.

You made a statement to Reuters in October 2018:

> It has been 22 years that I have been involved with foreign direct investment in Cuba. Of all transactions and achievements, I believe this one has been the most difficult one to accomplish and at the same time the one that will likely have the greatest positive impact on Cuba's economic future...[6]

This indicates to me that you love a challenge. Your statement, to "have the greatest positive impact on Cuba's economic future." Why is this important to you? There have been other investors who hoped to invest in Cuba during what I would call, "the years of hype" from December 2014 to the beginning of the Trump administration. CEIBA is still there. This is interesting.

Mr. Berger: In 2017, we structured and carried out the merger of two Cuban joint venture companies, which was a legal novelty in Cuba and extended surface rights of all our hotel properties by 25 years. In 2018, we raised additional funds, listed CEIBA on the London Stock Exchange and became managed by Aberdeen Standard Investments, one of Europe's leading asset managers.

Those events, and especially the listing of a company that has a demonstrated track record of investing in Cuba, making profits, distributing cash dividends to our shareholders, and staying out of trouble, allow the international investor community to learn more about Cuba's foreign investment climate and that it may very well be worthwhile pursuing investments in the absence of U.S. competitors.

[6] Statement by Mr. Berger in an article written by Marc Frank. "Cuba Fund first to be listed on London Exchange". Reuters. from https://www.reuters.com/article/us-cuba-investment/cuba-fund-first-to-be-listed-on-london-exchange-idUSKCN1MW2JW.

Mr. Berger, I would like to thank you for taking the time to participate in this interview. Discussing the success your company has experienced with its projects on the Island is a beacon for other foreign investors of the limitless possibilities of what can be done in Cuba.

Follow-up to the Interview: January 2022

In late January 2022, I spoke again with Mr. Berger following an interview by RT's journalist Oliver Zamora Oria with Rodrigo Malmierca,[7] Minister of Foreign Trade and Foreign Investment, which discussed how U.S. sanctions affect Cuba's foreign investment scenario.

Why do investors, such as yourself, continue to invest in what is generally viewed as a country that is difficult to invest in, speaking of, for example, the wretched U.S. embargo/blockade. For this reason, Cuba is viewed as a less attractive investment destination. Yet, the investors come. But why? What are your thoughts on this?

Mr. Berger: That is a difficult question… but I also believe that you haven't thought it through…

Compare Cuba to other pre-emerging markets and you will conclude that there is presently not an abundance of foreign investors pursuing investments in pre-emerging markets, let alone in Cuba. As you know, the same was recently confirmed by Rodrigo Malmierca who in January 2022 gave a pretty accurate and surprisingly honest and open explanation of the reasons why. *No es fácil!*

I agree with you that the principal reason that Cuba is off-limits for many international investors is because of the U.S. Cuban embargo and the incorrect (continuing) inclusion of Cuba on the list of State Sponsors of Terrorism. On the other hand, it is evident that—in comparison to the U.S.—Cuba is undoubtedly less important for Europe, Canada, and others so that none of these potential investment partners will go "head-to-head" with the United States to choose a completely different path and not only engage politically but also take serious steps and substantial financial commitments to stimulate Cuba economically by promoting and

[7] Interview with Rodrigo Malmierca by Oliver Zamora Oria, (2022). *¿Cómo afectan las sanciones a las inversiones? ¿qué se ofrece al capital extranjero?*: Habla Rodrigo Malmierca, ministro del Comercio Exterior de Cuba. View at: https://actualidad.rt.com/programas/entrevista/417803-rodrigo-malmierca-ministro-comercio-exterior-cuba.

supporting trade and investment. And notwithstanding that the situation of the U.S. embargo may drive Cuba to elect to befriend countries that are perhaps not the most popular ones, that doesn't make it easier for countries of the Western Hemisphere to increase their engagement with Cuba.

Unfortunately, everything about Cuba is black or white and never grey. In Florida, the Republicans depict the Democrats as Communists, Socialists, *Chavistas*, and *Castristas*, and in Cuba, demonstrations are believed to be part of a months-long destabilization campaign by the United States. That makes it very difficult to think that we are nearing a time in which people will engage in a real dialogue, make efforts to heal wounds and jointly lift the embargo and existing hurdles, speak up to resolve matters instead of making divisions impossible to overcome, and start the change from both sides while at the same time respecting Cuba's sovereignty. As a Dutchman living in the United Kingdom, the horrible weather has taught me what is grey. Perhaps that is the intermediate color I hope will appear during my time of doing business in Cuba.

So why do I think people should invest? Because I believe in the country, its people, its geographical position, and in the opportunities that it offers. Because I like to make a difference and—like the Cubans—dislike that others tell me or dictate to me what to do. Because the U.S. embargo will go one day, Cuba could become a member of the Organization of American States and the Inter-American Development Bank (Cuba is presently the only country south of the United States that is not a member) and have access to the IMF, the World Bank, etc. Because the Cuban government is taking serious steps to open its economy, settle its debts, and climb out of the present liquidity crisis. And the more it realizes that it can and should be less afraid of different opinions and views, there will be more and more countries that should and will engage economically.

References

Berger, S. (2021, April 1). *An update from our investment manager, Sebastiaan Berger.* Latest article. Retrieved December 7, 2021, from https://www.ceibalimited.co.uk/en/latest-article.

Berger, S. (2022, February 22). *An update from our investment manager, Sebastiaan Berger*. CEIBA Investments Limited. Retrieved March 19, 2022, from https://www.ceibalimited.co.uk/en/latest-article

Berger, S. A. C., & Young, C. (2008). *Cuba—The Regulation of Foreign Investment / Cuba - Regulación de la Inversión Extranjera*. CEIBA Publications Ltd.

Berger, S. A. C., Maldonado J. & Winkler, A. (2012). *Cuba: Contemporary art*. Overlook Books.

Cubanacan. (n.d.). *About us. Cubanacan Group*. Retrieved February 27, 2020, from https://www.cubanacan.cu/en/articles/quienes-somos

Frank, M. (2018, October 22). *Cuba Fund first to be listed on London Exchange*. Reuters. Retrieved July 7, 2021, from https://www.reuters.com/article/us-cuba-investment/cuba-fund-first-to-be-listed-on-london-exchange-idUSKCN1MW2JW

MINTUR. (2018, March). *Business opportunities for foreign investment in the tourism sector*. Retrieved December 7, 2021, from https://www.gocuba.ca/wp-content/uploads/2018/03/180301-Folleto-Oportunidades-Ingles-ilovepdf-compressed.pdf

Zamora Oria, O., & Malmierca Díaz, R. (2022, January 24). *¿Cómo afectan las sanciones a las inversiones? ¿qué se ofrece al capital extranjero?*: Habla Rodrigo Malmierca, ministro del Comercio Exterior de Cuba. *RT*. other.

CHAPTER 37

Archipelago's Hotel Investment and Expansion in the Time of Pandemic: Interview with Managing Director, Gerard Byrne

Archipelago International, Southeast Asia's largest privately owned and independent hotel operator announced its recent expansion in Cuba in a press release in July 2020. Two properties were rebranded under Archipelago's ASTON trademark on December 1, the beginning of the high tourist season on the Island (Fig. 37.1).

Apart from showing strong growth in Indonesia, the Company has focused on international expansion primarily in the Middle East (Saudi Arabia and the UAE) and Cuba.

Today, Archipelago manages five hotels and resort projects at various stages of development throughout the Island. Those properties include the ASTON Panorama Hotel (Havana), ASTON Costa Verde Beach Resort (Holguin), and GRAND ASTON Cayo Las Brujas Beach Resort & Spa. Currently under construction and scheduled to open in 2021 are the GRAND ASTON Varadero Beach Resort and the GRAND ASTON La Habana Hotel.[1]

[1] The GRAND ASTON La Habana Hotel opened its doors in Havana on March 14, 2022. Archipelago International. (2022, March 14). *Archipelago Announces Opening of New Havana Hotel* [Press release]. https://www.archipelagointernational.com/en/page/pressdetail/363/archipelago-announces-opening-of-new-havana-hotel.

T. K. Hernández, *The Cuba Interviews*,
https://doi.org/10.1007/978-3-031-30203-9_37

Fig. 37.1 Archipelago International Overseas' Managing Director, Gerard Byrne (From the personal collection Mr. Byrne)

Archipelago's involvement in Cuba began in late 2015 following a meeting request from the Cuban ambassador in Jakarta. As a result of this event, Gerard Byrne and CEO John Flood were invited to Cuba to meet with the hotel company, Grupo de Turismo Gaviota S.A.

I decided to approach the company's Managing Director Gerard Byrne of Archipelago Overseas to request an interview.

Mr. Byrne, originally from Ireland, has 25 years of experience in the corporate banking, real estate, and consulting sectors, with a strong focus throughout his career on the hospitality and leisure industries.

He is an MBA graduate from the University College of Estate Management at the University of Reading (UK) and a Chartered Fellow of the Chartered Management Institute, UK.

Hernández: Tell us how Archipelago International, an Indonesian hotel chain, became involved in the Cuban hotel market?

Gerard Byrne: Back in late 2015, we were invited to a meeting with the Cuban Ambassador to Indonesia. At this meeting, an invitation was extended to visit Cuba to meet with key stakeholders in the Cuban hotel industry and inspect a number of hotel and tourism projects.

As a result, in early 2016, myself and our President and CEO John Flood visited Cuba for the first time. We were very impressed by the people, by the island's natural beauty, and by the amount of development that was happening in hotel and tourism projects. It was clear to us that Cuba had spent many years investing in and developing its tourism infrastructure.

It was also evident that they needed the assistance and investment of international hotel operators who could improve the quality and standards in their hotels on the island. Having grown our company in a developing country over a period of 20 years, we understood the many challenges the Cubans faced and knew that we could add significant value and assistance to the industry there.

It is fair to say that this initial visit to Cuba made a significant impression on us. At the time, I was finishing my MBA and decided to redirect the topic of my thesis paper to focus on what was happening there. The title of my paper was "Real Estate Development and Tourism in the New Cuban Revolution." The title referenced changes I was seeing at the time both geopolitically and culturally, but more importantly the paper gave us the research and knowledge essential to begin doing business in Cuba.

From there we started competing for management contracts on new hotel projects and, in 2018, our perseverance was rewarded with our appointment on a first project, Grand Aston Varadero Beach Resort, which is currently under construction and is due for completion mid next year.

An investment in Cuba's tourism sector brings jobs to the local economy. How does your investment benefit job creation and what opportunities do you bring to the Cuban employees who work at the ASTON hotels?

Mr. Byrne: Yes, it is true to say a hotel investment brings many jobs to the local economy. In fact, globally, travel and tourism is not only one of the biggest industries, accounting for 10.3% of global GDP),[2] but also one of the largest employers (330 million or one in ten jobs) (World Travel and Tourism Council, 2020). To clarify, the vast majority of the investment in and development of hotels in Cuba has been undertaken by the Cuban government. So, we are not investing in the real estate asset, but rather we are investing in the infrastructure and talent to support our operations on the Island and to ensure the effective training and transfer of knowledge to local Cuban staff in the hotels.

The Cuban staff benefit from extensive training to international standards, they get an insight into our culture and experience, together with having the opportunity to earn some valuable foreign currency through tips. Local businesses also benefit as we try to source as much as we can locally both in terms of products and services.

To support our hotel projects in Cuba and staff training in particular, we have sent several task forces to Cuba from Indonesia. Typically, these consist of 10 plus senior corporate staff who spend at least one month in Cuba at a time. In addition, during the COVID-19 crisis we made the decision to keep our foreign staff (department heads and corporate staff) in Cuba to continue to work on our ongoing projects and to assist with operations on the ground. We are also investing in the establishment of a regional corporate office in Havana, which will employ local as well as international staff when it is up and running.

Overall, our investment to date has been significant. However, we are investing for the future and see Cuba as a long-term part of our regional development strategy.

Archipelago recently received the "Safe Travels" certification from the World Travel & Tourism Council (WTTC). This certification recognized Archipelago's commitment to keeping guests and employees safe and healthy with the implementation of several "new normal" safety protocols for all your hotels. What strategies are in place to ensure the safe travel experience of guests and staff in Cuba?

Mr. Byrne: We as a company have taken a multi-layered approach to reassuring our guests, staff, and partners. Initially, we implemented new COVID-19 Standard Operating Procedures in each department, hotel,

[2] World Travel & Tourism Council (2021). Economic Impact | World Travel & Tourism Council (WTTC) [Online] wttc.org. Available at: https://wttc.org/Research/Economic-Impact.

and corporate office. These covered the full spectrum of hygiene, masking wearing, safety, and cleaning protocols.

In addition, we were the first hotel chain to implement company-wide testing for all staff. We now have clear and unequivocal data from our hotels and our corporate office that potential customers are choosing our hotels over other brands because they are seeing our "Safe Travels" certification and our "Trusted Safety Warranty" that all hotel employees are regularly tested. Guests and travel partners can be assured that the same levels of safety and hygiene will be experienced at our hotels in Cuba.

Did you work with the Ministry of Tourism on these safety protocols?

Mr. Byrne: Being based in Southeast Asia meant that our understanding of previous virus outbreaks (SARS & Swine Flu) and of early COVID-19 data gave us a head start in being able to react to the current crisis.

At a very early stage, we presented a paper to the President of Gaviota outlining the type of protocols and strategies that needed to be implemented in Cuba. We advised that Cuba needed to take a holistic approach that involved all sectors related to tourism, including hotels, airports, transport, etc.

As the crisis developed, we presented a second paper which outlined further detailed standard operating procedures and recommendations on a regular testing regime. We are proud that many of our recommendations have been incorporated in the protocols that are now in place.

Cuba also took advice from many other stakeholders in the aviation, travel, and transport sectors and today has a comprehensive playbook of policies across the entire tourism spectrum, which will ensure a very safe travel experience for guests.

In addition to all the now-standard social distancing, mask wearing, hygiene, and cleaning protocols, Cuba has utilized its excellent healthcare system to ensure that there are medical centers in all resorts and testing facilities in each destination, so that any localized outbreak can be traced and contained. This includes keeping local Cuba staff in resort destinations during work weeks and extensive staff testing, which ensures close monitoring of the situation in tourist destinations.

What does the future hold for Archipelago International's ASTON brand of hotels in Cuba? Are there plans for further investment?

Mr. Byrne: In addition to the Grand Aston Varadero Beach Resort, we have been awarded a further four hotel management contracts on projects in Cayo Santa Maria (Grand Aston Cayo Las Brujas Beach Resort & Spa—our first operational hotel), in Holguin (Aston Costa Verde Beach Resort—reopening December 2020), and in Havana (Grand Aston La Habana; opening in mid-2021 and Aston Panorama Hotel—reopening in December 2020). We will have 3,000 rooms under management in Cuba in the short run. However, I feel there is still plenty of room for growth of the Aston brand on the Island.

In addition to our trusted Aston brand, Archipelago has a further nine hotel brands which cover the full spectrum of hotel classifications, from hostels to luxury five-star hotels. We have the brands and the enthusiasm to grow our Cuban portfolio further. This is why we are establishing a corporate office in Havana and are investing for the future. As our brand recognition and reputation increases, I am confident that our success in Cuba will lead to further expansion opportunities, new partnerships in the region, and further growth in Latin America.

What in your view are Cuba's unique selling points (USPs) in a post-COVID context?

Mr. Byrne: Apart from the obvious one (great climate/weather), I think Cuba has several unique selling points. Firstly, in a post-COVID context I think the environment will be even more on traveler's minds given what we have seen with the likes of Venice where the canals became clean with no tourists visiting for several months. Cuba has a strong focus on protecting its natural habitats, and this is done at the master planning stage.

It's also admirable how they design and develop their resort hotels, with low-rise buildings barely visible from the sea. Mangrove protection, wildlife sanctuaries, and parks are prioritized, but these are just some examples. To me, Cuba's diverse ecosystem and strategic focus on environmental protection is very important.

Secondly, Cuba's global reputation for quality health care has been brought to the fore during this crisis, from its antiviral drugs being used in China at the beginning, to its teams of Cuban doctors working in the most dangerous epicenters of the virus. It has also been very successful at containing the virus, with very low case and death rates compared to many popular destinations globally. This will be an important consideration in the decision-making process of future guests.

Finally, Cuba has always been a very safe destination with zero incidences of terrorism. It is only a few years since tourism in places like Europe and Egypt was seriously disrupted by terrorism.

So, having those three USPs of environmental, health, and safety in one destination gives it a distinct advantage over many of its competitors.

Mr. Byrne, it was great talking with you. Thank you for taking the time to share your thoughts and discuss Archipelago's ASTON hotel expansion plans. It's good to see that despite the current limitations which include the COVID-19 pandemic, investment is moving forward in Cuba.

References

Archipelago International. (2022, March 14). *Archipelago announces opening of New Havana Hotel* [Press release]. Retrieved March 4, 2022, from https://www.archipelagointernational.com/en/page/pressdetail/363/archipelago-announces-opening-of-new-havana-hotel

WTTC. 2020. *World Travel and Tourism Council: Travel & Tourism—Global Economic Impact & Trends 2020—May 2020*. Retrieved December 7, 2021, from https://wttc.org/Research/Economic-Impact

PART X

Agriculture

CHAPTER 38

USACC Chair Talks Agricultural Trade with Cuba

Paul Johnson is the Chair of the United States Agriculture Coalition for Cuba (USACC). Over 100 agricultural organizations and corporations belong to the Coalition, focused on improving two-way trade with Cuba (Fig. 38.1).

I spoke with Mr. Johnson on agricultural trade between the United States and Cuba, the recent success of the Potato USA seed project, and the upcoming "Agricultural Export Expansion Act of 2021" bill to Congress.

Since 2014, he is also a Partner at Focus Cuba Consulting. He has led several business and political missions to the Island to improve trade and investment between the United States and Cuba.

In 2008, Mr. Johnson founded Chicago Foods International to export food products to the Cuban and tourism markets.

For the last 25 years, he has lived in and traveled frequently to the Island.

Mr. Johnson has a degree in international relations from the University of Wisconsin and a Master's from the University of Illinois in Chicago.

He lives in Chicago and, like many Americans, is longing for flights to Cuba to commence again.

T. K. Hernández, *The Cuba Interviews*,
https://doi.org/10.1007/978-3-031-30203-9_38

Fig. 38.1 Paul Johnson of the USACC (From the personnel collection of Mr. Johnson)

Hernández: First, let me thank you for the opportunity of this interview. Tell me, is it back to normal in the United States? Can you fly to Cuba again?

Paul Johnson: We're still stuck with the charter flights, once a week, so it's not good.

Is the "Agricultural Export Expansion Act of 2021" sponsored by Senator Michael Bennet (D-CO) and Senator John Boozman (R-AR) bill to Congress co-sponsored by other people?

Mr. Johnson: It hasn't been introduced yet. This week.

In preparing for this interview, I found the names of senators associated with the bill. There was John Boozman, Michael Bennett, John Hoeven, Tom Udall, Kevin Cramer, Angus King, Mark Warner, Susan Collins, Debbie Stabenow, Amy Klobuchar, Mike Enzi, and Patrick Leahy (Agricultural Export Expansion Act, 2019).

Mr. Johnson: Yes, that was from the last time it was introduced.

Are the same people going to co-sponsor it this time?

Mr. Johnson: I imagine. They're working on getting as many co-sponsors as possible. We'll see.

The original bill died in the previous Congress. Do you have hopes that the outcome will be different? What are the efforts behind the bill to ensure its success this time around?

Mr. Johnson: The last time they introduced it, President Trump was tightening the embargo and the rhetoric around Cuba, making it difficult for Congress to maneuver. There were no champions in Congress to support a Cuba bill that would go against the will of the president. Now that Biden is in office, we still don't have a true champion on the Hill and we don't have a president who has publicly stated his position on Cuba.

In some respects, we face similar challenges today as we did two years ago. While we don't have a policy direction from the White House, there isn't the same pushback either. Frankly, the real goal has always been to get Congress to act. We've seen executive regulations signed and unsigned over the past decades. What we need is a law that can't be overturned in the next election cycle.

Exactly. Business can't function with that on-again, off-again thing.

Mr. Johnson: Yes, exactly right. Business wants certainty and we don't have that. I think it's important to note that this is not the only bill that's circulating in Congress that would support or change our relations with Cuba. There are others.

What separates this bill is that it takes a very narrow approach. It only addresses trade finance of agricultural commodities to Cuba, so the narrowness of the bill works in its favor because it may draw less opposition.

However, there are other groups and even congressmen who would support a broader bill rather than having to alter the embargo piece by piece. But the real strength of this bill is in its bipartisan support. Senator Boozman is a Republican from Arkansas and the ranking chair of the Senate Agriculture Committee, and that carries a lot of weight. Senator Bennett is a Democrat out of Colorado. He has a great track record of working on both sides of the aisle. And, you know, let's face it, Congress needs to show us that they can find some common ground. And I think this bill fits that category.

And it's to the benefit of American farmers, of course. What do you think the efforts will be to ensure its success this time?

Mr. Johnson: We circulated a letter of support within our coalition, and we have great support at the national level (USACC, 2021). We had groups like the American Farm Bureau, Corn, Soy, Wheat, National Association of State Departments of Agriculture, National farm cooperatives, dry beans, Potatoes, Dairy, Cattle, you name it. There's a lot of support at the national and the state level. Cuba is an issue that has always had strong support across America, both in rural and urban America. That's what we're building from.

You sort of answered the next question I had. What kind of support have you received from the groups within the coalition?

Mr. Johnson: Yes, it's good. I mean, we've circulated letters of support in the past, but not all of them always sign onto every effort that we do. What was different about this letter of support is that we had some groups that I hadn't heard from in about four years. That was encouraging. That's positive.

If this bill is successful, what do you see foresee for the future of U.S.–Cuba agriculture?

Mr. Johnson: We would like to talk more about the future of U.S. and Cuba agricultural relations, but it's hard to talk about building a relationship from the ground up and learning from past years to build trust and confidence.

This future conversation of the agriculture relationship doesn't fit well in political circles where the focus, understandably so, is simply on how to get a bill through Congress or have the President sign an executive order. But it doesn't leave much room to talk about what we want or where we are going. But what we need to discuss is comprehensive agricultural reform. That entails a slew of things. I'll name some of them: balanced trade, support for agroecology and conventional farming where it works, supporting local Cuban agricultural production and allowing the United States to fill in the gaps where needed, and the improvement of Cuba's economy to aid trade.

We're not just talking about exports, but imports from Cuba and investment in Cuban agriculture to meet the recent changes within Cuba's policy to allow foreign direct investment in Cuban agriculture. We need to end travel restrictions. We need to suspend Title III. And we need a continued dialog between the United States Department of Agriculture (USDA) and the Ministry of Agriculture, particularly around the MOU they signed back in 2016. We need more agricultural trade promotion programs to allow the U.S. agricultural community to be more competitive. And of course, we need to open our embassy and ideally have USDA staff at the embassy.

Agreed. Biden—who knows when he's going to make an announcement–made promises in his campaign[1] **and everybody is waiting to hear from him.**

Mr. Johnson: They are currently reaching out to stakeholders in all sectors to gather notes and opinions and comments. And I suspect they will have an announcement when they feel the time is right. Obviously, Biden is more focused on domestic policy now.

Our concern is that we're still living under the Bolton policy toward Cuba, and it's terrible. To travel to Cuba right now is incredibly difficult. There's only one flight a week for a country of 11 million. You have lots of Cuban Americans and others who want to see their family and friends in Cuba, and they can't go back. That is related to COVID-19, but also the regulations in place, so we hope that Biden makes a move sooner rather than later. We'd hate to think that this would drag on until after the mid-term elections.

There are no commercial flights, it's just charter flights. I think there are about six charter companies that fly to Cuba now, and they're on a rotating basis. Every charter company gets to fly once a week. You can imagine the demand to get to Cuba. Of course, in Cuba, the current situation is bleak. But there is light at the end of the tunnel as all of Havana will be vaccinated by around the end of this month. Seventy percent of the country should be vaccinated by August. And 100% of the island will be vaccinated by September.[2] That will help a great deal.

You heard the news of June 21, Cuba's Abdala vaccine is 93.28% effective (Cubadebate, 2021) **in preventing COVID-19? Cuba is achieving great success with their vaccines.**

Mr. Johnson: Yes, and it's incredible to think of a country of 11 million people still living with the embargo and yet able to create a vaccine. I heard a lot of machinery they need for the production of

[1] Litz, S. (2020, September 5). https://www.nbcmiami.com/news/politics/decision-2020/biden-discusses-approach-to-cuba-in-nbc-6-interview/2287930/. *Biden Discusses Approach to Cuba* in NBC 6 Interview at: https://www.nbcmiami.com/news/politics/decision-2020/biden-discusses-approach-to-cuba-in-nbc-6-interview/2287930/.

[2] For updated vaccination rates, see Mathieu, E., Ritchie, H., Ortiz-Ospina, E. et al. *A global database of COVID-19 vaccinations*. Nat Hum Behav (2021).

vaccines and other critical equipment is old, and they have to band-aid it together to make it work. Yet they've created a successful vaccine to pull them out of this mess. That's commendable. I hope that the United States rewards Cuba for its efforts and sees it for what it is. It's a health issue and it's saving lives. I have family in Cuba and it's a relief knowing that my in-laws have all been vaccinated.

Agreed. The Cubans have created five vaccines for COVID (Yaffe, 2021). **One is a nasal application. They have also released the phase III test results of the Soberana, which is 63% efficient after two of a three-dose protocol. Cuba is suffering because of the U.S. embargo and has sent many teams of medical staff overseas. It's incredible what they've achieved in this awful situation.**

Should the outcome of this bill be successful in a two-way trade, what do you predict Americans would import from Cuba?

Mr. Johnson: Besides the obvious, rum and tobacco and maybe sugar down the line, there could be tropical fruit such as mangoes, guayaba, pineapple. Also aquaculture, I think, is certainly a sector to keep our eyes on. Coffee one day, winter vegetables, and organic products. Obviously, there's a market for that here in the United States. If Cuba can get their products certified and get production up, that could be a great export for them.

Can you share with us the present state of U.S. agricultural exports to Cuba numbers? Is it still one-way trade?

Mr. Johnson: Basically, two items are permitted to be imported into the United States, one is artisanal charcoal. The other is not a direct import into the United States, but Nespresso is shipping coffee to Europe, packaging it into those little capsules, and then selling it for their Nespresso machines.

Since 2000, when we passed the Trade Sanctions Reform and Export Enhancement Act of 2000 (TSRA), the United States has been allowed to export food products to Cuba. We've exported about $8 billion in food over those 20 years. Last year we only exported $160 million of food, which represents about 10% of what Cuba purchases from global suppliers around the world. In the first quarter of this year, we are at a $100 million, which is up 85% from the same period last year. Almost all of it is poultry meat. Cuba depends on poultry meat for about 40% of their protein needs so they can get it relatively inexpensively from the United States. They've increased their orders. How long that lasts, given their cash situation, I don't know. But chicken is cheaper to produce than pork or beef. So it's an inexpensive way to supply their protein needs and I hope that continues.

Do the Cubans need cash upfront now?

Mr. Johnson: TSRA stipulates we can only export food products on a cash basis and that is what the Bennet/Boozman bill would change. That would allow us the opportunity to offer trade financing terms. But it obviously goes hand in hand with Cuba's economy and if they have money to pay for our goods. And that's why we're always keen on talking about comprehensive agricultural reform. We estimate that under normal trade relations, we would capture about 60% of the Cuban market or roughly $1.2 billion annually. And that figure would grow over time as Cuba's economy and tourism increase.

Can you tell us about the recent success of Potatoes USA's project that shipped 16 tons of seed potatoes to Cuba? How did it come about?

Mr. Johnson: Yes, it's a great project! I worked on that as a consultant, and we were supportive as a coalition. Importantly, that project continued the discussion between the USDA and the Ministry of Agriculture (Cuba) around the MOU both groups signed back in 2016 (USDA, 2016). We were able to continue that effort under the Trump administration. It's incredibly important to have APHIS,[3] which is the USDA's animal and plant health inspection services, working with their scientist counterparts in Cuba.

Pests and diseases don't know political boundaries. It's vital to protect agriculture both in Cuba and the United States. Part of the process of getting the seed potato down to Cuba was finalizing the import permit. This included inviting Cuban scientists to visit Colorado, California, Minnesota, and North Dakota to show them how we operate, to get them comfortable with our standards. And then once those protocols were established, they become the railroad tracks for future trade. Those discussions were really nitty-gritty and didn't get a lot of attention. But it all starts there. It starts with negotiating the import permit. Why we had success was because it was a collaborative effort between USDA, industry, Potatoes USA, farmers, and their counterparts in Cuba. Once the protocol was signed, it built trust and confidence. It also encourages

[3] *Animal and Plant Health Inspection Service*, U.S. Department of Agriculture. See more at Animal and Plant Health Inspection Service. https://www.aphis.usda.gov/aphis/home/.

more dialogue. Once we had this permit in place, we shipped around 16 tons of seed. The trial itself was definitely successful. Some varieties performed better than others, and we learned from that. We are going to build on the information from the year one trial and ship another container for a year two trial sometime this fall.

We're going to have to get a few trials to find out what varieties work best in the Cuban environment and soils. Transporting and handling seeds, how to store them, plant and harvest them are all part of the learning process that always needs to be improved.

Do you have any similar projects with Cuba in the future?

Mr. Johnson: Yes, we're always looking to increase trade, help Cuba improve local production, and find ways to strengthen our agriculture relations. We're also looking for opportunities to invest in Cuban agriculture. So, yes, there are a number of projects that we continue to work on.

There are foreign investors there, and I believe the Cubans are opening investment to *Cuban Americans*.

Mr. Johnson: Well, you know, the law that just recently came out doesn't single out Cuban Americans. It allows for foreign direct investment in Cuban agriculture, which is something that we've been waiting for a long time. As their law changes to allow the private sector to grow, they are also allowing foreigners to invest directly with them.

I suppose they'll be set for when Biden makes his announcement.

Mr. Johnson: I'm just hoping for the best, and we're doing all we can. He made a promise on the campaign trail. If you're looking for a bipartisan bill that's going to get a lot of support across America, then a broad Cuba policy needs to be considered. Our coalition represents a lot of groups and individuals from across America, both urban and rural, Republicans and Democrats. There's a tremendous amount of support to change the present policy in Cuba.

That's positive. Thank you for your time, Paul. Nice to meet with you and discuss U.S.–Cuba agriculture relations, the upcoming Bill in Congress, and the success of the potato seed project.

Mr. Johnson: Thank you very much.

Follow-up to the Interview: April 14, 2022

Your organization, the USACC, ran its third conference in Havana recently in April 2022. How would you rate the experience, the expectations of this event, and the outcome?

Mr. Johnson: It was positive and a win for U.S. agriculture. I expect U.S. agriculture exports to Cuba to reach between $400 and $500 million this year, up from the roughly $300 million we sold last year. The Minister of Foreign Trade and Investment relayed that figure to us.

We also had the opportunity to meet with Cuba's President Miguel Díaz-Canel Bermúdez, the Minister of Agriculture, Minister of Foreign Affairs, Minister of Planning and the Economy, and the Minister of Foreign Trade and Investment. The message we received was the recognition of the Cuban people and government to work with American farmers to help normalize our relations. The President expressed their will to expand exchanges and acknowledged that U.S. agriculture is at the forefront of understanding, promotion, and the fostering of relations between the U.S. and the Cuban people.

He also highlighted the advantages of the U.S. agriculture market given its proximity, quality, price, and as an important option in times of natural disasters such as hurricanes.

The trip also provided an opportunity to get both the United States and Cuba on more solid ground so we can work to resolve larger problems of immigration, food insecurity, plant and animal health diseases, natural disaster preparedness, protecting our shared natural resources, support for civil society, and an opportunity to increase foreign direct investment to Cuba's emerging private sector.

In 2021, U.S. exports to Cuba reached nearly $300 million, an 88% increase since 2020. Although the Island is the 53rd largest market for the American agriculture sector, it is only 15% of what Cuba purchases from other nations.

What do you predict the market share would be if Cuba and the U.S. agriculture sector could trade normally? And similarly, do you have a projection for Cuban agri-industry exports to the United States? Is there a comparable market in the Latin American-Caribbean region to give us an idea of the potential?

Mr. Johnson: With normal trade relations, I expect the U.S. share to capture 60% of what Cuba imports from global suppliers. The advantages we offer include lower shipping costs, quality, competitive pricing, and the ability to ship less food more frequently, which helps alleviate stress on Cuba's existing supply chains.

Specifically, Cuba is a top three market for our poultry producers; top ten for wheat growers, top 12 for corn producers, and top two for rice producers. Cuba is a country of 11 million but could be a top 25 partner for U.S. agriculture exports. That is not an unrealistic estimate. It will take time, but with normal trade, and that includes offering credit on our exports, we can hit that mark.

Cuba has been actively pursuing reforms within the agricultural and the private sectors such as permitting the sector to import, export, and connect with foreign investment. Did the USACC conference result in the signing of any cooperation agreements, foreign investment initiatives, or new projects?

Mr. Johnson: No, but we certainly recommitted to expand our relations. During our private meetings with various ministers and heads of state, it was clear that FDI opportunities and Cuba's legal development of MSMEs, Local Development Projects or LDP's, and agricultural cooperatives are a legitimate form of economic growth and key to unleashing the talent of Cuban citizens who need to have a greater contribution to the Cuban economy. The state-run enterprises remain, but there is more competition from the private sector to challenge the efficiency and productivity of the traditional state entities. I wouldn't say that privatization has been completely embraced by the competing interests within Cuba, but clearly the privatization reforms initiated ten years ago by Raúl Castro are being cemented into Cuba's economy by President Diaz-Canel.

References

Anon. (2021, June 22). *Abdala, with three doses, demonstrates 92.28% efficacy*. CubaDebate. Retrieved March 7, 2022, from http://en.cubadebate.cu/news/2021/06/22/abdala-with-three-doses-demonstrates-9228-efficacy/

Litz, S. (2020, September 5). https://www.nbcmiami.com/news/politics/decision-2020/biden-discusses-approach-to-cuba-in-nbc-6-interview/2287930/. *Biden discusses approach to Cuba in NBC 6 interview*. Retrieved October 2, 2021, from https://www.nbcmiami.com/news/politics/decision-2020/biden-discusses-approach-to-cuba-in-nbc-6-interview/2287930/

S.1447—116th Congress (2019–2020): *Agricultural Export Expansion Act of 2019*. (2019, May 14). https://www.congress.gov/bill/116th-congress/senate-bill/1447

USACC. (2021, September 17). *USACC advocates for "Comprehensive agriculture reform"*. USACC. Retrieved July 30, 2021, from https://www.usagcoalition.com/post/usacc-advocates-for-comprehensive-agriculture-reform

Yaffe, H. (2021, March 31). *Cuba's five COVID-19 vaccines: The full story on Soberana 01/02/Plus, Abdala, and Mambisa: LSE Latin America and Caribbean.* LSE Latin America and Caribbean blog. Retrieved June 20, 2021, from https://blogs.lse.ac.uk/latamcaribbean/2021/03/31/cubas-five-COVID-19-vaccines-the-full-story-on-soberana-01-02-plus-abdala-and-mambisa/

PART XI

The Non-state Sector: Micro, Small, and Medium Enterprises (MSMEs)

CHAPTER 39

The Cuban Entrepreneurs: "Running Up That Hill," Interview: Marta Deus

The inspiration for the title of this interview comes from a 1985 song by Kate Bush called "Running Up That Hill." Released more than three decades ago, it soared to the top of the charts in the United Kingdom and the United States as a result of its inclusion in the Netflix series, *Stranger Things*. The powerful and timeless lyrics from the song are perfect to describe the present-day challenges of Cuba's relatively new emerging sector, the Micro, Small and Medium Enterprises (MSMEs) (Fig. 39.1).

Marta Deus is both a visionary and pathfinder of Cuba's new entrepreneurial sector. If she is not seen as an influencer today, she will be in the very near future. She is young, bright, and upcoming—if not already "arrived." Her background is evidence of this. Foreseeing new opportunities before they materialize, anticipating needs, she is a finder of solutions blended with imagination and wisdom.

We met at her office, a splendid white building on the Calle 2 in Vedado. She was noticeably tired that day, not surprising from someone who manages three successful business ventures with another one in the incubation stage.

Ms. Deus is the founder of *Deus Expertos Contables*, and co-founder of two other enterprises, *Negolution* magazine and *Mandao.*

T. K. Hernández, *The Cuba Interviews*,
https://doi.org/10.1007/978-3-031-30203-9_39

Fig. 39.1 Entrepreneur Marta Deus at her office in Vedado (Photo by the editor)

Ms. Deus was born in Havana. She took a summer course for entrepreneurs at the International University of Florida in 2018 and graduated with a Master's in Business Management and Administration from the Institución Universitaria Mississippi of Madrid in 2010.

In her earlier professional life, she worked in Europe at Más Móvil in Spain and France Telecom.

In 2013, she founded Deus Expertos Contables which provides consulting and financial services to Cuba's emerging entrepreneurial sector.

Ms. Deus founded *Negolution* magazine with a team of Spanish and English associates. Negolution magazine is an intelligent, glossy publication, targeting the self-employed sector.

Founded in September 2019 just months before the outbreak of the pandemic, her company Mandao, a food delivery service, works with 300 companies, is an app used by over 100,000 people. Mandao delivery staff are easily recognizable on their bikes and motorcycles, zipping through the streets of Havana with bright yellow boxes on the back rack bearing the brand name. Mandao began in the capital city and has expanded to Cienfuegos, Matanzas, Trinidad, Santa Clara, and Holguin.

On her future, she told me, there's a café in the works, a "work in process."

Besides her hectic schedule, Ms. Deus still finds time to organize private events for women entrepreneurs such as the *Ellos Hablan*, the *Hour of Code*, and the *Week of Innovation.*

For relaxation, she enjoys a daily morning swim in the sea and sometimes finds the time to read on weekends.

Since our meeting for this interview in May 2022, over 4,000 businesses[1] on the Island have come into legal existence. Some will make it and some will not, but that's the reality in the world of business, big and small.

Hernández: I understand entrepreneurs can now form joint ventures, international economic associations, open bank accounts outside of Cuba, and receive investment from investors. How will this be achieved and has any of this taken place yet in Cuba as far as you know?

Marta Deus: It's not possible yet for entrepreneurs to open bank accounts outside of Cuba.

Like almost everything, sometimes you don't have a specific answer for a specific question. This is something that is happening. There is no law for foreign investment for the MSMEs yet. We have the same law for

[1] The Ministry of Economy and Planning reported in its Twitter account that as of July of 2022, 4,859 economic actors had been approved since September 2021. Of the MSMEs, 4,750 are private, 51 are state-owned, and 58 are cooperatives. Fifty-two percent are reconversions of preexisting businesses and 48% are new ventures. The MSMEs are predicted to generate 82,836 new jobs to the Cuban economy. Retrieved from: https://twitter.com/MEP_CUBA/status/1562799342993301506.

state-owned companies that is used by foreign investors. It's a long and complicated process for a small company.

There are some companies that are trying to do international contract associations. The country is focusing on what they want to start with MSMEs that are producing, exporting, and providing services. What I believe is that this law must develop, and the Ministry should think of a specific law for the MSMEs in relation to foreign investment[2] because there are specific situations for these kinds of companies that state-owned companies don't have. State-owned companies and the MSMEs share the same law for foreign investment. Right now, I know that three or five companies are in the process of international economic association contracts, but we don't have any created yet.

So, it's in process as laws are being formed?

Marta: Yes, but I would like to add that this process should be specific to MSMEs. It shouldn't be the same process for all the companies because we are in different positions.

Since the enactment of reforms establishing the MSMEs last September, there have been many challenges on the path to success. These include the pandemic, the subsequent global economic fallout, monetary reform in 2021, and continuing U.S. sanctions. How do these obstacles affect have the success of nascent entrepreneurs?

Marta: In the case of Mandao during the pandemic, it was a challenge, but it was an opportunity for us to expand, for sure. But most of the companies, their services focus on tourism and because of the pandemic, it was super-complicated for them. It was hard. Many of them disappeared, they couldn't find a way out; many emigrated because of the situation.

With this pandemic, with monetary reforms, and the situation we have now with the inflation, and the lack of access to buy foreign currency, it is super-complicated for entrepreneurs to work in this situation.

U.S. sanctions don't help because when you are a Cuban, you have problems almost everywhere if you are trying to do a transaction, a wire transfer between countries. When they see it is for Cuba, that is a problem. There is always a problem in banking. You can't hire

[2] On July 21, 2022, At the ninth ordinary session of Parliament, the Minister of Economy and Planning, Alejandro Gil, made the announcement of 75 measures including the approval of foreign investment in the private sector. The measures are meant to boost Cuba's economic recovery. http://www.cubadebate.cu/noticias/2022/07/21/aprueban-nuevas-medidas-para-recuperar-la-economia-cubana/.

a service from U.S. companies such as Google or payment platforms. It is a problem for us because we are Cubans. It's really difficult for entrepreneurs to work in this environment. For sure, we have to be really flexible, but they are surviving and trying to work with all these situations that they have. It's complicated for them to scale, to take your business to another level with all these complications surrounding them. It's difficult for them.

It sounds overwhelming. I understand what Cuba's trying to do, what the entrepreneurs are trying to do and then there's this situation of challenges and complications. It's mind-boggling. But there have been successes since the regulations. Are there any success stories you could share with us?

Marta: Well, yes, Mandao is a success story. We are six partners, and we are under a company. We are under contract to hire the employees; we can do contracts with state-owned companies that were difficult to do before. I have many friends who are entrepreneurs who are producing paintings, or doing software, and they have many more opportunities to export, to import, to sell their products. For example, VeloCuba, is a company for bike rentals, so you can bike around Havana. The company is owned by a woman. There's also Juan Carlos Blain, Adriana Heredia, and Oniel Díaz.

Your company, Deus Expertos Contables, provides financial and business consulting services to businesses. What is your impression of the banking services available to new businesses?

Marta: We have the sense that the companies are growing in a way that banking is not at the level of the companies. It is still very complicated to open an account, to get a card, to do any online transactions online in the national currency. For an MLC account, you have to go in person to the bank and spend time at the bank.

What I believe is that our banking sector needs more technology, for sure, to provide a better service for the MSMEs. And international banking is super-complicated for us because we are Cubans, so, yes, it is hard.

Going forward, what changes would you like to see in the legal structures/institutions for the non-state sector? Do you have a "wish-list"?

Marta: We have a list of prohibited activities we can't do. On that list, there are many professional services. I would like this list not to focus on professional services. Maybe the military, health, and education should be included, but the rest should be open. That's very important, but the rest should be open for the development of the MSME sector in Cuba. The rest of the occupations such as architects and engineers, these kinds of professions, should have access to form companies. That's important.

For sure, I'd like to see a specific process for investment law. A process whereby you can bring an investor into our companies. An easy and specific process for everyone to understand and achieve what they want.

As it stands right now, let's say you have an investor, and this investor wants to invest $10,000, for example, in your company and expects a return on that investment. How is that done?

Marta: If you want to do it through the process that the country gives you, I think it makes little sense because $10,000 is not a lot of money, and you will have to spend a lot of time and effort to get $10,000 to your company legally. So, if you have a personal bank account in another country, maybe they can wire you the money and you can use it. There are ways. If you want to do it through the foreign investment law, it's really complicated. So that's why it's important to have a specific law for joining foreign investment with the entrepreneurs.

We share the same tax system for the MSMEs as the state-owned companies and that's something that, in my opinion, should change because the MSMEs need a specific law for taxes, and labor codes. But for taxes, they should do this for micro, small and medium businesses and create an institution that is not the Ministry of the Economy and Planning. Then people can go to that institution and ask what the process is, and they can provide information, help them create their companies and ask for a loan. An institution where the entrepreneurs can find resources and help for the company.

Do you ever meet with government representatives to discuss what's going on, what your sector needs to see?

Marta: Yes, sometimes. In my case, I have had opportunities to speak with the Ministry of Transport and the Vice Minister of Economy and Planning. It depends on the moment you meet. Sometimes these are not for discussions, they could be events. We have access and share our thoughts for sure. I also have access to the Minister of Foreign Investment, and I share all these concerns.

Thank you, Marta. Lovely to meet you in Havana. This interview was an "eye-opener" to the incredible challenges for the

entrepreneurs. Struggling to build a small business in today's environment reminds me of that song by Kate Bush, "Running Up That Hill."

References

Figueredo, O., et al. (2022, July 23). *Aprueban Nuevas Medidas Para recuperar La Economía cubana*. Cubadebate. Retrieved April 22, 2022, from http://www.cubadebate.cu/noticias/2022/07/21/aprueban-nuevas-medidas-para-recuperar-la-economia-cubana/

Ministerio de Economía y Planificación de Cuba. (2022, August 25). *Con esta decisión, Suman 4859 Los Actores Económicos aprobados desde que inició el proceso en septiembre de 2021. De Las mipymes, 4750 son privadas y 51 son estatales, y Además Hay 58 son Cooperativas*. Twitter. Retrieved August 30, 2022, from https://twitter.com/MEP_CUBA/status/1562799342993301506

PART XII

The Nonprofit Organizations

CHAPTER 40

Interview with James Williams, President of Engage Cuba

Everybody involved with the Cuba scene during the optimistic years of the Obama presidency knew of the U.S. organization Engage Cuba. In the spring of 2016, I visited Washington, D.C. for an event called the "Days of Action against the Blockade of Cuba," organized by the International Committee of Peace, Justice and Dignity, IFCO/Pastors for Peace, the National Network on Cuba, the Institute for Policy Studies, and the Venceremos Brigade at the University of the District of Columbia.

The forum, "*Through Cuban Eyes*," was the closing panel to several days of events. It was at this event I first met the Ambassador, José Ramón Cabañas, the writer and journalist, Stephen Kimber, and several prominent American human rights activists. Through my attendance, I was given the opportunity to speak with several U.S. representatives about the U.S. embargo.

I also visited the offices of Engage Cuba and spoke with President James Williams and his staff.

Engage Cuba was the bipartisan non-profit organization representing businesses and private companies working to end trade and travel restrictions against the Island. They were deeply committed to lobbying Congress to lift the blockade. Their primary focus was U.S.–Cuba legislative advocacy.

At that time, there were several bills in the House and Senate: S. 299/HR 664 Freedom to Travel to Cuba Act, S.491 Freedom to Export to

T. K. Hernández, *The Cuba Interviews*,
https://doi.org/10.1007/978-3-031-30203-9_40

Cuba Act of 2015, S. 1049 Agricultural Export Expansion Act of 2015, S. 1389/HR 3055 Cuba DATA Act, S. 1543/HR 3238 The Cuba Trade Act of 2015, and H.R. 3687 Cuba Agricultural Exports Act.

Hernández: Do you think that in this election year there will be any more progress toward lifting the embargo? Do you believe it's going to happen now?

James Williams: Within the past few months, we made history when a majority of senators co-sponsored the S.299 Freedom to Travel to Cuba Act. In June, the Senate Appropriations Committee passed four pro-engagement Cuba amendments. An amendment to allow American farmers to extend private financing for the export of agricultural commodities to Cuba passed by a vote of 22-8. An amendment to end the travel ban on Cuba then passed by voice vote. Additional amendments passed by voice vote to allow for the exportation of telecommunication services and the refueling of planes at Bangor Airport for international flights enroute to or from Cuba.

We believe that this momentum in the Senate is indicative of a general atmosphere on Capitol Hill to fully normalize U.S.–Cuba relations. While there is still work to be done in the House of Representatives, the historic compromise last week in the House Financial Services Committee to find a long-term solution to provide credit for the export of agricultural commodities to Cuba[1] is a promising sign of progress. Although the timeline for lifting the full embargo is uncertain, the wind is clearly behind our back in our effort to put an end to the half-century-long failed U.S. policy toward Cuba.

Let's discuss the first steps for a corporation that is interested in opening up in Cuba. The common knowledge is that a business should begin the process of investigating now, rather than later.

Mr. Williams: The Cuban Embassy in Washington plays a pivotal role for U.S. companies that wish to explore business opportunities on the Island. We bring members of our Business Council to the Embassy, and we develop proposals for our members to travel to Cuba to explore corporate ventures. Once a business delegation is approved to travel to Cuba, Engage Cuba works with the Embassy to develop an official agenda for the company and provides briefing materials prior to the trip.

[1] Wola (2016). *Financial Services Appropriations Bill Shows Support for U.S.-Cuba Policy Shift*. Available at: https://www.wola.org/2016/06/financial-services-appropriations-bill-shows-support-u-s-cuba-policy-shift/.

Engage Cuba staff accompany the business delegation throughout the trip to assist with logistical and content matters. We believe that corporate engagement is a vehicle to mobilize the business community in support of our legislative strategy to lift the embargo.

Even though the embargo still restricts economic activity in Cuba, it is important for U.S. companies to begin conversations now with their Cuban counterparts to prepare for the inevitable day when it is lifted.

In your view, which U.S. sectors are most prepared to start doing business in Cuba?

Mr. Williams: There is no shortage of interest from the business community for a change in U.S. policy toward Cuba. Some sectors that are particularly invested in seeing an end to the embargo are the agriculture, telecommunications, construction, and hospitality industries. There is interest, too, within the biotech and pharmaceutical sectors, as well as in renewable energy.

It has been fascinating to see a complementary relationship between various business sectors operating in Cuba. For example, Starwood,[2] a member of Engage Cuba's Business Council, just began operating the Quinta Avenida Hotel in Havana under its Four Points by Sheraton brand. Another Engage Cuba member, Stonegate Bank, enabled its MasterCard credit card for use in Cuba,[3] becoming the only U.S. credit card that will work on the island until more financial institutions agree to authorize transactions on the island. The ability for U.S. travelers—some of whom might stay at the Quinta Avenida—to use the card in Cuba will ease some of the burden for travelers who typically must carry cash.

[2] Starwood Hotels, now Marriott International, Inc. became the first American hotel corporation to sign a hotel deal with Cuba. The Starwood contract included the renovation and management of two other hotels, the Hotel Inglaterra and the Santa Isabel in Havana. In June of 2020, the Trump administration ordered Marriott to close its Four Points by Sheraton hotel operations by August 31. The hotel company was warned its government license would not be renewed. The order included the other hotels the company had been renovating. *Trump administration orders Marriott to cease Cuba hotel business*. (2020). Reuters. Available at: https://www.reuters.com/article/us-cuba-usa-hotel-exclusive-idUSKBN23C298.

[3] On June 14, 2016, the AP news agency reported that Stonegate Bank of Pompano Beach in Florida would issue the first U.S. credit card intended for use in Cuba. Available at: https://apnews.com/article/b325b8b31f8640bb9e0e350df43c8e5e.

Does your organization feel optimistic at this point in time that it will become easier for American businesses to open up in Cuba this year, an election year (2016)?

Mr. Williams: We are in a moment of presidential electoral politics that most pundits would have not predicted. The presumptive candidates from both the Democratic and Republican parties are in favor of normalized relations with Cuba. Although businesses will likely maintain a degree of caution in their approach toward Cuba, they can bet that the progress in U.S.–Cuba relations will continue rather than backtrack under the next administration, whoever that president might be.

Engage Cuba works with American agribusiness. Credit issues are a hindrance to increasing U.S. agriculture exports, (Cuba being a natural market for U.S. AG). U.S. agriculture exports are down for the fiscal year 2014 and 2015.

What's the short-term solution to increasing American agriculture exports to Cuba, or is there a quick solution at all?

Mr. Williams: The United States used to be the number one supplier of agricultural goods to Cuba, but has fallen to number five behind the EU, Brazil, Argentina, and Vietnam as of the end of 2015. U.S. policy that prohibits the extension of credit for U.S. agricultural exports to Cuba makes American products less competitive, even though there are some that still go to Cuba in spite of the restrictions (such as poultry, and very recently, soy oil). The U.S. agribusiness community has been very active in trying to stimulate congressional action on these policies—which is the only way that they can be changed. Different states, like Arkansas and Louisiana, and commodity groups, like rice and wheat, have been seeking engagement and greater ties, but all is contingent on policy change. In the near-term, if U.S. products are more competitive through the ability to extend credit, the United States could recapture lost market share relatively quickly.

Does Cuba appear to have any preferences in terms of which sectors Americans should invest first? Is Cuba offering any preferential treatment to certain sectors? Which sector has the easiest entry for U.S. businesses in Cuba?

Mr. Williams: Cuba has a portfolio of investment opportunities that is revised annually and contains a variety of projects for which they are seeking foreign direct investment in sectors ranging from agriculture to manufacturing.

Given the current influx of visitors to Cuba and the strains that place on the hospitality sector, Cuba has an immediate need for hospitality infrastructure, for example, hotels. In addition, there are increasing needs in the energy sector because of the loss of oil supply from Venezuela, hence Cuba's priority of investment in renewable energy projects.

There is no such thing as "easiest entry" for U.S. businesses in Cuba, given the complex regulatory environment on the U.S. side and the bureaucratic approval process on the Cuban side. That said, some important approvals we have seen are within the hospitality sector, such as hotel management and cruise ships sailing; finance agreements like that of Stonegate Bank; and several entertainment projects like the filming of Fast & Furious 8.[4]

How enthusiastic is Cuba to have American corporations doing business in Cuba?

Mr. Williams: Cuba is very interested in securing investment from U.S. companies. The Embassy of Cuba in Washington has been overwhelmed with requests for business meetings and travel to Cuba. Indeed, Cuba is well aware that the more concrete, tangible ties there are between Cuba and the American business community, the more permanent the current normalization process will be.

Companies from other countries are already well-established in Cuba. Will American business be able to compete with these companies, and do you think American corporations possess any competitive advantages?

Mr. Williams: American companies will absolutely be able to compete with foreign entities. American firms are some of the best in the world—no matter the competition—and that will hold true in Cuba, too, once the embargo is lifted. Even with restrictions, American media and brands that make their way onto the island are very popular. American companies have the advantage of proximity, cultural affinity, and a shared history—albeit a tumultuous one. The ties that bind the Cuban and American people permeate the embargo, and once that barrier is removed, commerce and exchange will flow freely.

[4] Producer Michael Fottrell arranged for an OFAC license to do business in Cuba. "We also had to get a BICS license from the Department of Commerce," he said, "that allows you to export and import all your equipment." Location Managers Guild International. (2017). *The Fate of the Furious*. Available at: https://locationmanagers.org/the-fate-of-the-furious/.

Where do you feel the greatest problems lie for Americans once they are established in Cuba, or is it a smooth process after obtaining a license from the U.S. government?

Mr. Williams: Obtaining a license from the United States is only part of the process; there are necessary approvals on the Cuban side as well. Cuba is a new market for many American companies, and some of the challenges that are common in other emerging markets will surely be present in Cuba as well. Cuba has an advantage of excellent human capital, which is not common in most emerging markets but there are some factors such as lack of internet connectivity, that will make doing business difficult (or at least different) in the short-term.

Let's hope the upcoming talks in September yield positive results. James Williams, thank you.

References

Marsh, S. (2020, June 5). *Trump administration orders Marriott to cease Cuba Hotel Business.* Reuters. Retrieved December 7, 2021, from https://www.reuters.com/article/us-cuba-usa-hotel-exclusive-idUSKBN23C298

Mills, N. (2017, November 7). *The fate of the furious.* Location Managers Guild International. Retrieved September 10, 2021, from https://locationmanagers.org/the-fate-of-the-furious/

Weissenstein, M. (2016, June 14). *Florida bank issues first US credit card for use in Cuba.* AP NEWS. Retrieved December 7, 2021, from https://apnews.com/article/b325b8b31f8640bb9e0e350df43c8e5e

Wola. (2016, July 20). *Financial services appropriations bill shows support for U.S.-Cuba policy shift.* WOLA. Retrieved July 7, 2021, from https://www.wola.org/2016/06/financial-services-appropriations-bill-shows-support-u-s-cuba-policy-shift/

CHAPTER 41

Environmental Defense Fund and Cuba's Long-Term Mutually Beneficial Relationship, Dan Whittle

Élise C. Hartill

In 2020, the Environmental Defense Fund (EDF) celebrated 20 years of cooperation with Cuba in marine ecosystems conservation and rebuilding fisheries. In honor of this anniversary of scientific collaboration, we approached EDF's Senior Director and Attorney, Dan Whittle, to understand how EDF became involved in this long-term mutually beneficial relationship (Fig. 41.1).

Mr. Whittle is involved in Latin American and Caribbean projects to promote sustainable fisheries, coral reef, marine, and coastal ecosystems preservation. Since 2007, he has worked with the Tri-National Initiative on Marine Sciences and Conservation that facilitates collaborative research and conservation projects between scientists in Cuba, the United States, and Mexico.

É. C. Hartill (✉)
Whitefield, ME, United States
e-mail: eliseh@mycj.org

T. K. Hernández, *The Cuba Interviews*,
https://doi.org/10.1007/978-3-031-30203-9_41

Fig. 41.1 Dan Whittle, Senior Director, and Attorney at EDF.org at the Encuentro de Pesca Sostenible en Cuba event, 2018 (From Mr. Whittle's personal collection)

He has been active in promoting scientific exchange, environmental dialogue, and cooperation between the United States and Cuba. In 2011, he organized a fact-finding delegation to the Caribbean Island with William Reilly, co-chair of former President Obama's national oil spill commission.

Currently, Mr. Whittle directs EDF's efforts in Puerto Rico advocating for clean energy policies and collaborating with rural communities to design and build low carbon microgrids to harness clean energy.

Mr. Whittle has taught environmental law at Wake Forest University Law School and is a former policy advisor for the North Carolina Department of Environment and Natural Resources. He also practiced environmental and energy law with Van Ness, Feldman, and Curtis in Washington, D.C.

EDF has the mission to preserve natural systems and find sustainable solutions to serious environmental problems. The organization maintains relationships with scientists, managers, NGOs, and policymakers in the United States, Cuba, and around the world.

Dan Whittle spoke with Élise C. Hartill, a marine scientist from Maine in a Zoom conference on June 8th, 2020. This is an in-depth interview and was originally published in three parts on Cuba Business Report.

Élise Hartill: How did EDF become involved in conservation efforts in Cuba? What did that work look like initially, and what does it look like today?

Dan Whittle: We got involved in Cuba conservation efforts by accident, about 20 years ago, when I was part of our oceans program working from North Carolina to Florida on two things, trying to end overfishing and protecting essential fish habitats.

We were working with U.S. federal advisory councils to come up with rules to ensure that fishing levels were not excessive and that fish stocks could rebound. We were spending a lot of time on that. Then in the year 2000, we hired a fisheries' biologist from Miami to help us out on that effort. He said, "you know, I've spent some time studying reef fish with Cuban scientists, especially snappers, groupers, grunts, and others that spawn off the southwest coast of Cuba and get carried by the currents up to the southeast coast of the U.S." It became clear to us that our success in managing fisheries in the United States depends upon what Cuba does.

That was the first seed of an idea to reach out and work in Cuba. We got invited to give a series of papers in December 2000 in Havana at an international marine conference. The moment we walked into that conference, Cuban scientists and lawyers (I'm a lawyer, not a scientist) were very welcoming and seemed eager to work with an American group like EDF on just about anything related to the environment and science.

We just started as a one off and after that trip, it was clear that there were opportunities to collaborate on science and possibly to compare ideas on management, law, and policy as well. In the mid to late nineties, Cuba had an environmental Renaissance where they developed ambitious environmental laws, policies, and programs. In 1995, they established the Ministry of Science, Technology and Environment, which was the first ever cabinet level position for the environment. In 1997, the government adopted Law 81 of the Environment, and then in the late nineties, they developed several additional environmental policies and laws, including measures on protected areas, coastal zone management, and environmental review and licensing.

It was interesting for me as a lawyer to see how ambitious Cuba was being at a time when their economy was just beginning to come out of a serious economic crisis.

After that, I had several conversations with lawyers there about how they could implement those laws successfully. In other words, the question was, "these environmental laws could just be paper tigers, how do you plan to implement and enforce them?"

On the science side, there was so much to learn from each other. Cuba was just barely in the process of trying to develop a national park system for the ocean. They had a pretty good network of green protected areas on land, and they wanted to extend that notion of protecting important habitats around the Island.

Our first opportunity was working to protect essential fish habitats, just like we were trying to do in the United States and so we decided we could, if nothing else, compare notes on the science. EDF could bring resources to the country to host workshops, and get scientists talking to each other to identify which coastal types, which marine ecosystems, were most important to protect and how to prioritize their protection. So that's how we started, and it just never stopped. We found that there was a real value in collaborating on marine protected areas.

Fast-forward 20 years, and Cuba has already protected almost 25% of their insular platform, the coastal and marine waters. Many of those protected areas include mangroves and shorelines, which are critically important to the life history of fishes and other marine life.

That early collaboration produced valuable science that has resulted in conservation on the ground. That's a legacy that we've built upon. We continue primarily to serve as a science-based organization that facilitates scientific collaboration that can inform management and policy.

In 2002, we were part of an exchange between the United States and Cuba on environmental law. Unfortunately, the exchange did not fully happen. The Cuban professionals were not able to get visas to come to New Orleans in 2002 because of U.S. policy, but all the U.S. professionals got permission to go to Cuba. So, we had the entire exchange in Havana, and that provided an opportunity for lawyers and policy experts to talk about the challenges of implementing these various environmental laws. I remember at the end of that exchange, there was a list of what factors would be necessary for Cuba to be successful in implementing these ambitious laws while still growing its economy.

There seemed to be a consensus that what's needed is good science, good law and policy. You also need the political will to implement them and collaboration on the Island among all the different agencies to work together and not work in silos. Public awareness and support is also key and not just within the Island.

I have to say, the Cubans know what they've got; they know that they have incredibly a bio-diverse, rich, special place. Every Cuban knows that Columbus said when he landed on the Island years ago, "this is the most beautiful land human eyes have ever seen." And Cubans take a pride in that, but you need public awareness and support in order to protect the environment, in a time when the economy is really most important to people, you need money and there has to be a way to pay for it, and finally, you also need international collaboration.

Since we share waters, we share the environment. It's critically important, not just for the United States and Cuba, but Cuba and The Bahamas, Mexico, and the entire region. And again, that's been a reality that's guided us over the years.

I can talk more about where we are now. We focused more and more over time on fisheries, how to rebuild fish populations and protect habitats. Along the way, we focused on conservation of coastal areas more broadly. We've worked on renewable energy in Cuba and, after the BP oil spill in 2010, EDF was able to facilitate exchange of information between two governments that had no diplomatic relations and therefore weren't officially talking to each other. In 2011, we were able to facilitate a delegation of experts to Cuba to talk about how to collaborate on oil spill prevention and response. That delegation was led by former Environmental Protection Agency (EPA) administrator, William Reilly, who was the EPA administrator under the first Bush administration in the early nineties.

That part of the approach is dialogue, science and goodwill, and collaboration. Basically, science diplomacy. But in terms of subject matter, our work in Cuba has really aligned with our work in the United States and now around the world, to end the dire threat of overfishing. Billions of people around the world depend upon fish protein, and many small communities around the world depend upon fishing for their economy and jobs. How do you work with government officials, scientists, and fishermen, and fishing families to end overfishing in a manner that doesn't sacrifice their livelihoods. How can you catch fewer fish and make more money, essentially.

After the reestablishment of diplomatic relations in 2015, EDF began thinking about other areas like sustainable agriculture and renewable energy where we have experience in the United States and elsewhere that might be beneficial in Cuba. And then finally, I'll say that something that often gets overlooked or forgotten is that this is a two-way street. We've never seen our work as being aid or assistance. We benefit as much as our Cuban partners do. We've learned a lot from our Cuban partners on why their coral reefs are generally healthy and resilient to coral bleaching and various other things. We've studied their corals to bring those lessons elsewhere. They have some of the most impressive mangrove forests in the world that are incredibly important buffers to sea level rise and intensifying hurricanes. We see Cuba as a classroom for U.S. scientists and experts in conservation.

Does EDF collect its own data, conduct its own research in Cuba? Does EDF employ scientists, or is it mostly funding and collaboration/consulting? How exactly does the collaboration take form?

Mr. Whittle: Yes, that's a good question because it's changed over the years. We're limited on how we spend money through the U.S. law, basically Department of Treasury regulations. We're allowed to legally conduct research, and we've had specific licenses over the years, and in recent years, we've had what they call general licenses that allow research, and that extends to collaborative research.

We've spent a fair amount of time on the water with Cuban scientists in the Gardens of the Queen National Park (Jardins de la Reina) and the Gulf of Batabano conducting fieldwork, and that's the best approach. We prefer to do it that way, where scientists are in the field together. Sometimes that's difficult to do, not because of U.S. rules, but because of all the permitting challenges and the time involved.

Also, we've helped facilitate other groups. We either participate in or help facilitate U.S.–Cuba collaborative science in the field. We have provided support for Cuban researchers in the Gardens of the Queen and elsewhere to conduct the research, provided it's part of a joint work effort.

You already touched on a few of the questions I have. It sounds like EDF's work in Cuba is multifaceted and based on collaboration, which is great. Well managed fisheries can be an asset to conservation. Can you explain how fishers and the community take part in the work that you do? Or, how EDF takes part in the work that the community is doing regarding stewardship and conservation of coral reefs?

Mr. Whittle: That's a great question. Historically, there have been lots of conflicts over commercial fisheries and even recreational fisheries, where typically fishermen feel like they're pitted against the government and environmental groups. The feeling is that there are just too many rules. Fishers know the water better than anyone else, and may think, "just leave us alone to do our work." But as we've seen in the United States since the late seventies, and in Canada, with the collapse of cod in the North Atlantic and around the world, overfishing is a serious problem. Good science and good regulations are needed to ensure that sustainability is achieved. The mistake that was made historically is that government just kind of came in and tried to solve the problem unilaterally. And for years, environmental groups would too.

The government would basically say "here's the limit. You can't fish over that limit. Here are the rules." There was no real dialogue. Fishermen felt further and further disenfranchised.

Starting in the mid to late nineties in the Gulf of Mexico, and eventually in New England and the West Coast, fishermen and environmental groups discovered that if they work together, they can achieve common ground solutions. Everyone has an interest in ensuring that fish stocks are sustainable. Fishermen have an economic interest. The public has an interest in making sure that ecologically, marine life is intact for all the many benefits they provide, consumers want to make sure they have a steady supply of local seafood. There's a common interest.

We and other groups started working in the United States with fishermen in the late nineties and early 2000s to figure that out and, over time, the United States has become a success story; overfishing of most stocks has ended, in many cases, because conservation groups and commercial fishermen are working together.

So much of the conflict, though not all of the conflict, is gone. In a place like Cuba, it's a similar approach. Historically, decisions have been made in Havana by the agencies responsible for managing the fish stocks. Even with the small scale fisheries they have in Cuba, and fishermen don't have sophisticated technology or sophisticated boats, they still saw fish stocks steadily decline since the 1980s, and scientists in Cuba kept pointing the finger to overfishing and saying, "we have to stop doing that."

But there was a real tension between imposing more rules on fishermen who were just barely making a living. The government was reluctant to choose between jobs, food, and the environment. When we began working with Cuban scientists and Cuban policymakers on this, they said, "we know there's a problem, but we need the science to back it up and we don't have the data." So, one thing we began doing is using something scientists called data-poor methodologies. Basically, it's a way to assess the status of fish populations without having a lot of empirical data by looking at the life histories of different species, for example. And so we collaborated with Cuban scientists and managers on that. Through that collaboration, they were able to develop a national fisheries' assessment that evaluated how vulnerable fish populations around the Island were to overfishing.

The key to that exercise was that they did not operate in a vacuum. At each and every workshop, there were either fishermen or representatives of the seafood and fishing industries. They were able to provide so much information that the scientists didn't have access to or didn't know. Scientists were relieved and surprised to find out that fishermen were worried too.

They didn't want to just give up or reduce fishing for the sake of it, but they knew something had to be done. It was an opportunity to have a conversation of what to do. And, as in the United States, everyone began to realize that everyone should have a voice. Through that dialogue, relationships would happen. Collaborations would happen. So that's what the approach was. Now fast-forward to the present. Cuba adopted a new fisheries law in 2019 that requires science-based fisheries management for the first time ever, embraces the private commercial fishing sector, legitimizes them, and gives private, commercial fishers retirement benefits, among other things.

The new law is an official recognition that fishermen have a voice in management and in the science process, both of which have become highly participatory. That's just one result of collaboration and exchange. We also, I should mention, over the years have facilitated exchanges between Cuban fishermen, scientists, decision-makers, conservationists, with counterparts in the United States and beyond, in Mexico, Latin America, and parts of Europe. The theory behind those exchanges is you just get people in the same room. Though the fisheries in Cuba are nothing like the fisheries off the northwest coast of the United States, fishers all over the world speak the same language. And it's remarkable when you get people in the same room, how much they can learn from each other. And again, that's been a really effective way to make a change in the environment.

Finally, I'll want to mention a floating workshop we hosted in 2011 off the south coast of Cuba, in the Gulf of Batabano. We invited government officials from the United States, Cuba, and Mexico, fishers from all three countries, scientists, and conservationists. We got everyone on a boat, 21 of us. We spent four days at sea and two days on land talking to each other. We even had a senior government official for National Oceanic and Atmospheric Administration (NOAA). This was in 2011, when things like that didn't happen. And it worked! One of the Cuban fishermen said, "we have to talk together because we share the same ocean." That 2011 floating workshop was really the foundation, in my opinion, for eventual relationships between government officials in the United States and Cuba, when those relationships were few and far between, and those relationships ultimately blossomed once diplomatic relations were restored.

That sounds like a success story in the Caribbean. What would you attribute the successful preservation of healthy marine ecosystems to in Cuba, given that Cuba has some of the few healthy coral reefs in the Caribbean? Would you call it a success or a work in progress?

Mr. Whittle: That's a good question. I would say it's both. I would say comparatively Cuba is a success story, and it's a work in progress because nothing's permanent, changes are happening beyond Cuba's control—climate change, for example. But there's a lot within its control as it grows its economy. It's imperative to continue to strike the right balance, to recognize that coral reef ecosystems are just like capital, natural capital, that fuels the economy, and protects people's lives and livelihoods. I think there's a pretty strong recognition of that. The Cuban people, as well as their government, see climate change as an existential threat to people living on the coast around the country. For years, they've devoted a lot of the resources to better understanding the potential impacts of climate change and in developing models for the impacts of sea level rise.

And they've taken steps to mitigate impacts. Along the way, Cuban scientists have indicated that one of our greatest protections against climate change is helping coral reefs, which are healthy for a variety of reasons, not because of some accident, not because Cuba is lost in history, not because of its isolation. While all of that may have played some role, Cuba hasn't developed in the same ways as most of the rest of the Caribbean, possibly in part because of politics but more importantly, starting 30 years ago, Cuba started affirmatively and proactively putting policies in place to protect its natural capital.

I think the coral reefs on the whole are in pretty decent shape because scientists understand, the people understand, and more and more of the people making decisions on the economic development understand the importance of their conservation.

The Gardens of the Queen, the national park off the south-central coast, which I encourage you as a diver to go check out, is considered by many to be the most spectacular marine park in the entire Caribbean. Not only because of its incredibly vibrant corals and diversity, but because of its abundance of fish, big fish. You can dive in other places in the Caribbean and see remarkable corals, but the Gardens of the Queen have the biomass that scientists talk about, the abundance that's been achieved by protecting the area for over 25 years. They've seen the fish rebound, and they've seen the spillover. Fish leave the park and provide benefits to fishermen fishing outside of the park. That's been a real success story. It's something that's caught the attention of Havana since the Gardens of the Queen is now known around the world. It is a hugely a sought-after destination, for diving and fly-fishing and the Cuban government has understood that it makes good sense to protect this area.

One interesting statistic is that people will pay a lot of money to come to the Gardens of the Queen to dive with big sharks. An economist in Cuba did a study, and I can't remember the exact figures but it determined that a live shark in the national park was worth two to three hundred one thousand dollars versus a shark on the dock, which is worth about a hundred bucks. Placing a value on ecosystems and the services they provide has also helped make the case that if you want to successfully grow the economy, you've got to focus on protecting the environment. But now, looking ahead, they must write the next chapter.

That's a great segue to my next question. What do you think the future of ecotourism is and balancing responsible economic development with conservation?

Mr. Whittle: I think it almost comes back down to the list we made back in 2002. For good science, you have to have laws and policies, not just the ones that were written in the late nineties; laws need to be updated. They have the new fisheries law I mentioned, which mandates that science drive fisheries management, you've got to have the political will. As things change, it's imperative that leaders throughout the country believe in and respect the importance of conservation and environmental protection. The collaboration we've talked about is fundamental, public awareness and support within Cuba and outside of Cuba. I think one reason that they've done such a good job of conserving the Gardens of the Queen park is that it has an international reputation. And then, of course, money is a big issue.

The economy in Cuba at the moment is hurting. I think it's in everyone's best interest that it has the wherewithal to grow its economy. It's important for the people living in Cuba to have good jobs and put food on the table. Without growing the economy, it will be hard to invest in, to finance conservation. And that's critically important. I think maybe the number one thing that Cuba has done is that they've earned a reputation as a biodiversity hotspot, a place where many of its natural areas still look like they did a hundred years ago in the Caribbean. They can truly have their cake and eat it too.

People want to come to Cuba for its history, music, sports, architecture, etc. They really stand alone in the Caribbean, it's a truly special place. Closing the door to collaboration, closing the door to Americans who want to visit, taking away opportunities for Cuban entrepreneurs to make a living off tourism or conservation is the wrong way to go. We saw in 2014 and then 2015 through early 2017, real progress being made that was beneficial not only to the Cuban people, by the way, but also to people in the U.S. As we mentioned at the outset, Cuba was doing a good job of protecting its environment and we're down current of Cuba. We benefit from that. And again, we also have a lot to learn from their success. The goal is to get things back on track. We're treading water now, but hopefully we can soon get back to normal again.

There is a fear of big developers coming to Cuba and building large hotels or resorts on the shores and destroying mangroves and other habitats that are important not only to the fish that end up in coral reefs but also to the integrity of the shoreline. If there's the political will to protect the environment, hopefully that takes precedent over big developers wanting to come in.

Mr. Whittle: That's the principal question. That was the question people were asking, as diplomatic relations were getting back on track during the Obama administration. That was the question, and it continues to be the question, and ultimately, it's up to the Cuban people and their government to strike the right balance. I think the advantage they have and have had is that they've been able to learn from mistakes made throughout the region. All the issues you described, that have happened from Cancun to other Caribbean destinations and their lessons for what not to do. I think Cuban scientists certainly, but many people in Cuba in general, are aware of those cautionary tales. Over the years there are best practices that have allowed developers to build resorts more sustainably, hotels, etcetera, in a manner that does not undermine the environment and conservation. It's always a challenge.

Arguably, Cuba made some decisions in the last few years that may or may not have been the best in terms of where to site hotels or new development. The cruise ships were controversial around the Caribbean and have had a tremendous impact on the natural environment. The Cuban government decided to allow cruise ships in, which was an understandable decision, as they brought thousands of American tourists and others to the island, which was critically important for the economy. They were aware of the potential drawbacks. There were decisions made not to allow cruise ships in certain areas of Cuba, but moving forward, those are the questions. Provided that the process is inclusive and transparent and, as science leads the way, they've got the potential to grow the economy in a manner that works.

So that's the big one and that's why it's in our interest. It's certainly in our interest that we support Cuba in protecting its environment and in developing its economy in an environmentally sustainable way. Therefore, it's in our interest to encourage scientific collaboration among experts and investment in renewable energy.

We all benefit as Cuba tries to transition to renewable sources of energy and away from the use of dirty, imported, and expensive fossil fuels. Cuba has also led the way, in recent years, on sustainable agriculture, agroecology, where the farm to table movement happened for a variety of reasons. Now during this pandemic, the farmers who are prospering the most are local organic and sustainable farmers. I think there are many lessons out that demonstrate there's a right way and a wrong way. But it's always going to be up to governments to adapt, and for decision-makers to change the approach to development and conservation over time. Maintaining political will is critically important. Again, the best way to move forward is by dialogue and collaboration, not by isolation.

With regard to the sustainable development of hotels and resorts, big industry leaders are taking initiative. Meliá, for instance, has won several awards for sustainability recently.[1] I think that's the trend in

[1] In 2019, Meliá Hotels International, S.A. was named the most sustainable hotel company in the world by the SAM Corporate Sustainability Assessment (CSA). www.hospitalitynet.org/news/4095337.html.

hotels because consumers will look for that kind of respect for the environment.

Mr. Whittle: That's a really important point because it underscores the importance of partnerships. When we were talking earlier about the issues in the U.S., the game changer was that fishermen started partnering with conservation groups and business groups. EDF's approach has always been finding the ways that work, often through unconventional partnerships. We partnered with McDonald's back in the early nineties to get rid of their styrofoam clam shell boxes; if there's a willingness to join forces with people or entities that have traditionally been your opponents, then there's real opportunity to change.

That includes cruise ships, but also hotels, especially because Meliá and others have done a good job in responding to consumer demand for a more sustainable product. They have to be a part of the solution. They must drive that same thing with U.S. agriculture, a huge opportunity for agribusiness and other agricultural interests in the United States. In my opinion, they only succeed if they wave the flag of sustainability.

Thank you, Dan, for taking the time to do this interview.

Mr. Whittle: Well, thank you for everything you guys are doing! I'm glad you're still spreading the word about Cuba.

Reference

Melia Hotels International. (2019, October 4). *Meliá hotels international named the Most Sustainable Hotel Company in the world* [Press Release]. Hospitality Net. Retrieved December 8, 2020, from https://www.hospitalitynet.org/news/4095337.html

Index

A

Aberdeen Standard Investments, 353, 359
Academy of Sciences, Cuba, 323, 325, 327
Acasta Cuba Capital Inc., 227
Agriculture
  agribusiness, 225, 400
  Agricultural Export Expansion Act of 2021, 374, 375, 378
  collaboration in, 114, 380
  exports, 400
  FDI and, 376, 380, 382
  opportunities, 349, 351
  Potatoes USA project, 379
  production, 134, 376
  sustainable agriculture, 414
  Trade Sanctions Reform and Export Enhancement Act of 2000 (TSRA), 378
  US-Cuba agriculture, 376, 380
  US exports, 378, 381, 400
Airbnb, Inc., 344
Altintas, Ahmet, 111
Altozano, Hermenegildo, 191–197
Amazon.com, Inc., 195
American Association for the Advancement of Science, 305, 323
Archipelago International, 365–367
  ASTON Hotels, 363, 365, 367, 369
  WTTC Safe Travels' certification, 366, 367

B

Banking. *See also* Central Bank of Cuba
  banking reforms, 197
  Resolution 73/2020, 197
Barceló Hotels, 67
Bennett, Michael, 374, 375
Berger, Sebastiaan, 353–361
Biden, Joe R., 133, 235, 348, 375, 377
  administration, 2, 324
  and Helms-Burton litigation, 186. *See also* Helms-Burton Title III

T. K. Hernández, *The Cuba Interviews*,
https://doi.org/10.1007/978-3-031-30203-9

impediments to a Cuba policy (analysis), 235, 236
predictions for a Biden presidency, 133, 235, 352
BioCubaFarma, 116, 292, 311, 318
exports, 318
joint ventures with China, 315, 316
joint ventures with Russia, 124, 316, 317, 333
joint ventures with Turkey, 115, 116
joint venture with Roswell Park Comprehensive Cancer Center. *See* Roswell Park Comprehensive Cancer Center
pharmaceutical products, 116, 134, 287, 307, 308, 313–317
Biopower S.A., 91
Biotechnology, 115, 287, 305, 307, 318. *See also* BioCubaFarma
Bird & Bird, Spain, 191
Blockade (U.S. economic embargo against Cuba), 54, 89, 103, 221, 229, 230, 303
Cuban perspective of, 54
economic cost of, 13
economic effects, 87
extraterritoriality, 230, 232
failure of, 104, 125, 225, 398
impact on agriculture and food security, 351
impact on Americans, 16, 104, 308, 348
impact on Cubans, 16, 88, 124, 234, 303, 349, 359
impact on economy, 12, 124, 349
impact on entrepreneurs, 390
impact on FDI, 57, 65, 206, 263, 272, 340
impact on human rights, 17
intention of, 19–21
policy formation and, 54
violation of international law, 188
Bolton, John, 11
Troika of Tyranny, 11, 16
Boozman, John, 374, 375
Brazil, 70
Brothers to the Rescue, 232
Bush, George W., 305
Bustamente, Michael, 54
Byrne, Gerard, 363–369

C
Cabañas Rodríguez, José Ramón, 101–105, 397
Callejón, Luis, 193
Canada, 103
and Helms-Burton Title III, 188, 230, 232, 233
Atlantic Canada Opportunities Agency, 262
business in Cuba, 64, 109, 230, 231, 261, 263
Canadian tourism, 65, 109, 263
development cooperation, 109
Foreign Extraterritorial Measures Act (FEMA), 187, 232
Global Affairs Canada, 107, 110
relations with Cuba, 65, 107–109, 263
trade with Cuba, 109
Cancer treatments, 6, 287, 292, 305, 315, 333. *See also* BioCubaFarma; Roswell Park Comprehensive Cancer Center
clinical trials, 314
Castro, Fidel, 53, 57, 86, 87, 113, 224, 265
Castro, Raúl, 7, 54, 57, 68, 86, 224, 227, 337
meeting with Obama, 7, 345
Çavuşoğlu, Mevlüt, 114
CEIBA Investments Limited, 353, 355–359

and London Stock Exchange, 359
Center for Genetic Engineering and Biotechnology (CIGB), 311, 313
Center for Neuroscience (CNEURO), 317
Center for Research and Development of Medicines (CIDEM), 331–333
Center for the Study of the Cuban Economy, 130
Central Bank of Cuba, 63, 141, 169–176, 203. *See also* Micro, small and medium-sized enterprises (MSMEs)
cryptocurrencies and, 174, 175
educational strategy, 171, 173
establishing a financial instititution in Cuba, 175
FATF and, 171
FDI and, 174–176
foreign currency accounts, 174, 176
impact of US blockade, 172
lending to enterprises and MSMEs, 171–174
microcredits, 174
modernization of banking system, 171, 172
MSMEs and, 173
payment platforms, 172
technology acquisition, 172
Chelovskiy, Dmitry Dr., 331–333
Chevalier, Felix, 219–222, 224, 225
China, 67, 273
BGP China, 275
Changchun Heber Biological Co., Ltd., 315
Greatwall Drilling. *See* Greatwall Drilling Company
Guangxi Fukang, 316
International Pilot Medical Development Zone of Fangchenggang, 316
joint ventures with Cuba, 67, 315
research projects with Cuba, 316
Chretien, Jean, 109
Clinton, Bill, 232, 343
Comercializadora de Servicios Médicos Cubanos (CSMC S.A.), 285, 287, 288, 291, 293–300
business alliances, 116, 292
ethics/principles of, 289
future direction, 292
international academic and medical services, 285
program delivery, 291
Communist Party of Cuba (PCC), 53, 81
Couillard, Phillipe, 65
Council of Ministers (CECM), 206
COVID-19, 111, 134, 311, 377
conducting business during, 112, 115, 118, 281
Cuban vaccines, 17, 313, 377
impact on economy, 12, 17, 131, 134, 139
impact on foreign investment, 42, 193, 206, 280, 340, 366
impact on tourism, 139, 194
protocols, 280, 313, 366, 367
Cuba. *See also* Cuban society
bureaucracy, 138, 306
cost of living, 64
history, 52, 55, 104
national identity, 52, 55
politics, 53, 54, 56
socialism, 306
sovereignty, 55
Cuba Cooperation France, 265
Cuba Initiative Trade and Investment Forum, 75, 91, 95
CUBANACAN Group, 296, 358
Cuban Americans, 104, 133, 235, 345, 377, 380
Cuban Industrial Property (OCPI), 223, 224

Cuban National Assembly, 81
Cuban Revolution, 52, 69, 81, 82, 85, 86, 89, 105, 183
Cuban society. *See also* Women in Cuba
aging population, 56, 82
Cuban exceptionalism, 55
Family Code, 83
gender equality, 84, 85. *See also* Women in Cuba
gender violence, 84
human rights, 225
literacy, 234
racism, 52, 89
religious freedom, 89
social contract theory, 55, 56, 58
Cuentapropistas. *See* Micro, small and medium-sized enterprises (MSMEs)
CUPET (La Unión Cuba-Petróleo), 73, 270, 275, 280
Cuba Energy Oil and Gas Conference (CEOG), 73, 191
Currency, 45
dual currency economy, 91
exchange rate distortion, 45, 47, 143, 144
Currency reform, 57, 62, 137, 138. *See also* Economy
foreign exchange, 137, 139
impact on foreign investors, 42, 57, 94, 132, 164, 197
impact on the economy, 42, 132, 143
currency unification. *See* Economy, *Ordenamiento monetario*

D

de Armas Águila, Dr. Yamila, 291–300
de Cossio, Carlos Fernandez, 17
Deus, Marta, 350, 387–393
Deus Expertos Contables, 387
Mandao, 389–391
Negolution (magazine), 389
Díaz-Canel, Miguel, 88, 224, 264, 381, 382

E

Economist Intelligence Unit (EIU), 135
Economy
currency reform and. *See* Currency reform
debt payment crisis, 35, 41, 57, 194
economic development, 58, 87, 88, 97, 134, 135, 154, 233
economic performance, 37, 42, 141
economic reforms, 18, 136, 137, 139
economic reforms, impact on foreign investors, 42, 43, 47, 132, 138
environmental protection and, 411, 412, 414. *See also* Environment Defense Fund (EDF)
FDI and, 35, 37, 38, 42–45, 47, 57, 97, 98, 233
Food security, 351
GDP, 36, 37, 51, 131, 136, 137, 139, 144
global recession and, 41
Gross Capital Formation (GCF), 37, 44
impact of COVID-19, 41. *See also* COVID-19 impact on economy
inflation and, 19, 141–143
macroeconomic factors, 36, 39, 47, 56
National Economic and Social Development Plan until 2030, 93, 96, 97, 123, 149, 154, 172

Non-state sector and. *See* Micro, small and medium-sized enterprises (MSMEs)
Ordenamiento Monetario and, 41, 42, 136, 137, 139, 302
performance, 21
policy formation, 55, 56
predictions for, 137, 139–143
price controls, 43, 141, 142
scientific collaboration, 414
strongest sectors, 134
Ekinci, Berris, 111–119
Embassy of Canada, 65, 109, 326, 327
Embassy of Cuba in Washington, DC, 79, 398, 401
Embassy of Turkey, 111
Emigration, 12, 57, 143, 390
Energy sector, 221, 401
joint ventures, 115, 270
renewable energy transition, 414
Russian projects, 123, 124
Engage Cuba, 10, 219, 224, 225, 397–399
Entwistle, Mark A., 51–58, 227–236
Environmental Defense Fund (EDF), 403, 405–409, 411, 413, 414
BP oil spill, 407
collaboration with Cuba, 406, 407, 410
renewable energy in Cuba, 407
scientific collaboration, 403
Environmental protection, 368, 406
achievements in, 406
challenges implementing law/ policies, 406
economic development, 412
fisheries law, 412
hotel development, 368, 413
impact of climate change, 411
international collaboration and, 407
marine ecosystems in Cuba, 411
policies, 405
sustainable development, 414
Erdoğan, Recep Tayyip, 113
Espin, Vilma, 86
European Union, 76, 92
Blocking Statute, 94, 187
Helms-Burton and, 88, 196, 232, 358
Political Dialogue Cooperation Agreement (PDCA), 76
Exports, 98, 155
FDI and, 98
Expropriations, 55, 189, 202

F

Federation of Cuban Women, 83–86
Feinberg, Richard E., 147, 149
Fireworks FX Inc, 261, 262, 264, 265
Foreign debt, 41, 45, 57, 143. *See also* Paris Club
Foreign direct investment (FDI), 8, 35–47, 66, 203, 205–207, 233. *See also* Economy, FDI and; Helms-Burton Title III; Micro, small and medium-sized enterprises
advantages for investors, 39, 202, 203, 361
agriculture and. *See also* Agriculture
attracting new investment, 42, 96–98, 149, 154, 202, 204
benefits of, for Cubans, 365, 366
constraints on, 45, 46
development strategy, 150
disadvantages, 39, 40, 46, 57, 231
economy and, 68, 97, 138, 359
Helms-Burton Title III and, 196, 233, 340
historical view of, 38
how to invest, 196, 221, 263, 272
improving conditions for, 40, 47, 204, 205

inflows, 19, 39, 41, 44, 95, 96, 205
International Economic Associations, 96
investment climate and, 359
investment facilitation and, 38, 40, 41, 44, 47
joint ventures, 58, 138, 194, 203, 357, 359
Local Development Projects and, 47, 382
medical tourism and. *See* Medical tourism
most successful foreign investor in Cuba, 355
MSMEs and, 46, 47, 206, 381, 382, 389, 390
opportunities for, 349, 351
Portfolio of Opportunities for Foreign Investment, 66, 138, 205, 207. *See also* Portfolio of Opportunities for Foreign Investment
prioritized sectors, 93, 98
protections for investors, 94, 150, 151, 202–207
reasons for low levels, 88, 138
reforms, 58, 197, 203, 206
sustainable development and. *See* Environmental protection
tax benefits, 203
U.S. sanctions and, 138. *See also* Blockade (U.S. economic sanctions against Cuba)
ZED Mariel and, 350. *See also* Mariel Special Development Zone (ZEDM)

Foreign Investment Law Decree No. 14/2020 ("Pledge and Mortgage"), 96, 203
Foreign Investment Law Decree No. 15/2020 ("Guarantee Trust"), 96, 97, 203, 204
Foreign Investment Law, No.118, 2014, 39, 66–68, 94, 202, 205, 233

G

Gardens of the Queen National Park, 408
protection of, 412
Garmendía Peña, Julio, 61–71
Gaviota S.A. (Grupo de Turismo), 364, 367
General Electric, 9, 223
GeoMinera S.A., 194
Global Ports Holding, 114
Golf course development, 338–340, 357
Carbonera Golf & Beach Resort, 338–340
Gonzalez Fraga, Ana Teresita, 111
Google, 9, 223
Grandal, Dr. Aldo, 111
Greatwall Drilling Company, 74, 273, 275, 276
Guskov, Andrei Anatolyevich, 121–125

H

Habana 500 anniversary, 261, 264
Hammond, Philip, 74
Hasbiotech, 116
Havana International Trade Fair (FIHAV), 68, 262
Havana Syndrome, 14, 305, 323, 324, 326, 328
Canadian joint research with Cuba, 327
CDC Report on, 326
CIA evaluation of, 16
evidence of Canadian scientists, 327
FBI conclusions, 14, 16, 324, 328
HAVANA Act, 16

health complaints of US diplomats, 14, 323
Is There a Havana Syndrome? meeting, 324
JASON Report, 16
lack of collaboration with Cuba, 323, 324
lack of motive for Cuba, 328
microwave theory, 14, 15, 325
NASEM Report, 322, 325, 327, 328
pesticide intoxication, 15, 327
psychogenic factors, 15, 327, 328
reaction by other countries, 327
U.S. scientists silenced, 324
Healthcare sector, 116, 303, 304, 306, 367. *See also* BioCubaFarma; Biotechnology; Medical internationalism; Medical tourism; Pharmaceuticals
collaboration, 308
development of, 307
export of healthcare professionals, 69, 307
funding of, 307
impact of U.S. embargo, 306
infant mortality, 306
NGO collaboration, 302, 303
outcomes, 305
salaries of medical staff, 64
universal access to, 286
U.S. cooperation, 305
what the U.S. can learn from Cubans, 307
Heber Biotec S.A., 311
Héctor Ardisana, Dr. Osvaldo, 285–289, 291
Helms-Burton Title III, 91, 94, 110, 188
defendants, 187, 194
extraterritoriality, 45, 188, 191, 192, 195, 196
FDI and, 88, 352, 358
plaintiffs, 186, 194, 195, 233
protecting foreign investors. *See* Foreign investment protections for investors
violation of international law, 88
Henry Reeve Medical Brigade, 286, 291. *See also* Medical internationalism
support to other countries during the pandemic, 17
Houston Trade Mission to Cuba, 219, 220

I
Iberostar Hotels, 67, 296
IFCO/Pastors for Peace, 397
Igarza Martínez, Ana Teresa, 147–154
Innovative Immunotherapy Alliance BioCubaFarma, 314
insightCuba, 343, 346
Inter-American Development Bank, 135
International Committee of Peace, Justice and Dignity, 397
Iran, 186
ITALSAV, 265

J
Johnson, Paul, 373, 374, 376, 377, 379–382
Chicago Foods International, 373
Focus Cuba Consulting, 373
USACC Conference, 381, 382
Journalism, 8, 301, 305, 306

K
Kartet Karadeniz Toptan Elektrik Ticareti A S, 115
Kimber, Stephen, 397

Kong, Xiangzhong, 274–276
Kruger, Judy, 224

L
Latin American School of Medicine (ELAM), 307
Leahy, Patrick, 374
London & Regional Properties Ltd. (UK), 337–340

M
M & C Latin Trade Consulting, 262
Malmierca Díaz, Rodrigo, 18, 68, 91–99, 360, 381
Malmström, Cecilia, 188
Mariel Special Development Zone (ZEDM), 18, 39, 44, 66, 67, 92, 93, 103, 148–155, 159–161, 163, 165, 318, 350
  advantages of, 151, 152
  benefits to surrounding communities, 24, 153, 163, 164
  committed investment, 18, 154
  comparison to other countries, 154
  development strategy, 154
  economic development plan, 154
  financial operations, 151
  history of, 149, 150
  housing program for employees, 153
  investments, 96
  membership in Free Trade Zones Association of the Americas (AZFA), 151
  One-Stop Shop system, 93, 151, 161
  protection of investors, 150
  regulatory framework, 149, 151
  reinvestments, 150, 151
  success of, 155
  wages, 153, 154
Marriott International, Inc., 9, 344, 352
Mauri Pérez, Dr. Mayda, 311–316, 318
Medical internationalism, 69, 288, 307, 308
Medical tourism, 285–288, 291, 293, 295–299, 307
  conferences, 299
  countries of origin, 288, 294, 297
  foreign investment and, 298, 299
  promotion of, 296, 297, 299
  safety and security, 293, 295
  statistics, 294, 295
  thermal/spas, 298
  treatment programs, 287, 288, 294–296, 298
MEDICC, 301, 303, 305, 309
  conferences in Cuba, 304
  cooperation in health, 304
Medina González, Marcelino, 107–110
Melbana Energy Limited, 269–272, 277, 282
  and Sherritt International, 277, 280, 281
  and Sonangol, 278, 279
Meliá Hotels International, S.A., 67, 195, 296, 353, 356, 357
  sustainable development and, 415
Menendez, Bob, 236
Micro, small and medium-sized enterprises (MSMEs), 64, 142, 206, 349, 382, 392, 413. *See also* Foreign direct investment (FDI)
  banking and, 173, 391
  challenges for the sector, 390, 391
  foreign investment and, 46, 47, 98
  legal reforms, 98, 390
  requirements for success, 143
  successful entrepreneurs, 391

Mining sector, 194. *See also* GEOMinera S.A.; Ministry of Energy and Mines (MINEM); Panterra Gold Limited
Ministry of Agriculture (MINAG), 376, 379
Ministry of Economy and Planning (MEP), 173, 392
Ministry of Foreign Affairs (MINREX), 87, 101
Ministry of Foreign Trade and Investment (MINCEX), 91, 93, 111
Ministry of Health, 291, 292
Ministry of Justice (MINJUS), 206
Ministry of Science, Technology and Environment (CITMA), 130, 405
Ministry of Tourism (MINTUR), 296, 338, 367
Ministry of Transport (MITRANS), 123
Miramar S.A., 355, 358
Mogherini, Federica, 89, 188
Morris, Dr. Emily, 135, 137–143

N

National Academy of Sciences, Engineering, and Medicine (NASEM). *See* Havana Syndrome
National Council of Churches, 104
National Development Program, 93
National Institute of Sports, Physical Education and Recreation (INDER), 292
National Network on Cuba, 104, 397
National Office of Statistics and Information (ONEI), 44, 137
Nestlé Nespresso S.A., 378
NEYROS (Russia), 331–333
Nguyen, Huong, 157–165
Non-state sector, 136, 349, 350, 382. *See also* Foreign direct investment (FDI); Micro, small and medium-sized enterprises (MSMEs)
  foreign investment and, 382
  inflation and, 140
  negative list of self-employment, 41
  regulatory restrictions, 139
  tourism and, 134, 345, 366

O

Obama, Barack, 70, 227
  administration, 2, 89, 230, 323, 413
  détente with Cuba, 235, 343, 344, 346, 401
  meeting with Raúl Castro, 54, 345
Oil and gas industry. *See also* CUPET (La Unión Cuba-Petróleo);Melbana Energy Limited
  Alameda-1, 281
  assessment of oil in Cuba, 271
  Block 9, 269, 280, 281
  Greatwall Drilling Company. *See* Greatwall Drilling Company
  Motembo oil field, 281
  oil spill prevention and response, 407
  Peberco, 274
  PetroVietnam, 274
  potential in the industry, 275
  refineries, 221
  Sherritt International. *See* Sherritt International
  Zarubezhneft, 124
Ordenamiento Monetario. *See* Economy

P

Pan American Health Organization (PAHC), 306
Panterra Gold Limited, 194
Paris Club, 41, 57. *See also* Foreign debt
Parrilla, Bruno Rodríguez, 114
Popper, Tom, 343–352
 82° West Consultants, 349
Portfolio of Opportunities for Foreign Investment, 93, 96, 205, 207, 297, 318, 400. *See also* Foreign investment
Purcell, Andrew G., 277–282

Q

Québec, 66, 110
 business in Cuba, 65, 110
 cooperation projects, 110
 Québec-Cuba Working Group, 110
 Québec tourism, 110

R

Reagan Administration
 Dames & Moore vs. Regan, 186
 executive order, 186
 International Emergency Economic Powers Act (IEEPA), 186
 Iran and, 186
Real estate sector
 CEIBA investment in, 357, 358
 London & Regional Properties Ltd. (UK), 337–340
Reed, Gail, 301–309
 life in Cuba, 304
Remittances, 15, 17, 35, 103
Rivas Saavedra, Déborah, 201–207
Roswell Park Comprehensive Cancer Center, 6, 305, 314
Rubio, Marco, 11, 15
Russia, 121–125
 Bioorganika Consortium, 317
 collaboration with BioCubaFarma, 317
 collaboration with CIDEM, 331–333
 collaboration with CNEURO, 317
 collaboration with Cuba, 317
 energy sector projects, 123
 humanitarian aid, 124
 joint ventures with Cuba, 122, 123, 317, 331
 joint venture with BioCubaFarma. *See* BioCubaFarma; Joint ventures
 modernization of railways, 123
 MOUs with Cuba, 317
 NEYROS, 331–333
 relations with Cuba, 121, 124, 125
 Russian Railways, 123
 Skolkovo Innovation Center, 331–333
 Soviet Union (USSR), 228
 trade with Cuba, 122
 war in Ukraine, 125
 Zarubezhneft, 124

S

Services Santé International, 285, 287
Servicios Médicos Cubanos (SMC). *See* Comercializadora de Servicios Médicos Cubanos (CSMC S.A.); Medical internationalism; Medical tourism
Sherritt International, 68, 70, 274, 280
 Melbana partnership, 277
Sierra Maestra Cruise Port, 114
Sonangol E.P. (Angola), 277–279
South Africa, 70
Spain, 103, 191, 350
 Business in Cuba, 67

Special Period, 228, 287, 303, 306, 405
Stickland, Peter, 269–272
Stokes, Dr. Antony, 73–77
Stonegate Bank, 399, 401
Sustainable development, 204. *See also* Environmental protection; Foreign direct investment (FDI)
  economic development, 414
  fisheries, 410
  hotel development and, 414

T

Taljaard, Desmond, 338–340
Technology Parks in the Universities, 41
Territorial Development Strategy, 41, 46
Tourism, 62, 134, 346
  cruise industry, 11, 225, 343, 344, 346, 352, 401, 414
  Cuba as a safe destination, 347, 368–369
  development, 193, 263, 347, 365, 401
  ecotourism, 293
  golf courses. *See* Golf course development
  job creation, 365
  people-to-people travel, 11, 343
  real estate development. *See* Real estate sector
  recovery 2022, 143
  Support for the Cuban People Travel, 343, 346, 348
  travel statistics, 10–11, 22
  unique selling points (USP), 368
  U.S. tourism, 11, 133, 345, 346. *See also* United States: restrictions on US travel
Triana Cordoví, Juan, 35–47, 129–134
Triesman, Lord David, 95
Tri-National Initiative
  collaborative research and conservation, 403
Trudeau, Justin, 109
Trudeau, Pierre Elliott, 109
Trump, Donald J., 70, 133, 223–225, 232, 355
  administration, 2, 104, 105, 185, 322, 345, 379
  exploring business opportunities in Cuba, 10
  Havana Syndrome, 14
  implementation of Helms-Burton, 12, 14, 35, 88, 229
  measures against Cuba, 14–16, 133, 235, 343, 345, 348, 375
Turkey
  agriculture projects, 115
  business in Cuba, 112, 114–116
  delegations to Cuba, 114
  history in Cuba, 112
  Karpowerships, 111
  MomentumCuba, 116
  OKAN Group, 116
  relations with Cuba, 111–113, 115, 117
  research collaboration, 116
  Technical Follow-up Committee, 114, 116
  trade volume, 117
  Turkish Cooperation and Development Agency, 115
  Turkish position on US sanctions, 116
Turkish Airlines, 111, 114

U

UCL Institute of the Americas, 135
UNICEF, 302, 306
United Kingdom

Biopower S.A., 92
business with Cuba, 73–76
foreign direct investment (FDI), 91, 95
Helms-Burton and, 358
joint ventures, 91, 338
relations with Cuba, 73, 76, 94
Royal visit to Cuba, 92, 94
solar parks, 92
trade with Cuba, 92
U.S. embargo and, 184
United Nations, 84, 113, 306
United Nations General Assembly (UNGA), 110, 117
United States. *See also* Blockade; Helms-Burton Title III
agreements with Cuba (MOUs), 105, 379
American exceptionalism, 55
business community and Cuba, 9, 12, 221, 224, 225, 398, 400–402
Cuban Adjustment Act (1966), 12
Cuban Democracy Act, 303
Department of Agriculture (USDA), 376, 379
Department of Justice, 196
Department of the Treasury, 221, 346
Foreign Claims Settlement Commission, 196
funding of dissidents, 19
House and Senate bills, 397, 398
laws, regulations in collaborative research, 408
Office of Foreign Assets Control (OFAC), 221, 231
restrictions on US travel, 11, 15, 184, 186, 187, 343, 345, 346, 348, 377
sanctions against Cuba, 102, 09, 117. *See also* Blockade (U.S. economic embargo against Cuba)
State Department, 15, 323
U.S. airlines, 225
U.S. Chamber of Commerce, 232
U.S.-Cuba collaboration in science, 404, 408
U.S.-Cuba policy, 9, 15, 16, 54, 235, 236, 345, 380
U.S.-Cuba relations, 9, 17, 55, 88, 89, 101, 105, 224, 225, 398, 400, 411
United States Agriculture Coalition for Cuba (USACC), 373, 375, 376, 378–382
University of Havana, 116

V

Valdés-Sosa, Dr. Mitchell, 322–328
Varadero, 270, 281, 355, 357
Venezuela, 11
Vidal Ferreiro, Josefina, 79–90
Vietnam, 157–164, 350
relations with Cuba, 159
ViMariel S.A., 18, 157–164, 350
benefits to surrounding communities, 163, 164
concrete manufacturing, 162
employment and wages, 163, 164
infrastructure, 160
investing at, 161–163
"three-in-one" infrastructure, 160
VUCE, 138
VUINEX (One-Stop Shop), 41, 88, 91, 93, 96, 138, 161, 204, 205, 207. *See also* Foreign direct investment (FDI)

W

Wade, Fred, 261–265

Wages in Cuba, 43, 63, 64, 86, 89, 136, 141, 307
  taxes, 307. *See also* Mariel Special Development Zone
Whittle, Dan, 403–415
Williams, James, 224, 225, 397–402
Wilson González, Marta Sabina, 169–176
Women in Cuba
  in government, 81, 82, 89
  in the professions, 86
  maternity law, 82, 83
  reproductive rights, 86, 89
  status of women, 82–85, 87, 89
World Bank, 131, 306
World Health Organization (WHO), 94, 306
World Trade Organization (WTO), 187

Z

Zim, Daniel R., 183–189
  Zim Travel Law, PLLC, 183

Printed in the USA
CPSIA information can be obtained
at www.ICGtesting.com
LVHW021302291023
762471LV00008B/683

9 783031 302022